BISHOPS'
COMMITTEE
ON THE
LITURGY
NEWSLETTER

Published by Liturgy Training Publications, 1800 North Hermitage Avenue, Chicago IL 60622-1101. Phone: 1-800-933-1800. Fax: 1-800-7094.

Cover design by Jill Smith.

Printed in the United States of America.
ISBN 1-56854-014-0
BCL
$22.00

INTRODUCTION

The Bishops' Committee on the Liturgy is a standing committee of the National Conference of Catholic Bishops with a history dating back to November 1958. It was then that the Bishops' Commission on the Liturgical Apostolate, taking a name which was suggested by Pope Pius XII's 1947 encyclical *Mediator Dei* (see no. 109) was established. Since 1965, the Bishops' Commission on the Liturgical Apostolate and since 1967, the Bishops' Committee on the Liturgy has issued a monthly newsletter in order to communicate news and events of liturgical interest to bishops, diocesan liturgical commissions, offices of worship and all who are interested in liturgical renewal. The *Newsletter* of the Bishops' Committee on the Liturgy also serves as a public record for the official and authoritative statements of the Apostolic See and of the National Conference of Catholic Bishops concerning the liturgy.

In 1976 the issues of the *Newsletter* that were published from 1965–1975 were reissued in a single bound collection. In 1981 a second collection which contained all issues of the *Newsletter* issued from January 1976 through December 1980 was published. It also contained a number of statements of the Bishops' Committee on the Liturgy originally issued separately: *The Sign of Peace* (1977), *A Call to Prayer* (1978), *Commemorative Statement on the Fifteenth Anniversary of the Constitution on the Sacred Liturgy* (1978), and *General Intercessions* (1979). A third collection, containing the issues of the *Newsletter* published from January 1981 through December 1985, was released in 1986.

This fourth bound collection contains all the issues of the *Newsletter* of the Committee on the Liturgy published from January 1986 through December 1990 and marks the completion of the twenty-sixth volume of the *Newsletter*. It contains a thorough index which should facilitate easy access to the information contained in the collection.

In the five years represented in this volume, a number of significant events in the history of the liturgical renewal in the United States are chronicled. In 1986 the Federation of Diocesan Liturgical Commissions published the results of the national study on the Order of Mass which took place in 1981 and 1982. The

Committee on the Liturgy was represented at a meeting of the national liturgical commissions of all the countries where Spanish is used as a liturgical language. The chairman of the Hispanic Liturgy Subcommittee, Bishop Ricardo Ramirez, attended the meeting along with Father John A. Gurrieri, Executive Director of the Secretariat for the Liturgy. The Subcommittee on the *Book of Blessings* met for the first time at the beginning of the year. It was ultimately to compose 40 new blessings which were added to the Roman *De Benedictionibus* to produce the U.S. edition of the *Book of Blessings*, as well as a book for use in the home, *Catholic Household Blessings and Prayers*. In cooperation with the Lutheran Churches in the United States, a Lutheran-Roman Catholic Service of the Word was published for use on occasions when common prayer is desirable. Father Ronald F. Krisman, Associate Director of the Liturgy Secretariat, was appointed Coordinator of the Relocation of the NCCB/USCC Conference Headquarters in May 1986, and Monsignor Alan F. Detscher, a priest of the Diocese of Bridgeport, Connecticut, began working in the Secretariat two days a week as a staff consultant. The adaptations approved by the NCCB for the rite of ordination of deacons were confirmed by the Apostolic See and published in the *Newsletter*. Also in May, Augustin Cardinal Mayer, prefect of the Congregation for Divine Worship, visited both the NCCB Liturgy Secretariat and the offices of the International Commission on English in the Liturgy. The first African American Catholic hymnal, *Lead Me, Guide Me*, and the third edition of *Worship* were both published by GIA Publications. The Secretariat produced a summary of the *Ceremonial of Bishops* under the title, *The Bishop and the Liturgy*, to assist bishops until the full English translation was available. Bishop Joseph P. Delaney was elected chairman of the Committee on the Liturgy at the November plenary meeting of the National Conference of Catholic Bishops. At the same meeting the bishops approved the American edition of the *Rite of Christian Initiation of Adults* and the *National Statutes on the Catechumenate*. They also approved the Spanish common text ("*texto único*") for the Order of Mass and the eucharistic prayers. In December, the Navajo translation of the Order of Mass was confirmed by the Congregation of Divine Worship. The *Guidelines for Receiving Communion*, approved by the NCCB in November, were published. Publishers of missalettes were directed to include them in each issue of their missalettes.

Pope John Paul II declared the Marian Year at the beginning of 1987, and the Secretariat published *Celebrating the Marian Year* as a pastoral resource. A joint committee composed of members of the Liturgy and the Doctrine Committees was established to study the issue of inclusive language in translations of Scripture proposed for use in the liturgy; this was a result of concerns raised at the November 1984 meeting of the NCCB concerning the revised *Grail Psalter.* The joint committee completed its work at the end of 1990. In February 1987, Monsignor Alan F. Detscher was appointed a full-time Associate Director of the Secretariat for the Liturgy. The Secretariat published a statement in the *Newsletter* on the washing of feet on Holy Thursday. The Congregation for Divine Worship confirmed the *Book of Divine Worship* for the use of Catholics coming from the Anglican tradition (the so-called "Pastoral Provision"). The Congregation for Divine Worship approved the Choctaw translation of the Order of Mass and also the use of Pima-Papago in the liturgy. The Secretariat prepared the liturgical books to be used in the Holy Father's pastoral visit to the United States and assisted in both the planning and the actual celebration of the various papal liturgies. The Secretariat published a collection of the various statements of the Committee with a commentary by Monsignor Frederick R. McManus under the title, *Thirty Years of Liturgical Renewal.* The Committee revised its guidelines for concelebration and published them in the *Newsletter.* The Congregation for Divine Worship confirmed the Spanish translation of the *Book of Blessings: El Bendicional.* The NCCB approved the ecumenical marriage rite, which had been prepared by the North American Consultation on Common Texts (CCT), and requested the confirmation of the Apostolic See.

The Congregation for Divine Worship confirmed the new Mass formulary for the feast of Our Lady of Guadalupe at the beginning of 1988. The *Rite of Christian Initiation of Adults* was also confirmed by the Congregation and published in the latter part of the year. *In Spirit and Truth,* a statement prepared by the Black Liturgy Subcommittee, was published by the Secretariat. It reflects on the various options contained in the Order of Mass and how they relate to the celebration of the eucharist in African American Catholic parishes and communities. *Catholic Household Blessings and Prayers* was published by the USCC Publications Office. On December 1, 1988, Father John A. Gurrieri completed his ten years of service to the Secretariat: three years as Associate Director and seven years as Executive Director. Father Ronald F. Krisman succeeded Father Gurrieri as Executive Director, and Father Kenneth F. Jenkins was appointed an Associate Director of the Secretariat. December 1988 also marked the 25th anniversary of the promulgation of the Constitution on the Sacred Liturgy, *Sacrosanctum Concilium.*

God's Mercy Endures Forever, guidelines of the Committee on the Liturgy on the presentation of Jews and Judaism in Catholic preaching, was published in early 1989. In June the NCCB/USCC moved into its new headquarters building near the Catholic University of America. The *Order of Christian Funerals,* after many delays, was finally published. The American edition of the *Book of Blessings*, containing 40 new blessings for use in the United States, was also published. The Congregation for Divine Worship confirmed new liturgical texts for the Liturgy of the Hours for the feast of Our Lady of Guadalupe. And the NCCB established December 3, 1989, as the effective date for the use of the new *"texto único"* Spanish translation of the Order of Mass and the eucharistic prayers.

Early in 1990 the *Ordinario de la Misa*, the Order of Mass in Spanish, was published for use in the United States of America. The Congregation for Divine Worship confirmed the use of Lakota as a liturgical language in this country. The Order for the Reception of the Holy Oils was published in the *Newsletter.* The Mass in Celebration of the Fifth Centenary of the Evangelization of the Americas was confirmed by the Apostolic See in both English and Spanish versions. The Joint Committee on Inclusive Language presented its report at the November meeting of the NCCB and the resulting *Criteria for the Evaluation of Inclusive Language Translations of Scriptural Texts Proposed for Use in the Liturgy* was approved. The *Criteria* were published at the beginning of 1991. The Congregation for Divine Worship and the Discipline of the Sacraments confirmed the Spanish translation of the *Rite of Christian Initiation of Adults*, which conforms to the previously confirmed English edition of the same liturgical book. The Most Reverend Wilton D. Gregory was elected to replace Bishop Joseph P. Delaney at the November plenary meeting of the NCCB.

Staff changes took place during this five-year period: Father John A. Gurrieri, after seven years of service as Executive Director of the Secretariat, was succeeded by Father Ronald F. Krisman. From 1986 to 1987 Monsignor Alan F. Detscher assisted the Secretariat as a staff consultant, and in 1987 he was appointed as an Associate Director. In January 1989, Father Kenneth F. Jenkins joined the Secretariat staff as an Associate Director. Monsignor Frederick R. McManus, whose many years of association with the Bishops' Committee on the Liturgy has afforded both the Secretariat and Committee with invaluable insights and experiences, continued as staff consultant.

In November 1984, Bishop John S. Cummins completed his three-year term as Chairman of the Bishops' Committee on the Liturgy. Archbishop Daniel E. Pilarczyk of Cincinnati was elected the succeeding Chairman. However, when he was elected Vice President of the National Conference of Catholic Bishops/United States Catholic Conference in November 1986, Bishop Joseph P. Delaney of Fort Worth was elected to complete his term. Bishop Delaney was then elected in November 1987 to a three-year term of his own. Bishop Wilton D. Gregory, Auxiliary Bishop of Chicago, was elected as the first Chairman-elect of the

Committee at the November 1989 meeting of the NCCB, and took office as the new Chairman of the Liturgy Committee at the conclusion of the November 1990 meeting of the episcopal conference.

It is appropriate to call to mind the names of those who died during this five year period who faithfully sought to strengthen and develop the liturgical life of the Church in the United States: Bishop John L. Dougherty, Auxiliary Bishop of Newark, who served on the ICEL Episcopal Board from 1968–1976 as the representative of the National Conference of Catholic Bishops; Dr. Ralph A. Keifer, who served as the acting Executive Secretary of ICEL for a brief period and was involved in the preparation of the *Roman Missal* and the *Liturgy of the Hours* and who later taught in various seminaries and schools of theology; Mr. John N. Dwyer, who was the business manager of The Liturgical Press and also served on the Board of Directors of the Federation of Diocesan Liturgical Commissions; Reverend Niels K. Rasmussen, OP, who taught in the liturgical studies programs of the Catholic University of America and Notre Dame University; Reverend Eugene A. Walsh, SS, who taught liturgy to generations of seminarians and was noted for his writings and workshops directed towards the improvement of parish liturgy; Reverend Stephen J. Hartdegen, OFM, who served the NCCB in various capacities related to the Bible and particularly as the editor of the *New American Bible* and who assisted the Secretariat in the preparation of the second edition of the *Lectionary for Mass*.

Chairmen of the Bishops' Committee on the Liturgy

1965–1966	Cardinal John F. Dearden
1966–1968	Archbishop Paul J. Hallinan
1968–1969	Archbishop Leo C. Byrne
1969–1972	Bishop James W. Malone
1972–1975	Bishop Walter W. Curtis
1975–1977	Archbishop John R. Quinn
1977–1978	Bishop Rene H. Gracida
1978–1981	Archbishop Rembert G. Weakland, OSB
1981–1984	Bishop John S. Cummins
1984–1986	Archbishop Daniel E. Pilarczyk
1986–1990	Bishop Joseph P. Delaney
1990–1993	Bishop Wilton D. Gregory

Executive Directors

1965–1975	Reverend Monsignor Frederick R. McManus
1975–1978	Reverend John A. Rotelle, OSA

1978–1981	Reverend Thomas A. Krosnicki, SVD
1981–1988	Reverend John A. Gurrieri
1988–	Reverend Ronald F. Krisman

Associate Directors

1968–1971	Reverend Joseph M. Champlin
1970–1975	Reverend John A. Rotelle, OSA
1972–1978	Reverend Thomas A. Krosnicki, SVD
1978–1981	Reverend John A. Gurrieri
1981–1988	Reverend Ronald F. Krisman
1987–	Reverend Monsignor Alan F. Detscher
1989–1991	Reverend Kenneth F. Jenkins
1991–	Sister Linda Gaupin, CDP

Administrative Assistant

| 1976–1980 | Sister Luanne Durst, FSPA |

Staff Consultants

| 1975– | Reverend Monsignor Frederick R. McManus |
| 1986–1987 | Reverend Monsignor Alan F. Detscher |

BISHOPS' COMMITTEE ON THE LITURGY

NEWSLETTER

NATIONAL CONFERENCE OF CATHOLIC BISHOPS

1986
VOLUME XXII
JANUARY

Final Report of the 1985 Synod of Bishops

At the conclusion of its November 24-December 8, 1985, meetings in Rome, the participants to the 1985 extraordinary session of the world Synod of Bishops issued both a pastoral "Message to the People of God" and a "Final Report" to His Holiness, Pope John Paul II. The release of the latter document marks the first time that a synod's full report to the Roman pontiff has been made public by the Holy See.

The report is divided into two parts, the first emphasizing the central theme of the 1985 Synod, "Celebration, Verification, and Promotion of Vatican Council II." The second part addresses many of the particular themes which emerged at the Synod: the mystery of the Church, the universal call to holiness by the People of God, the Word of God in the life of the Church, evangelization, the Church as Communion, and the Church's mission to the world. Included with the Word of God in the section dealing with "Sources of life for the Church" was a treatment of the Church's sacred liturgy. Reprinted below are those comments of the Synod Fathers, in the Vatican's English-language translation of the report. (For the complete text of the "Final Report," cf. Origins: NC Documentary Service, [Vol. 15: no. 27, December 19, 1985], pp. 444-450.)

1. Internal renewal of the liturgy

The liturgical renewal is the most visible fruit of the whole conciliar effort. Even if there have been some difficulties, it has generally been received joyfully and fruitfully by the faithful. The liturgical renewal cannot be limited to ceremonies, rites, texts, etc. The active participation so happily increased after the council does not consist only in external activity, but above all in interior and spiritual participation, in living and fruitful participation in the paschal mystery of Jesus Christ (cf. *Sacrosanctum Concilium,* 11). It is evident that the liturgy must favor the sense of the sacred and make it shine forth. It must be permeated by the spirit of reverence, adoration and the glory of God.

2. Suggestions

The bishops should not merely correct abuses but should also clearly explain to everyone the theological foundation of the sacramental discipline and of the liturgy.

Catecheses must once again become paths leading into liturgical life (mystagogical catecheses), as was the case in the church's beginnings.

Future priests should learn liturgical life in a practical way and know liturgical theology well.

Decree of the Apostolic Penitentiary regarding Indulgences

On December 14, 1985, the Apostolic Penitentiary issued a decree conceding to diocesan bishops the right to impart the papal blessing with a plenary indulgence to those who cannot be physically present but who follow the sacred rites at which the blessing is imparted by radio or television transmission. This concession expands Norm 11, par. 2, of the 1967 Enchiridion of Indulgences, which states: "Diocesan bishops, and others equated to them in law, have the right from entrance upon their pastoral office to impart in their respective dioceses, according to the prescribed formula, the papal blessing with a plenary indulgence three times a year on solemn feasts of their own choice, even if they only assist at the solemn Mass."

This concession, it should be noted, does not apply to the Urbe et Orbe *blessing of the Holy Father, which could already be received even by radio transmission. Rather, it refers to the three solemn celebrations during the year in the diocese on which occasions the bishop has determined to impart the papal blessing.*

Following is the text of the decree, in an unofficial translation made by the Secretariat of the Bishops' Committee on the Liturgy.

Requests from various places have come to the Holy See to the effect that, since the television and radio media are being employed more frequently and effectively in spreading the good news of salvation—undoubtedly a gift of Divine Providence, who directs all things toward the goal of salvation—so likewise they should serve for the lavishing of spiritual gifts, in so far as the nature of their functions allows.

Some bishops have specifically proposed this with regard to the plenary indulgence attached to the papal blessing which, according to Norm 11, par. 2, of the *Enchiridion Indulgentiarum,* can be imparted three times a year by a diocesan bishop. This has been requested, of course, in order that the Christian faithful committed to their care might be able to receive the indulgence if, for a reasonable circumstance, they are not physically present at the sacred rites during which the papal blessing is imparted. In such cases they are to follow those rites with pious attention while they are being transmitted live by television or radio and receive the blessing, properly fulfilling the usual conditions of confession, communion and prayer for the intentions of the Holy Father.

The Apostolic Penitentiary had gladly recommended that this proposed accommodation of the present discipline be accepted, all the more so because the esteem of the Christian people for indulgences will be greatly fostered by it, and they will thus be piously inspired to receive or increase sanctifying grace through the sacraments, and be more firmly united in mind with the bishop.

In an audience granted to the undersigned Major Penitentiary on 13 December, Pope John Paul II graciously deigned to approve that the Christian faithful would be able to gain the plenary indulgence in the above-mentioned manner, and he decided that this concession should be made public.

By this decree the Apostolic Penitentiary puts into effect this reported decision of the Supreme Pontiff.

All thing to the contrary notwithstanding.

Given at Rome, from the Apostolic Penitentiary, 14 December 1985.

+ Luigi Cardinal Dadaglio
Major Penitentiary

Luigi De Magistris
Regent

1985 National Meeting of Diocesan Liturgical Commissions

The annual National Meeting of Diocesan Liturgical Commissions took place in Grand Rapids, Michigan, October 7-10, 1985. Cosponsored by the Committee on the Liturgy and the Federation of Diocesan Liturgical Commissions, the meeting considered the theme of liturgical spirituality and related questions.

The meeting participants, representing diocesan liturgical commissions and offices of worship from throughout the United States, heard keynote speaker, Father Gerard Austin, OP, Chairman of the Department of Theology at the Catholic University of America, address the topic, "Spirit through Word." He explained that it is through the Word of God that a liturgical assembly gathers together in the Spirit; it is that same Spirit which forms the Eucharistic assembly into the one Body of Christ.

Sister Theresa Koernke, IHM, a member of the faculty of Mount Saint Mary's Seminary in Cincinnati, challenged her listeners to reject the kind of liturgical spirituality which is only another form of individualism. Rather, she stated, an authentic liturgical spirituality must be primarily ecclesial, leading the participants to "live morally, to live in the justice of God."

Benedictine Sister Mary Collins, president of the North American Academy of Liturgy, addressed the connection between devotions and renewal movements and the Church's liturgy. Noting how devotions and spiritual movements, such as RENEW, Cursillo, and Marriage Encounter, have arisen as responses to human concerns, she invited her hearers "to be aware of human concerns which give rise to devotions" and to "pay attention to the fruits of liturgical celebrations and devotional practices to test their authenticity."

Dr. Louis Weil, professor of Liturgy at Nashotah House in Wisconsin, presented the closing talk on the topic "The Arts: Language of the Spirit." Stating that the gifts of the Spirit are widely diverse in each local community, he asked that conscious attempts be made in each community to discern artistic gifts which may be used in service of the Church's liturgical prayer.

Three Position Statements and three Resolutions of Immediate Concern were adopted by the delegates during business sessions at the National Meeting. In the position statements (drafted by various regional groupings of diocesan liturgical personnel at their spring 1985 meetings) the delegates asked the Bishops' Committee on the Liturgy to "issue a document similar to *Music in Catholic Worship* dealing with the ministry of the presider at liturgical celebrations, not only in its functional but also in its spiritual dimensions." They also requested that the Bishops' Committee on the Liturgy, the Bishops' Committee on Priestly Formation, and diocesan offices and/or commissions "urge individual bishops to insure that seminaries with which they are associated provide programs of liturgical and musical formation and study as required in the *Constitution on the Sacred Liturgy,* nos. 15-17, and the 1979 *Instruction on Liturgical Formation in Seminaries* from the Sacred Congregation for Catholic Education which are most recently reflected in *Liturgical Formation in Seminaries: A Commentary* (1984) from the Bishops' Committee on the Liturgy and the Bishops' Committee on Priestly Formation." In addition they asked that "the FDLC National Board direct the Liturgical Arts Committee to initiate ongoing dialog with the NCEA and the NCDD concerning the support and promotion of Christian Spirituality rooted in Liturgical Prayer through the formal study of the related arts and their accompanying skills in all Catholic Schools and in Catechetical and Religious Education Programs."

In the three resolutions of immediate concern, which were drafted during the course of the National Meeting at "hearing sessions," the delegates requested that "in order to help simplify the work of liturgical planners and that the just compensation of both composers and publishers could be assured, the delegates urged the establishment of a central clearing-house for facilitating copyright permissions and payments." By unanimous votes they also commended the leadership of the American Bishops for effectively promoting the spiritual growth of the Church in the United States through their vigorous implementation of the liturgical reforms of the Second Vatican Council, and they gave a special tribute posthumously to Father Robert Doppler, priest of the Diocese of Toledo, for his long and dedicated service to the Federation of Diocesan Liturgical Commissions (FDLC) for several years. Father Doppler died October 3 following a brief illness with cancer.

The 1986 National Meeting will be held October 13-16 in Portland, Maine. Joseph Cardinal Bernardin, Archbishop of Chicago, is scheduled to be one of the speakers at that meeting and will examine the future of penance and reconciliation in the Church.

FDLC Board of Directors Elects New Offices

At the semiannual meeting of the Board of Directors of the Federation of Diocesan Liturgical Commissions, held in Grand Rapids, Michigan, in October 1985, the following were elected to two-year terms on the Board's Executive Committee: Reverend Joseph McMahon (Portland in Oregon), Chairman; Reverend Richard Ward (Pittsburgh), Vice-Chairman; Reverend Steve Moore (Anchorage), Treasurer; Sister Elizabeth Meagher, RSM (Gaylord), Delegate-at-Large East; and Sister Norita Lanners, OSB (Salt Lake City), Delegate-at-Large West.

Results of Order of Mass Study Published

The Federation of Diocesan Liturgical Commissions recently has published *The Order of Mass Study: A Report,* which presents the results of the 1981-1982 study of the structural elements of the Order of Mass. Parish representatives from 97 dioceses and archdioceses participated in the project.

The 43-page booklet gives a summary of comments submitted on each section of the *Ordo Missae,* statistical data, conclusions, and comparative tables.

For pricing information write: FDLC National Office, P.O. Box 29039, Washington, D.C. 20011.

Ceremonial of Bishops: New Publication

In order to assist bishops and masters of ceremonies to familiarize themselves with the new *Caeremoniale Episcoporum* (Ceremonial of Bishops) the Secretariat of the Bishops' Committee on the Liturgy is preparing a descriptive commentary on the principal sections of the book, treating the nature and importance of episcopal liturgy, offices and ministries in episcopal liturgies, the stational Mass of a diocesan bishop, notable days in the life and ministry of a bishop, the rites of ordination, blessings given by a bishop, and the use of insignia and vestments.

In addition the commentary will contain translations of two studies which appeared in recent issues of *Notitiae:* "The New *Ceremonial of Bishops,*" by Archbishop Virgilio Noe, Secretary of the Congregation for Divine Worship and former Papal Master of Ceremonies; and "Features of the *Caeremoniale Episcorporum,*" by A.G. Martimort. An outline of the contents of the Ceremonial of Bishops and a Bibliography and list of Resources will also be included.

Resources from Diocesan Worship Offices

Proclaiming the Passion. The Office of Sacred Worship of the Diocese of La Crosse, WI, has recently published its *Proclaiming the Passion* series in a new one-volume edition. The narratives are divided for readers and offer suggestions for optional musical interludes. A revised commentary on the four Passion accounts is also included. Cost: $9.00 each; $35.00 for four copies, plus 15% postage and handling. While the supply lasts, copies of the original books are still available for $2.50 each or $9.00 for four copies, plus $15.00 postage and handling. Contact: Office of Sacred Worship, P.O. Box 4004, La Crosse, WI 54602-4004. Telephone: 608/788-7700, ext. 221.

Other Resources for Lent and Eastertime

A Crucified Christ in Holy Week, by Father Raymond E. Brown, SS, presents essays on the four Gospel passion narratives. Originally appearing as a series of articles in *Worship* magazine, this collection will be of special assistance to homilists preparing for the Passion Sunday and Good Friday liturgies. Cost: $3.95. Order from: The Liturgical Press, Saint John's Abbey, Collegeville, MN 56321. Phone 612/363-2213.

Parish Path through Lent and Eastertime, edited by Mary Ann Simcoe, presents planning suggestions for parish liturgy teams for the seasons of Lent and Easter. The 138-page paperbook presents articles on the lectionary and sacramentary texts for the seasons, along with treatment of environment and art, music, preaching, and *The Rite of Christian Initiation of Adults.* Cost: $5.25 ($4.50 each for 5 or more). Order from: Liturgy Training Program (LTP), 1800 North Hermitage Avenue, Chicago, IL 60622. Phone 312/486-7008.

BISHOPS' COMMITTEE ON THE LITURGY
NEWSLETTER

NATIONAL CONFERENCE OF CATHOLIC BISHOPS

1986
VOLUME XXII
FEBRUARY

New Commission for the Spanish Translation of Liturgical Books

At the International Congress of Presidents and Secretaries of National Liturgical Commissions which took place in Rome in October 1984 [cf. *Newsletter,* Volume XIX, March 1984, p. 12], Cardinal Marcelo Gonzalez Martín, Primate of Spain and president of the Episcopal Liturgical Commission of Spain, suggested that a new commission for the translation of liturgical books into Spanish be established so that, like other language groups such as English, French and German, those who worship in Spanish might achieve unity in their liturgical language. Several Latin American conferences of bishops agreed to this proposal which also received the support of the Congregation for Divine Worship.

As a follow-up to the Cardinal's suggestion a meeting of representatives of CELAM and Spain took place in Bogota, Colombia in June 1985, at which time three items were discussed: (1) a single Spanish translation of the newly-promulgated *De Benedictionibus* (Book of Blessings); (2) a single Spanish translation of the Order of Mass, the Lord's Prayer, and the nine eucharistic prayers; (3) the establishment of a new international commission for Spanish liturgical translation.

New translations of the Mass texts noted in no. 2 were prepared on the basis of the five existing translations of the Roman Missal, those of Argentina, Chile, Colombia, Mexico and Spain. A Spanish translation of *De Benedictionibus,* with minor adaptations, was also prepared by the CELAM-Spain group. These were to be examined and voted upon at a special meeting of presidents and secretaries of the Spanish and Latin American national liturgical commissions.

That meeting took place under the sponsorship of the Congregation for Divine Worship in the old Synod Hall at the Vatican, February 3-7, 1986. The following conferences of bishops sent representatives: Argentina, Bolivia, Chile, Colombia, Dominican Republic, Ecuador, El Salvador, Guatemala, Honduras, Mexico, Nicaragua, Panama, Paraguay, Peru, Puerto Rico, Spain, Uruguay, United States of America, and Venezuela. (Representatives of Costa Rica and Cuba were unable to attend.) Representatives of the Liturgy Department (DELC) of CELAM were also present.

Cardinal Paul Augustine Mayer, OSB, Prefect of the Congregation, presided over the sessions with the assistance of Archbishop Virgilio Noè, Secretary, and Monsignor Piero Marini, Under-Secretary, of the Congregation. Cardinal Agostino Casaroli, Vatican Secretary of State, sent greetings to the participants, in which he emphasized the importance of their deliberations and assured them that His Holiness Pope John Paul II was praying for the success of the meeting.

The purpose of this special meeting was threefold: (a) to approve the Spanish translation of *De Benedictionibus* for submission to the respective conferences of bishops; (b) to reach agreement on a single common Spanish-language translation of the Order of Mass, the Lord's Prayer, and the nine eucharistic prayers for use in Spain, Latin America, and the United States; (c) to establish a new commission for the translation of Latin liturgical books into Spanish. By the end of the meeting the representatives had agreed to all three objectives, approving the translation of the *Book of Blessings,* and of the new translation of the Order of Mass, the Lord's Prayer, and Eucharistic Prayers I-IV. (Work remains to be done on the Eucharistic Prayers for Masses with Children I-III and the Eucharistic Prayers for Masses of Reconciliation I-II.) Each member conference will be asked to approve the new translations for mandatory use on March 8, 1992, the fifth centenary of the evangelization of the Americas. The Hispanic Liturgy Subcommittee and the Liturgy Committee itself will review this work with a view toward making recommendations to the National Conference of Catholic Bishops at the earliest possible time.

The National Conference of Catholic Bishops (USA) was asked to send non-voting observers to the meeting. In the course of the meeting, however, a motion was made jointly by the representatives from Chile and the Dominican Republic that the NCCB representatives be given full voting status. That motion was carried unanimously and was approved by the Congregation.

Report of the Liturgy Committee on the Use of Spanish in the Liturgy

The following report was given by the Most Reverend Ricardo Ramirez, CSB, Bishop of Las Cruces (New Mexico) and Chairman of the Hispanic Liturgy Subcommittee, at the meeting of presidents and secretaries of national episcopal liturgical commissions of conferences where Spanish is used in worship. Bishop Ramirez represented the Liturgy Committee Chairman, Archbishop Daniel E. Pilarczyk. Father John Gurrieri of the Liturgy Secretariat also attended the Rome meeting from February 3-7, 1986.

Status of Spanish as a Liturgical Language in the USA

1. English is the official language of the United States of America and, as such, is the principal language of the Church in the United States. Translations of the liturgical books into English are prepared by the International Commission on English in the Liturgy (ICEL), a Joint Commission of Catholic Bishops' Conferences. However, by a decree of the National Conference of Catholic Bishops enacted on April 2, 1964 and subsequently confirmed by the Apostolic See, vernacular languages other than English are permitted "in liturgical services celebrated with a congregation of another language . . . according to a translation approved by a competent territorial ecclesiastical authority of that language . . . " That decree has provided a general and pastorally suitable approbation on the part of the episcopal conference for the use of any approved and confirmed liturgical language in the United States.

2. As a consequence those who celebrate the liturgy in Spanish have been permitted to use the liturgical books approved by the episcopal conferences of Spain, Mexico, Colombia, Argentina, *et al.* However, because the translations vary or differ significantly one from the other, even in the parts of the liturgy belonging to the people, unity in Spanish-speaking liturgical assemblies is often difficult to achieve. Likewise it has been impossible for Spanish-speaking Catholics to avail themselves of the liturgical adaptations approved for other Americans in the English translations of the liturgical books. In most situations the liturgical books used by the clergy and the participation aids used by the people (missals, missalettes, etc.) also differ in translation, causing greater confusion in parishes. For these and many other reasons the National Conference of Catholic Bishops of the United States sought to have *a single adapted version of Spanish language liturgical books approved for use in the United States.*

3. Because of the growth of the Spanish-speaking community, the increasing numbers of immigrants from Mexico, Central America, and South America (there are nearly twenty million Hispanics, people of Spanish or Latin American descent or origin, in the United States), and the greater acceptance and prestige accorded to the Spanish language in the United States, on September 11, 1984 the National Conference of Catholic Bishops approved Spanish as an official liturgical language of the Church in the United States. This enactment was confirmed by the Apostolic See by decree of the Congregation for Divine Worship on January 19, 1985 (Prot. CD 382/84).

4. The principal effect of this decree enables the Conference to approve and adopt a single version of Spanish-language liturgical books as approved by a competent episcopal conference, but adapted to local circumstances, for uniform use throughout the dioceses of the United States. Sacramental formulae, of course, would be those common to all Spanish translations.

5. Because the Spanish language is so important in the Church in the United States many conference documents are issued in Spanish as well as English. For example, on December 4, 1983 the Conference issued its pastoral statement commemorating the twentieth anniversary of *Sacrosanctum Concilium* in Spanish as *La Iglesia en Oración, un Templo Santo del Señor.* Important statements of the national liturgical commission have also been issued in Spanish, e.g. *La Música en el Culto Católico, La Música Liturgica Hoy,* etc.

Hispanic Liturgy Subcommittee

6. With this goal in view the Bishops' Committee on the Liturgy established an *Hispanic Liturgy Subcommittee,* now chaired by the Most Reverend Ricardo Ramirez, CSB, Bishop of Las Cruces (New Mexico). The subcommittee works closely with national Hispanic organizations, especially the Instituto de

Liturgia Hispana. The subcommittee has been studying the various Spanish translations of liturgical books, especially of the Roman Missal, so that it may eventually recommend a common translation to the conference of bishops. A consultation among the diocesan liturgical commissions will be conducted later this year to determine which Spanish translation of the Roman Missal to recommend. The subcommittee is also studying the question of cultural adaptation of the liturgy, the addition of feasts of Spain and Latin America to the particular calendar of the United States, and other liturgical matters.

Liturgical Books in Use in the United States

7. As noted above, any approved Spanish translation of liturgical books may be used in the United States. However, the following are the most commonly accepted in American parishes:

Roman Missal:	Spain, Mexico, Colombia
Roman Ritual:	Spain, Mexico, Argentina
Roman Pontifical:	Spain, Argentina
Roman Lectionary:	United States, Spain

8. The first volume of the *Leccionario, Edición Hispanoamericana* was prepared by the Centro Católico para Hispanos del Nordeste (New York) in 1982 with the approval of the National Conference of Catholic Bishops. (A second volume will soon be published.) This edition uses the *La Biblia Latinoamericana* translation, while language usage was drawn from the Peruvian lectionary, *Pueblo de Dios.*

9. In cooperation with the Liturgy Secretariat of the Mexican Conference of Bishops, a Spanish translation of the rites of anointing and viaticum, as adapted for English-speaking conferences, was prepared and published as *Cuidado Pastoral de los Enfermos: Ritos de la Unción y del Viatico.* A bilingual edition of excerpts of *Cuidado Pastoral de los Enfermos* will soon be published for the use of ministers for whom Spanish is only a second language.

Conclusion

10. The National Conference of Catholic Bishops of the United States of America is interested in this new initiative to establish a *CELAM-España Commission for the Translation of Liturgical Books.* The Chairman of the Bishops' Committee on the Liturgy, the Most Reverend Daniel E. Pilarczyk, Archbishop of Cincinnati (Ohio), expresses his gratitude and that of the entire Committee for the invitation to participate as observers in the meeting of February 3-7, 1986 in Rome.

11. We share the goals of this new commission, which will greatly benefit the liturgical life of Spanish-speaking Catholics in the United States of America. For it is our experience in the English-speaking world that a common translation of the liturgical books not only unifies worship in each country, but also forges common bonds between countries of the same language. The work of the International Commission on English in the Liturgy (ICEL) has brought the English-speaking world together in worship.

12. It is our hope that a common Spanish translation will not only unify the Spanish-speaking liturgical communities in the United States, but that it will also bind Hispanic American Catholics closer to their ancestral roots and to their authentic cultural and liturgical traditions. For language, culture, and the religious imagination are intimately tied to one another. As our conference stated in 1983: "We must continue to search for appropriate ways to enrich our liturgies both by retrieving our artistic tradition and using it appropriately, being open to new forms of the artistic imagination, and by utilizing the cultural heritage of the diverse ethnic and racial groups of the Church in America" (*The Church at Prayer, A Holy Temple of the Lord,* no. 45).

Most Reverend Ricardo Ramirez, CSB
Bishop of Las Cruces
Chairman, Hispanic Liturgy Subcommittee

Reverend John A. Gurrieri
Executive Director, Liturgy Secretariat

22 January 1986
Washington, DC

Liturgia Horarum, Second Typical Edition

The first volume of the second typical edition (*editio typica altera*) of the Liturgy of the Hours (*Liturgia Horarum*), issued by decree of the Congregation for Divine Worship on Easter Sunday, April 7, 1985, has recently been made available by the publisher, the Vatican Polyglot Press. This first volume covers the Advent and Christmas seasons.

A number of important new features are found in the second edition. The Neo-Vulgate translation of the Scriptures is used throughout the various hours in the biblical readings and in the Old Testament and New Testament canticles. In addition the psalm texts, which already in the first edition were from the Neo-Vulgate translation, include the recent revisions made in the latest edition of that translation. Many of the responsories in the Office of Readings also follow the Neo-Vulgate translation unless for a particularly forceful reason, such as composition, traditional usage or musical setting, the older version has been retained. The antiphons to the *Benedictus* and *Magnificat* for Sundays and solemnities also employ the new translation.

The texts of the hymns have been edited in conformity with *Te Decet Hymnus.* And an appendix includes additional texts for the solemn blessing and penitential rite taken from the Roman Missal.

The remaining volumes in the second edition will be issued during the next several months. Copies of the first volume may be ordered directly from: Libreria Editrice Vaticana, 00120 Vatican City State, Europe. Price: 50,000 Italian lire (approximately US $32.00) plus shipping.

The Time for the Celebration of the Easter Vigil

The practice has appeared lately whereby the celebration of the Easter Vigil is begun before nightfall as though it were an "anticipated Mass" of Easter Sunday. This practice is contrary to liturgical law and goes against the whole history and symbolism of the Easter Vigil, restored to its proper time by Pope Pius XII.

It is worth recalling what the *General Norms for the Liturgical Year and the Roman Calendar* states on this subject: "The Easter Vigil, during the holy night when Christ rose from the dead, ranks as the "mother of all vigils"[Augustine, *Sermo* 219: PL 38, 1088]. Keeping watch, the Church awaits Christ's resurrection and celebrates it in the sacraments. Accordingly, the entire celebration of this vigil should take place *at night,* that is, it should either begin after nightfall or end before the dawn of Sunday" [*Ergo tota huius sacrae Vigiliae celebratio nocte peragi debet, ita ut vel incipiatur post initium noctis vel finiatur ante die dominicae diluculum*] (no. 21).

The Sacramentary also indicates the *nocturnal character of the Easter Vigil:* "The entire celebration of the Easter Vigil takes place at night. It should not begin before nightfall; it should end before daybreak on Sunday" (Sacramentary, Easter Vigil, no. 3).

The Easter Vigil begins and ends in darkness. It is a *nocturnal vigil,* retaining its ancient character of vigilance, and expectation, when the Christian people await the resurrection of the Lord during the night. Fire is blessed and the paschal candle is lighted to illumine the night so that all may hear the Easter proclamation and listen to the word of God proclaimed in the Scriptures. For this reason the Service of Light takes place before the Service of the Word.

Christ the Light is symbolized in and praised by means of the paschal candle. Only the light of his resurrection illumines the darkness of the night and enlightens the assembled Church. The Easter Vigil marks Christ's passing from darkness to light, from death to life. To celebrate the Easter Vigil before nightfall or to conclude it with the light of dawn at a "sunrise service" misses the mark of this symbolism. (See "The Hour for the Vigil Celebration" in *Celebrating the Easter Vigil* edited by Rupert Berger and Hans Hollerweger, Pueblo Publishing Company, NY, 1983, pp. 96-97, 38-42, 101; see also Secretariat of the Bishops' Committee on the Liturgy, Study Text 9, *The Liturgical Year: Celebrating the Mystery of Christ and His Saints,* Washington, DC: USCC Office of Publishing and Promotion Services, 1985, pp. 49-53; for the liturgical norms, see Secretariat of the Bishops' Committee on the Liturgy, Liturgy Documentary Series 6: *Norms Governing Liturgical Calendars,* Washington, DC: USCC Office of Publishing and Promotion Services, 1984.)

BISHOPS' COMMITTEE ON THE LITURGY

NEWSLETTER

NATIONAL CONFERENCE OF CATHOLIC BISHOPS

1986
VOLUME XXII
MARCH

Blessings Subcommittee Meeting in San Diego

The Blessings Subcommittee of the Bishops' Committee on the Liturgy met at the University of San Diego's Kolbe Center, San Diego, CA, from January 10-13, 1986. Bishop Patrick R. Cooney, Auxiliary Bishop of Detroit, is Chairman.

The subcommittee reviewed the work done thus far on Part I (Daily Blessings) of *Household Blessings and Prayers,* the family/home edition of the Book of Blessings. Parts II and III (Occasional Blessings and Prayers) are being prepared by one of the subcommittee's working groups. The subcommittee also reviewed the structure and contents of the minister's edition of the *Book of Blessings.* This edition is based on the English translation of *De Benedictionibus,* now being prepared by the International Commission on English in the Liturgy (ICEL), and additional blessings which are being added by the Blessings Subcommittee.

The following particular rites, not found in the Roman ritual, were also reviewed by the subcommittee: Blessing of an Advent Wreath, Blessing of a Christmas Creche or Manger Scene, Epiphany Blessing of Homes, Visit to a Cemetery on All Souls' Day, Blessing of Foods on Holy Saturday or on Thanksgiving Day, Blessing of the Saint Joseph Table, Blessing of Fishing Boats and Gear, Blessing of Seeds at the Time of Planting, Blessing at the Time of Miscarriage, Blessing of a Victim of Crime or Oppression, Blessing of a Person Suffering from Substance Abuse, Blessing on the Occasion of a Birthday, Rite of Installation of a Pastor, Rite of Commissioning a Catechist. These and other new rites are being included in the American edition as a consequence of the consultation of diocesan liturgical commissions conducted by the Liturgy Secretariat in 1984. It is the subcommittee's hope that a few of these rites (particularly those related to the liturgical year) will be published in provisional form this year.

The Blessings Subcommittee is scheduled to meet again in Boston, October 17-19, 1986.

New Blessings for the American Edition of *De Benedictionibus*

The Blessings Subcommittee is in the process of preparing new rites or orders of blessing for the American edition of the *Book of Blessings (De Benedictionibus).* The "green book" or provisional translation of the Latin text is being prepared by the International Commission on English in the Liturgy (ICEL). When the translation is complete, the particular blessings for use in the dioceses of the United States will be incorporated into the appropriate sections of the *Book of Blessings.* (Blessings related to the liturgical year will be collected under a new title not found in *De Benedictionibus:* "Blessings Related to the Liturgical Feasts and Seasons.")

The addition of these new rites is in keeping with the principles enunciated in the General Introduction (*praenotanda*) of the recently promulgated *Book of Blessings.* No. 39 of the Introduction states that in this matter the conference of bishops has the following responsibilities:

a) to decide on adaptations, in keeping with the principles established in the present book, and preserving the proper structure of the rites;

b) to weigh carefully and prudently what elements from the traditions and culture of individual peoples may be appropriately admitted into divine worship, then to propose further adaptations that the conference considers to be necessary or helpful;

c) to retain or to adapt blessings belonging to particular rituals or those of the former Roman Ritual that

1312 MASSACHUSETTS AVENUE, N.W. • WASHINGTON, D.C. 20005

are still in use, as long as such blessings are compatible with the tenor of the Constitution on the Liturgy, with the principles set out in the present Introduction, and with today's mentality;

d) to add different texts of the same kind to the various orders of blessing whenever the present book gives the choice between several alternative texts;

e) not only to translate in their entirety but also, where necessary, to expand the Introductions in this book, so that the ministers will fully understand the meaning of the rites and carry them out effectively and the faithful will take part more intelligently and actively;

f) to supply elements missing from this book, for example, to provide other readings that may be useful, to indicate what songs are suited to the celebrations;

g) to prepare translations of the texts that are adapted to the idiom of the different languages and to the genius of the diverse cultures;

h) to arrange the contents of editions of a book of blessings in a format that will be as convenient as possible for pastoral use; to publish sections of the book separately, but with the major introductions always included.*

The following is a list of those new rites or orders of blessings now being written for the American edition of *De Benedictionibus*. Being based on the results of a survey conducted among diocesan liturgical commissions by the Liturgy Secretariat, it received initial approval of the Bishops' Committee on the Liturgy in June 1985. In keeping with no. 39c of the Introduction, several of the blessings on the list will be adapted from the previous edition of the Roman Ritual approved for the United States (*Collectio Rituum pro dioecesibus Civitatum Foederatum Americae Septentrionalis*, 1964).

1. Blessing of Parents Before Childbirth
2. Blessing of Mothers on Mother's Day
3. Blessing of Fathers on Father's Day
4. Blessing of Foster Parents and Adopted Children
5. Blessing on the Occasion of a Birthday
6. Blessing of Parents After a Miscarriage
7. Blessing of a Person Suffering from Substance Abuse
8. Blessing of a Victim of Crime or Oppression
9. Blessing of Teachers
10. Blessing of Students
11. Blessing of a Meeting
12. Blessing of an Ecumenical Gathering
13. Blessing of an Interreligious (Interfaith) Gathering
14. Blessing at the Inauguration of a Public Official
15. Blessing of Fishing Boats and Gear
16. Blessing of Seeds at the Time of Planting
17. Blessing of Food on Holy Saturday
18. Blessing of Food on Thanksgiving Day
19. Blessing of Throats
20. Blessing upon Visiting a Cemetery on All Souls' Day
21. Blessing of an Advent Wreath
22. Blessing of a Christmas Creche or Manger Scene
23. Blessing of a Christmas Tree
24. Blessing of a Home on the Solemnity of the Epiphany
25. Blessing of a Home in the Easter Season
26. Blessing of Foods and Other Elements related to Religious Devotions (e.g., Bread, Wine, Flowers, Candles, Oil)
27. Easter Proclamation on the Solemnity of the Epiphany
28. Christmas Proclamation (Roman Martyrology)

Comments and suggestions concerning the above list should be sent to the Liturgy Secretariat, 1312 Massachusetts Avenue, NW, Washington, DC 20005-4105.

Ministry of Blessing

Q. Who may exercise the ministry of blessings?

R. The ministry of blessings is treated in the General Introduction of the Book of Blessings (*De*

---

*This English translation of responsibilities of a conference of bishops (a-h) is from the General Introduction of *De Benedictionibus*, (c) 1985, International Committee on English in the Liturgy, Inc. All rights reserved. Used with permission.

Benedictionibus, no. 18) and will be clearly indicated in the American edition when it is published, possibly in 1987. While a bishop, priest or deacon will ordinarily exercise the ministry of blessing, the following extended quotation from the General Introduction* indicates that participation in this ministry is understood to be more extensive.

"The ministry of blessing involves a particular exercise of the priesthood of Christ and, in keeping with the place and office within the people of God belonging to each person, the exercise of this ministry is determined in the following manner:

a) A *bishop* is the minister to whom it belongs to preside at celebrations that involve the entire diocesan community and that are carried out with special solemnity and with many of the faithful in attendance. The bishop, accordingly, may reserve certain celebrations to himself, particularly those that are celebrated with special solemnity.

b) A *presbyter or priest* is the minister to whom it belongs, in keeping with the nature of his service to the people of God, to preside at those blessings especially that involve the community he is appointed to serve. Priests, therefore, may preside at the celebration of all the blessings in this book, unless a bishop is present with the intention of presiding.

c) A *deacon* is the minister to whom it belongs to preside at those blessings that are so indicated *in loco* in this book, because, as the minister of the altar, of the word, and of charity, the deacon is the assistant of the bishop and of his presbyterate.

But whenever a priest is present, it is more fitting that the office of presider be assigned to him and that the deacon assist by exercising his proper functions within the liturgical service.

d. An *acolyte* and a *reader* who by formal institution has this special office in the Church is rightly preferred over other laypersons as the minister designated to impart certain blessings, at the discretion of the local Ordinary.

Other *laymen and laywomen,* in virtue of the universal priesthood, a dignity they possess because of their baptism and confirmation, may celebrate certain blessings, as indicated in the respective orders of blessing, by use of the rite and formularies provided for laypersons. Such laypersons exercise this ministry in virtue of their office (for example, parents on behalf of their children) or because they are exercising some special liturgical ministry or they are fulfilling some particular charge in the Church, as is the case with religious or catechists in many places at the discretion of the local Ordinary, once their proper pastoral formation and prudence in the apostolate has been ascertained.

But whenever a priest or deacon is present, the office of presider should be left to him."

A Lutheran-Roman Catholic Service of the Word

A Lutheran-Roman Catholic Joint Liturgical Group was established in January 1984 for the purpose of following up on the suggestion of Bishop David Preuss of the Lutheran Church in America and the Most Reverend James W. Malone, President of the National Conference of Catholic Bishops, that a joint service of the word drawn from the Roman Catholic and Lutheran traditions be prepared for use in ecumenical worship services in which Lutherans and Roman Catholics participate. A draft of that service received the commendation of representative Roman Catholic and Lutheran bishops at a meeting in Washington, DC, in October 1984. The service was used for the first time at Reformation Lutheran Church in Washington in November 1985.

A Lutheran-Roman Catholic Service of the Word, as that joint worship service is now entitled, contains the structure of a Liturgy of the Word similar to that used in Roman Catholic and Lutheran eucharistic celebrations though not exactly resembling either. The service contains the following elements: Gathering Song; Greeting (Dialogue); the Promise of the Word; Hymn of Praise (optional); Prayer; First Reading; Silence; Psalm (or hymn or psalm paraphrase); Second Reading; Silence; Gospel Acclamation/Gospel Hymn; Gospel; Homily; Silence; Intercessory Prayers; Sign of Peace; Lord's Prayer; Offering (for a Common Ministry)—anthem or instrumental music; Prayer of Praise; Hymn; and Departure of the Ministers.

---

*This English translation is from the General Introduction of *De Benedictionibus,* (c) 1985, International Committee on English in the Liturgy, Inc. All rights reserved. Used with permission.

Suggested readings, hymns and alternate patterns of worship for use with the basic structure have been prepared for the following: The Season of the Incarnation—Advent, Christmas, Epiphany; The Paschal Season—Lent, Easter, Pentecost; Reformation Sunday/Reconciliation/Reunion; Week of Prayer for Christian Unity; Justification by Faith; Thanksgiving; Baptismal Renewal; Sanctoral feasts.

An Introduction spells out the primacy of the Word of God and Christ's presence in his word, contains guidelines for planning and making good use of the service by Lutheran and Roman Catholic parishes and suggests occasions when the service might best be used.

Service of the Word is being published by Augsburg Publishing House, 426 South Fifth Street, Minneapolis, MN 55440. It will be available for sale from both the publisher and from the USCC Office of Publishing and Promotion Services, 1312 Massachusetts Avenue, NW, Washington, DC 20005-4105.

Individual Communion Cups

Since the promulgation of the 1969 *Missale Romanum* by Pope Paul VI, various questions have arisen with regard to the reception of Holy Communion under both kinds. Recently the Secretariat of the Bishops' Committee on the Liturgy was asked whether it is permissible to use "individual communion cups" at Mass.

The General Instruction of the Roman Missal authorizes only four methods for the reception of the precious blood for the Latin Church: (1) directly from the chalice, (2) by intinction, (3) by using a silver tube, and (4) by using a spoon (GIRM, nos. 240-252; see also the norms approved by the National Conference of Catholic Bishops and confirmed by the Apostolic See, *This Holy and Living Sacrifice: Directory for the Celebration and Reception of Communion under Both Kinds,* nos. 44-52). In the description of the Rite of Communion under Both Kinds directly from the chalice (nos. 244-245), it is clear that the chalice is to be of such a size as to permit a number of communicants to receive the precious blood.

While individual communion cups are used in certain other Christian Churches, they have never been approved for use in Roman Catholic eucharistic celebrations. Nor can the use of such vessels be understood as authorized by the current provisions of the General Instruction of the Roman Missal when it speaks of "chalices." Proper concerns for health and hygiene may in certain instances require another form of administration of the precious blood. However, such concern cannot be said to legitimate the use of individual communion cups as a replacement for the chalice (see the statement of the Bishops' Committee on the Liturgy, "Communion Under Both Kinds and Certain Health Concerns," *Newsletter,* December 1985, pp. 45-46).

Liturgical Programs/Conferences

Rensselaer Program of Church Music and Liturgy

The 1986 summer session of the Rensselaer Program of Church Music and Liturgy will be held June 24-August 8. More than thirty courses in graduate and undergraduate music theory, history and practice, and liturgy will be offered. Students may choose any of the following specializations: organ, voice, piano, guitar, composition, conducting, or music education. Available also is a three-summer sequence, leading to a Diploma in Pastoral Liturgy.

In the area of liturgical music course offerings will include: Theory, Composition, Conducting, History, and Applied Music. Liturgy courses will include the following: Music as Pastoral Prayer; Children's Liturgies; Rites of Christian Initiation; Symbol, Ritual, and Celebration; The Eucharist in Christian Tradition; and The Liturgical Year.

For further information and applications for the summer session, contact: Rev. Lawrence Heiman, C.PP.S., Director of the Rensselaer Program of Church Music and Liturgy, Saint Joseph's College, P.O. Box 815, Rensselaer, IN 47978. Telephone 219/866-7111.

BISHOPS' COMMITTEE ON THE LITURGY
NEWSLETTER
NATIONAL CONFERENCE OF CATHOLIC BISHOPS

**1986
VOLUME XXII
APRIL/MAY**

Choctaw Translation Approved by NCCB Administrative Committee

On March 18, 1986, the Administrative Committee of the National Conference of Catholic Bishops approved *ad interim* the translation of the Order of Mass and eucharistic prayers in the Choctaw language.

Choctaw was approved as a liturgical language by the NCCB Administrative Committee on September 13, 1984. This action was confirmed by the Apostolic See by decree of the Congregation for Divine Worship on October 1, 1984 (Prot. CD 1677/84). Soon after that time, a translation of the Mass was prepared by Father Robert Goodyear, S.T. and Ms. Roseanna Tubby of Mississippi. The translation was independently reviewed for accuracy by Ms. Thalis Lewis of the Tribal Council of the Mississippi Band of Choctaw Indians and was then approved by the Bishops' Committee on the Liturgy for submission to the Administrative Committee on November 10, 1985.

The translation was presented to the Administrative Committee in two sections: (a) *Literal Interlinear Translation,* a word-for-word and line-by-line translation; and (b) a parallel running English translation of the Choctaw.

An appendix to the translation contained a background paper concerning the history of the Choctaw people and their language. Choctaw is the primary language of 97% of the Choctaw people of Mississippi. It is also spoken, with dialect variants, in Alabama, Oklahoma, and Louisiana.

Confirmation of the liturgical translation by the Apostolic See has been requested.

Father Ronald F. Krisman Appointed Conference Relocation Coordinator

On April 18, 1986 Monsignor Daniel F. Hoye, NCCB/USCC General Secretary, announced the appointment of Father Ronald F. Krisman, Associate Director of the Liturgy Secretariat, as Coordinator of the Relocation of NCCB/USCC Conference Headquarters.

Construction of a new building housing the national headquarters of the National Conference of Catholic Bishops and the United States Catholic Conference in northeast Washington (near The Catholic University of America) is tentatively slated to begin in October 1986. Father Krisman's responsibilities include acting as liaison between conference staff directors and the architectural firm in the designing of the building. He will also oversee special task groups established to provide input regarding a number of critical areas: library, food service, telecommunications, chapel, finance and administration, security and fire suppression, etc. And while the building is being constructed, he will assist Mr. Ralph Clark of Arlington, who has been selected as the on-site supervisor of construction for the NCCB/USCC. Finally, toward the end of the construction period, Father Krisman will participate in coordinating staff activities leading up to the actual move to the new building on about the first weekend of June 1988.

Over the next two years Father Krisman will continue to work, on a part-time basis, in his position as Associate Director of the Liturgy Secretariat.

Monsignor Alan F. Detscher Appointed Secretariat Consultant

Monsignor Daniel F. Hoye, NCCB/USCC General Secretary, has named Monsignor Alan F. Detscher as Consultant to the Secretariat of the Bishops' Committee on the Liturgy. Msgr. Detscher will assume

1312 MASSACHUSETTS AVENUE, N.W. • WASHINGTON, D.C. 20005

several of Father Krisman's duties in the Secretariat while the latter serves as Coordinator of Relocation for the Conference.

Monsignor Detscher is Secretary to the Most Reverend Walter Curtis, Bishop of Bridgeport. He also directs the diocesan office of worship in Bridgeport. He holds licentiate and doctoral degrees in liturgy, both awarded *summa cum laude,* from the Pontifical Liturgical Institute of San Anselmo in Rome, and has served as an advisor to the Bishops' Committee on the Liturgy for the past six years and as a member of various subcommittees of the International Commission on English in the Liturgy.

As a member of the staff, Msgr. Detscher will assist the Secretariat in its projects and in its day-to-day activities. As of May 1, 1986, he will ordinarily work at the Secretariat in Washington on Tuesday and Wednesday each week.

The Bishops' Committee on the Liturgy and its Secretariat are grateful to Bishop Curtis for allowing Msgr. Detscher to assist the Secretariat.

Consultation on the Order of Mass and Eucharistic Prayers

In late 1982, as part of its Comprehensive Revisions Program, the International Commission on English in the Liturgy (ICEL) began the process of consultation with the member and associate member conferences of bishops of the English-speaking world to revise the translation of *The Roman Missal.* Responses from the 1982 consultation workbook were reviewed by ICEL's Episcopal Board and Advisory Committee and, as a result, the translation of the presidential prayers of the *Missal* (opening prayers, prayers over the gifts, prayers after communion, solemn blessings, etc.) are presently being revised by ICEL's subcommittee on translations and revisions.

The next phase in this process of revision entails a review of the current translation of the Order of Mass, the nine eucharistic prayers, and the prefaces. To facilitate this phase of the revisions process, ICEL has issued a second workbook on *The Roman Missal,* entitled *Consultation on Revision: The Roman Missal, Order of Mass.* Copies have already been sent to each bishop and diocesan liturgical commission/office of worship in the United States.

It is ICEL's goal to present the revised translation of *The Roman Missal* to the conferences of bishops in late 1990 or early 1991. A great deal of work remains to be done to revise the more than 1600 texts of the *Missal.* For this reason, and so that the revision process may continue at a reasonable pace, the conferences of bishops having membership in ICEL have been asked to review the present translations contained in the workbook and to forward their responses directly to the ICEL Secretariat. Model response sheets are found on pages 134-135 in the workbook. Because many questions have arisen over the last decade with regard to the various elements of the Order of Mass and related questions, respondents are also asked to answer the questionnaire found on page 136 of the workbook. The Foreword of the workbook explains the process in some detail (see pp. v-vii).

The comments of experts in Scripture, Latin, English, liturgy, literature, the classics, etc., as well as the suggestions of those who proclaim the texts and those who hear them are especially welcome. The Liturgy Secretariat has a few extra copies of the Consultation booklet. Those wishing a copy may request one. However, it should be noted that the workbook may be reproduced as needed.

Responses should be sent no later than January 1, 1987 either to the Bishops' Committee on the Liturgy (1312 Massachusetts Avenue, NW, Washington, DC 20005) or directly to the ICEL Secretariat (1275 K Street, NW, Suite 1202, Washington, DC 20005).

Adaptations Approved in the *Rite of Admission to Candidacy for Ordination as a Deacon* and in the *Rite of Ordination of a Deacon*

On April 18, 1986 the National Conference of Catholic Bishops received confirmation from the Congregation for Divine Worship for several adaptations in the *Rite of Admission to Candidacy for Ordination as Deacons* and the *Rite of Ordination of a Deacon.*

These adaptations were prepared by the Bishops' Committee on the Liturgy at the request of and with the concurrence of the Bishops' Committee on the Permanent Diaconate. Subsequently they received the approval *ad interim* of the Administrative Committee of the National Conference of Catholic Bishops on September 10, 1985. One text was later amended to reflect the suggestions of the Congregation for Divine Worship (January 16, 1986/Prot. N. 1330/85) and was approved by the NCCB Administrative Committee on March 18, 1986.

The newly approved adaptations, which are printed below, are to be inserted into *The Roman Pontifical* (ICEL, 1978), and other editions of these rites, and may be implemented immediately.

Rite of Admission to Candidacy for Ordination as Deacons

EXAMINATION (Roman Pontifical, p. 145)

(After the Bishop asks the candidates about their resolve to prepare themselves, etc., the following title, rubrics and texts are added:

For married candidates

You have been sealed and strengthened in the sacrament of marriage in mutual and lasting fidelity. Therefore, it is proper to ask the consent of your wife, who is united to you in the communion of love and life. Your ministry will not only make demands upon your life together, but will become the source of new blessings in your family.

Then the bishop turns to the wife (wives) of the married candidate(s) and asks:

Are you resolved to help your husband continue to grow in faith and to support his desire to serve the Church in the order of deacons?

Wife/Wives:

I am.

INTERCESSIONS (Roman Pontifical, p. 146)

(The following text is added in brackets after the third intercession.)

Deacon or minister:

That the wives and families of these candidates may continue to support and help them by their love and prayer as the candidates prepare for ministry in the Church, let us pray to the Lord:

R. Lord, hear our prayer.

Approved by the NCCB Administrative Committee on September 10, 1985 and March 18, 1986. Confirmed by the Congregation for Divine Worship on January 16, 1986 and April 18, 1986 (Prot. N. 1330/85).

Rite of Ordination of Deacons and Rite of Ordination of a Deacon

HOMILY

(The following rubrics are to replace those found at number 14 under the heading "Homily"—Pontifical, pages 159 and 177.)

Page 159, Ordination of Deacons - The Rubric is changed to read as follows: "Then all sit, and the bishop gives the homily. He begins with the text of the readings from Scripture and then speaks to the people and the candidates about the office of deacon. *The bishop should take into consideration the state in life (married, celibate) in which the various candidates will exercise their ministry, and speak about the meaning and importance of celibacy and Christian marriage in the Church.* He may use these words:"

Page 177, Ordination of a Deacon - The rubric is changed as follows: "Then all sit, and the bishop gives the homily. He begins with the text of the readings from Scripture and then speaks to the people and the candidate about the office of deacon. *The bishop should take into consideration the state in life (married, celibate) in which the candidate will exercise his ministry, and speak about the meaning and importance of celibacy and/or Christian marriage in the Church.* He may use these words:"

Approved by the NCCB Administrative Committee on September 10, 1985. Confirmed by the Congregation for Divine Worship on January 16, 1986 (Prot. N. 1330/85).

In Memoriam: Bishop John J. Dougherty

The Bishops' Committee on the Liturgy notes with sadness the death of Bishop John J. Dougherty, former auxiliary bishop of Newark, New Jersey, and former president of Seton Hall University, South Orange, New Jersey. Bishop Dougherty, who was 77, served as the representative of the National Conference of Catholic Bishops on the Episcopal Board of the International Commission on English in the Liturgy from 1968 to 1976.

A noted biblicist and preacher, Bishop Dougherty was for a number of years a member of the faculty of Immaculate Conception Seminary, Darlington, New Jersey. He became auxiliary bishop of Newark in 1963 and retired from that post in 1982.

> O God,
> from the ranks of your priests
> you chose your servant John
> to fulfill the office of bishop.
> Grant that he may share
> in the eternal fellowship of those priests
> who, faithful to the teachings of the apostles,
> dwell in your heavenly kingdom.
>
> We ask this through Christ our Lord.
> Amen.

NALR *Assemblybook 1986*

The North American Liturgy Resources, 10802 North 23rd Avenue, Phoenix, AZ, has recently published a new annual participation aid called *Assemblybook 1986* along with its companion *Scripturebook 1986*. *Assemblybook 1986* contains the following notice on the acknowledgment page: "*Edited and developed in consultation with the Bishop's [sic] Committee on the Liturgy.*"

While it is true that all participation aids containing approved liturgical texts must be reviewed by the Secretariat of the Bishops' Committee on the Liturgy to determine if they fulfill the requirements established by the Bishops' Committee on the Liturgy in the Committee's *Guidelines for the Publication of Liturgical Books* (see *Newsletter,* June/July 1985, pp. 22-26) and/or the Committee's *Guidelines for Missalettes* (see *Newsletter,* August/September 1985, pp. 31-35), such review does not constitute an endorsement of those publications. In the case of *Assemblybook 1986* the page proofs were reviewed by the Secretariat, but the above-mentioned notice was neither included in those proofs nor authorized for later insertion into the acknowledgments.

In the course of its review of *Assemblybook 1986,* the Secretariat asked the NALR editors to make certain changes in and additions to the booklet. But this did not constitute "editing" or "development" of the booklet. Nor is it correct to state that the Bishops' Committee on the Liturgy or its Secretariat endorses *Assemblybook 1986* or, for that matter, any other participation aid.

When a liturgical book or a minister's edition of an excerpt of a liturgical book is published it is required to add the following statement: *Published by authority of the Bishops' Committee on the Liturgy, National Conference of Catholic Bishops.* No other statement of authorization is generally required from the Bishops' Committee on the Liturgy. For participation aids the Committee or its Secretariat notifies the International Commission on English in the Liturgy that the conditions in its *Guidelines* have been fulfilled. ICEL then grants its permission for the reprinting of copyrighted liturgical texts. There is generally no other statement of authorization required by the Bishops' Committee on the Liturgy.

Recently, a pamphlet entitled "Liturgical Directives" was mailed by an anonymous source to priests and religious in several parts of the United States. The document consists of highly selective excerpts from official liturgical documents of the Church.

While this pamphlet contains a number of current liturgical norms for the Roman Rite, it betrays a misunderstanding of the nature of liturgical law, the manner of its legislation, the subject and object of liturgical law, and the authority of liturgical norms. Likewise it betrays a misconception of the nature of ecclesiastical authority as it relates to liturgical law. Thus, because the pamphlet may already have caused a certain amount of confusion, it should be pointed out that this document does not have the sanction of the National Conference of Catholic Bishops in those areas in which the conference is competent to legislate.

"Liturgical Directives" is a defective document for many reasons. For example, it omits all relevant particular norms and decrees approved and enacted by the National Conference of Catholic Bishops for the dioceses of the United States and confirmed by the Apostolic See. Neither are special indults granted by the Apostolic See to the NCCB included in the pamphlet. And while the pamphlet appears to have the sanction of the Holy See, this is not actually the case.

The following points concerning authority over the liturgy should be noted. *Sacrosanctum Concilium,* the Constitution on the Sacred Liturgy, states that the bishop is the chief liturgist in his diocese. It is the bishop's role to govern, promote, and teach the liturgy. "Liturgical Directives" was circulated without the prior approval or knowledge of the bishops in the United States. Moreover, it was circulated anonymously. Thus, the document has caused confusion to pastors who did not know the source or origin or reason for which the pamphlet was sent.

It should also be kept in mind that liturgical law grants regulation over certain aspects of the liturgy to national or regional conferences of bishops. This regulation is confirmed by the Apostolic See. The author/compiler of "Liturgical Directives" is obviously unaware of this aspect of the liturgical norms of the Church.

Finally, the pamphlet called "Liturgical Directives" does not have the endorsement of the Bishops' Committee on the Liturgy and was circulated without the knowledge of the Committee or of any other organism within the National Conference of Catholic Bishops. Besides the Holy See, only the diocesan bishop or the conference of bishops are authorized to issue documents of liturgical norms, directives, and legislation.

Hispanic Liturgy Subcommittee

The Hispanic Liturgy Subcommittee met in special session at the Washington Plaza Hotel, Washington, DC, on March 20-21, 1986, to review and respond to the proposed new Spanish translation of the Eucharistic Prayers for Masses of Reconciliation, the Eucharistic Prayers for Masses with Children, and the Eucharistic Prayers of the "Swiss Synod." The following members were present: Most Reverend Ricardo Ramirez, CSB, Chairman; Most Reverend Rene Valero, Sister Rosa Maria Icaza, CCVI (new member), Reverend Jose Rubio, Reverend Juan Sosa, and Reverend John A. Gurrieri.

The subcommittee considered the following agenda items: (1) review of the meeting of presidents and secretaries of National Liturgical Commissions of Spanish-Speaking Conferences of Bishops; (2) review of the new Spanish translation of the Eucharistic Prayers for Masses of Reconciliation (= EP-R), for Masses with Children (= EP-C), and of the "Swiss Synod" ("Sinodo Suisso"/= EP-SS); (3) strategy for implementation of the new common Spanish translation; (4) consultation workbook on a Spanish Sacramentary for the dioceses of the USA; (5) the use of the term "hombres" in the eucharistic prayers.

The subcommittee discussed the meeting of presidents and secretaries of national liturgical commissions of countries where Spanish is spoken which took place at the Old Synod Hall at the Vatican, February 3-7, 1986. Bishop Ramirez explained that the National Conference of Catholic Bishops had been elected to full membership in the consultation and in the future commission.

The subcommittee also reviewed the various positions relating to the usage of *Vosotros* and *Ustedes* in the written liturgical text and in spoken proclamation.

The subcommittee then studied the translations of EP-R and EP-C and the document containing variations from the five Spanish language versions of the Sacramentary. The subcommittee's suggested *variantes* were subsequently forwarded to the Congregation for Divine Worship. After a review of EP-SS the subcommittee made recommendations for revision in the texts, which also were submitted to the Holy See. The subcommittee next discussed the possibility of seeking approval of EP-SS by the NCCB for use in the USA, although these texts are not approved in English translation. The reasons advanced for this recommendation were the following: (a) unity with the Spanish-speaking Church throughout the world; (b) EP-SS responds to the "signs of the times" as expressed at the Tercer Encuentro. The recommendation will be reviewed by the Bishops' Committee on the Liturgy.

The subcommittee next turned its attention to the production of the Hispanic Sacramentary Consultation workbook which must be revised in light of the Roman meeting. It was decided to add examples from the Chilean Sacramentary, to remove the eucharistic prayers, Gloria, Lord's Prayer, and Creeds. The workbook is presently being revised as a result of the subcommittee meeting.

Also discussed at the meeting was the project to compose original texts for the Hispanic Sacramentary, especially the following: alternative opening prayers, blessings, *monitiones,* invocations for the penitential rite. The criterion for composing these texts is to make the Hispanic Sacramentary as similar as possible to the American (English) Sacramentary.

Lead Me, Guide Me: The African American Catholic Hymnal

Bishop James Lyke, OFM, has announced the imminent publication of *Lead Me, Guide Me: The African American Catholic Hymnal.* The new hymnal, to be dedicated to Father Clarence Joseph Rivers of Cincinnati, will be published by GIA Publications (7404 South Mason Avenue, Chicago, IL 60638).

As the first hymnal published for Black Catholics, *Lead Me, Guide Me* marks a milestone in Catholic liturgical publishing. The hymnal was the inspiration of Bishop Lyke, who formed the Black Catholic Hymnal Committee. The project was sponsored by the National Black Catholic Clergy Caucus and was supported by various other national Black Catholic organizations. *Lead Me, Guide Me* was also sponsored by the Black Liturgy Subcommittee of the Bishops' Committee on the Liturgy. The Subcommittee is chaired by Bishop Wilton Gregory of Chicago.

Liturgical Programs/Conferences

National Association of Pastoral Musicians

The 1986 regional conventions of the National Association of Pastoral Musicians will be held between June and August in the following locations: Richmond, VA (June 16-19), New Orleans, LA (June 30-July 3), Rochester, NY (July 14-17), Indianapolis, IN (July 21-24), Sacramento, CA (July 28-31), and Bismarck, ND (August 4-7). Each conference includes lectures and special interest sessions, music showcases, special musical events and liturgical celebrations.

For further information, write: NPM Conventions, 225 Sheridan Street, NW, Washington, DC 20011. Telephone: 202/723-5800.

Notre Dame Center for Pastoral Liturgy

The Notre Dame Center for Pastoral Liturgy will sponsor its Fifteenth Annual Conference from June 9-12, 1986 on the University of Notre Dame campus. Having as its theme, "Reconciliation: The Continuing Agenda," the program is designed to expand and deepen the knowledge and appreciation of reconciliation in the life and mission of the Church. Keynote speaker Reverend James Lopresti, SJ, will consider "The Church as Sinful Reconciler." Other major presenters will be Reverend James Dallen ("Theological Foundations of Reconciliation") and Sister Kathleen Hughes, RSCJ ("Ritualizing Reconciliation: Cultural and Christian Dimensions").

Focus Sessions will develop topics associated with the theological dimensions of reconciliation as well as liturgical and pastoral themes related to the ritualizing of reconciliation.

For information on program and speakers, contact: Notre Dame Center for Pastoral Liturgy, P.O. Box 81, Notre Dame, IN 46556. Telephone: 219/239-5435. For information on registration and accommodation fees, contact: Pastoral Liturgy Conference, Center for Continuing Education, P.O. Box 1008, Notre Dame, IN 46556. Telephone: 219/239-6691.

New York School of Liturgical Music

The New York School of Liturgical Music will sponsor its seventh annual summer seminar at the Catholic Center at New York University from July 7-10, 1986. Presentors will include Father Gabriel Coless, OSB; Robert Hebble; Dr. Fred Moleck; Sr. Norita Lanners, OSB; Michael Hay; and Larry King. Advanced registration (before June 27) is $150.00. Housing is available at the New York University Dormitory ($160.00 double occupancy) or at Southgate Tower Hotel.

For further information, write: The Registrar, New York School of Liturgical Music, 1011 First Avenue, New York, NY 10022. Telephone: 212/371-1000, Ext. 2291 or 2292.

Great Lakes Liturgical Conference

The Great Lakes Liturgical Conference, sponsored by the Office of Worship, Diocese of Grand Rapids, will be held August 4-6, 1986, at the Amway Grand Plaza Hotel in Grand Rapids, MI. The theme for the three-day conference is "Ancient Rites, Future Signs: A Sacramental People Celebrate." General session speakers include: Rev. Regis Duffy, OFM; Rev. Edward J. Dietrick, Dr. Tad Guzie, and Rev. John Melloh, SM.

Seminar sessions will explore such topics as Eucharistic spirituality, sacramental reconciliation, season and sacraments, initiation and music, sacramental preparation and celebration with the developmentally impaired, and sacred spaces. Seminar speakers include Rev. Gaspar F. Ancona, Rev. Giles Pater, Mr. Lucio Caruso, Charmaine A. Kulczyk, Marty Haugen and Austin Lovelace.

Registration fee is $80 (before July 14), $90 after that date. Individual daily rates are also available.

For further information and registration forms, write: Conference Services by Loretta Reif, P.O. Box 5226, Rockford, IL 61125. Telephone: 815/399-2140.

Loyola Pastoral Institute

The Loyola Pastoral Institute, in cooperation with the Seminary of the Immaculate Conception, Huntington, NY, has announced two summer workshops. "Music in Worship: Contemporary Issues and Historical Roots" will be held on June 30-July 3, 1986. By examining the way earlier church communities responded to their own needs by utilizing the gifts available to them, this seminar proposes to offer sound pastoral approaches to meet today's needs. Presenters include Reverends Edward Foley and James Lopresti and Sister Mary Alice Piil. A variety of lectures, discussions and demonstrations, along with morning and evening prayer and Eucharist, will be offered each day.

Tuition is $100, room and board $75, and meals only $40. Special group and parish rates are also available.

"Liturgical Preaching" will be held on July 7-10, 1986. Under the direction of Father James Lopresti, SJ, this seminar will examine the place of the Word in the liturgy. With special attention to the demands of the liturgical year and the prayers of the eucharistic liturgy, participants will discuss the unique place of preaching in the liturgy. All sessions will be held daily from 9:00-11:30 a.m.

Tuition is $50, room and board (at the seminary) is $25 per night.

For further information on both conferences, write: Loyola Pastoral Institute, 980 Park Avenue, New York, NY 10028. Telephone: 212/861-2686.

Christian Initiation Subcommittee Meeting

The Christian Initiation Subcommittee of the Bishops' Committee on the Liturgy met at the Techny Towers Conference Center, Divine Word International, Techny, IL, on March 12-13, 1986. The members of the Subcommittee include: Most Reverend John S. Cummins, Bishop of Oakland; Reverend James Dunning and Ms. Karen Hinman, North American Forum on the Catechumenate; Reverend Raymond B. Kemp, Washington, DC; and the following directors of diocesan worship offices—Reverend Robert Duggan, Washington, DC; Sr. Luanne Durst, OSF, La Crosse; Reverend Donald Neumann, Galveston-Houston; Reverend James Notebaart, Saint Paul and Minneapolis; Reverend Ronald Lewinski, Chicago; and Sister Barbara O'Dea, DW, Pueblo, CO.

Under the chairmanship of the Most Reverend Joseph A. Ferrario, Bishop of Honolulu, the subcommittee discussed the "white book" (final translation) of the *Rite of Christian Initiation of Adults* (hereafter "*RCIA*"), released by the International Commission on English in the Liturgy in early 1986, and proposals for American adaptations of the ritual book. The subcommittee also discussed the presentation of these materials to the members of the National Conference of Catholic Bishops, tentatively set for November 1986, within the context of a national strategy for the full implementation of the *RCIA* in the United States.

One of the issues which the Subcommittee is studying is that of liturgical rites for celebrations with baptized but uncatechized adults who are seeking reception into the full communion of the Catholic Church. Members of the subcommittee noted the common experience in the United States of having numerous baptized but uncatechized adults involved in catechetical formation along with catechumens. Rites adapted from and analogous to those found in the *RCIA* are being composed throughout the country. It was the desire of the subcommittee to recognize the need for these rites by providing them as appendices to the *RCIA*. Including such rites would not preclude their further development, but it could assist greatly in preserving the fundamental theological distinctions between the baptized and unbaptized persons coming into the Catholic Church.

In the proposed amendments to the ritual book, the subcommittee has identified: 1) ritual decisions to be requested of the National Conference of Catholic Bishops in response to no. 33 of the Introduction to the *RCIA*; 2) editorial changes in the *RCIA* "white book" necessitated by these ritual decisions; 3) proposed adaptations to the ritual book and corresponding editorial changes.

Possible adaptations which the Subcommittee may recommend for approval by the Bishops' Committee on the Liturgy for presentation to the National Conference of Catholic Bishops include: a Parish Rite preceding the Rite of Election, when the latter is to be celebrated by the bishop in the Cathedral; an Optional Rite of Election for Children of Catechetical Age; a Rite of Welcome for Baptized but Uncatechized Adults as they begin their catechetical formation; an Adaptation of the Scrutinies for Baptized but Uncatechized Adults.

The subcommittee also is preparing a pastoral commentary on the *Rite of Christian Initiation of Adults,* and it has produced the first draft of national statutes regulating the catechumenate (called for by canon 788 of the 1983 Code of Canon Law), which it will refer to the NCCB Committee on Pastoral Research and Practices and the Committee on Canonical Affairs.

The next meeting of the Subcommittee will be held on June 5-7, 1986, in Saint Paul, Minnesota.

BISHOPS' COMMITTEE ON THE LITURGY
NEWSLETTER
NATIONAL CONFERENCE OF CATHOLIC BISHOPS

**1986
VOLUME XXII
JUNE/JULY**

Meeting of the Bishops' Committee on the Liturgy

The Bishops' Committee on the Liturgy met with its advisors and consultants at Saint John Vianney Seminary in Saint Paul, MN, June 7-8, 1986. Information reports were given on the following items: (1) the visit of Cardinal Paul Augustin Mayer, Prefect of the Congregation for Divine Worship, to the NCCB Liturgy Secretariat; (2) the projects of the Hispanic Liturgy Subcommittee, the Black Liturgy Subcommittee, the Blessings Subcommittee, the Subcommittee on Christian Initiation, and the Lectionary Subcommittee; (3) the projects of the International Commission on English in the Liturgy; (4) the publications of the Liturgy Secretariat; (5) the projected plans and programs of the Bishops' Committee on the Liturgy and its Secretariat in 1987; (6) the Federation of Diocesan Liturgical Commissions; and (7) the Instituto de Liturgia Hispana.

The following agenda items were considered by the Committee: (1) approval of the "white book" (final translation) of the *Rite of Christian Initiation of Adults* for submission to the members of the National Conference of Catholic Bishops in November 1986; (2) proposed new texts to be added to the *Rite of Christian Initiation* for the dioceses of the USA; (3) canonical statutes for the catechumenate; (4) preliminary sketch of a national plan for the implementation of the *Rite of Christian Initiation of Adults* in the dioceses of the USA; (5) the outline, new liturgical texts, and graphics for *Household Blessings and Prayers;* (6) the American edition of the proposed *Book of Blessings* (English translation of *De Benedictionibus*); (7) the results of the consultation on the Eucharistic Prayer of Saint Basil; (8) the draft of a volume in the Study Text series on eucharistic worship and devotion; (9) the Spanish translation of the "Swiss Synod" eucharistic prayers; (10) a proposed statement of guidelines on the various options permitted in the celebration of the Mass; (11) a proposed Lectionary for Masses with Children being prepared by a committee of the Federation of Diocesan Liturgical Commissions; (12) Sunday celebrations in the absence of a priest.

The Committee approved a number of new texts for incorporation into the ICEL "white book" version of the *Rite of Christian Initiation of Adults* to be submitted with the "white book" to the National Conference of Catholic Bishops in November 1986. Among these additional chapters are the following: a Rite of Sending of the Catechumens for Election by the Bishop; and an optional Rite of Election for Children of Catechetical Age. Four optional rites for celebrations with baptized but previously uncatechized Catholics preparing for reception of the sacraments of confirmation and eucharist have also been approved: Welcoming the Candidates; Sending the Candidates for Recognition by the Bishop; Calling the Candidates to Continuing Conversion (analogous to the Rite of Election of catechumens); and a Penitential Rite (Scrutiny). And three combined celebrations involving rites with catechumens and rites with baptized but previously uncatechized adult Catholics have been proposed for inclusion with the one combined rite (the Easter Vigil celebration) already a part of the "white book." These three new chapters are: Celebration of the Rite of Acceptance into the Order of Catechumens and of the Rite of Welcoming Adult Catholics who Seek to Complete their Christian Initiation; Parish Celebration Sending Catechumens for Election and Candidates for Recognition by the Bishop; and Celebration of the Rite of Election of Catechumens and of the Call to Continuing Conversion of Candidates who Seek to Complete their Christian Initiation.

In certain cases, it will be proposed that the rites composed for celebrations with baptized but previously uncatechized adult Catholics (authorized by nos. 299-303 of the Latin *editio typica* of the *Rite of Christian Initiation of Adults*) may also be used in celebrations with baptized but previously uncatechized adult non-Catholics who are preparing to be received into the full communion of the Catholic Church.

1312 MASSACHUSETTS AVENUE, N.W. • WASHINGTON, D.C. 20005

In accord with canon 888.3 of the 1983 Code of Canon Law, canonical statutes for the catechumenate will be proposed to the NCCB for its approval. The Committee reviewed a first draft of the statutes which will be revised during the summer. The first draft has also been reviewed by the following other NCCB committees: Committee on Canonical Affairs, Committee on Pastoral Research and Practices, Committee for Ecumenical and Interreligious Affairs.

A national plan to implement the final version of the RCIA is also under preparation. The Bishops' Committee on the Liturgy reviewed and discussed a variety of ideas suggested by its Subcommittee on Christian Initiation.

In 1987 the Bishops' Committee on the Liturgy will propose two forms of the Book of Blessings for the NCCB's approval: first, a translation of *De Benedictionibus* which incorporates particular blessings for the dioceses of the United States (see *Newsletter*, March 1986, pp. 9-10); secondly, *Household Blessings and Prayers,* a book of blessings, liturgical prayers, and devotions for the family and home. At the June meeting the Committee approved the final version of the tables of contents of the two books. The Blessings Subcommittee will continue its work toward their completion.

After a careful review of the responses forwarded by bishops, diocesan liturgical commissions and offices of worship, and other consultants, the Bishops' Committee on the Liturgy decided not to propose the Eucharistic Prayer of Saint Basil for use in the dioceses of the United States. (On March 14, 1986 the Committee approved the submission of Eucharistic Prayer A, an original English composition, to the NCCB.) Having reviewed the Spanish translation of the "Swiss Synod" eucharistic prayers (already approved and confirmed for the dioceses of Spain and a number of Latin American conferences), the Committee decided to submit the prayers to the NCCB in November 1986 for approval and subsequent confirmation by the Holy See.

Concerning Sunday worship in the absence of a priest, a growing phenomenon in the United States, the Committee decided upon several courses of action: (a) it will review a document prepared by the Archdiocese of Portland over the next several months; (b) an interim set of guidelines will be prepared for the Committee's review later this year; (c) final guidelines will be issued upon the publication of the norms now being prepared by the Congregation for Divine Worship.

The Committee also approved the direction being taken by the Federation of Diocesan Liturgical Commissions in its project to prepare a *Lectionary for Masses with Children.* The Committee also discussed the following: (1) the manner of celebrating the *mandatum* at the Mass of the Lord's Supper on Holy Thursday; and (2) a Catholic-Jewish colloquium on preaching scheduled to take place in January 1987 under the aegis of the Liturgy Secretariat and the Anti-Defamation League of B'nai B'rith.

Pope John Paul II on Popular Piety and Liturgy

On Thursday, April 24, 1986, His Holiness Pope John Paul II received in audience the eleven bishops of the Episcopal Conference of Abruzzo and Molise on their "ad limina" visit. After commending the bishops on the level of liturgical renewal achieved in the region in response to the Second Vatican Council, the Holy Father addressed the matter of popular piety in its relation to the Church's liturgical life. An extended excerpt from the translation of the Pope's address follows. (For the complete text see the English-language edition of L'Osservatore Romano, *May 12, 1986, pp. 8-9).*

I would like to draw your attention as pastors to one point in particular: that of popular piety and its relation to the liturgical life.

The Constitution on the Sacred Liturgy of the Second Vatican Council contains an explicit reference to the problem, when in no. 13 it speaks of the "pious practices of the Christian people," praising them and recommending them, provided that they are "in conformity with the laws and norms of the Church." It follows from this that those manifestations of piety and of devotion which are still alive among the Christian people, for example, the pastoral feasts, pilgrimages to shrines, the various forms in which devotion to the saints is expressed, cannot be ignored or treated with indifference or contempt.

Popular piety or popular devotion is, in fact, as already noted by Paul VI in the Apostolic Exhortation *Evangelii Nuntiandi,* rich in values. "It manifests a thirst for God that only the simple and the poor can know. It makes people capable of generosity and sacrifice even to the point of heroism, when it is a matter of manifesting belief. It involves an acute awareness of the profound attributes of God: fatherhood, providence, loving and constant presence. It engenders interior attitudes rarely observed to the same degree elsewhere: patience, the sense of the cross in daily life, detachment, openness to others, devotion" (no. 48).

Certainly, however, not everything in these religious manifestations is of the same elevated quality.

Because they are human, their motivations can be mixed with feelings of powerlessness in face of the events of life, with a simple desire for security rather than a lively confidence in Providence or a feeling of gratitude and adoration. Furthermore, they are expressed in signs, gestures and formulas which sometimes take on an excessive importance, to the point of seeking the spectacular. Nevertheless, they are essentially manifestations that express the nature of man, and a recognition of man's basic dependence as a creature on his Creator.

The fact that popular piety is at the same time a richness and a danger should stimulate the vigilance of the pastors of the Church. However, they should carry out their duty of providing orientation with a great degree of patience, because, as Saint Augustine already warned in reference to certain forms of the cult of the saints in his time, "We teach one thing: we are forced to tolerate another (*Contra Faustum,* 20, 21: CSEL 25, 263).

What really matters, revered brothers, is that we take note of the permanence of the religious need of man, underlying the diversity of its expressions, and make a continuous effort to purify it and to elevate it through evangelization.

This method has always been followed by the Church, whether with regard to problems of inculturation, or regarding problems of popular piety and popular devotions. This is the way the Church acted when she had to receive a host of new converts after the edict of Constantine. This happened too in the case of the barbarian peoples of Europe. Again the same thing happened with the peoples of the new world to whom the Gospel had to be preached. And the same thing happens today too, in the necessary adaptation to the nature and to the traditions of the various peoples (cf. the Constitution on the Sacred Liturgy, *Sacrosanctum Concilium,* 37-40). We need never forget the orders that Pope Gregory the Great gave to the Apostle of England, Saint Augustine of Canterbury: they were not to destroy, but were to purify and consecrate to God the pagan temples and also the religious customs with which the people were accustomed to celebrate the annual religious festivals of their life (cf. Gregory the Great: Jaffé, *Regesta Pontificum,* no. 1848, letter of 10 July, 601).

In a country of ancient Christian traditions like Italy, the popular religious manifestations have an undeniable Christian character. Many customs of this country had their origin in the feasts of the Church and are still linked to them. This fact must be pointed out, and in the event that these festivities should stray too far from their point of departure, every effort should be made to bring them back to their ancient origins.

It is our task as pastors to see to it that these acts of devotion be corrected if necessary, and especially that they do not degenerate into a false type of piety, superstition, or magical practices. Thus, the devotion to the saints expressed in the patronal feasts, pilgrimages, processions and so many other forms of piety, should not sink to the level of a mere search for protection for material goods or for bodily health. Rather, the saints should be presented to the faithful as models of life and of imitation of Christ, as the sure way that leads to him.

The best remedy against deviations, which are always possible, is to permeate these manifestations of popular piety with the word of the Gospel, leading those who thrive on these forms of popular piety from an initial and sometimes faltering belief to an act of authentic Christian faith.

The evangelization of popular piety will free it gradually of its defects; it will consolidate it through a process of purification so its ambiguities may acquire a character more clearly marked by faith, hope and charity. We must by no means underestimate the value of this word of catechesis. The people in general are undernourished in the matter of Christian doctrine: it will be necessary to nourish them with the Word, especially on these occasions when even those who normally never, or almost never, participate in the life of the Church are present.

In conclusion, it could be affirmed that in the lives of the faithful and of the Christian communities there is and there should be a place for forms of piety that do not strictly come under the category of liturgical celebration. This implies a requirement: these forms of piety should not be superimposed on the times for liturgical celebration; they should not be allowed to compete with the most important solemnities of the liturgical year. If there is a devotion that has a value superior to all the others it is the devotion of the Church, namely, the cult it renders to God, its liturgical life, in the mysteries and in the seasons which follow each other in succession in the course of the year of the Lord.

A last practical consequence is that referred to in 1958 by Pope Pius XII: liturgical celebrations and pious exercises should never be mixed (cf. Congregation of Rites, *Instructio de Musica et Sacra Liturgia,* 3 September 1958, no. 12).

As you can see, an authentic liturgical ministry will never be able to neglect the riches of popular piety, the values proper to the culture of a people, so that such riches be illuminated, purified and introduced into the liturgy as an offering of the people.

I encourage you in this effort to make popular piety become a kind of teaching through which the Christian people can attain to an ever more conscious, active and fruitful participation in the liturgy of the Church. Assuring you of my most cordial affection, I impart my Blessing to you and to the faithful entrusted to your pastoral care.

Perpetual Exposition of the Blessed Sacrament

Recently the Secretariat has been asked by several bishops and diocesan liturgical commissions to comment on the new practice of "perpetual exposition" of the blessed sacrament in parish churches. The Secretariat has reviewed the question. The matter was also extensively discussed by the Bishops' Committee on the Liturgy at a meeting on March 14, 1986, and again during the Committee's meeting with its advisors and consultants on June 7-8, 1986. The Committee asked that the Secretariat publish the following response in its Newsletter. *The Secretariat is also preparing a volume in the Study Text series, to be issued later this year, which covers the history, theology, and liturgical practice of eucharistic devotion. That volume will also offer pastoral guidelines on eucharistic exposition.*

Question: Is perpetual exposition of the eucharist in parish churches permitted by liturgical and canon law?

1. Because eucharistic worship is so important to the devotional and spiritual life of the Church, but also in order to avoid the abuses of the past, the Church today carefully and strictly regulates the exposition of this holy sacrament. The present discipline regarding all aspects of eucharistic worship and devotion is governed by the *Roman Ritual: Holy Communion and Worship of Eucharist Outside Mass,* promulgated by decree of the Congregation for Divine Worship, 21 June 1973, and also by the revised Code of Canon Law, canons 934-944.

2. The Church situates its traditional teaching on eucharistic worship and devotion in its doctrine on the Mass. This teaching is stated succinctly in the Congregation of Rites' 1967 instruction *Eucharisticum mysterium* and is repeated in the decree promulgating *Holy Communion and Worship of the Eucharist Outside Mass:* "the celebration of the eucharist in the sacrifice of the Mass is the true origin and purpose of the worship shown to the eucharist outside Mass." Moreover, "the principal reason for reserving the sacrament after Mass is to unite, through sacramental communion, the faithful unable to participate in the Mass, especially the sick and the aged, with Christ and the offering of his sacrifice." The "practice of adoring this sacrament and offering to it the worship which is due to God" resulted from eucharistic reservation, "which became customary in order to permit the reception of communion."

3. The decree also states: "Once the sacrifice is offered and while the eucharist is reserved in churches and oratories," Christ Jesus is present; "he is truly Emmanuel, 'God with us.' He is in our midst day and night; full of grace and truth he dwells among us." Therefore, because "the veneration and adoration which is due to God himself" is to be shown to this holy sacrament, "as has always been customary in the Catholic Church," the Church must strictly regulate the reservation of the eucharist.

4. With regard to exposition, the Ritual states the following: "Exposition of the eucharist, either in the ciborium or in the monstrance, is intended to acknowledge Christ's marvelous presence in the sacrament." Through exposition we are invited to that "spiritual union with him that culminates in sacramental communion." Thus exposition "fosters very well the worship which is due to Christ in spirit and in truth" (no. 82).

5. With regard to the length of time during which the sacrament may be exposed, besides brief periods of

exposition, *Holy Communion and Worship of the Eucharist Outside Mass* permits and encourages lengthier periods of exposition and adoration in the following two cases only:

   a. exposition for an extended period of time once a year but with the consent of the local Ordinary and only if suitable numbers of the faithful are expected to be present (no. 86);

   b. exposition ordered by the local Ordinary for a grave and general necessity for a more extended period of supplication but where the faithful assemble in large numbers (no. 87).

6. With regard to perpetual exposition, this form is permitted only in the case of those religious communities of men or women who "according to the constitutions and regulations of their institute have the general practice of perpetual eucharistic adoration or adoration over extended periods of time" (no. 90). In other instances perpetual exposition is not permitted.

7. The following statement of the Congregation for Divine Worship is worth recalling: "if the sacrament were exposed continuously, there would be a lessening in the value of these occasions [exposition and adoration] as reminders of their proper place in the spiritual life and of their character as high points for reflection on the eucharist" (Response of the Congregation for Divine Worship, *Notitiae* [1971] 414-415).

8. Therefore, perpetual exposition of the blessed sacrament in parish churches and other oratories, except where permitted by law, is not permitted. With regard to all aspects of exposition, adoration, and benediction of the eucharist, the norms of *Holy Communion and Worship of the Eucharist Outside Mass,* nos. 82-100, and canons 941-943 of the Code of Canon Law are to be observed diligently.

9. While pastors are to make every effort possible to enable the faithful to worship Christ present in the eucharist, this must be done according to the norms laid down by the Roman Ritual and the Code of Canon Law, as cited above.

Visit of Cardinal Mayer to the Liturgy Secretariat

On May 13, 1986, Cardinal Paul Augustine Mayer, OSB, Prefect of the Congregation for Divine Worship, once again paid a courtesy visit to the NCCB Liturgy Secretariat in Washington. (Cardinal Mayer also visited Washington in the Spring of 1985.) The visit, which lasted an hour, was an opportunity for the Prefect to discuss a number of questions which have come up recently in the ongoing work of the Congregation, and which are of particular interest to the Church in the United States. Among the topics which the Cardinal raised were the following: the *Order of Christian Funerals;* the composition of new eucharistic prayers; catechesis and practice of the sacrament of Penance, especially questions relating to general absolution; reverence in the celebration of the liturgy; the Secretariat's statement on "clown ministry" and liturgy; inculturation; inclusive language; the role of women in the liturgy; and the various projects in which the Congregation is presently engaged, e.g., revision of the rites of ordination, Sunday celebrations in the absence of a priest, the second typical edition of the *Liturgy of the Hours,* etc.

Cardinal Mayer's visit was an opportunity for open and frank dialogue on the above-mentioned items, as well as a chance for the members of the Liturgy Secretariat to voice their concerns about these and various other pastoral and liturgical matters. Besides Father Gurrieri, Father Krisman, and Monsignor Detscher, Monsignor Daniel F. Hoye, NCCB/USCC General Secretary, and Monsignor Richard Malone, Executive Director of the Secretariat of the NCCB Committee on Pastoral Research and Practices, were present.

Guidelines for Multi-lingual Masses

The Instituto de Liturgia Hispana and the Federation of Diocesan Liturgical Commissions recently collaborated to produce Guidelines for Multi-lingual Masses. *The purpose of these guidelines is to assist parishes and other communities faced with multi-cultural and multi-lingual celebrations of the eucharist. These guidelines arise out of the experience of many parish liturgists, priests, and diocesan worship offices in their planning and celebration of such liturgies, and from a respect for the liturgical principles which comprise the rites of the Roman Missal. These guidelines are reprinted with the permission of the Federation of Diocesan Liturgical Commissions.*

The United States of America is composed of multi-cultural and multi-lingual groups. This multiplicity is reflected in the Roman Catholic community, especially when diverse groups assemble on significant occasions for liturgical celebration. Such assemblies may provide opportunity to employ the rich diversity of cultural and linguistic expressions into one common act of worship.

The following guidelines for liturgical celebrations of multi-cultural and multi-lingual assemblies are offered to assist in the preparation and celebration of these special occasions. Such serious concern for the diversity of culture and language should express the unity which flows from liturgical celebration.

It is presumed that liturgical planners understand that the goal of Masses which blend multiple languages and other cultural expressions is to unite people of shared faith in common prayer around the word and the eucharistic table, and that the extraordinary feature of such celebrations is that only some, not all, of the elements of the celebration of the Mass will be understood by those assembled.

An explanation or understanding of these special features will be occasion for those assembled for common worship to enter more freely and deeply into the meaning and structure of the rites of the Mass, respecting the order of worship with which they are already acquainted, and respecting the linguistic or cultural expression of these rites even when they may not be their own.

It is also presumed that, on ordinary Sundays, multi-lingual parishes provide eucharistic celebrations to meet the linguistic needs of their people. Therefore, multi-lingual liturgies have particular value in the celebration of major feasts, weddings, funerals, and other important parish and diocesan events.

A. General Norms

1. The cultural and ethnic diversity of those assembled for eucharistic celebrations should be reflected throughout the celebration in the choice of gestures, postures, vesture and environmental design, as well as in the choice of musical texts and styles and in the determination of languages which will be used to proclaim the scripture readings and prayers of the Mass.

2. Multi-lingual celebrations may require the moderate use of a commentator at appropriate points which do not impede the natural rhythm of the structure of the Mass:

      a. before the celebration, for instruction concerning the celebration;
      b. before or during the liturgy of the word, as indicated in B. 2b;
      c. following the prayer after communion, for announcements.

B. Norms for Specific Rites during Mass

1. *The Introductory Rite*

"The introductory rite of Mass has the purpose that the faithful, assembling in unity, should constitute a communion and should prepare themselves properly for hearing the word of God and celebrating the eucharist worthily" (GI, no. 24). Therefore, every effort should be made to create this disposition in those assembled.

      a. The choice of processional music, introductory greetings and of music for the penitential intercessions and the Gloria can elicit an awareness of the cultural diversity of those gathered for the liturgy.

      b. The invitation to pray before the opening prayer can be given in the diverse languages spoken by those assembled. The opening prayer itself should be prayed in one language to preserve its integrity.

2. *The Liturgy of the Word*

"When the Scriptures are read in the Church, God himself is speaking to his people, and Christ, present in his own word, is proclaiming the Gospel."

"The readings must therefore be listened to by all with reverence; they make up a principal element of the liturgy. In the biblical readings God's word addressed all people of every era and is understandable to them, but a living commentary on the word, that is, the homily, as an integral part of the liturgy, increases the word's effectiveness" (GI, no. 9).

In order that the scriptures can be heard with reverence and understood by all, attention should be given to the language(s) in which they are proclaimed and commented upon in the homily.

a. One or both of the readings preceding the gospel should be proclaimed in the language spoken by the majority of those assembled. If two readings are to be proclaimed, one may be proclaimed in another language appropriate to those assembled.

b. Printed booklets which provide translations of the scripture readings do not enable active listening. A brief commentary may be offered in other languages before each proclamation of the scripture readings to assist those who do not understand the language in which the reading(s) will be proclaimed, providing some understanding, appreciation, and reverence for the chosen biblical text.

c. In multi-lingual Masses the antiphon for the responsorial psalm may be sung in one of the languages not spoken by the majority, while the verses may be sung by the cantor or choir in the languages represented by the assembly. In bilingual Masses the antiphon for the responsorial psalm may be in either language (consistent throughout the response), while the verses may be sung in both languages.

d. The gospel, which Christ himself proclaims, should be announced in the language of the majority of those assembled. Portions of the gospel, upon which the homily will be based, should also be announced in the other languages spoken by those assembled. The repetition of the entire gospel text in another or other languages unduly prolongs and makes awkward the proclamation.

e. The homily, ordinarily, should be preached in the language of the majority. A short summary may be given in other languages. The homilist may reflect the same theme in his summary while incorporating a different development or cultural illustration.

f. The invitation to each of the general intercessions may be given in the various languages spoken by those assembled (e.g., "Let us pray for the Church" and "Let us pray for the sick," etc.) Following each invitation, a pause will allow for the assembly to unite in prayer for particular concerns. The conclusion to each intercession should be spoken or sung in the same language throughout to allow for the consistent, flowing pattern of the response among the assembled.

3. *The Liturgy of the Eucharist*

a. *Preparation of the Gifts.* "At the beginning of the liturgy of the eucharist the gifts, which will become Christ's body and blood, are brought to the altar" (GI, no. 49). These gifts of bread and wine, and gifts for the Church or the poor brought by the faithful or collected at Mass, are appropriate. Other symbolic gifts are not appropriate.

b. *Eucharistic Prayer.* To preserve the integrity of the eucharistic prayer, the chief elements of its composition should be maintained even when the multiple languages spoken by those assembled are chosen for its proclamation. When such a choice is made, only one language should be used for each of the chief elements, namely: Thanksgiving; Acclamation; Epiclesis; Institution Narrative; Anamnesis; Offering; Intercessions; Final Doxology.

c. *Communion Rite.* Because the Lord's Prayer is common to all Christians, members of the assembly may be invited to recite the prayer in his or her own language simultaneously with others. (This same principle applies to the recitation of the Creed.)

4. *The Concluding Rite*

When the more solemn forms of blessing are chosen, each of the blessing prayers may be given in alternating languages appropriate to those assembled.

C. Norms for Music

1. Members of multi-lingual assemblies can join in the singing of short texts even if the language is foreign to them (e.g., "Lord, have mercy," "Hosanna in the highest," psalm antiphons, etc.). Repetitious 'ostinato' styles of music, like Taizé, provide a style of music which allows for the texts to become familiar and easy to sing; such a form of music can also foster a sense of unity among those assembled.

When Latin chants or antiphons are known, understood, and can be sung well, these can be an effective means of bringing about musical unity.

2. The languages of those assembled should be expressed in song. Music proper to each culture, however, should be preferred to the practice of translating texts to accompany melodies which express a different culture. An integrity of musical styles, however, should be respected throughout the liturgy.

An effort should be made to promote the expertise of poets and musicians of each cultural group toward the development of original music which can be incorporated into these celebrations.

3. Some familiar hymns are known in several languages. Alternating verses in each of the languages represented by those in the assembly can be effective. Care should be taken to balance instrumental accompaniment with the language of the culture, as well.

4. Antiphonal selections can be used effectively when the verses are sung by cantor or choir in several languages, while the antiphon is sung by all present in a common language.

5. Eucharistic acclamations should reflect an integral musical style and may include a blend of the diverse languages of those assembled. Composers must give special attention to the blending of multiple languages in such musical settings.

6. Choirs assembled for special occasions must work together in the development of a common repertoire and in the development of a unified choir for the exercise of music ministry.

Pastoral Care of the Sick/Cuidado Pastoral De Los Enfermos, Bilingual abridged edition

This ritual book contains, with English and Spanish on facing pages: the rites of visiting the sick, taking communion to and anointing of the sick either at home or in a hospital, and the rites for emergencies and special circumstances. An appendix gives the rite for reconciliation of individual penitents. The introductions to the rites are in English only. A publication of LTP and the Mexican American Cultural Center. Soft leather-grain paper cover, 216 pp. Cost $8.00. Order from: Liturgy Training Publications, 1800 North Hermitage Avenue, Chicago, IL 60622-1101. Phone: (312) 486-7088.

BISHOPS' COMMITTEE ON THE LITURGY
NEWSLETTER
NATIONAL CONFERENCE OF CATHOLIC BISHOPS

**1986
VOLUME XXII
AUGUST**

1986 National Meeting of Diocesan Liturgical Commissions

The nineteenth annual National Meeting of Diocesan Liturgical Commissions, sponsored by the Bishops' Committee on the Liturgy and the Federation of Diocesan Liturgical Commissions, will take place in Portland, Maine, October 13-16, 1986. This year's meeting, hosted by Region I (New England) and by the Diocese of Portland, will focus on the theme "God has given us the ministry of reconciliation" (2 Cor. 5:18).

The following topics will be treated: "Binding up Wounds in a Healing Community," Dr. Doris Donnelly, Saint Mary's College, Notre Dame, IN; "The Good News of Repentance and Conversion," Reverend Kevin Irwin, The Catholic University of America, Washington, DC; "Reconciliation: Disquieting Pastoral Reflections," Sister Kathleen Hughes, RSCJ, Catholic Theological Union, Chicago, IL; "The Future of Reconciliation in the Church: Learning a New Art," Most Reverend Patrick R. Cooney, Auxiliary Bishop of Detroit. Various workshops are scheduled during the four day meeting. A typical Maine clambake is also planned.

For additional information and registration forms, write to: Federation of Diocesan Liturgical Commissions, P.O. Box 29039, Washington, DC 20017.

Notice: *Order of Christian Funerals*

Many diocesan offices have called to inquire about the current status of the *Order of Christian Funerals*. The OCF was approved by the National Conference of Catholic Bishops on November 14, 1985. At that time the NCCB established November 2, 1986, All Souls Day, as the effective date of implementation in the dioceses of the United States of America. September 1, 1986 was likewise set as the publication release date, the day on which publishers could offer the new ritual book for sale. However, these dates were dependent on the confirmation of the NCCB's decree of approval by the Apostolic See.

The decree of confirmation has not yet been received from the Congregation for Divine Worship. Accordingly, the release date for these publications has had to be postponed. Should there be the need to change the mandatory effective date for use of the new ritual, publishers and dioceses will be informed.

Order of Crowning an Image of the Blessed Virgin Mary

In June 1986 the International Commission on English in the Liturgy (ICEL) issued the provisional translation ("green book") of the *Order of Crowning an Image of the Blessed Virgin Mary*. Copies of this text have been sent to English-speaking episcopal conferences for study and comment. In the United States a copy was sent to each bishop on July 31, 1986 with a cover letter from Archbishop Daniel E. Pilarczyk, Chairman of the Bishops' Committee on the Liturgy. On the same day a copy was sent to each diocesan liturgical commission or office of worship.

The Latin *editio typica* of the *Ordo coronandi imaginem Beatae Mariae Virginis* was issued by the Congregation for the Sacraments and Divine Worship on March 25, 1981. The book contains a theological-liturgical Introduction (*praenotanda*), followed by three chapters: (1) Crowning of an Image of the Blessed Virgin Mary within Mass; (2) Crowning of an Image of the Blessed Virgin Mary within Evening Prayer; (3) Crowning of an Image of the Blessed Virgin Mary within a Celebration of the Word of God.

The *Order of Crowning* is ordinarily celebrated by the bishop (no. 8) and is "fittingly held on solemnities and feasts of Mary or on other festive days. But the rite is not to be held on the principal solemnities of the Lord or on days having a penitential character" (no. 9).

The Introduction to the rite explains the significance of the *Order of Crowning an Image of the Blessed Virgin Mary:* "Coronation is one form of reverence frequently shown to images of Mary" (no. 2). "Both in the East and in the West the practice of depicting the Blessed Virgin Mary wearing a regal crown came into use in the era of the Council of Ephesus (A.D. 431). Since then Christian artists have often portrayed the glorified Mother of the Lord seated on a throne, dressed in royal robes, and surrounded by a court of angels and saints" (no. 3). "The growth of the custom [of coronation] led to the composition of a special rite for crowning images of Mary, and in the 19th century this was incorporated into the Roman liturgy" (no. 4). The rite had been composed in the 17th century and was incorporated into the *Pontificale Romanum* under the title *Ritus servandus in coronatione imaginis Beatae Mariae Virginis.*

In the liturgy and in popular devotion the Church recognizes and invokes Mary as queen because she is the Mother of the Son of God, the "chosen companion of the Redeemer," "the perfect follower of Christ," and the "foremost member of the Church" (no. 5). For this reason, it is fitting that the Church crowns images of Mary.

The Introduction also states the following: "It is the responsibility of the diocesan bishop, together with the local community, to decide on the opportuneness of crowning an image of the Blessed Virgin Mary. But it should be noted that it is proper to crown only those images to which the faithful come with a confidence in the Mother of the Lord so strong that the images are of great renown and their sites centers of a genuine liturgical *cultus* and of religious vitality" (no. 6).

The rite itself consists of the following elements: (1) prayer of thanksgiving and invocation; (2) the crowning; and (3) the general intercessions or a litany. These elements are always preceded by the proclamation of the Word of God whether within Mass, Evening Prayer, or a special celebration of the Word.

The following texts illustrate the nature of the new *Order of Crowning an Image of the Blessed Virgin Mary.*

Thanksgiving and Invocation*

Blessed are you, Lord, God of heaven and earth,
for in your mercy and justice
you cast down the mighty and exalt the lowly.
Your marvelous wisdom is shown above all
in the Word made flesh and in his Virgin Mother.
For he, your Son,
who freely humbled himself even unto death on the cross,
now sits at your right hand and is radiant with unending glory,
the King of kings and Lord of lords;
and she, the Virgin who wished to be called your servant,
was singled out to be Mother of the Redeemer
    and true Mother of all the living:
now she is exalted above the choirs of angels
and reigns in glory with her Son,
praying for all of us,
the Queen of mercy, pleading for grace.

Merciful Lord, look upon us your servants,
who by crowning this image of the Mother of your Son,
[*or:* who by crowning this image of Christ and his Mother,]
proclaim him as King of all creation
and approach her as our queen.

Give us the grace to follow them in serving you;

---

to do what love demands
for the sake of our brothers and sisters;
to deny ourselves and spend ourselves,
so as to win our neighbors for you;
to be lowly on earth,
so as to be exalted in heaven
where you reward your faithful servants with a crown of life.

We ask this through Christ our Lord.

R. Amen.

Crowning

Mary, Virgin for ever,
most worthy Queen of the world,
pray for our peace and salvation,
for you are the Mother of Christ,
the Lord and Savior of all. [Easter season: Alleluia]

It is the intention of the Bishops' Committee on the Liturgy to review the *Order of Crowning an Image of the Blessed Virgin Mary* at its next meeting in November 1986, with a view towards its eventual submission for approval by the National Conference of Catholic Bishops. Therefore, all comments from bishops, diocesan liturgical commissions or offices of worship, and other consultants should be forwarded to the Liturgy Secretariat no later than *October 1, 1986.*

Meeting of the ICEL Advisory Committee

The following notice is reprinted from the ICEL Newsletter *(July-December 1985/January-June 1986) with permission.*

The Advisory Committee of the International Commission on English in the Liturgy met in London from 24 to 28 April 1986. A major focus of their discussions was the revised translations of eighty-four opening prayers from the Proper of Seasons section of *The Roman Missal.* The revised translations were prepared by the subcommittee on translations and revisions. The other main topic on the Advisory Committee agenda was the plan for the contents and arrangement of the revised Missal. This plan was prepared by the subcommittee on the presentation of texts.

Though criticisms were made of some of the revised prayers under review, the revisions were for the most part fully endorsed by the Advisory Committee. Prayers returned to the subcommittee for further work will be dealt with at the August 1986 meeting of the subcommittee. The Advisory Committee directed that articles explaining ICEL's work on the revision of the collects and giving some examples of the revised prayers be prepared for publication. The Episcopal Board of ICEL has also asked that articles on the revision of the collects be prepared. It is hoped that the first article will be published in September.

The Advisory Committee also discussed in detail the plan drawn up by the presentation of texts subcommittee for the contents and arrangement of the revised Missal. The present plan calls for a two-volume Missal, a volume for Sundays and a volume for weekdays. A complete plan of the contents of each volume was endorsed by the Advisory Committee. Decisions were made at the meeting on the arrangement of the Easter Triduum, the placement of various texts in the Order of Mass, the arrangement and placement of ministerial chants, etc.

The Advisory Committee reviewed a draft translation of the entire *De Benedictionibus.* After a full discussion of the draft, the Committee appointed a three-member subcommittee to put the draft into a finished form towards publication of the Green Book or interim text. The subcommittee will meet in late October. The decision of the Advisory Committee on the Book of Blessings means that the book will not be ready by late 1986 as originally planned. The new target date for the publication of the Green Book is May 1987.

The Advisory Committee made recommendations for further work to be done on the Eucharistic Prayer of Hippolytus following upon the consultation that ICEL held on its translation of the prayer. The Advisory

Committee discussed also the work in progress on the translation of the *Caeremoniale Episcoporum*. Work on the Ceremonial—a text of approximately 400 pages—will be completed by mid-1987. The Advisory Committee approved the Green Book text of the *Order of Crowning an Image of the Blessed Virgin Mary*. The Latin text was published by the Holy See in 1982. The Order of Crowning is principally for the use of a diocesan bishop in crowning a Marian image which is of great renown and whose site is a center of a genuine liturgical *cultus*.

New Appointments

Three priests, active in the liturgical renewal in various English-speaking countries, have recently been appointed to new positions of responsibility. Father Joseph L. Cunningham, for many years the Director of the Liturgy Office of the Diocese of Brooklyn, has been named Rector of St. Vincent de Paul Regional Seminary, Boynton Beach, Florida. Father Cunningham has served two terms as a member of the ICEL Advisory Committee and continues as a member of ICEL's presentation of texts subcommittee. He holds a degree in liturgical studies from the University of Notre Dame.

Father John Fitzsimmons, Chairman of the Advisory Committee of the International Commission on English in the Liturgy, has been appointed Rector of the Scots College, Rome, by the Scottish Episcopal Conference. Father Fitzsimmons, who will continue as chairman of the Advisory Committee, holds a degree in biblical studies from the Pontifical Biblical Institute, Rome.

Father Murray Kroetsch, a priest of the diocese of Hamilton, Ontario, has been named by the Canadian Conference of Catholic Bishops to succeed Father Regis Halloran as Director of the National Liturgy Office of Canada. Father Kroetsch, ordained in 1978, holds a degree in liturgical studies from the University of Notre Dame. He has been active on diocesan and regional levels in liturgy and music, and served as a member of the National Council for Liturgy of Canada, 1983-1986.

Anticipated Masses on All Saints and All Souls 1986

On November 2, 1986 All Souls Day occurs on a Sunday. Mass celebrated that day is taken from the section entitled "Masses for the Dead" in the Sacramentary. The Liturgy of the Hours is that of the Thirty-first Sunday in Ordinary Time. However, when Morning Prayer and Evening Prayer are celebrated with the people, these hours may be taken from the Office for the Dead.

The solemnity of All Saints begins with Evening Prayer I on Friday, October 31, and concludes with the celebration of Evening Prayer II of the solemnity on November 1st. (Evening Prayer II of the solemnity takes precedence over Evening Prayer I for the 31st Sunday in Ordinary Time.) If the Eucharist is celebrated on the evening of Friday, October 31st, the Mass is that of the solemnity of All Saints. If the Eucharist is celebrated on Saturday evening, November 1st, the Mass is that of All Souls' Day and is taken from "Masses for the Dead" in the Sacramentary.

New Secretariat Publications

The following three publications of the Liturgy Secretariat are now available from the USCC Office of Publishing and Promotion Services: (1) *The Bishops and the Liturgy: Highlights of the New Ceremonial of Bishops* (Pub. No. 996, $8.95); (2) *Liturgical Calendar and Ordo 1987 United States of America* (Pub. No. 986, $6.95); (3) *Liturgy Documentary Series 7: Penance and Reconciliation in the Church* (Pub. No. 104, $5.95). The usual discounts for large orders are available. For copies, order from: Office of Publishing and Promotion Services, United States Catholic Conference, 1312 Massachusetts Avenue NW, Washington, DC 20005. Phone orders: 800/235-USCC.

BISHOPS' COMMITTEE ON THE LITURGY
NEWSLETTER
NATIONAL CONFERENCE OF CATHOLIC BISHOPS

**1986
VOLUME XXII
SEPTEMBER**

Instituto de Liturgia Hispana: III Conferencia Nacional

The third National Conference of the Instituto de Liturgia Hispana will take place at the Ramada O'Hare Hotel, Chicago, IL October 23-26, 1986. The theme for the conference is "*La Liturgia en la Parroquia*" ("Liturgy in the Parish"). Major addresses and their presentors will be the following: "Rite of Christian Initiation of Adults," Most Reverend Ricardo Ramirez, CSB, Bishop of Las Cruces, NM; "Liturgical Ministries," Father Domingo Rodriguez, ST, Cleveland, OH; "Environment and Art in the Liturgy," Father Jaime Lara, Brooklyn, NY; "Liturgy and Social Justice," Sister Dominga Zapata, SH, Chicago, IL; "New Spanish Translations," Father Andres Pardo, Director of the National Liturgical Commission, Madrid, Spain. All conferences will be given in Spanish.

For registration and information, write: Instituto de Liturgia Hispana, P.O. Box 23210, Chicago, IL 60623-0210.

NCCB November Agenda: *Eucharistic Prayer A*

The Bishops' Committee on the Liturgy has proposed that the National Conference of Catholic Bishops, at its November 1986 plenary assembly, approve the use of *Eucharistic Prayer A,* an original composition in English prepared by the International Commission on English in the Liturgy.

At present nine eucharistic prayers in English are approved for use in the dioceses of the United States of America: Eucharistic Prayers I-IV (Roman Missal), Eucharistic Prayers for Masses of Reconciliation I-II, and Eucharistic Prayers for Masses with Children I-III. These prayers have been included in the 1985 edition of the American Sacramentary.

Since the issuance of the Circular Letter *Eucharistiae participationem* by the Congregation for Divine Worship in 1973, other language groups have added newly-composed eucharistic prayers to their own editions of the Missal or Sacramentary. These are: (a) Eucharistic Prayers "of the Swiss Synod" V-A, V-B, V-C, V-D (original language = French), now approved for the following: Switzerland (French, German, Italian), France, Germany, Austria, Spain (recently approved also for a number of Latin American conferences of bishops), Italy, The Netherlands, etc.; (b) Eucharistic Prayer V "of the Congress of Manaus" (Brazil); (c) Eucharistic Prayer for Marriage, French-speaking Canada; (d) Eucharistic Prayers A-B, *Altaarmissal voor de Nederlandse Kerkprovincie,* The Netherlands and Flanders (Flemish-speaking Belgium).

In 1980 the International Commission on English in the Liturgy established a subcommittee on eucharistic prayers to revise the translation of the eucharistic prayers contained in the Roman Missal, to produce translations of ancient and modern eucharistic prayers, and to respond to the desire of the English-speaking world by composing original eucharistic prayers in English. For ICEL, as for other language groups, the mandate for such new texts comes both from the wish of the member and associate member conferences of ICEL and from the 1969 Instruction on the Translation of Liturgical Texts (*Comme le prévoit*) which states: "Texts translated from another language are clearly not sufficient for the celebration of a fully renewed liturgy. The creation of new texts will be necessary. But translation of texts transmitted through the tradition of the Church is the best school and discipline for the creation of new texts so 'that any forms adopted should in some way grow organically from forms already in existence' [*Sacrosanctum Concilium,* art. 23]" (no. 43).

1312 MASSACHUSETTS AVENUE, N.W. • WASHINGTON, D.C. 20005

In May 1984 ICEL issued *An Original Eucharistic Prayer: Text 1,* the first eucharistic prayer composed in the English language, for the purpose of study and comment. The text of this eucharistic prayer was the fruit of ICEL's subcommittee on eucharistic prayers. New English translations of the Eucharistic Prayer of Hippolytus and the Eucharistic Prayer of Saint Basil were also issued for study and review.

In the introduction of *An Original Eucharistic Prayer: Text One* the following was noted: "In recent years original prayers in languages other than English have been approved for liturgical use in several conferences of bishops and confirmed by the Apostolic See. The English text contained in this booklet has been submitted to an intensive process of scrutiny and preparation under the direction of the Advisory Committee of ICEL. It is being made available for purposes of widespread consultation and study by bishops and consultants throughout the English-speaking world."

A copy of *An Original Eucharistic Prayer: Text One* was sent to all the bishops of the United States, to each diocesan liturgical commission or office, and to other liturgical, biblical, theological, and literary consultants. The responses to this consultation were examined by the Committee on the Liturgy and were forwarded to ICEL. The Committee recommended that the eucharistic prayer be approved by the National Conference of Catholic Bishops and asked that it be placed on the agenda of the November 1984 plenary assembly of the bishops. However, at a meeting just prior to the November 1984 NCCB meeting, the Committee on the Liturgy decided to withdraw the eucharistic prayer from the agenda, since a number of bishops in the United States and in other English-speaking conferences had proposed changes in the prayer and it was felt that it would be advantageous to submit these also to ICEL when the consultation period ended in April 1985. The comments made by individual bishops and other consultants were then sent to ICEL in May 1985.

In January 1986 ICEL issued the final or definitive version of this eucharistic prayer under the convenient title *Eucharistic Prayer A.* The foreword of this edition states the following: "Numerous comments on this eucharistic prayer were received from bishops and consultants throughout the English-speaking world. These were studied by ICEL's subcommittee on original texts, which then made proposals for several revisions in the text to ICEL's Advisory Committee. The Advisory Committee after a full consideration of the proposals for revision voted to approve the text at its meeting in August 1985. Both the subcommittee on original texts and the Advisory Committee took great care to make only the most necessary revisions, revisions that would not violate the internal coherence and original character of the prayer. Meeting in Rome in November 1985, the Episcopal Board of ICEL voted to approve the text, now entitled *Eucharistic Prayer A,* in final form and to submit it to the conferences of bishops that participate in the work of ICEL for their review and possible vote." (Subsequently the prayer has been approved by the ICEL member conferences of bishops of Australia, Canada, India, New Zealand, and South Africa and submitted for the confirmation of the Apostolic See.)

Contents and Structure of Eucharistic Prayer A

Eucharistic Prayer A is envisioned for use on Sundays and weekdays as permitted by the rubrics of the Roman Missal and by the General Norms for the Liturgical Year and Roman Calendar. Insofar as other eucharistic prayers of the Roman Missal are thematic, this prayer focuses on the "themes" of creation and redemption, the healing of creation in Christ. These themes are the dominant motives of the text.

Eucharistic Prayer A follows the structure required for a eucharistic prayer of the Roman Rite (see *General Instruction of the Roman Missal 54-55*). The *preface* offers praise of God the Creator and narrates the account of creation in biblical and poetic language. The *post-sanctus* begins with a proclamation of God's greatness for having restored creation after the Fall. Then, alluding to the covenant relationship between God and his people, the prayer focuses on the coming of Christ who embodied the longings of the people of Israel and fulfilled their hopes by his passion and death. The *epiclesis,* in language reminiscent of the creation account, calls upon the Holy Spirit to sanctify the bread and wine that they may become the body and blood of Christ. The *institution narrative* is worded in the language of blessing while the *words of consecration* are the same as those in the other eucharistic prayers. The *memorial acclamation* follows. The *anamnesis* focuses on the redeeming sacrifice of Jesus Christ, his resurrection, his exaltation, and his coming again in glory, with the petition that the Church be watchful, strong, and faithful. The *first intercession* is for the pope and bishop and is couched in the language of praise and thanksgiving. The *second intercession* is for the Church "here present" and for the entire world. The *third intercession,* for the dead, follows with the petition that the dead be forgiven and eventually participate in communion with Mary and the saints.

Finally, the eucharistic prayer looks to the final times when creation is healed and made one in Christ. The usual *final doxology* and Amen follow.

The Bishops' Committee on the Liturgy feels that the addition of this eucharistic prayer to the present collection of eucharistic prayers will be of great benefit to the celebration of the Eucharist in the United States. The text is both biblically and theologically sound; it is liturgically correct in its structure and content; it is sufficiently poetic and literary without being beyond the people's comprehension; it relies neither on novel expressions nor on unusual metaphors and similies as have so many unauthorized compositions of eucharistic prayers in the last twenty years. The consultation with bishops and hundreds of other consultants in the English-speaking world have demonstrated the utility and need for a prayer such as *Eucharistic Prayer A.*

Site for the New NCCB/USCC Building: Blessing and Groundbreaking

The blessing and groundbreaking of the site for the new NCCB/USCC headquarters building, to be located on Fourth Street, NE, directly behind Theological College at The Catholic University of America, took place on August 18, 1986. Bishop James W. Malone, Bishop of Youngstown and President of the National Catholic Conference of Bishops and the United States Catholic Conference, presided at the ceremony.

The Rite of Blessing and Groundbreaking of a New Site was taken from a provisional translation of *De benedictionibus* (Book of Blessings), promulgated by the Congregation for Divine Worship in May 1984. The rite is structured in the following manner: (1) Introductory Rites: Psalm 127 with the antiphon *May the Lord watch over this house, and keep us in peace,* followed by the Sign of the Cross, the Greeting, and Introductory Remarks; (2) Reading of the Word of God: 1 Corinthians 3:9-11 (*You are God's Building*) and Homily; (3) Intercessions; (4) Prayer of Blessing; Sprinkling of the Site with Holy Water, during which is sung a hymn or psalm (At the groundbreaking, the hymn *Christ's Church Shall Glory in His Power* [*Worship* 616] was sung); (5) Conclusion of the Rite: Blessing, Dismissal and Groundbreaking (a ritual element not found in *De benedictionibus* but customary in the United States).

The following *Prayer of Blessing* was used in the ceremony:

> All-powerful and all-merciful Father,
> You have created all things through your Son
> and have made him the unshakeable foundation of your Kingdom.
> Grant, we pray, that the undertaking we begin today
> for your glory and our own well-being
> may go forward through the gift of your eternal wisdom
> to its successful completion.
> We ask this through Christ our Lord. Amen.*

Eleventh International Congress of the Societas Liturgica

The eleventh International Congress of the Societas Liturgica will take place at the Kardinal-Nikolaus—Cusanus-Akademie in Brixen (Bressanone), Italy, August 17-22, 1987. The theme of the Congress will be "A Worshiping Church: Penitent and Reconciling." The following description of the theme is excerpted from the Summer 1986 issue of the *Newsletter* of the Societas Liturgica.

"In a broken world the Christian message proclaims the forgiveness of sins and the reconciliation of human beings to God and one another. Entrance into this new life is by way of repentance, faith and love. The first sacramental sign of salvation is baptism, by which people are incorporated into the body of Christ. Since the early centuries the Church has provided means for the reconciliation of its members who have fallen away and for the renewal of its own corporate life. The forms of this practice have varied historically

---

*Excerpt from the provisional English translation of *De benedictionibus*, © 1985 International Committee on English in the Liturgy, Inc., Toronto, Canada. All rights reserved. Used with permission.

(e.g., public reconciliation of apostates and grave sinners; private confession of individuals; general confession and absolution; penitential services). At the present time we observe many attempts to reinvigorate this practice of forgiveness and reconciliation and to adapt it to current conditions. In the secular world also, we see evidence of the need to deal with guilt and a longing for integral community. Such reconciliation, Christians believe, finds its goal and expression in the assembly of the people of God and their eucharistic communion. But as long as the several churches themselves remain divided, their witness to the Gospel of forgiveness and reconciliation is obscured.

"In its approach to these issues the 1987 Congress of the *Societas Liturgica* will structure its reflections according to the following pattern: 1. Penance in Contemporary Scholarship; 2. Penance in the Churches: Current Practice and Experience; 3. The Church's Ministry of Reconciliation: a Service to Humanity throughout the Ages; 4. The Need to be Reconciled: Contemporary Non-ecclesial Forms of Reconciliation; 5. A Forgiven and Forgiving Community: the Baptismal and Eucharistic Church; 6. The Reconciliation of Divided Churches: a Witness to the Gospel."

For further information on the Societas Liturgica, write to the Secretary: Mr. Artur Waibel, Liturgisches Institut, Postfach 26 28, D-5500 Trier, West Germany. Telephone: (0651) 4-81-06.

Southwest Liturgical Conference

The Southwest Liturgical Conference, which comprises the 24 dioceses of the states of Arizona, Colorado, New Mexico, Oklahoma, Texas and Wyoming, will hold its 25th annual study week at the Beaumont Plaza Holiday Inn, Beaumont, TX, on January 19-22, 1987. The theme of the conference is "Sacraments of Initiation: The Rite Connection."

Major topics and speakers will include: "Sacraments of Initiation: The Rite Connection," the keynote address by the Reverend Raymond Kemp, Secretary for Parish Life and Worship and Director of the RENEW program for the Archdiocese of Washington, DC; "Celebrating the Sacraments of Initiation within the Liturgical Year," Dr. Mark Searle, Coordinator of the Graduate Program in Liturgical Studies at the University of Notre Dame; "Sacraments of Christian Initiation: Builders of Community," Karen Hinman, Executive Director of the North American Forum on the Catechumenate, Arlington, VA; "Mystagogia: The Fourth Day," Sister Teresita Weind, SND Pastoral Minister in Oak Park, IL; and "Eucharist: Ultimate Sacrament of Commitment," Reverend Ronald Lewinski, Director of the Office of Divine Worship and Director of the Catechumenate for the Archdiocese of Chicago.

The Most Reverend John S. Cummins, Bishop of Oakland, will offer a special one-day session for bishops and the *RCIA*. Bishop Cummins, immediate past chairman of the Bishop's Committee on the Liturgy, will also present a general workshop on "Preaching—THE Catechesis."

Nineteen special interest sessions will cover such topics as beginning to use the RCIA; catechetical content of catechumenal formation; the content and task of the period of mystagogia; shaping catechumens in the prayer of the Church; celebrating sacraments of initiation with children, with teenagers and with the handicapped; planning the rites; music and environment for the rites; special views on the sacraments of reconciliation and confirmation; presiding at the RCIA celebrations; and forming the catechumenate in small parishes.

Two panel sessions will also be held. "Ministries for the Process of Christian Initiation" will address the functions of evangelizers, sponsors, and catechists. "Will the Real Catechumens Please Stand Up?" will deal with the distinctions between catechumens and baptized candidates for confirmation and eucharist, the pastoral care of uncatechized or lapsed adult Catholics, and the use of the dismissals at Mass.

The early registration fee for the week is $75. For more information, contact: SWLC Study Week, P.O. Box 3948, Beaumont, TX 77704-3948. Telephone: (409) 838-0451.

BISHOPS' COMMITTEE ON THE LITURGY
NEWSLETTER

NATIONAL CONFERENCE OF CATHOLIC BISHOPS

**1986
VOLUME XXII
OCTOBER**

NCCB November Meeting Agenda: Liturgical Items

At its meeting on September 9-10, 1986, the Administrative Committee of the National Conference of Catholic Bishops approved the inclusion of a number of liturgical items on the agenda of the plenary assembly of the National Conference of Catholic Bishops (November 10-13, 1986). In addition to seeking the approval of *Eucharistic Prayer A* [see *Newsletter,* September 1986, pp. 33-34], the Bishops' Committee on the Liturgy will propose the adoption of the final translation ("White Book" edition) of the *Rite of Christian Initiation of Adults* (RCIA) and ask that, pending confirmation by the Apostolic See, the implementation date be set for February 21, 1988, the First Sunday of Lent.

Relating to the approval of the final translation of the RCIA, the NCCB will be asked to approve a number of ritual decisions authorized by no. 33 of the *praenotanda* of the RCIA (no. 75 in the Latin *editio typica*). The bishops will also be asked to approve and authorize a number of additional liturgical texts and rites which come out of the American Catholic experience with the previous edition of the RCIA (1974 "Green Book"). These include the following rites: a parish Rite of Sending Catechumens for Election by the Bishop; in the rites for the Christian initiation of children, an optional Rite of Election; in Part II, Chapter 4 "Preparation of Uncatechized Adults for Confirmation and Eucharist," the following rites: Welcoming the Candidates (4A), Sending the Candidates for Recognition by the Bishop (4B), Calling the Candidates to Continuing Conversion (4C), Penitential Rite (Scrutiny) (4D); in Part III, "Additional Rites," the following combined rites: Celebration of the Rite of Acceptance into the Order of Catechumens and of the Rite of Welcoming Baptized Adults who seek to complete their Christian Initiation; Parish Celebration Sending Catechumens for Election and Candidates for Recognition by the Bishop; Celebration of the Rite of Election of Catechumens and of the Call to Continuing Conversion of Candidates who seek to complete their Christian Initiation.

The bishops will also be asked in November to approve *National Statutes for the Catechumenate*— norms dealing with the rights and obligations of catechumens, the minister of the sacraments of initiation, the catechesis of adult Catholics preparing for confirmation and eucharist, the reception of baptized Christians into the full communion of the Catholic Church, etc.—as well as a plan for the national implementation of the *Rite of Christian Initiation of Adults* and the catechumenate in the years from 1987 through 1992.

To assist the bishops in dealing with these action items on the RCIA, a workshop for the bishops will be offered on Monday, November 10, 1986. The workshop will focus on evangelization, the role of the RCIA in episcopal ministry, how to integrate the catechumenate into parish life, the American experience with the RCIA over the last decade, and a description of the additional rites being presented for the bishops' approval. Archbishop Roger Mahony of Los Angeles and Father James Dunning of the North American Forum on the Catechumenate will be the featured presentors.

The Bishops' Committee on the Liturgy will also seek the approval of a new common Spanish translation of the Order of Mass, the Eucharistic Prayers, and several other Roman Missal texts for use in the dioceses of the United States of America in all celebrations of the Mass in Spanish by March 30, 1992.

Resulting from the desire for one single Spanish translation which was expressed during the 1984 Congress of Presidents and Secretaries of National Liturgical Commissions at the Vatican, in early 1985 the Congregation for Divine Worship, with the approval of the Holy Father, convened an ad hoc commission of translators from Spain and the liturgy department (DELC) of CELAM for the purposes of preparing a single unified and common Spanish translation of the Order of Mass, the Lord's Prayer, and the Eucharistic Prayers which would eventually replace all existing Spanish language versions of these elements of the Mass. This new translation was to be based on the five existing Spanish versions of the texts.

Once the translation was completed by the commission, the Congregation invited the presidents (chairmen) and secretaries of the national liturgical commissions of the twenty-two conferences of bishops where Spanish is used—the United States included—to participate in a meeting at the Vatican, February 2-7, 1986 [see *Newsletter,* February 1986, pp. 5-6; and *Notitiae,* nos. 236-237 (March-April 1986)]. At that meeting the representatives reviewed the work of the ad hoc commission, submitted their own critique of the translations, and promised to inform their conferences of the progress of this project.

On August 6, 1986, the Congregation for Divine Worship informed the president of the NCCB (and the other Spanish-language conferences) that work on the new Spanish translation had been completed and put into final form. A copy of the texts was forwarded with that letter. The twenty-two conferences were asked to approve the translation by December 31, 1986 so that the Holy See could confirm the texts in early 1987.

The new Spanish translation includes the following texts: (1) Order of Mass; (2) new prefaces (translations from the Italian Missal): Advent III, Advent IV, Lent V, After Ascension, Sundays in Ordinary Time X, Blessed Virgin Mary IV, Blessed Virgin Mary V, Common VII-IX, Baptism, Confirmation, Holy Eucharist III, Penance, Anointing of the Sick, Ordinations II; (3) Eucharistic Prayers: Eucharistic Prayer I-IV (Roman Missal); V/a to V/d ("Swiss Synod"); Reconciliation I-II, Masses with Children I-III; (4) Rite of Blessing and Sprinkling Holy Water on Sundays (translations from the Italian Missal); (5) Collects for the Common of the Blessed Virgin Mary (translations from the Italian Missal).

In accordance with the August 6 letter of the Congregation for Divine Worship, since *ustedes* is used by Spanish-speakers in the United States, the Bishops' Committee on the Liturgy will also propose that a note be included in all future U.S. editions of Spanish liturgical books which contain this new translation by which it will be possible to use the less formal *ustedes* instead of *vosotros* in the salutations and admonitions. *Vosotros* will remain the liturgical usage for other texts.

As a consequence of NCCB approval and the subsequent confirmation of the Holy See, this new translation will become the only approved and authorized version of these texts for use in Spanish liturgical celebrations in the United States and in all Spanish-speaking countries.

With regard to the collects, other presidential prayers, antiphons, etc., of the Roman Missal, the Hispanic Liturgy Subcommittee of the Bishops' Committee on the Liturgy will conduct a consultation to determine which of the five existing translations of these texts should be adopted for use alongside the new translation of the Order of Mass and Eucharistic Prayers in an eventual complete edition of the Missal for Spanish celebrations of the Eucharist in the United States. This consultation will take place in 1987.

New Committee Advisors

Archbishop Daniel E. Pilarczyk, Chairman of the Bishops' Committee on the Liturgy, has announced the appointment of new advisors to the Committee to replace outgoing advisors Sister Arlene Bennett, RSM (formerly acting director of the Detroit Archdiocesan Department of Christian Worship) and Father Edmund J. Siedlecki (pastor of Saint Wenceslaus Church, Chicago). A replacement for Mr. Lawrence Johnson, formerly an *ex officio* advisor to the Committee by reason of his position as Executive Secretary of the Federation of Diocesan Liturgical Commissions, has also been announced.

Appointed to three-year terms as at-large advisors to the Committee are Sister Kathleen Loewen, OP, director of the Office of Worship of the Archdiocese of Milwaukee, and Reverend William M. Cieslak, OFM Cap, professor of liturgy at the Franciscan School of Theology at Berkeley, CA. Reverend Michael J. Spillane, a priest of the Archdiocese of Baltimore, will become an *ex officio* advisor to the Committee after November 3, when he assumes the position of Executive Secretary of the FDLC.

The role of an advisor is to assist the Committee in its review of agenda items, study papers, etc., and generally to participate in the deliberations of the Committee according to their particular liturgical, pastoral or theological expertise.

Sister Kathleen Loewen is a member of the Dominican Sisters of Racine, WI. She received the M.A. in liturgical studies from Webster University in 1968 and has served in the Milwaukee Office of Worship since

1977, becoming director in 1978. Father Cieslak, who received his doctorate in systematic theology from the Graduate Theological Union, has served as professor of liturgy at the Franciscan School of Theology since 1979. Father Michael Spillane has served as founding pastor of Saint Elizabeth Ann Seton Catholic Church in Crofton, MD, since 1975. A graduate of the North American College in Rome, he served part-time for five years as secretary to the late Cardinal Lawrence Sheehan in Baltimore, and for the past six years he has chaired the Building Commission of the Archdiocese of Baltimore.

The Bishops' Committee on the Liturgy and its Secretariat express their gratitude for the assistance and advice given by Sister Arlene Bennett, Father Siedlecki and Mr. Johnson during their terms as advisors and looks forward to the future collaboration of its newly appointed advisors.

Questions Concerning the *Order of Crowning an Image of the Blessed Virgin Mary*

On July 31, 1986 a copy of the provisional translation ("Green Book") of the *Order of Crowning an Image of the Blessed Virgin Mary* was sent to each bishop and diocesan liturgical commission or office of worship along with the request that comments concerning the proposed translation be forwarded to the Liturgy Secretariat by October 1, 1986. [For a description of and sample prayers from the *Order of Crowning,* see the August 1986 issue of the Bishops' Committee on the Liturgy *Newsletter,* pp. 29-31.]

Several bishops and commissions have responded to this consultation with a number of observations and questions about the translation of the *Order of Crowning* and about the rites themselves. Frequently asked is whether these rites may be used in situations other than those mentioned in the ritual, specifically whether they may be used in celebrations of "May crownings" or in similar devotional services.

The *Order of Crowning an Image of the Blessed Virgin Mary* is celebrated under the presidency of the diocesan bishop or, if he is unable to do so, the responsibility is entrusted to another bishop or to a priest, "particularly one associated with him [the diocesan bishop] in the pastoral care of the faithful in whose Church the image to be crowned is venerated" (no. 8). If the image is to be crowned in the name of the pope, "the directives of the authorizing papal brief are to be followed" (no. 8). It is not envisioned that the rites in the *Order of Crowning* may be led by other priests, deacons, or lay persons, since the *Order of Crowning* is a pontifical rite.

The Introduction (*praenotanda*) of the *Order of Crowning* further specifies that the image to be crowned is to be one of great renown and whose site is the center of a genuine liturgical *cultus* (no. 6). It is implied that the image of Mary (or of Christ and Mary) is one which attracts pilgrims. Clearly then this *Order of Crowning* is not intended for the crowning of an "ordinary" image of the Blessed Virgin which may be found in every parish church or chapel. However, the crowning of such images may be the object of a devotional service which takes its inspiration from the various texts and rites of the *Order of Crowning an Image of the Blessed Virgin Mary.* "May crownings" and other laudable pious practices expressing devotion to the Mother of God which are in keeping with the norms of Pope Paul VI's Apostolic Exhortation *Marialis cultus* (February 2, 1974) may indeed be led by priests, deacons, and laypersons.

It has also been asked whether the new *Order of Crowning* is truly a liturgical rite. Such is demonstrated by the decree of promulgation of this liturgical book. Furthermore, the custom or tradition of crowning or blessing an image of Christ, Mary, or one of the saints during a liturgical celebration such as the Liturgy of the Hours, a liturgy of the word, or even during Mass, although of relatively recent origin, traces its origins to the Roman Pontifical (see *Order of Crowning,* no. 4, note 4).

Finally it has also been asked whether the *Order of Crowning* is consonant with the teaching of *Sacrosanctum Concilium* and *Marialis cultus.* In the latter document Pope Paul VI stated the following: "If one studies the history of Christian worship, one notes that both in the East and in the West the highest and purest expressions of devotion to the Blessed Virgin have sprung from the liturgy or have been incorporated into it. We wish to emphasize the fact that the veneration which the universal Church today accords to blessed Mary is a derivation from and an extension and unceasing increase of the devotion that the Church of every age has paid to her, with careful attention to truth and with an ever watchful nobility of expression. From perennial tradition kept alive by reason of the uninterrupted presence of the Spirit and continual attention to the Word, the Church of our time draws motives, arguments, and incentives for the veneration that she pays to the Blessed Virgin. And the liturgy, which receives approval and strength from the Magisterium, is a most lofty expression and an evident proof of this living tradition" (*Marialis cultus* no. 15).

The publication of the *Order of Crowning an Image of the Blessed Virgin Mary,* once it has been approved by the National Conference of Catholic Bishops and confirmed by the Apostolic See, might well serve as an occasion for a renewed catechesis on the nature of devotion to the Mother of God which finds expression not only in *Marialis cultus* but also in *Behold Your Mother, Woman of Faith* (November 21, 1973), the pastoral letter of the National Conference of Catholic Bishops.

Newsletter Subscription Renewals

Computerized renewal notices will be sent to all subscribers to the Bishops' Committee on the Liturgy *Newsletter* in November. Subscribers are asked to return the completed renewal forms with their payment before December 20, 1986. (Subscriptions which have not been renewed by the time the January 1987 *Newsletter* goes to press will be placed on an inactive list and reinstated once payment is received.) The single subscription prices for 1987 will be $8.00 domestic mail (an increase of $1.00) and $10.00 foreign airmail. Bulk rates will be increased by 5 percent.

In order that subscribers' accounts may be properly credited, the instructions accompanying the renewal forms should be followed. The "renewal coupon" portion of the invoice must be included with payment. Coupon and payment should be returned in the self-mailer envelope which has been provided. This envelope is preaddressed for direct mail deposit to the bank. Payment should not be sent to the Liturgy Secretariat, since this needlessly slows down the renewal process.

Subscribers who have not received a renewal form by November 30, 1986 should contact the Liturgy Secretariat and a duplicate invoice will be sent. (*Newsletter* recipients whose subscription number is 205990, 205995, or 205999 are receiving *gratis* copies. Therefore, they will receive no renewal invoice.)

The Liturgy Secretariat expresses its thanks to all subscribers for their cooperation in the renewal process.

Worship: A Roman Catholic Hymnal and Service Book

Worship: A Roman Catholic Hymnal and Service Book, the revised successor to the *Worship II* hymnal, has recently been published by GIA Publications, Inc., Chicago, IL.

Unlike the second edition of *Worship* (1975) in which the hymns, listed alphabetically, are followed by the Order of Mass and the sacramental rites, the revised edition "has been organized to mirror who we are and how we pray as Roman Catholics within the larger Christian community" (Preface, *Worship*). The contents of *Worship* are presented in the following order: Morning and Evening Prayer from the *Liturgy of the Hours,* the psalter, the rites of the Church, the Order of Mass, hymns (arranged according to liturgical season, general use and ritual celebrations), the Lectionary (sung settings of responsorial psalms and gospel acclamations; the readings themselves are contained only in the "A" edition of *Worship*), and finally prayers of the individual and household. Several indices offer a thorough and helpful guide to the various sections and entries, as well as to the scriptural sources for many of the hymn texts.

Worship contains 486 hymns, psalms and canticles (as opposed to 311 in *Worship II*) and 126 entries for the various sung elements of the Order of Mass. The editors of *Worship* have avoided exclusive or archaic language in hymn texts.

Despite its differences from the previous two editions, *Worship: A Hymnal and Service Book for Roman Catholics* remains an important resource for Roman Catholic liturgical celebration in the United States.

BISHOPS' COMMITTEE ON THE LITURGY
NEWSLETTER
NATIONAL CONFERENCE OF CATHOLIC BISHOPS

**1986
VOLUME XXII
NOVEMBER**

Bishop Joseph P. Delaney Elected Liturgy Committee Chairman

On November 13, 1986, the Most Reverend Joseph P. Delaney, Bishop of Fort Worth, was elected to a one-year term as chairman of the Liturgy Committee of the National Conference of Catholic Bishops. This will complete the unexpired term of the previous chairman, Most Reverend Daniel E. Pilarczyk, Archbishop of Cincinnati, who was elected Vice President of the National Conference of Catholic Bishops/ United States Catholic Conference on November 11, 1986. (Archbishop John L. May of St. Louis was elected the new NCCB/USCC President.) A statute of the NCCB/USCC states that an officer of the Conference may not also hold a committee chairmanship.

Bishop Delaney was ordained in 1960 for the Diocese of Fall River. In 1966 he became a priest of the Diocese of Brownsville, Texas, where he served as Chancellor for many years. In 1981 he was chosen Bishop of Fort Worth.

Bishop Delaney was appointed a member of the Bishops' Committee on the Liturgy by Bishop John S. Cummins in 1981. In 1984 he was reappointed to a three-year term by Archbishop Pilarczyk. From 1981 until 1984 he served as chairman of the Committee's Hispanic Liturgy Subcommittee.

The staff of the Liturgy Secretariat congratulates Archbishop Pilarczyk upon his election to the office of Vice President of the Conference and wishes both Bishop Delaney and him well in their new responsibilities.

NCCB Approval of Liturgical Items on Agenda

On Tuesday, November 11, 1986, the National Conference of Catholic Bishops approved a number of liturgical items submitted for their discussion and action by the Bishops' Committee on the Liturgy [see *Newsletter,* October 1986, pp. 37-38]. Four of the five action items approved by a two-thirds majority of the *de iure* members of the Conference dealt with the *Rite of Christian Initiation of Adults.* The bishops approved: the final translation ("White Book" edition) of the *RCIA;* various ritual determinations (eleven in number) authorized by no. 33 of the *praenotanda* of the *RCIA* (no. 65 in the Latin *editio typica);* a number of additional liturgical texts and rites for inclusion in the U.S. edition of the ritual; and *National Statutes for the Catechumenate.* A mandatory effective date of February 21, 1988, the First Sunday of Lent, was set for each of these items.

The NCCB also approved by a two-thirds majority of its *de iure* members a new common Spanish translation of the Order of Mass, the Eucharistic Prayers, and several other Roman Missal texts, along with the inclusion of a note in all future U.S. editions of Spanish liturgical books which contain this new translation stating that it is possible to use the less formal *Ustedes* instead of *vosotros* in the salutations and admonitions.

No mandatory effective date was set for the new Spanish liturgical texts by the NCCB. (The Apostolic See is allowing this mandatory effective date to occur as late as March 30, 1992.) Such a date will be determined once plans for a complete edition of the Missal are made by the Hispanic Liturgy Subcommittee of the Liturgy Committee. This will follow upon the 1987 consultation with US bishops, diocesan liturgical commissions, et al., concerning the translation of collects, other presidential prayers, antiphons, etc., of the Missal to be adopted for use in the United States.

By a required simple majority the bishops approved a national plan and strategy for the implementation of the *Rite of Christian Initiation of Adults* and the catechumenate in the years from 1987 through 1992.

1312 MASSACHUSETTS AVENUE, N.W. • WASHINGTON, D.C. 20005

One action item submitted by the Liturgy Subcommittee failed to gain the required two-thirds majority vote of the NCCB, namely, *Eucharistic Prayer A*, the eucharistic prayer composed in English under the direction of the International Commission on English in the Liturgy.

Address of Archbishop Pilarczyk

On October 13, 1986 the Most Reverend Daniel E. Pilarczyk, Archbishop of Cincinnati and Chairman of the Bishops' Committee on the Liturgy, addressed the delegates to the annual National Meeting of Diocesan Liturgical Commissions and Offices of Worship in Portland, Maine. The text of Archbishop Pilarczyk's address follows.

One of the basic questions of all reality is the question of the one and the many, being and becoming, order and diversity. This is the question that the founding fathers of western philosophy addressed. The Eleatic Parmenides taught that being is one, and that change, becoming, multiplicity are merely illusory. *Ens est, non ens non est.* Heraclitus of Ephesus had earlier laid stress on becoming. There is one basic being, fire, but change, becoming, tension are essential to the existence of the One. Plato was dealing with the same question when he taught that the multitudinous objects of sense perception are not the objects of true knowledge, since they do not possess the necessary stability. Rather, the objects of true knowledge are ideal, subsistent, immaterial forms, hierarchically arranged and culminating in the one form of the good. Aristotle's teaching about potency, something between being and non-being, yet real, was an attempt to preserve the reality of change and multiplicity while preserving the stability of being.

In recounting all this it is not my intent to give a mini-lecture on ancient philosophy, but to point out that the tension between the one and the many, between uniformity and diversity has been with us for a long time. I believe that much of what is going on in the context of liturgy these days can be understood, at various levels and in various ways, in that same frame of reference.

To begin with, there is the *Rite of Christian Initiation of Adults* which comes before the National Conference of Catholic Bishops in November. There are no less than five different items, each of major import, that have to be dealt with. There is the approval of the ICEL "white book"; the approval of the ritual adaptations for the United States; the approval of new texts arising, for the most part, from the experience of the RCIA over the past decade in our country; the approval of national canonical statutes for the catechumenate; and the approval of a national plan for the implementation of the RCIA. When the members of our Administrative Committee were presented with all this in September, the terms "morass" and "labyrinth" were bandied about. One could also look on this complicated series of items as rampant multiplicity.

But there is multiplicity at a profounder level also. The RCIA basically deals with preparing, receiving, and welcoming non-baptized persons into the community of faith. Yet there is also provision made for non-catechized persons who have been baptized as Catholics, for non-catechized Christians of other ecclesial communities, for catechized Christians who wish to enter the Church, for children of catechetical age. Can all these be accommodated in one uniform process of formation, one uniform series of liturgical rites? Obviously not. The RCIA itself calls for adaptation to individual pastoral requirements. But how is this to be expressed ritually? The proposed canonical statutes indicate that as a general rule, those already baptized should be received into full communion when they are ready and do not need to be kept waiting until the Easter Vigil. But should those already baptized *ever* be received at the Vigil, especially when there are catechumens in the strict sense to be baptized at the same ceremony? There are strong feelings and strong arguments on both sides of this question. The point at issue is how much multiplicity is acceptable before it undermines the basic significance of what is going on.

The sacrament of reconciliation is a veritable bonanza of tensions between unity and multiplicity. There is the tension between the sinner, by definition individual, whose life has been fragmented into a multiplicity of warring components and the community of the Church which has been undermined by the individual's unfaithfulness. In sacramental practice in the past, we tended to underline the individual dimension of reconciliation: one sinner, one priest, in a dark and secret place when God's forgiveness was given. The community dimension was downplayed almost to the point of disappearance. Since the renewal of the sacrament we have given greater emphasis to the communitarian aspect of sin and forgiveness to the point that in some places the individual aspect of reconciliation runs the risk of being lost entirely. Both elements need to be respected if we are going to be faithful to the realities with which we are dealing.

Another item on our NCCB agenda this November is the approval for submission to the Holy See of an original eucharistic prayer from ICEL, entitled, not very poetically, *Eucharistic Prayer A* to distinguish it from the four standard eucharistic prayers already in the sacramentary. This is an event of some historical importance since *Eucharistic Prayer A,* if confirmed by the Congregation for Divine Worship, will be the first authorized anaphora originating in English since the Church began. A Pentecostal event, one might say. Yet even here, the dialectic between the one and the many is operative. Have we reached the point when eucharistic prayers are becoming too many? Is more always better? What is the ecclesial significance of a eucharistic prayer that is to be used by only one language group in the Church? Are we on the threshold of a new kind of unity or are we opening the door to increasing fragmentation? I have my answers to those questions, but perhaps not everyone everywhere would agree with them.

In the context of another language, the picture is just the opposite. Thanks to the initiative of the Congregation for Divine Worship last February, a uniform world-wide Spanish translation of the Order of Mass and the approved eucharistic prayers has been prepared. It is being offered to our bishops' conference for approval in November, with the hope that the whole project, world wide, can be concluded by the end of the present calendar year. Without the participation of the center of Catholic unity, this endeavor would have taken years and years to complete.

These are all matters presently on the agenda of our bishops' conference at various stages of completion. For the future, our Bishops' Committee on the Liturgy is working on such projects as the study of cultural adaptation of the liturgy for use among Black Catholics and for use among Hispanic Catholics in the United States. We are drawing closer to the publication of the liturgical *Book of Blessings* in two versions, one a ministerial edition, the other a version for families called *Household Blessings and Prayers.* We continue to collaborate with a committee of the Federation of Diocesan Liturgical Commissions in the preparation of a lectionary for Masses with children. A multiplicity of projects, each of which is replete with mulitiplicities of its own, all in the context of one worshiping church community.

In addition to all that, it has been suggested that our committee undertake several new studies. One would be the preparation of one or more nationally approved formulas for the act of contrition to be used for personal prayer, but more importantly in the sacrament of reconciliation. This request adverts to the multiplicity of options now available and also to the mobility of contemporary American society. Another suggestion that we have received urges us to prepare national guidelines for concelebration of the Eucharist: who should be invited to concelebrate, under what circumstances, by whom, etc. This suggestion arises out of a wide variety of practice around the country, but it also alludes to limitations on Eucharistic concelebration which sometimes leave priests and bishops asking themselves for what purpose they have been invited to attend certain events. I am aware that there are other dynamics in play here. In any case, it is an issue charged with implications about unity and diversity in the Church.

What I have been saying has been concerned mainly with issues that face the National Conference of Catholic Bishops in matters liturgical. Yet the liturgy is not planted primarily in bishops' conferences, but in local diocesan churches and local congregations. And that is where your role as staff persons and members of diocesan liturgical commissions is so important. It is your responsibility to assist the local leadership of the Church in your dioceses to understand the multiplicity of practices and needs that exist in the local church and to assist the leadership to respond to local situations in ways that respect pastoral realities but which at the same time preserve and foster the unity that is absolutely essential for the life of the universal as well as of the particular church. In the name of the bishops of our country, I wish to offer today a word of thanks for what you do to assist our Catholic people to "be Church." We bishops rely on you and your expertise more often than you may think. Know today that we are grateful.

Last year when I had the privilege of addressing your gathering in Grand Rapids, I spoke about maturity, about a second age of liturgical development in which deepening and developing had succeeded innovation. Today I have cast my remarks in the context of the metaphysical tension between the one and the many. These two approaches are not without connection, because one of the signs of maturity is the ability to deal with tension. There has always been tension between unity and diversity, between consistency and change, between centripetal and centrifugal. There always will be. But if twenty-five centuries of western thought have given us any lesson, it is that neither element suppresses the other. The resolution of the tension is neither in a Parmenidean uniformity nor in a Heraclitean flux. The resolution is to respect each element and realize that each is essential to reality. And to say that one of the signs of maturity is the ability to deal with tension is also to say that the mature person is one who is willing to come to grips with reality.

Rite of Exorcism in the Church

On September 29, 1985 the Congregation for the Doctrine of the Faith issued a Letter to Local Ordinaries Reminding Them of the Current Norms Regarding Exorcism (Prot. N. 291/70). The circular letter, which refers to the use of prayers of exorcism by lay persons during prayer meetings, was signed by Joseph Cardinal Ratzinger, Prefect of the Congregation, and Archbishop Albert Bovone, Secretary. Following is an unofficial translation of the letter.

For some years now certain groups in the Church have been meeting more and more to pray for deliverance from evil spirits, even if this does not represent exorcism properly defined. These meetings are conducted under the leadership of lay persons, even when a priest is present.

The Congregation for the Doctrine of the Faith has been asked what is to be thought of such activities. It feels obliged to inform all ordinaries of its response, which is as follows:

1. Canon 1172 of the Code of Canon Law states that no one can legitimately perform exorcisms over the possessed unless he has obtained special and express permission from the local ordinary (para. 1), and it determines that this permission from the local ordinary is to be granted only to a presbyter endowed with piety, knowledge, prudence and integrity of life (para. 2). The bishops therefore are strongly asked to urge the observance of these laws.

2. It follows from these prescriptions that the Christian faithful are not allowed to employ the formula of exorcism against Satan and the apostate angels taken from the ritual promulgated by the Supreme Pontiff Leo XIII, much less to use the entire text of this exorcism. When necessary, bishops are to admonish the faithful of this fact.

3. Lastly, for these reasons, bishops are asked to exercise care—even in cases were real diabolical possession has been ruled out but some sort of evil influence is nevertheless apparent—to ensure that those lacking the proper authority do not take charge of gatherings in which prayers are said to obtain deliverance, in the course of which devils are addressed directly and attempts are made to learn their identity.

The publication of these norms should in no way discourage the faithful from praying, as Jesus taught us, to be delivered from evil (cf. Mt. 6:13). In fact, pastors can use the opportunity offered here to recall what the tradition of the Church teaches about the role which the sacraments and the intercession of the Blessed Virgin Mary and the angels and saints properly enjoy in the spiritual struggle of Christians, even against evil spirits.

Resources

How To Form A Catechumenate Team. In this 72-page paperback book, Karen M. Hinman, the director of the North American Forum on the Catechumenate, addresses the issues of recruiting, forming and strengthening those involved in catechumenate teams: catechists, pastors, sponsors, welcomers, directors. Written in pastoral and practical language. Cost: $4.75. Order from: Liturgy Training Publications, 1800 North Hermitage Avenue, Chicago, IL 60622-1102. Phone: 312/486-7008.

Guidelines for Building and Renovating Churches. This 26-page, 8½ x 11 inch publication of the Liturgical Commission of the Diocese of Buffalo includes general principles and specific guidelines regarding building and renovating churches in accord with the 1983 Code of Canon Law and official Church statements. An alphabetical index serves as a handy reference to each topic covered in the guidelines. Cost, including postage and handling: $4.50 per copy. Contact: Reverend Edward Grosz, Office of Worship, 795 Main Street, Buffalo, NY 14203-1250. Phone: 716/847-5545.

BISHOPS' COMMITTEE ON THE LITURGY

NEWSLETTER

NATIONAL CONFERENCE OF CATHOLIC BISHOPS

1986
VOLUME XXII
DECEMBER

Navajo Translation of Mass Confirmed by the Apostolic See

On December 9, 1986 the National Conference of Catholic Bishops received the decree of the Congregation for Divine Worship, dated November 25, 1986, confirming the decision of the Administrative Committee of the NCCB to approve the Navajo translation of the Order of Mass, Eucharistic Prayers I and II of the Roman Missal, Eucharistic Prayer I for Masses with Children, and the sacramental formulas for the consecration of the bread and wine. The Congregation also approved the request of the National Conference of Catholic Bishops that Eucharistic Prayer I for Masses with Children may be used for Masses with adults in the Navajo communities. The confirmed Navajo translation may be implemented immediately in Navajo communities.

The following is an unofficial English translation of that decree.

Prot. N. 231/86

At the request of His Excellency James W. Malone, Bishop of Youngstown and President of the National Conference of Catholic Bishops, on January 22, 1986, and in virtue of the faculties granted to this Congregation by Pope John Paul II, we gladly approve, that is, confirm the Navajo translation of liturgical texts, as they appear in the appended copy, namely:

> The Order of Mass together with the formularies applying to the consecration of the bread and the wine in the celebration of the Eucharist;
>
> Eucharistic Prayer I and II from the *Missale Romanum*;
>
> Eucharistic Prayer I for Masses with Children.

In the publication of these texts mention should be made of the confirmation granted by the Apostolic See. In addition two copies of these printed texts are to be sent to this Congregation.

Anything to the contrary notwithstanding.

From the Congregation for Divine Worship, 25 November 1986.

+ Paul Augustin Cardinal Mayer
Prefect

Piero Marini
Subsecretary

Address of Archbishop Roger Mahony on the *Rite of Christian Initiation of Adults*

On Monday, November 10, 1986, Archbishop Roger Mahony of Los Angeles addressed the members of the National Conference of Catholic Bishops during a special workshop dealing with the Rite of Christian Initiation of Adults. *Other speakers included Father James Dunning, President of the North American Forum on the Catechumenate, and Bishop Joseph A. Ferrario, Bishop of Honolulu and chairman of the Christian Initiation Subcommittee. The purpose of the workshop was to highlight the importance of the* Rite of Christian Initiation of Adults *in the sacramental life of the Church, and to provide an overview of the many items dealing with the RCIA being proposed for the approval of the members of the NCCB. Archbishop Mahony's address follows.*

1312 MASSACHUSETTS AVENUE, N.W. • WASHINGTON, D.C. 20005

One of the greatest treasures of our ancient tradition, and one of the best kept secrets in recent centuries, is the power and potential of the catechumenate for the life of the Church.

The New Testament mandate to preach the Good News and to make disciples of all nations, baptizing them in the name of the Lord, is both strong and compelling. It is a mandate which carries with it an urgency and challenges us anew today as it challenged the early Christian communities: how do we proclaim Jesus as Lord, and call people to conversion and faith? How do we prepare them for initiation into the full life of the Church? It is through the process of the *Rite of Christian Initiation of Adults* that we can facilitate a response to this challenge.

It is clear to me that the *RCIA* is in no way just another "program" to be implemented in the Church, nor even another creative option for parish renewal. It is, rather, an essential element of the life of the Church which has profound implications in the areas of evangelization and liturgical life. The catechumenate affects spiritual and apostolic development—particularly in the areas of ministry and service—and develops personal and communal consciousness of and identification with the universal Church. It is clear to me as well that the role of the bishop is key in the implementation and effectiveness of the rites themselves and the entire catechumenate for the local Church.

There is a paradox evidenced in those parishes where a fully developed catechumenate has been implemented to evangelize and initiate new members. It is the "converts" who call the Catholic community to conversion. Evangelization begins with an invitation, a welcome—in the words of Jesus, "Come and see" (John 1:39).

The local Church welcoming new members must examine its sense of hospitality, its Gospel values, its attractiveness, and, ultimately, the authenticity of its Christian life and witness. There is a self-scrutiny inherent in being a community of evangelization: is the life of the Risen Jesus incarnated and celebrated in the life, worship, and service of this local Church? Do—or can—others look at this local Church and see how these Christians love one another? Can they recognize the Lord Jesus in the breaking of the Bread and living of the Good News within that local community?

The catechumens themselves become evangelizers for the parish community in which they pursue their faith journeys. Parishioners become aware of adults who are asking questions, seeking meaning, and making a commitment to actively explore the Gospel and the teachings of the Church. As a consequence, they are led to reflect anew upon their own faith lives. They reaffirm the significance of their own baptism and confirmation. "I always took my faith for granted," they tell us, "but when I saw other adults freely choosing what I have, it really made me appreciate and want to learn more about my religion."

Families, friends, and co-workers are also evangelized by the catechumens who, in the enthusiasm of their inquiry and newly discovered faith, are often candidly open in proclaiming the Lord Jesus and his actions in their lives. Countless are the stories of catechumens who have brought friends into the Church with them. Many are the catechumens whose non-practicing Catholic spouses experience a new conversion and a return to the sacramental life through their witness.

Most powerful of all, perhaps, is the common experience of the sponsors who have come to companion a catechumen along the journey of faith. They come, they say, to share the faith with another. They stay, they say, because in doing so, they experience a new conversion. They rediscover the richness and power of the faith they have professed for years—even a lifetime. Indeed, while the catechumenate is a means of evangelization for newcomers to the faith, this process serves to evangelize our own Catholic people and, therefore, to intensify the life of the Church.

As bishops it is our responsibility to attend to the life and growth of our local Churches, with particular concern for new members. We are concerned with the quality of Catholic life today. We are concerned about moral decision-making among our people. We are concerned about the inroads of fundamentalism, which often confuses and challenges our people. We are concerned with the need to call our young people to truly live the Gospel, the Gospel of justice and peace. We are concerned.

How do we touch people's hearts? How do we move people to Christian action? How do we build vibrant, attractive communities of faith? We need to look at the heart of the matter, and the heart of the matter is *conversion*—individual and communal. My brother bishops, the *RCIA* is *about conversion*. It is not a simplistic solution. But it is the direction in which we need to be moving. I believe it is the direction in which the Spirit is moving the Church. We as bishops must take the lead, and our pastors will follow. The laity are crying out for our leadership. The initiation of adults involves a variety of ministries, and we must affirm and develop the gifts of all the baptized who share in the priesthood of Christ. Pastors must be encouraged to implement the full catechumenate and to celebrate the proper rites as a normal, necessary aspect of parish liturgical life.

For example, the incorporation of the Dismissal Rite at Mass has a profound effect on the catechumens and on the assembly of the faithful alike. Those preparing for initiation are dismissed after the Liturgy of the Word to share the Word of God, to discern its meaning for their lives, while at the same time fasting from and increasing their hunger for the Eucharist. They learn to make life decisions based on Gospel values. Presently in the Archdiocese of Los Angeles we have ongoing catechumenates in some seventy-five parishes, with many more now beginning.

The catechetical-liturgical integrity of the initiation process is to be maintained not only on the parochial level, but in a particular way through the visible presence of the bishop. Our presence and participation as Shepherd of the local Church manifests clearly the connection between the life and faith of the parish community and that of the universal Church. This happens formally—liturgically—and informally.

For example, the bishop's leadership, especially during the Rite of Election, emphasizes that election is truly the activity of the whole Church. The local community which has been involved with the formation of the catechumens joins with the diocesan community of faith under the leadership of the presiding bishop. In the Rite of Election we celebrate the choice on the part of the Church of those to be admitted to the Easter sacraments. Often this takes place at the Cathedral to celebrate the unity of the Church. In Los Angeles the Rite of Election takes place in each of our five pastoral regions, after individual testimonies of faith are shared at a parish celebration.

Another celebration appropriate to the Cathedral is the liturgy for the neophytes at the end of the Eastern Season, near Pentecost, to close the period of postbaptismal catechesis. The newly baptized who have lived the Easter mysteries and are prepared to enter fully into the mission and ministry of the Church come together in festive celebration with their local bishop. Again, their identity with the whole Church is reaffirmed. And the profound joy, enthusiasm, and powerful witness the neophytes give to one another and to us cannot be underestimated. Last Pentecost, our Cathedral in Los Angeles was filled with song and sounds of praise in Spanish and English, from a rainbow of races and cultures. More than sixty parishes were able to participate, involving some 680 newly baptized, 130 who were received into full communion with the Church, and 220 baptized but uncatechized Catholics who were confirmed, together with their sponsors, catechumenate leaders, and their families. The Church is alive and well! Such gatherings are tangible Pentecost experiences in our day—experiences of the Spirit moving within and among us, breathing new life and energy into God's Church.

The catechumenate is not something "new" in our Church. It is something very old, something which is rooted in the New Testament communities. It reclaims our earliest traditions of Christian initiation and our episcopal role in that process.

Rediscovered and revised for today's Church, the catechumenate responds to the Gospel mandate to tell the Good News to all people. It facilitates the process of conversion, recognizing the stages of adult faith development and understanding faith not merely as dogma, but as a way of living the Gospel in the world. The *RCIA* generates new life in the Church not only through new members, but through the development of ministries, the enrichment of liturgical life, and the involvement of the total faith community.

Yes, my brother Bishops, the Gospel mandate to go and make disciples of all nations is urgent and challenging. It is a mandate which we can accept with enthusiasm and joyful hope as we exercise leadership in the implementation of the *RCIA* and look forward to its integration into the total rhythm of the Church's life.

Guidelines for the Publication of Missalettes, Addendum: *Guidelines on Receiving Communion*

On November 8, 1986 the Administrative Committee of the National Conference of Catholic Bishops approved a proposal of the Bishops' Committee on Pastoral Research and Practices to issue *Guidelines for Receiving Communion* for circulation among the bishops and for inclusion in all missalettes and other participation aids published in the United States.

The goal of the Committee on Pastoral Research and Practices was threefold: to remind Catholics of the proper dispositions for receiving Communion, including the use of the sacrament of Penance when there is a consciousness of serious sin; to remind Christians not in full communion with the Catholic Church that the present state of division precludes offering a general invitation to receive Communion when they join Roman Catholics in the celebration of a Marriage or Funeral or other eucharistic liturgy; and to invite those who cannot receive Communion to be united with Catholics in prayer on these occasions.

These *Guidelines for Receiving Communion* are to be inserted into the *Guidelines for the Publication of Missalettes* as an *Addendum* immediately after the signatures of the Chairman and the Executive Director. The *Guidelines for Receiving Communion* are then followed by the following attribution: *National Conference of Catholic Bishops/ November 8, 1986/ Washington, D.C.*

The text of the guidelines as approved by the Administrative Committee is given below.

ADDENDUM
Guidelines for Receiving Communion

Publishers are to reproduce the following Guidelines for Receiving Communion in a prominent place in missalettes in the same type used for the responses of the assembly. They should consult with the Secretariat of the Bishops' Committee on the Liturgy prior to the issuance of the Guidelines for Receiving Communion *in their publications.*

For Catholics

Catholics fully participate in the celebration of the Eucharist when they receive Holy Communion in fulfillment of Christ's command to eat His Body and drink His Blood. In order to be properly disposed to receive Communion, communicants should not be conscious of grave sin, have fasted for one hour, and seek to live in charity and love with their neighbors. Persons conscious of grave sin must first be reconciled with God and the Church through the sacrament of Penance. A frequent reception of the sacrament of Penance is encouraged for all.

For Other Christians

We welcome to this celebration of the Eucharist those Christians who are not fully united with us. It is a consequence of the sad divisions in Christianity that we cannot extend to them a general invitation to receive Communion. Catholics believe that the Eucharist is an action of the celebrating community signifying a oneness in faith, life, and worship of the community. Reception of the Eucharist by Christians not fully united with us would imply a oneness which does not yet exist, and for which we must all pray.

For Those Not Receiving Communion

Those not receiving sacramental Communion are encouraged to express in their hearts a prayerful desire for unity with the Lord Jesus and with one another.

For Non-Christians

We also welcome to this celebration those who do not share our faith in Jesus. While we cannot extend to them an invitation to receive Communion, we do invite them to be united with us in prayer.

National Conference of Catholic Bishops
November 8, 1986
Washington, DC

Survey of Newsletter Subscribers

In January 1987 a survey will be made of a random sampling of subscribers to the Bishops' Committee on the Liturgy *Newsletter* to determine usefulness of the publication, readership satisfaction, and the respondents' use or non-use of the other thirteen newsletters published by various offices of the National Conference of Catholic Bishops or United States Catholic Conference. If you receive a copy of this survey, please respond to the NCCB/USCC Office of Planning, which has initiated this project. Thank you.

BISHOPS' COMMITTEE ON THE LITURGY

NEWSLETTER

NATIONAL CONFERENCE OF CATHOLIC BISHOPS

1987
VOLUME XXIII
JANUARY

Marian Year in 1987 Proclaimed

On January 1, 1987, the solemnity of Mary, Mother of God, Pope John Paul II proclaimed the celebration and observance of a Marian Year beginning on Pentecost Sunday, June 7, 1987, and concluding on the solemnity of the Assumption, August 15, 1988. The last Marian Year was celebrated in 1954.

As Archbishop John L. May, NCCB/USCC President, said in a statement released on January 5, 1987, "This observance in Rome and in the local churches offers Catholics and other Christians an opportunity to renew their devotion to the Blessed Virgin, deepen their understanding of her divinely given role in the work of redemption accomplished by her Son, and achieve further insight into the privileged position which she occupies in the community of faith."

To assist dioceses and parishes to celebrate the Marian Year, the Liturgy Secretariat has commissioned several devotional services to be composed according to the spirit and directives of *Marialis cultus* of Pope Paul VI and the NCCB's 1973 pastoral letter, *Behold Your Mother*. These services will be structured according to a liturgy of the word or an order of blessing and will focus on such elements as the Litany of Loreto, the communal recitation of the Rosary, crownings and processions with an image of Mary, and an adaptation of the Liturgy of the Hours (a brief Office of the Blessed Virgin Mary). The collection will also include traditional and contemporary prayers to Mary and St. Joseph, other forms of intercessory prayer, and new collects translated from the *Messale Romano,* the second edition of the Italian Sacramentary (1983).

When completed, the collection of Marian devotions will be available from the Office of Publishing and Promotion Services, United States Catholic Conference, 1312 Massachusetts Avenue NW, Washington, DC 20005.

Bishop Richard Sklba Named Committee Member

With the election of the Most Reverend Joseph P. Delaney, Bishop of Fort Worth, as Chairman of the Bishops' Committee on the Liturgy, a position for a new member of the Committee was opened. Bishop Delaney has appointed Bishop Richard J. Sklba, Auxiliary Bishop of Milwaukee, a member of the Committee. Bishop Sklba, who is also a member of the Bishops' Committee on Doctrine, had been a consultant to the Liturgy Committee since November 1984. He holds a degree in biblical studies from the Pontifical Biblical Institute and is a member of the ad hoc Committee for the Revision of the New Testament of the *New American Bible*.

Consultation on the Roman Missal in Spanish

On January 5, 1987 a copy of *Consulta sobre el Misal Romano en Espanol,* a consultation workbook concerning the Roman Missal in Spanish, was sent to each diocesan liturgical commission or office of worship. A copy was also sent to each bishop in the United States on January 6, 1987 with a cover letter signed by Bishop Joseph P. Delaney, Chairman of the Bishops' Committee on the Liturgy, and Bishop Ricardo Ramirez, CSB, Chairman of the Hispanic Liturgy Subcommittee.

The Introduction of the *Consulta* workbook delineates the aims and goals of the consultation. The main purpose of the consultation is to determine which version or translation of the collects and other presidential prayers will be chosen from among the present five Spanish translations of the Roman Missal (Argentina, Chile, Colombia, Mexico, Spain) for inclusion in an eventual *Hispanic Sacramentary* for use in the dioceses of the United States of America. Since such an edition of the Sacramentary will contain the new international translation of the Order of Mass or eucharistic prayers ("*texto unico*") which was approved by the National Conference of Catholic Bishops in November 1986 and earlier approved by other conferences which use Spanish in the liturgy (see *Newsletter,* volume 22, October 1986, pp. 37-38, and November 1986, page 41), this consultation does not pertain to those texts.

Since it is not the intention of the Bishops' Committee on the Liturgy to prepare yet another Spanish translation of the collects and other presidential prayers of the Missal, the Committee, through its Hispanic Liturgy Subcommittee, upon examining the results of the *Consulta,* will recommend one of the current translations of these texts for approval by the members of the National Conference of Catholic Bishops. To that end, therefore, each bishop and diocesan commission or office of worship is asked to consult with those who minister to the Spanish-speaking and respond to the questions of the *Consulta* by *April 24, 1987.*

Additional copies of the workbook are available from the Liturgy Secretariat at $2.00 per copy (prepaid, postage and handling included).

Perpetual Adoration of the Blessed Sacrament: Clarification

The attention of the Secretariat of the Bishops' Committee on the Liturgy has been drawn to an inadvertent non-substantive omission from the response concerning "Perpetual Exposition of the Blessed Sacrament" in the June/July 1986 issue of the *Newsletter* of the Bishops' Committee on the Liturgy, pp. 24-25.

No. 90 of *Holy Communion and Worship of the Eucharist outside Mass,* a section of the Roman Ritual, under the heading, "Adoration in religious communities," mentions not ony religious communities but also "other pious groups" (*aliisque piis coetibus*) in which the "constitutions or norms of their Institute" call for perpetual eucharistic adoration or adoration protracted over a long period of time. No. 90 states: "It is strongly recommended that they pattern this holy practice in harmony with the spirit of the liturgy. Then, with the whole community taking part, the adoration before Christ the Lord will consist of readings, songs, and religious silence to foster effectively the life of the community . . . "

Thus, no. 6 of the response given in the *Newsletter* (p. 25) may be applied to other communities or institutes which are not canonically considered religious institutes. This possibility of perpetual adoration within a religious community, institute, or the like, in accord with the canonical constitution or norms of such a body is in no way applicable to parish churches or other oratories.

It is to be noted, moreover, that no. 90 of the ritual, quoted above, is speaking of perpetual *adoration* in general and not explicitly of eucharistic *exposition* (treated in nos. 84-89). Adoration is understood to include the worship of the Holy Eucharist reserved in the tabernacle, as well as adoration during the exposition of the Eucharist contained in a ciborium or in a monstrance.

Readers may wish to review the entirety of the Roman Ritual's treatment of this matter in nos. 79-112 of *Holy Communion and Worship of the Eucharist outside Mass.* Concerning canons 941-943 of the 1983 Code of Canon Law, which summarizes the law of the ritual, see *The Code of Canon Law: A Text and Commentary* (New York/Mahwah, NJ: Paulist Press, 1985), pp. 666-667.

Inclusive Language Lectionaries

Q. What is the status of the new inclusive-language lectionaries? May they be used in the celebration of the eucharistic liturgy?

R. While there is a growing concern that liturgical and biblical texts used in Christian worship should not contain exclusive or discriminatory language, the requirement remains that only those texts approved and authorized by the competent authority of the Church may be used in liturgical celebrations. This is as true for versions of *The Lectionary for Mass* as it is for other liturgical books, such as the Sacramentary or Ritual.

Recently the Pueblo Publishing Company of New York announced the publication of a *Lectionary for the Christian People*. It is advertised as containing the "readings and gospels emended in inclusive American English for cycle A of the Roman, Episcopal, Lutheran lectionaries." It uses the Revised Standard Version (RSV) of the Bible.

Another version of the lectionary, *An Inclusive-Language Lectionary,* was prepared by the Inclusive-Language Lectionary Committee established at the recommendation of the Task Force on Biblical Translation and authorized by the Division of Education and Ministry of the National Council of the Churches of Christ. It was published for the Cooperative Publication Association by John Knox Press (Atlanta), the Pilgrim Press (New York), and the Westminster Press (Philadelphia). And it too uses the Revised Standard Version (RSV) of the Bible.

While the Catholic edition of the Revised Standard Version is approved for use in the lectionary, emended versions of the RSV—such as those used in the above-mentioned lectionaries—have not been authorized by the National Conference of Catholic Bishops.

An approved edition of *The Lectionary for Mass* is to contain a translation of the Scriptures approved by the National Conference of Catholic Bishops (and subsequently confirmed by the Apostolic See) and be "published by authority of the Bishops' Committee on the Liturgy." It may then be used to proclaim the readings in the celebration of the eucharistic liturgy in the dioceses of the United States of America.

Three translations of the Scriptures have been so approved by the National Conference of Catholic Bishops for use in *The Lectionary for Mass:* New American Bible, The Jerusalem Bible, and the Revised Standard Version-Catholic Edition. (The New Jerusalem Bible has not yet been authorized by the NCCB for liturgical use). The revised translation of the New Testament of the New American Bible will be included in future editions of *The Lectionary for Mass* which use the NAB version. At present no other English translation or version of the Scriptures is authorized for use in the celebration of the Mass or in another liturgical rite.

Saint Giuseppe Maria Tomasi, Liturgical Scholar

On October 12, 1986, Pope John Paul II canonized Blessed Giuseppe Maria Tomasi of the Order of Clerics Regular (Theatines) at St. Peter's Basilica at the Vatican. St. Giuseppe Maria Tomasi had been beatified in 1803 by Pius VII.

During the homily at the Mass of Canonization Pope John Paul II stated that this canonization was especially timely because of the new saint's importance in the field of liturgical studies "which he greatly promoted in his life and with his writings. The witness of this new saint is *particularly opportune in these days,* twenty years after the Second Vatican Council, which gave so much emphasis to the renewal of the liturgical life. The saint whom we proclaim today helps us *to understand and bring about this renewal in its proper sense.*"

St. Giuseppe Maria Tomasi was born in Licata, Sicily on September 12, 1649. Ordained in 1673, after having entered the Theatines in 1655, Tomasi became a scholar in classical and Oriental langauges, working in Messina, Ferrara, and Rome. His studies of the liturgy took him to the Vatican Library's collection of unedited manuscripts, especially the *Codices Sacramentorum nongentis annis antiquiores* (Rome, 1680) containing the *Sacramentarium Gelasianum,* the *Missale Gothicum,* the *Missale Francorum,* and the *Gallicum Vetus.* Among other scholarly editions of ancient liturgical books which Tomasi edited and published were: *Psalterium* (Rome, 1683), a comparison of the Gallican and Roman psalters; *Responsalia et Antiphonaria Romanae Ecclesiae* (Rome, 1686); *Antiqui libri Missarum Romanae Ecclesiae* (Rome, 1691).

St. Giuseppe Maria Tomasi, who was named a cardinal in 1712, was known for his erudition in the history of worship and liturgical manuscripts, and for his personal holiness. His liturgical scholarship, however, was also applied in the pastoral promotion of liturgical formation and education. "A true minister of the altar, Tomasi understood that it was necessary to seek Christ, most of all, as the psalmist says, 'in his sanctuary' (Ps. 63:3), '*dwelling in the house of the Lord*' (cf. Ps. 23:6); he gave due honor to the sacred liturgy, not limiting it to a ritualistic external action, but making the divine worship a *supreme fount of light and operative energy* for the Christian's entire day, making the day nothing else than the prolongation of the liturgical act, especially the Eucharistic sacrifice" (John Paul II, Homily, Canonization of St. Giuseppe Maria Tomasi).

Music Competition

In 1989 the Catholic Church in the United States will mark the 200th anniversary of the founding of the hierarchy in the country. In the light of the forthcoming anniversary, the National Conference of Catholic Bishops (NCCB) has appointed an episcopal Bicentennial Committee to formulate plans for this observance with the Most Reverend William D. Borders, Archbishop of Baltimore, serving as chairman.

As part of the preparations for the commemoration, the Bicentennial Committee has appointed a special music committee. Bishop Eugene Marino, Auxiliary Bishop of Washington, DC, serves as chairman of the committee and is being assisted by Monsignor Michael Di Teccia Farina, President of the Paul VI Institute for the Arts.

The committee is sponsoring a competition for the composition of a special musical setting of the Mass to highlight the anniversary. The competition is open to all. An award of $10,000 will go to the winning composer.

The competition will be conducted through the provinces of the Catholic Church in the United States and is limited to members within these provinces. Each diocese is to invite entrants and select one representative to be considered for the provincial candidate. The province will then select one contestant for consideration by a panel of national recognized authorities in the area of Church music. The national panel will make the final award.

Following are the regulations covering the competition:

1. The Mass must reflect the nature of the celebration, the meaning of the Church, its growth and influence upon the lives of the people. It must conform to the guidelines contained in the publications "Music in Catholic Worship" (1983 edition) and "Liturgical Music Today" (1982).

2. The work must be composed with congregational participation as well as choir in mind. Organ accompaniment is required, but other instrumentation may be considered. It must be composed with the regular Church choir and people in mind and not planned as a complex or dramatic piece.

3. The Mass should be conceived as one usable in all parishes for many occasions, not merely for solemn ceremonies or one-time-only events.

5. The composer will retain the copyright property of the Mass. But the National Conference of Catholic Bishops (NCCB) will reserve the right to retain a set of the parts and the right to performance without royalty or fees in each diocese of the United States for a limited time.

7. Charges for copying parts will be the responsibility of the music committee of the Bicentennial Committee on the Celebration of the Establishment of the American Hierarchy.

8. The finalist panel or judges reserve the option to declare no winner, and their decision is final.

All entries for the special music competition are to be received by the various dioceses by December 31, 1987. The Bicentennial Committee will announce the winning composition on November 1, 1988.

Joint Committee on Scripture and Inclusive Language

The Bishops' Committee on the Liturgy and the Bishops' Committee on Doctrine have formed a joint committee to study inclusive language in biblical translations. Bishop Raymond Lessard, Chairman of the Committee on Doctrine, has appointed Bishop Richard Sklba and Bishop Paul Waldschmidt, CSC, to represent the Committee on Doctrine, while Bishop Wilton Gregory and Bishop Patrick Cooney were appointed by Bishop Delaney to represent the Liturgy Committee. Father Michael Buckley, SJ, Executive Director of the Secretariat of the Doctrine Committee, and Father John Gurrieri, Executive Director of the Secretariat of the Liturgy Committee, will staff the joint committee.

The establishment of the joint committee on inclusive language and Scripture was occasioned by a *varium* presented to the National Conference of Catholic Bishops in November 1985 and at the subsequent direction of the NCCB Administrative Committee. The purpose of the joint committee is to establish criteria and guidelines by which the bishops may judge new translations of the Scriptures which are attentive to inclusive or non-discriminatory language, especially when such translations are proposed for liturgical use.

BISHOPS' COMMITTEE ON THE LITURGY
NEWSLETTER
NATIONAL CONFERENCE OF CATHOLIC BISHOPS

**1987
VOLUME XXIII
FEBRUARY**

Monsignor Alan F. Detscher Named Associate Director

Monsignor Alan F. Detscher, who has served as Staff Consultant to the Secretariat of the Bishops' Committee on the Liturgy since May 1986 was named an Associate Director of the Secretariat by Reverend Monsignor Daniel F. Hoye, General Secretary of the NCCB/USCC on February 9, 1987.

Monsignor Detscher holds licentiate and doctorate degrees in liturgy from the Pontifical Liturgical Institute of Saint Anselm in Rome. He has served in advisory and consulting roles with the Bishops' Committee on the Liturgy, the International Commission on English in the Liturgy, and the Liturgical Office of the Diocese of Saint Maron (Maronite Rite). A priest of the Diocese of Bridgeport, Connecticut, he has served as the Director of the Office of Liturgy and as secretary to Bishop Walter W. Curtis.

Monsignor Detscher has been a member of the Board of Directors of the Federation of Diocesan Liturgical Commissions and is a member of the North American Academy of Liturgy.

Time of Celebration of the Easter Vigil in 1987

In the February 1986 issue of the Bishops' Committee on the Liturgy *Newsletter* (Volume 22, page 8), the norm of the *General Norms for the Liturgical Year and the Roman Calendar* was recalled: "The entire celebration of [the Easter] vigil should take place *at night,* that is, it should either begin after nightfall or end before the dawn of Sunday" (no. 21). This clarification went on to state that to celebrate the Easter Vigil before nightfall or to conclude it with the light of dawn at a "sunrise service" runs counter to the symbolism of Christ the Light in the vigil liturgy.

Readers should be advised that daylight savings time begins this year on April 5, and Holy Saturday falls on April 18. While sunset in most parts of the United States will occur between 7:30 and 8:30 p.m. on Holy Saturday evening, the darkness suitable for the celebration of the Vigil will not occur until about 90 minutes after that. Local agencies should be contacted in order to determine the appropriate time when the Easter Vigil might be scheduled to begin.

The Washing of Feet on Holy Thursday

In response to a number of inquiries from bishops, diocesan liturgical commissions, and offices of worship concerning the rite of washing of feet on Holy Thursday, the Chairman of the Bishops' Committee on the Liturgy, after a review of the matter by the Committee, has authorized the following response prepared by the Secretariat. The matter is being referred to the competent Roman Congregation which is already studying various questions relating to Holy Week.

Question: What is the significance of the Holy Thursday footwashing rite?

Response:

1. The Lord Jesus washed the feet of his disciples at the Last Supper as a sign of the new commandment that Christians should love one another: "Such as my love has been for you, so must your love be for each other. This is how all will know you for my disciples: by your love for one another" (see John 13, 34-35). For

1312 MASSACHUSETTS AVENUE, N.W. • WASHINGTON, D.C. 20005

centuries the Church has imitated the Lord through the ritual enactment of the new commandment of Jesus Christ in the washing of feet on Holy Thursday.

2. Although the practice had fallen into disuse for a long time in parish celebrations, it was restored in 1955 by Pope Pius XII as a part of the general reform of Holy Week. At that time the traditional significance of the rite of footwashing was stated by the Sacred Congregation of Rites in the following words: "Where the washing of feet, to show the Lord's commandment about fraternal charity, is performed in a Church according to the rubrics of the restored Ordo of Holy Week, the faithful should be instructed on the profound meaning of this sacred rite and should be taught that it is only proper that they should abound in works of Christian charity on this day."[1]

3. The principal and traditional meaning of the Holy Thursday *mandatum,* as underscored by the decree of the Congregation, is the biblical injunction of Christian charity: Christ's disciples are to love one another. For this reason, the priest who presides at the Holy Thursday liturgy portrays the biblical scene of the gospel by washing the feet of some of the faithful.

4. Because the gospel of the *mandatum* read on Holy Thursday also depicts Jesus as the "Teacher and Lord" who humbly serves his disciples by performing this extraordinary gesture which goes beyond the laws of hospitality,[2] the element of humble service has accentuated the celebration of the footwashing rite in the United States over the last decade or more. In this regard, it has become customary in many places to invite both men and women to be participants in this rite in recognition of the service that should be given by all the faithful to the Church and to the world. Thus, in the United States, a variation in the rite developed in which not only charity is signified but also humble service.

5. While this variation may differ from the rubric of the *Sacramentary* which mentions only men ("*viri selecti*"), it may nevertheless be said that the intention to emphasize service along with charity in the celebration of the rite is an understandable way of accentuating the evangelical command of the Lord, "who came to serve and not to be served," that all members of the Church must serve one another in love.

6. The liturgy is always an act of ecclesial unity and Christian charity, of which the Holy Thursday footwashing rite is an eminent sign. All should obey the Lord's new commandment to love one another *with an abundance of love,* especially at this most sacred time of the liturgical year when the Lord's passion, death, and resurrection are remembered and celebrated in the powerful rites of the Triduum.[3]

Secretariat
Bishops' Committee on the Liturgy
16 February 1987

Notes

1. Sacred Congregation of Rites, *Instruction on the Correct Use of the Restored Ordo of Holy Week,* November 16, 1955 (Washington, DC: National Catholic Welfare Conference Publications Office, 1955), page 6.

2. In biblical times it was prescribed that the host of a banquet was to provide water (and a basin) so that his guests could wash their hands before sitting down to table. Although a host might also provide water for travelers to wash their own feet before entering the house, the host himself would not wash the feet of his guests. According to the *Talmud* the washing of feet was forbidden to any Jew except those in slavery.

In the controversies between Hillel and Shammai (cf. *Shabbat* 14a-b) Shammai ruled that guests were to wash their hands to correct "*tumat yadayim*" or "impurity of hands" (cf. Ex 30, 17 and Lv 15, 11). Priests were always to wash their hands before eating consecrated meals. The Pharisees held that all meals were in a certain sense "consecrated" because of table fellowship.

Jesus' action of washing the feet of his disciples was unusual for his gesture went beyond the required laws of hospitality (washing of hands) to what was, in appearance, a menial task. The Lord's action was probably unrelated to matters of ritual purity according to the Law.

3. For a brief overview of the restoration of the footwashing rite in 1955, see W.J. O'Shea, "Mandatum," *New Catholic Encyclopedia,* Volume IX, 146, and W.J. O'Shea, "Holy Thursday," *New Catholic Encyclopedia,* Volume VII, 105-107; Walter D. Miller, *Revised Ceremonial of Holy Week* (New York: Catholic Book Publishing Company, 1971), p. 43. See also Prosper Gueranger, OSB, *The Liturgical Year,* Volume VI, *Passiontide and Holy Week* (Westminster, Maryland: Newman Press, 1949), pp. 395-401. For the historical background of the many forms of this rite, see the following studies: Pier Franco Beatrice, *La lavanda dei piedi: Contributo alla storia delle antiche liturgie cristiane* (Rome: C.L.V. Edizioni Liturgiche, 1983); "Lotio pedum" in Hermann Schmidt, *Hebdomada Sancta,* Volume II (Rome: Herder, 1956-1957); Annibale Bugnini, CM, and C. Braga, CM, *Ordo Hebdomadae Sanctae Instauratus* in Biblioteca *"Ephemerides Liturgicae" Sectio Historica* 25 (Rome: Edizioni Liturgiche, 1956), pp. 73-75; Theodor Klauser, *A Short History of the Western Liturgy: An Account and Some Reflections,* second edition (New York: Oxford University Press, 1979), p. 81.

Projects of the Congregation for Divine Worship

In the December 1986 issue of *Notitiae,* the Congregation for Divine Worship gives a brief summary of the projects it is presently pursuing. Among these are the following.

1. A working group has been entrusted with the revision of the *Ordo Celebrandi Matrimonium (Rite of Marriage).* The group has already prepared a new *praenotanda* or introduction to the rite which is more developed and in greater harmony with other liturgical books. The liturgical texts and the rubrics of the rite have also been reviewed. The intention is to publish a revised edition of the Rite of Marriage.

2. A committee has been formed to examine the problems regarding the adaptation of the liturgy to various cultures. The committee has studied the principles upon which liturgical adaptations are to be based. A primary concern is that such adaptations be true expressions of the Church's faith and be faithful to the spirit and letter of the Constitution on the Sacred Liturgy. The goal of this work is the production of a directory on adaptation and the liturgy.

3. A working group engaged in an analysis of youth vis-a-vis the Church and its liturgical life has sent a questionnaire to all the national liturgical commissions in order to gather information of the status of youth and the liturgy, as well as suggestions regarding necessary liturgical provisions. This working group envisions a directory on liturgy for young people which would contain recommendations for celebrations of the word, norms for eucharistic celebrations, a special lectionary, and eventually a special eucharistic prayer.

4. Work is continuing on a fifth volume of the Liturgy of the Hours which will contain a two-year lectionary and psalm prayers.

5. A committee working on the revision of the Roman Martyrology has revised the text for the month of January after having reviewed the comments submitted by its consultants. It has also prepared the martyrology for the month of February which it also sent to consultants throughout the world. In addition, the committee discussed some of the areas of difficulty in its work.

Meeting of Consultors of the Congregation for Divine Worship

A meeting of the consultors of the Congregation for Divine Worship took place in Rome on October 13-15, 1986. The following subjects were discussed by the consultors and staff of the Congregation.

Eucharistic Prayers: The consultors discussed the legislation, praxis and prospects for the future regarding eucharistic prayers. Extended discussion focused on the circular letter of 27 April 1973, "*Eucharistiae participationem,* " and particular attention was given to the phrase "in special circumstances" which is found in no. 6 of that document and which speaks of the preparation of new eucharistic prayers.

Holy Week: In the last several years various difficulties and abuses have come to light regarding the celebration of Holy Week, especially the celebration of the Easter Vigil, e.g., the hour of the celebration, repetition of the rite, etc. The Congregation has prepared a preliminary document which recalls the spirit and norms of the rites of Holy Week. The consultors reviewed this document and gave a positive response to it.

Sunday and Feasts during the Week: Another problem area receiving the Congregation's attention is the celebration of various feasts and thematic days on Sunday. In recent years these have tended to multiply and have obscured the principle of Sunday being the primordial feast. Other feasts, unless they be of the greater importance, must not have precedence over Sunday (see the Constitution on the Sacred Liturgy, no. 106).

The publication of the new Code of Canon Law has extended the Sunday precept to the vigil Mass on Saturday evening has enlarged the number of solemnities that episcopal conferences can transfer to Sunday (see CIC, c. 1248,1; c. 1246,2). These questions will continue to be studied. As of yet there are no concrete proposals.

Concerts and Other Artistic Activities in Churches: In recent years there has been an increase in the number of concerts and other artistic activities (plays, dramas, etc.) in churches which often are detrimental to the sacredness of the place. Guidelines on this activity appeared in the 1958 document, *De Musicae sacrae disciplina,* but were not carried over into the Vatican II reforms. A first draft of revised guidelines has been prepared.

Youth and Liturgy: The consultors examined the question of youth and the liturgy and agreed that the Congregation should do further study on this subject. In October the Congregation sent a questionnaire to all the national liturgical commissions which asked for a status report on the issue and for suggestions on how to respond to the needs regarding young people and the liturgy.

Liturgy and the Communications Media: The question of liturgy and radio and television was studied many years ago and has been taken up once again. A first draft of guidelines on the objectives of radio and television broadcasts, on those responsible for them, and on the various parts of the celebrations was examined.

In Memoriam: John N. Dwyer

John N. Dwyer, 65, for many years the business manager of The Liturgical Press at Saint John's Abbey in Collegeville, MN, passed away on December 21, 1986, in Saint Cloud.

In 1952, Mr. Dwyer began his employment with The Liturgical Press, publisher of numerous works in the areas of liturgy, Scripture, lay ministry, family life and monastic studies. He retired in April 1986.

In 1969 Dwyer and his wife, Rita, founded the North Star Press, which in succeeding years published nearly 50 books on Midwestern Americana, including poetry, ballooning, lumbering, Indian wars and a guide that he wrote on amateur prospecting.

He was a founding member and three-year board member of the Minnesota Book Publishers Round Table, book chairman of the Catholic Press Association for five years, and coordinator of a reading program at the Saint Cloud Reformatory for three years.

He is survived by his wife, Rita, six sons and a daughter, a sister, and 11 grandchildren.

Requiescat in pace.

Mother Katherine Drexel and Edith Stein Declared Venerable

In a January 26 ceremony attended by His Holiness, Pope John Paul II, Mother Katherine Drexel and Edith Stein were declared venerable, advancing their causes for sainthood by the Vatican Congregation for Causes of the Saints.

Mother Katherine Drexel, a member of a wealthy Philadelphia family, renounced her fortune and in 1891 founded the Sisters of the Blessed Sacrament for Indians and Colored People in an effort to meet the spiritual and material needs of native Americans and blacks in the United States.

Edith Stein, whose Carmelite name was Sister Teresa Benedicta of the Cross, was raised in a Jewish family in what is present-day Poland. An atheist before her conversion to Catholicism at the age of 31, she entered the Carmelite order eleven years later in 1933. As Nazi anti-Semitism grew, the order sent her to a convent in Holland. Following the German conquest of Holland, she and sister Rose, who had followed her into the Church, were sent to Auschwitz and executed on August 9, 1942.

In decrees published on January 27, the Congregation for Causes of the Saints designated Katherine Drexel and Edith Stein as possessors of heroic virtues. In addition, it declared Sister Teresa Benedicta of the Cross a martyr of the church. This latter declaration of martyrdom means no proof of miracles is required for the beatification of Edith Stein as is the case for the cause of Mother Katherine Drexel.

BISHOPS' COMMITTEE ON THE LITURGY

NEWSLETTER

NATIONAL CONFERENCE OF CATHOLIC BISHOPS

1987
VOLUME XXIII
MARCH

Book of Divine Worship Confirmed by Apostolic See

On March 17, 1987 the National Conference of Catholic Bishops received the decree of the Congregation for Divine Worship, dated February 13, 1987, confirming the text of the *Book of Divine Worship*, which had been approved "ad interim" by the Administrative Committee of the National Conference of Catholic Bishops in March 1984 (see *Newsletter*, April 1985, page 13).

Use of the *Book of Divine Worship* is limited to the priests and laity of the "Pastoral Provision" under the direction of the Ecclesiastical Delegate appointed by the Apostolic See, His Eminence Bernard Cardinal Law, Archbishop of Boston. The book at present exists only in photocopied form and *is not* available from the Bishops' Committee on the Liturgy.

Following is the text of the decree, which was issued in English.

Prot. N. 1038/83

Liturgical Elements of the "Pastoral Provision"

A number of former Episcopalian clergy and laity in the United States of America having been received into full communion with the Catholic Church and sharing in the special "Pastoral Provision" of "Common Identity" parishes approved by the Holy See, have expressed the wish to retain certain elements of their Anglican liturgical heritage, in so far as this would be compatible with Catholic doctrine.

The implications of such a desire have appeared both to the Apostolic See and to the National Conference of Catholic Bishops of the United States of America to be of pastoral value for such parishes and so consequently there has been prepared, under the direction of His Eminence Bernard Cardinal Law, Ecclesiastical Delegate for the Pastoral Provision, a collection of such texts under the title: *Book of Divine Worship.*

At the request of His Excellency the Most Reverend James W. Malone, President of the National Conference of Catholic Bishops of the United States of America, this Congregation, by special mandate of Pope John Paul II approves and confirms the said *Book of Divine Worship* for interim use only within the Pastoral Provision until such time as other arrangements be made.

From the Congregation for Divine Worship 13 February 1987.

+ Paul Augustin Cardinal Mayer, OSB
Prefect

+ Virgilio Noè
Titular Archbishop of Voncaria
Secretary

New Publications of the Bishops' Committee on the Liturgy

Bishops' Committee on the Liturgy Newsletters 1981-1985, the third bound edition of past issues of the *Newsletter,* has recently been published by the Office of Publishing and Promotion Services of the United States Catholic Conference. The volume contains each issue of the *Newsletter* published from January 1981

1312 MASSACHUSETTS AVENUE, N.W. • WASHINGTON, D.C. 20005

through December 1985. In addition it contains the written report of the Bishops' Committee on the Liturgy and the oral report of Bishop John S. Cummins given at the Congress of Presidents and Secretaries of National Liturgical Commissions which took place at the Vatican on October 23-28, 1984. Containing 284 pages, the volume is priced at $9.95 a copy before discounts.

The *1988 Liturgical Calendar and Ordo for the Dioceses of the United States of America,* prepared by the Secretariat of the Bishops' Committee on the Liturgy, will be available in April 1987. Price: $7.50.

To order a copy of *Bishops' Committee on the Liturgy Newsletter 1981-1985* (Publication No. 138-5) or *1988 Liturgical Calendar and Ordo* (Publication No. 141-5), write to the Office of Publishing and Promotion Services, United States Catholic Conference, 1312 Massachusetts Avenue NW, Washington, DC 20005. Telephone: 1-800-235-USCC.

Eleventh Biennial Congress of the Societas Liturgica

Father Robert Taft, SJ, President of the Societas Liturgica, has announced the Eleventh Congress of the Societas to be held from August 17-22, 1987 at the Kardinal-Nikolaus-Cusanus-Akademie in Brixen (Bressanone), Italy.

Marking the twentieth anniversary of the Societas, the Brixen Congress will have as its theme "A Worshiping Church, Penitent and Reconciling." The principal conferences and speakers at the Congress will be as follows: (1) "Penance in Contemporary Scholarship," Robert F. Taft, SJ, Rome and Notre Dame (presidential address); (2) "Penance in the Churches: Current Practice and Experience," David R. Holeton, Vancouver (Anglican); Ottfried Jordahn, Hamburg (Lutheran); Bernard Marliangeas, Paris (Roman Catholic); Paul Meyendorff, New York (Orthodox); Raymond George, Bristol (Evangelical); (3) "The Church's Ministry of Reconciliation: A Service to Humanity throughout the Ages," Georg Kretschmar, Munich; (4) "The Need to be Reconciled: Contemporary Non-ecclesial Forms of Reconciliation," Karl-Heinrich Bieritz, Berlin; (5) "A Forgiven and Forgiving Community: The Baptismal and Eucharistic Church," Paul De Clerck, Brussels-Paris; (6) "The Reconciliation of Divided Churches: A Witness to the Gospel," Geoffrey Wainwright, Durham, NC; (7) Panel and Summary: Moderator, Hermann Wegman, Geldermalsen.

For additional information and to register, write: Secretariat, Societas Liturgica, Jesuitenstrasse 13c, Postfach 2628, D-5500 Trier, West Germany. Telephone: (0651) 48106.

Sr. Barbara O'Dea Named NCCB Delegate to 1989 Eucharistic Congress

Sister Barbara O'Dea, DW, a liturgist and author and member of the Executive Board of the Daughters of Wisdom, Islip, NY, has been appointed NCCB National Delegate to the 44th International Eucharistic Congress in 1989 in Seoul, Korea, by Archbishop John L. May of St. Louis, President of the National Conference of Catholic Bishops.

Sister O'Dea is a member of the Christian Initiation Subcommittee of the NCCB Committee on the Liturgy. Until June 1986 she served as Director of Liturgy in the Diocese of Pueblo and, previous to that, she was Coordinator of Liturgy in the Richmond diocese. She has also been active in the Federation of Diocesan Liturgical Commissions and other liturgical organizations.

A graduate of Saint John's University, Jamaica, NY, Sister O'Dea holds graduate degrees in systematic theology from the Graduate Theological Union, Berkeley, CA, and in French literature from Laval University, Quebec. She was principal author of *Study Text 10, Christian Initiation of Adults: A Commentary,* published by the USCC. Other books which she has written include *Of Fast and Festival,* on celebrating Lent and Easter, and *The Once and Future Church,* on the Rite of Christian Initiation of Adults. In addition she has contributed to numerous periodicals, has produced materials for audio-visual presentations, and has lectured extensively before liturgical and catechetical audiences.

Initiated in 1881 in Lille, France, International Eucharistic Congresses combine liturgical services with catechetical programs on devotion to Christ in the Eucharist and on the relationship between the liturgy of worship and witness to life. Participants are clergy, religious and laity and representatives of national and international Catholic organizations from throughout the world.

The most recent Congress took place in August, 1985, in Nairobi, Kenya, and attracted participants from 43 countries. Twenty cardinals, 200 bishops, and 700 priests concelebrated Mass opening the week-long observance. Pope John Paul II was principal concelebrant of the closing Mass.

Prayers to Prepare for the Visit of Pope John Paul II and Hymn to Welcome the Holy Father

The following prayers were prepared by the Secretariat of the Bishops' Committee on the Liturgy and may be used in private recitation or in special services of the word in preparation for the pastoral visit of Pope John Paul II to the United States of America on September 10-19, 1987. The hymn to welcome Pope John Paul II was commissioned by the NCCB Office for the Papal Visit. While the texts of the prayers and hymn may be reproduced without charge, the respective notice of copyright is always to be included.

Prayer to Prepare for the Visit of Pope John Paul II

Gracious God,
Creator of heaven and earth,
with faith and steadfast hope,
and mindful of our unity with all who believe in you,
we ask you to hear our prayers.

Help us by your grace to prepare
for the pastoral visit of Pope John Paul II
to the Church in the United States of America.
Renew in us the gift of your Holy Spirit
who unites us with bonds of love
and stirs within us the desire for reconciliation.

As the Vicar of Peter,
John Paul builds up the unity of the Body of Christ.
As the Vicar of Christ, your Son,
his ministry seeks out all those who profess the name of Jesus.
May we also become signs of reconciliation in the world
and builders of unity in the Church.

Lord God,
help us to use the gifts you have given to us
in loving service of one another,
in selfless concern for the poor,
and in the quest for world peace.

Send your blessing upon John Paul II
that he may always be strengthened to give you service.
Inspired by your Spirit of Truth,
may he continue his ministry to bring the human family,
with wisdom and compassion, into your loving embrace.

Let our hearts be filled with the same loving dedication and service
which filled the Blessed Virgin Mary, the Mother of your Son,
whose prayers we also seek.

We ask this through our Lord Jesus Christ, your Son,
who lives and reigns with you and the Holy Spirit,
one God, for ever and ever.
Amen.

Prayer for Pope John Paul II

Lord God,
source of eternal life and truth,

look with love upon your servant, John Paul II,
the pastor of your Church.

Give him a spirit of courage and right judgment,
a spirit of knowledge and of love,
that his words and example,
as he visits the United States of America,
may be a source of unity,
a sign of love,
and a witness to peace in the service of all nations.

Grant this through Christ our Lord.
Amen.

Hymn to Welcome Pope John Paul II

Stanza One

One in faith and one in service,
Let God's people sing his praise!
To the Lord of earth and heaven
Hearts and hands and voices raise:
Word of Christ, the world's Redeemer,
Rich in mercy, truth and grace.
In his kingdom love shall triumph,
Peace and justice shall embrace.

Stanza Two

Spirit-called to form one Body,
Firm in Christ our unity;
Spirit-blest with gifts abundant,
Rich our land's diversity!
Gather we, apostles, prophets,
Teacher, pastors, young and old:
All of us are Gospel heralds,
Many, yet one faithful fold.

Stanza Three

Enemies no more, nor strangers,
Sons and daughters all are we;
Such was God's good will and pleasure
Many hearts—one family.
Pierced and healing hands embrace us,
Word of life bids conflict cease;
If we but accept his challenge,
Christ himself will be our peace!

Stanza Four

Broken still do we assemble:
That God's pow'r might make us one;
Darkness yet though Light has claimed us:
May our lives reflect God's Son.
May this time of prayer refresh us,
Cleanse and heal, renew, refine,
Send us forth again as servants,
Instruments of love divine.

Stanza Five

Praised be God our gracious Father;
Glory to his risen Son;
Equal honor to the Spirit;
Ever blest, God Three-in-one!
Celebrate his love unfailing
And the living faith we share
With the servant of God's servants,
Here with us from Peter's chair!

Text by Reverend Peter J. Scagnelli

Suggested hymn tunes (8 7 8 7 D meter):
Hyfrydol (Alleluia! Sing to Jesus)
Hymn to Joy (Joyful, Joyful, We Adore You)
Pleading Savior (Sing of Mary)
Nettleton (God, We Praise You)

BISHOPS' COMMITTEE ON THE LITURGY
NEWSLETTER
NATIONAL CONFERENCE OF CATHOLIC BISHOPS

**1987
VOLUME XXIII
APRIL**

Collectio Missarum de Beata Maria Virgine

By the decree *Christi mysterium celebrans,* dated August 15, 1986, the Congregation for Divine Worship promulgated the *Collectio Missarum de Beata Maria Virgine,* a collection in two volumes of forty-six (46) Mass formularies in honor of the Blessed Virgin Mary. The collection is intended principally for use at Marian shrines. Each Mass formulary contains the following elements: entrance antiphon, opening prayer, prayer over the gifts, preface, communion antiphon, and prayer after communion. The *Collectio* also includes a volume of readings related to those formularies.

These Masses may be used in accord with the norms of the General Instruction of the Roman Missal and the General Norms for the Liturgical Year and Calendar (see *Collectio, praenotanda,* no. 19), namely, on days during the year when the General Instruction of the Roman Missal permits *"missae ad libitum"* (see GIRM 316c) or on the optional memorials of Mary on Saturday.

The International Commission on English in the Liturgy is presently preparing an English translation of a number of the new formularies for use in the Marian Year.

For copies of the *Collectio Missarum de Beata Maria Virgine* (Latin edition), write to: Libreria Vaticana Editrice, 00120-Vatican City State, Europe. Price: 70,000 Lire.

Revised NAB New Testament and the Lectionary

On April 5, 1987, the U.S. Catholic Biblical Apostolate of the United States Catholic Conference announced the publication of a revised translation of the New Testament of the New American Bible (NAB). The revised translation reflects changes indicated by some fifteen years of liturgical and other usage of the 1970 translation. The revision was overseen by an ad hoc committee of bishops which included Archbishop John Whealon of Hartford (Chairman), Archbishop Theodore McCarrick of Newark, Archbishop J. Francis Stafford of Denver, and Auxiliary Bishop Richard J. Sklba of Milwaukee. Father Stephen J. Hartdegan, Director of the Catholic Biblical Apostolate and Mr. Charles Buggé served as staff to the bishops' committee and to the committee of revisors.

The threefold purpose for the revision was to provide a version of the New Testament more suitable for liturgical proclamation, for private reading, and for purposes of study. Special attention was given to liturgical usage because of the demands of oral proclamation for American liturgical assemblies. Likewise, the committee of revisors gave special attention to the question of discriminatory language, particularly with regard to anti-Jewish language and language which discriminates against minorities. Special efforts were made to be particularly attentive to inclusive language with regard to women. However, in dealing with these matters the committee was above all concerned with fidelity to the original Greek text.

The use of the revised NAB New Testament in the liturgy has yet to be determined. The Bishops Committee on the Liturgy will review the matter in June 1987 in order to make a recommendation to the Administrative Committee of the National Conference of Catholic Bishops in September 1987. The Lectionary Subcommittee of the Bishops' Committee on the Liturgy is working in cooperation with the committee of revisors to prepare the Lectionary pericopes. (Archbishop Whealon is also Chairman of the Lectionary Subcommittee.) Once this work is completed, a new edition of the Lectionary for Mass, based on the *Ordo Lectionum Missae* (1981), which incorporates the revised NAB New Testament, will be submitted to the National Conference of Catholic Bishops for approval. The timetable for this project will be established by the Bishops' Committee on the Liturgy in consultation with publishers of the Lectionary for Mass.

Ad Hoc Committee for the Marian Year

The Most Reverend John L. May, Archbishop of Saint Louis and President of the National Conference of Catholic Bishops, has named Bishop Edward Head of Buffalo to chair an ad hoc Committee for the Marian Year. Other members of the Committee are Archbishop Francis M. Zayek, Bishop of Saint Maron, Bishop William Bullock of Des Moines, and Bishop Arthur Tafoya of Pueblo. Father John A. Gurrieri was appointed staff to the ad hoc Committee by NCCB/USCC General Secretary, Monsignor Daniel F. Hoye. The ad hoc Committee will seek ways to assist dioceses in the celebration of the Marian Year. Its first meeting will be held in Chicago on April 27, 1987.

New Publications for the Marian Year

The Secretariat of the Bishops' Committee on the Liturgy has prepared a collection of devotional services, entitled *Celebrating the Marian Year: Devotional Celebrations in Honor of Mary, Mother of God.* The collection consists of six services which may be led by a priest, deacon, or layperson: (1) "Celebration of the Litany of Loreto," a service which focuses on the litany and on Mary's various titles; (2) "Celebration of Petition and Invocation for the Intercession of Mary"; (3) "Procession with an Image of the Blessed Virgin Mary"; (4) "Crowning an Image of the Blessed Virgin Mary," a crowning service distinct from the episcopal liturgy of *Order of Crowning an Image of the Blessed Virgin Mary;* (5) "Celebration of the Rosary," a communal celebration of the rosary of our Lady; (6) "Evening Prayer" from the Common of the Blessed Virgin Mary of the Liturgy of the Hours. Each of the devotional services includes a liturgy of the word.

Celebrating the Marian Year also contains a collection of traditional and contemporary Marian prayers, biblical and non-biblical readings, and a listing of musical resources (hymns, anthems and instrumental music).

The purpose of the collection is, as Pope Paul VI stated in *Marialis cultus,* to foster "the faithful's devotion and acts of veneration toward the Mother of God [and] to retain what is of enduring value, and integrate those truths that have been reached from theological investigation and affirmed by the Church's magisterium" (no. 24). The collection will also help parishes celebrate the Marian Year with devotion. For, as Pope John Paul II states in his newly promulgated encyclical, *Redemptoris Mater* ("Mother of the Redeemer"), "the Marian Year is meant to promote a new and more careful reading of what the Council said about the Blessed Virgin Mary, Mother of God, in the mystery of Christ and of the Church . . . Marian *spirituality*, like its corresponding *devotion*, finds a very rich source in the historical experience of individuals and of the various Christian communities present among the different peoples and nations of the world" (no. 48).

Another publication which has been prepared for use in the Marian Year is the *Book of Mary*, a collection of prayers and biblical readings for personal prayer and devotion. This collection is made up principally of excerpts from *Celebrating the Marian Year.*

Celebrating the Marian Year is available in separate editions for ministers and people from the United States Catholic Conference Office of Publishing and Promotion Services. Prices: Minister's Edition, $5.95; People's Edition, 50 copies at $22.00. Also available from the USCC Office of Publishing and Promotion Services are the *Book of Mary* (Price: $1.95) and Pope John Paul II's encyclical letter *Redemptoris Mater* (Price: $3.95). Order from: USCC Office of Publishing and Promotion Services, 1312 Massachusetts Avenue, NW, Washington, DC 20005. Telephone: 1-800-235-USCC.

Liturgical Programs/Conferences

Rensselaer Program of Church Music and Liturgy

The 27th annual summer session of the Rensselaer Program of Church Music and Liturgy will be held

June 23-August 7, 1987. Graduate and undergraduate courses in music theory, history and practice, and liturgy will be offered, with specializations in organ, voice, piano, guitar, composition, conducting, or music education. A three-summer sequence, leading to a Diploma in Pastoral Liturgy, is also available. Graduate tuition is $82 per credit hour: undergraduate, $75.

In the area of liturgical music course offerings will include: Theory, Composition, Conducting, History, and Applied Music. Liturgy course offerings will be: Historical and Theological Perspectives of Christian Worship; Music as Pastoral Prayer; Liturgy Planning and Coordination of Ministries; Children's Liturgies; and Liturgical Art and Architecture.

For further information and applications for the summer session, contact: Rev. Lawrence Heiman, C.PP.S., Director of the Rensselaer Program of Church Music and Liturgy, Saint Joseph's College, P.O. Box 815, Rensselaer, IN 47978. Telephone: 219/866-7111.

New York School of Liturgical Music

The eighth annual summer seminar sponsored by the New York School of Liturgical Music will be held from July 6-9, 1987. Seminar '87 will provide an opportunity for exploring varied musical media and will include as speakers Dr. Alice Parker, Dr. Fred Moleck, Rev. Andrew Ciferni, Robert MacDonald, Don Campbell, David Weck, and Reverend Jerome Hall, SJ.

For further information and registration form, write: The Registrar, New York School of Liturgical Music, 1011 First Avenue, New York, NY 10022. Telephone: 212/371-1000, Ext. 2291 or 2292.

National Association of Pastoral Musicians

The 1987 national convention of the National Association of Pastoral Musicians, with the theme "As Grain Once Scattered," will be held on June 22-26 in Minneapolis, MN. Principal speakers will include Sr. Teresita Weind, Reverend John Gallen, Rabbi Lawrence Hoffman, Rosemary Haughton, and Dr. Martin Marty. The program also will feature a "Music Industry Exposition Day," 64 special interest sessions, music showcases, special musical events and liturgical celebrations.

For further information, write: National Convention, National Association of Pastoral Musicians, 225 Sheridan Street, NW, Washington, DC 20011. Telephone: 202/723-5800.

North American Worship Conference

The first North American Worship Conference, having as its theme "Hearing, Celebrating and Witnessing: Liturgy for 1988," will be held from August 10-13, 1987, at the Shoreham Hotel, Washington, DC. Speakers will include: Robert Batastini, David Haas, Robert Rambusch, Sr. Theresa Koernke, and the Reverends John Buscemi, Austin Fleming, John Gallen, Robert Dufford, Michael Joncas, Eugene LaVerdiere, David Power, and David Stanley.

For further information, write: Time Consultants, 650 Ritchie Highway, Severna Park, MD 21146. Telephone: 301/647-8145.

Notre Dame Center for Pastoral Liturgy

The Notre Dame Center for Pastoral Liturgy will sponsor its Sixteenth Annual Conference from June 15-18, 1987 on the University of Notre Dame campus. The theme for the event is "Forming the Worship Community: An Owner's Guide." The program will examine the liturgical life of the laity in the contemporary parish, exploring the issues of participation and prayer, community formation by and for the liturgy and the challenges of lived discipleship that flow from worship. Keynote speaker is the Most Reverend Kenneth Untener, Bishop of Saginaw. Other major presenters will include Dr. Mark Searle and Dr. Marchita Mauck.

For further information and registration materials, contact: Notre Dame Center for Pastoral Liturgy, P.O. Box 81, Notre Dame, IN 46556. Telephone: 210/239-5435.

Blessings Subcommittee

The Blessings Subcommittee of the Bishops' Committee on the Liturgy met in Washington, DC, on February 27-March 1, 1987. During the course of the meeting, chaired by Bishop Patrick Cooney of Detroit, the subcommittee gave final shape to the new blessings which are to be included in the American edition of *De Benedictionibus* or *Book of Blessings*. At the same time the subcommittee reviewed in detail the family or home edition of the *Book of Blessings* known as *Household Blessings and Prayers*. Both collections will be submitted to the Bishops' Committee on the Liturgy in June for approval. It is hoped that the *Book of Blessings* (ICEL translation and American supplement) and *Household Blessings and Prayers* will be submitted to the Administrative Committee of the National Conference of Catholic Bishops in September 1987 for approval "ad interim."

The subcommittee has now completed its three-year task. The Bishops' Committee on the Liturgy and its Secretariat wish to express their gratitude to the subcommittee's chairman, Bishop Patrick Cooney, and to the members: Sister Arlene Bennett, RSM (Detroit), Deacon Richard Bowles (Denver), Mr. Gabe Huck (Chicago), Sister Kathleen Huettner, RSM (Detroit), Rev. Dennis Krouse (San Diego), Rev. Joseph McMahon (Portland, Oregon), Rev. Msgr. Anthony S. Sherman (Brooklyn), and Rev. Thomas G. Simons (Grand Rapids), and Msgr. Alan Detscher, now a member of the Secretariat, who edited much of the material.

Archbishop Pilarczyk Named NCCB Member of the ICEL Episcopal Board

On March 26, 1987 the Administrative Committee of the National Conference of Catholic Bishops confirmed the nomination of Archbishop Daniel E. Pilarczyk of Cincinnati as the new representative of the National Conference of Catholic Bishops on the Episcopal Board of the International Commission on English in the Liturgy (ICEL) for a period of five years. Archbishop Pilarczyk replaces Bishop James W. Malone of Youngstown who represented the NCCB on the ICEL Episcopal Board since 1976. As the new American Episcopal Board member, Archbishop Pilarczyk will also serve as a consultant to the Bishops' Committee on the Liturgy.

El Bendicional, Spanish Book of Blessings

El Bendicional, the first Spanish-language edition of *De Benedictionibus,* was recently published by Coeditores Liturgicos in Spain. The new Spanish Book of Blessings contains a translation of the Latin texts prepared by the new international commission for Spanish liturgical texts. It also contains several new blessings not found in the Latin *editio typica,* such as the blessings of an advent wreath, a Christmas creche, a Christmas tree, banners, etc.

According to the decree of the Congregation for Divine Worship, dated May 7, 1986 (Prot. n. 338/86), *El Bendicional* may be used in all Spanish-speaking countries, the United States included, once the appropriate episcopal conferences have approved its use and requested the Apostolic See's confirmation. In the United States of America, *El Bendicional* will be submitted for NCCB approval at the earliest opportunity.

For copies of *El Bendicional* (704 pages), write to: Coeditores Liturgicos, E. Jardiel Poncela 4, Apartado 19.049, 28016-Madrid, Spain. Price: 1,450 pesetas.

Other new publications from Coeditores Liturgicos are the following: *Evangeliario, dominical y festivo* (Book of Gospels, Sundays and feasts), illuminated pages, bound in leather, 19,700 pesetas; and *Libro del Salmista* (antiphons and psalms for Sundays and feasts; 416 pages, 1,700 pesetas.

Resources

Assembly 1986-1987. Published five (5) times per year by the Notre Dame Center for Pastoral Liturgy. A central theme is used for each issue. Recent topics include: Liturgical Language, Idea Feasts, Laying on of Hands, Eucharistic Devotion, Formation of the Assembly. To subscribe, send $6.00 ($7.00 Canada) to: Notre Dame Center for Pastoral Liturgy, P.O. Box 81, Notre Dame, IN 46556. Telephone: 210/239-5435.

BISHOPS' COMMITTEE ON THE LITURGY

NEWSLETTER

NATIONAL CONFERENCE OF CATHOLIC BISHOPS

1987
VOLUME XXIII
MAY

Choctaw Translation of Mass Confirmed by the Apostolic See

On May 7, 1986 the National Conference of Catholic Bishops received the decree of the Congregation for Divine Worship, dated April 25, 1987, confirming the decision of the Administrative Committee of the NCCB to approve the Choctaw translation of the Order of Mass, Eucharistic Prayer II of the Roman Missal, and the sacramental formulas for the consecration of the bread and wine. The confirmed translation may be implemented immediately in Choctaw communities.

The following is an unofficial English translation of that decree.

Prot. N. 779/86

At the request of His Excellency James W. Malone, Bishop of Youngstown and President of the National Conference of Catholic Bishops of the United States of America, on July 2, 1986, and in virtue of the faculties granted to this Congregation by Pope John Paul II, we gladly approve, that is, confirm *ad interim* the Choctaw translation of liturgical texts, as they appear in the appended copy, namely:

The Order of Mass with a congregation;

The sacramental formularies for the consecration of the bread and the wine;

Eucharistic Prayer II.

In the publication of these texts mention should be made of the confirmation granted by the Apostolic See. In addition two copies of these printed texts are to be sent to this Congregation.

Anything to the contrary notwithstanding.

From the Congregation for Divine Worship, 25 April 1987.

+ Paul Augustin Mayer
Prefect

+ Virgilio Noè
Titular Archbishop of Voncaria
Secretary

Pope John Paul II on the Anointing of the Sick

On the solemnity of Christ the King, November 23, 1987, His Holiness Pope John Paul II, as part of his pastoral visit to the Church in New Zealand, met the sick, elderly and disabled in Wellington and celebrated the sacrament of the anointing of the sick. An excerpt from his homily which deals with the mystery of human suffering and the healing presence of Christ follows. (For the full text, see L'Osservatore Romano *[English edition], December 1, 1986, pp. 7-8.)*

. . . Dear brothers and sisters in Christ: "The Kingdom of God is very near to you!" (Luke 10:9).

The only time Jesus was asked: "Are you a king?" (John 18:28) was during his Passion, at the time of his greatest suffering. Indeed, it was by his suffering and death that he won for us the gift of the Redemption and definitively established his Kingdom. Perhaps this helps us to understand better why Jesus gave the following instructions to his disciples when he first sent them forth: "Whenever you go into a town where they make you welcome, eat what is set before you. Cure those in it who are sick, and say, "The Kingdom of God is very near to you" (Luke 10:8-9). God wishes to draw near to every human person, but with particular tenderness to those who are sick.

Mystery of Suffering

2. Human suffering, however, tempts us to doubt the words of Jesus that the Kingdom of God is near. When pain dulls the mind and weighs down body and soul, God can seem far away; life can become a heavy burden. We are tempted not to believe the Good News. "For," as the Book of Wisdom says, "a perishable body presses down the soul, and this tent of clay weighs down the teeming mind" (Wisdom 9:15).

The mystery of human suffering overwhelms the sick person and poses disturbing new questions: Why is God allowing me to suffer? What purpose does it serve? How can God who is good permit something which is so evil? There are no easy answers to these questions asked by the burdened mind and heart. Certainly, no satisfying answer can be found without the light of faith. We must cry out to God, our Father and Creator, as did the author of the Book of Wisdom: "With you is wisdom, she who knows your words . . . Despatch her from the holy heavens . . . to help me and to toil with me and teach me what is pleasing to you" (Wisdom 9:9-10).

3. Our Savior knows well the many special needs of those who suffer. From the beginning of his public ministry, together with his preaching of the Good News of the Kingdom, "he went about doing good and healing" (Acts 10:38). When he sent forth his own disciples on their mission, he gave them a special power and clear instructions to follow his example.

In his preaching, Jesus makes it clear that, although illness is linked to the sinful condition of humanity, in individual cases it is certainly not a punishment form God for personal sins. When asked whose sin had caused a man to be born blind, Jesus replied: "Neither he nor his parent sinned; he was born blind so that the works of God might be displayed in him" (John 9:3). What unexpected Good News this was for his followers! This suffering is not divine retribution. On the contrary, it is intended for a good purpose: "so that the works of God might be displayed"!

The Strengthening and Healing Presence of Christ

And indeed, it was the suffering and death of Christ that displayed the works of God most eloquently. By his Paschal Mystery, Jesus won for us our salvation. Suffering and death, when accepted with love and offered with trust to God, become the key to eternal victory, the triumph of life over death, the triumph of life through death.

4. By means of a special sacrament, the Church continues Jesus' ministry of caring for the sick. Thus, the Liturgy of the Anointing of the Sick which we are celebrating today faithfully continues the example of our loving Savior.

This sacrament is best understood within the context of the Church's overall concern for the sick. For it is the culminating point of the many and varied pastoral efforts made for the sick in their homes, in hospitals and in other places. It is the climax of an entire program of loving service in which all the members of the Church are involved.

What we are doing today is faithful to the example of Jesus and to the instructions of Saint James, who wrote: "If one of you is ill, he should send for the elders of the Church, and they must anoint him with oil in the name of the Lord and pray over him. The prayer of faith will save the sick man and the Lord will raise him up again; and if he has committed any sins, he will be forgiven" (John 5:14-15). Today in New Zealand, the Successor of Peter continues this tradition of the anointing of the sick, which the Church teaches to be one of the Seven Sacraments of the New Testament instituted by Christ.

It is good for all of us, even the elderly and sick, to remember that good health is not something to be taken for granted but a blessing from the Lord. Nor is it something we should endanger through the misuse of alcohol or drugs or in any other way. For, as Saint Paul says, "Your body, you know, is the temple of the Holy Spirit . . . That is why you should use your body for the glory of God" (1 Cor 6:19-20). Doing what we can to maintain our own good health makes it possible for us to serve others and fulfill our responsibilities in the world. However, when illness does come, we have this special sacrament to assist us in our weakness and to bring the strengthening and healing presence of Christ.

5. Those who are seriously ill feel deeply their need for the assistance of Christ and the Church. Besides the physical pain and weakness, illness brings powerful anxieties and fears. The sick are vulnerable to temptations which they may never have faced before; they may even be led to the verge of despair. The Anointing of the Sick responds to these precise needs, for it is a sacrament of faith, a sacrament for the whole person, body and soul.

Through the laying on of hands by the priest, the anointing with oil and the prayers, new grace is given: "The sacrament provides the sick person with the grace of the Holy Spirit by which the whole individual is brought to health, trust in God is encouraged, and strength is given to resist the temptations of the Evil One and anxiety about death. Thus the sick person is able not only to bear his or her suffering bravely, but also to fight against it. A return to physical health may even follow the reception of this sacrament if it will be beneficial to the sick person's salvation" (*Pastoral Care of the Sick: Rites of Anointing and Viaticum,* 6).

The Anointing of the Sick brings particular consolation and grace to those who are near death. It prepares them to face this final moment of earthly life with lively faith in the Risen Savior and firm hope in the Resurrection. At the same time, we must remember that the Sacrament is meant not only for those about to die but for anyone who is in danger of death through sickness or old age. Its purpose is not to prepare us for death, which will inevitably come to all of us, but also to strengthen us in our time of illness. For this reason, the Church encourages the sick and elderly not to wait until the point of death to ask for the Sacrament and to seek its grace.

6. Today's Liturgy says that the Lord is the Good Shepherd who leads us beside restful waters to refresh our drooping spirits. The Psalmist says to God:

"You have prepared a banquet for me in the sight of my foes. My head you have anointed with oil; my cup is overflowing" (Ps 22[23]:5).

Anointing with oil has been used to signify healing, but at the same time to signify a particular mission among God's people. In the Scriptures we often find that people whom God has chosen for a special mission receive a special anointing. So it is with you who are sick or elderly. You have an important role in the Church.

First of all, the very weakness which you feel, and particularly the love and faith with which you accept that weakness, remind the world of the higher values in life, of the things that really matter. Moreover, y our sufferings take on a special value, a creative character, when you offer them in union with Christ. They become redemptive, since they share in the mystery of the Redemption. That is why Saint Paul could say: "Now I rejoice in my sufferings for your sake, and in my flesh I complete what is lacking in Christ's afflictions for the sake of his body, that is, the Church" (Col 1:24).

Through the pain and the disabilities that restrict your life, you can proclaim the Gospel in a very powerful way. Your joy and patience are themselves silent witnesses to God's liberating power at work in your lives . . .

Unauthorized Eucharistic Prayers

Recently the Liturgy Secretariat has received several requests for clarification about the liturgical use of unauthorized eucharistic prayers, especially *Spoken Visions,* a privately published collection of twenty-five eucharistic prayers. A similar question has been asked with regard to the liturgical use of eucharistic prayer texts legitimately issued for purposes of consultation.

The Congregation for Divine Worship addressed the subject of unauthorized eucharistic prayers in the Circular Letter *Eucharistiae participationem,* 27 April 1973 (see *Documents on the Liturgy 1965-1979: Conciliar, Papal, and Curial Texts* [=DOL], nos. 1975-1993) in which it stated that only those eucharistic prayers approved by the competent authority may be used in the liturgy [see nos. 6, 11, (DOL 1980, 1985)].

With regard to eucharistic prayers in English, only those texts approved by the National Conference of Catholic Bishops of the United States of America and confirmed by the Apostolic See may be used in the celebration of the Eucharist. These eucharistic prayers have been so approved and confirmed for use in the dioceses of the United States of America: Eucharistic Prayers I-IV of the Roman Missal (Sacramentary),

Eucharistic Prayers I-II for Masses of Reconciliation (Sacramentary, 1985 edition, Appendix VI), and Eucharistic Prayers I-III for Masses with Children (Sacramentary, 1985 edition, Appendix VI).

With regard to parishes and communities which legitimately celebrate the Eucharist in a language other than English, those additional eucharistic prayers contained in the approved liturgical books of the language of the celebration may also be used. For example, those celebrating in Italian or French or German may use the additional eucharistic prayers found in the Missals approved by the appropriate conference of bishops and confirmed by the Apostolic See.

In Memoriam: Very Reverend Canon Harold Winstone

The Very Reverend Canon Harold E. Winstone died on Easter morning, April 19, 1987. Born in London in 1917, Canon Winstone was ordained a priest of the diocese of Westminster in 1943. After taking a degree in Latin and Greek at Cambridge he served for many years as a classics master at St. Edmund's, Ware, and as headmaster at St. Hugh's, Nottingham. Over the years Canon Winstone became a major figure in the English liturgical movement. His knowledge of German enabled him to translate some of the classic twentieth century liturgical works, including Josef Jungmann's *The Liturgy of the Word,* and Pius Parsch's *The Liturgy of the Mass* and *Seasons of Grace.* A very able Latinist, he was responsible for the popular pre-Vatican II handmissal, *The Layman's Missal,* and prepared widely-used English translations of all the papal encyclicals issued between the years 1953-1966.

In 1969 Canon Winstone founded the St. Thomas More Centre for Pastoral Liturgy, the original vision of which was to be a national center for England and Wales. The St. Thomas More Centre has had and continues to have a major influence not only in Great Britain, but, especially through its music, throughout the English-speaking world.

In 1964 Father Winstone was asked by the founding bishops of the International Commission on English in the Liturgy to serve as a member of the "International Advisory Committee on English in the Liturgy." From 1968 to 1975 he served as Chairman of the Advisory Committee. He also served as co-chairman of the International Consultation on Common Texts (ICET). During that period when the major liturgical books were being issued by the Holy See in rapid succession, Father Winstone was instrumental in meeting the challenge to bring about a vernacular liturgy for the English-speaking Catholic Church.

In his later years Father Winstone was named a canon of Westminster Cathedral. Until his death, he served as parish priest (pastor) of Knebworth and as a member emeritus of the ICEL Advisory Committee. One of his last tasks with ICEL was to help in the final translation of the *Book of Blessings.*

> Eternal rest grant unto him, O Lord.
> And let perpetual light shine upon him.
> May his soul and the souls of all the faithful departed,
> through the mercy of God, rest in peace. Amen.

Centennial of the Pontifical Athenaeum of St. Anselm

On March 21, 1987, the solemnity of St. Benedict according to the calendar of the Order of St. Benedict, the Pontifical Athenaeum of St. Anselm began its centennial celebration. Erected in Rome by Blessed Innocent XI on March 22, 1687, the Collegio Sant'Anselmo was restored by Pope Leo XIII on January 4, 1887 with its ancient Faculties of Theology, Philosophy, and Canon Law. On June 17, 1961 the Congregation for Seminaries and Universities of Higher Studies canonically erected the Pontifical Liturgical Institute.

While the centennial will be marked by a number of celebrations, conferences, and lectures, the following stand out: November 11, 1987: inauguration of the new Library of Saint Anselm; December 5, 1987: Symposium of the Faculty of Philosophy, *The Philosophical Thought of St. Anselm - Its Relevance for Today;* February 19-20, 1988: Symposium of the Mosaic Institute, *Spirituality and Culture in Monastic Tradition;* May 9-13, 1988: Third International Liturgical Congress, *The Easter Triduum.*

For further information on the various events of the Centennial, write: Leonard J. Maluf; Segreterio del Centenario; Collegio Sant'Anselmo; Piazzi dei Cavalieri di Malta, 5; 00153 Rome, Italy. Telephone: (06) 575.00.73 or 574.35.69.

BISHOPS' COMMITTEE ON THE LITURGY
NEWSLETTER

NATIONAL CONFERENCE OF CATHOLIC BISHOPS

**1987
VOLUME XXIII
JUNE/JULY**

Order of Crowning an Image of the Blessed Virgin Mary Confirmed by the Apostolic See

On June 22, 1987 the National Conference of Catholic Bishops received the decree of the Congregation for Divine Worship, dated May 22, 1987, confirming the decision of the Administrative Committee of the NCCB to approve the English translation of *Order of Crowning an Image of the Blessed Virgin Mary* for use in the dioceses of the United States of America. The following is an unofficial English translation of that decree.

Prot. N. 623/87

At the request of His Excellency John L. May, Archbishop of Saint Louis and President of the National Conference of Catholic Bishops, on March 31, 1987, and in virtue of the faculties granted to this Congregation by Pope John Paul II, we gladly approve, that is, confirm *ad interim* the English translation of *Order of Crowning an Image of the Blessed Virgin Mary,* as it appears in the appended copy.

In the publication of this text mention should be made of the confirmation granted by the Apostolic See. In addition two copies of the printed text are to be sent to this Congregation.

Anything to the contrary notwithstanding.

From the Congregation for Divine Worship, 22 May 1987.

> \+ Paul Augustin Cardinal Mayer, OSB
> Prefect
>
> \+ Virgilio Noe
> Titular Archbishop of Voncaria
> Secretary

June Committee Meeting of the Bishops' Committee on the Liturgy

The Bishops' Committee on the Liturgy met with its advisors at the Bishop Mason Retreat and Conference Center in Flower Mound, Texas, June 10-12, 1987. Bishop Joseph P. Delaney of Fort Worth chaired the meeting. Progress reports were given by the chairmen of the following subcommittees and task groups: Hispanic Liturgy Subcommittee (Bishop Ricardo Ramirez, CSB), Blessings Subcommittee (Bishop Patrick Cooney), Lectionary Subcommittee (Father Ronald Krisman, in place of Archbishop John Whealon), Black Liturgy Subcommittee (Bishop Wilton Gregory), Christian Initiation Subcommittee (Father Krisman, in place of Bishop Joseph Ferrario), the Task Group on Sunday Worship in the Absence of a Priest (Bishop Michael Sheehan). Sister Kathleen Hughes, RSCJ, Vice Chairwoman of the ICEL Advisory Committee, reported on the various projects and consultations of the International Commission on English in the Liturgy. Fathers Joseph McMahon and Michael Spillane gave an update on the Federation of Diocesan Liturgical Commissions, and Father Juan Sosa reported on the activities of the Instituto de Liturgia Hispana.

During the course of the meeting, the Committee reviewed and acted upon a number of action items which are in various stages of development. The Committee reviewed the position statements of the delegates of the 1986 National Meeting of Diocesan Liturgical Commissions (Portland, Maine) which requested action from the Bishops' Committee on the Liturgy. The first of these concerned Sunday worship in the absence of a priest. The Committee had already addressed this matter in November 1986 when a Task Group on Sunday Worship in the Absence of a Priest was established. The second position statement addressed to the Committee concerned continuing formation of liturgical ministers. After a lengthy discussion of this topic, the Committee decided to seek the collaboration of the NCCB Committees on Priestly Formation, Priestly Life and Ministry, and Permanent Diaconate in order to review once again current national and regional programs of continuing liturgical formation of priests and deacons.

The Committee reviewed a number of projects and requests concerning liturgy in languages other than English. At the request of the Diocese of Phoenix, the Committee reviewed the process for having Pima-Papago approved as a liturgical language in the United States. The matter will be presented to the NCCB Administrative Committee. The Committee also agreed to submit *El Bendicional*, the Spanish translation of *De Benedictionibus*, to the NCCB Administrative Committee for approval in the dioceses of the United States. At the request of the Hispanic Liturgy Subcommittee, the Committee agreed to begin the process of raising the rank of Our Lady of Guadalupe (December 12) from memorial to feast in the Proper Calendar for the Dioceses of the United States. The Committee reviewed the preliminary results of the *Consulta sobre el Misal Romano en espanol*, a consultation which took place from December 1986 through April 1987. The report indicated that those who participated in the consultation (bishops, priests, lay persons, *et al.*) expressed a preference for the Mexican translation of the *Missale Romanum*, and that this translation should be used in an eventual edition of the *Sacramentario* approved for the dioceses of the United States. (A detailed report is being prepared and will be circulated among the bishops and respondents.) As a consequence, the Committee approved the motion that the Mexican translation should be used as the "base translation" for the presidential prayers of the *Sacramentario*.

Other action items concerned the second edition of *The Lectionary for Mass* for the dioceses of the United States, revised translations of the Scriptures, the revised New Testament of the *New American Bible*, and a proposed *Lectionary for Masses with Children*. After a lengthy discussion it was decided that the second edition of *The Lectionary for Mass* should be targeted for completion in 1991 in connection with the ICEL revision of the English translation of *The Roman Missal* (Sacramentary). At that time, the lectionary will incorporate the revised New Testament of the *New American Bible*. The Committee gave initial approval of the pericopes for inclusion in the proposed *Lectionary for Masses with Children* and recommended that the new translation of the Bible for children currently under preparation by the American Bible Society be approved as the liturgical text for this lectionary.

Bishop Wilton Gregory presented two action items emanating from the Black Liturgy Subcommittee, *In Spirit and in Truth: Black Catholic Reflections on the Order of Mass* (tentative title) and *Black Americans and Catholic Worship*. These items were referred to the Secretariat for additional editorial work.

In January 1987, as a follow-up to the Holy See's 1985 *Notes on the Correct Way to Present the Jews and Judaism in the Preaching and Catechesis of the Roman Catholic Church*, the Bishops' Committee on the Liturgy commissioned *Guidelines on the Presentation of Jews and Judaism in Catholic Preaching*. The Committee reviewed the first draft of the *Guidelines* and the responses of a number of Catholic and Jewish biblical and liturgical scholars. As a consequence, a second draft is to be prepared and submitted to the Committee, and eventually to the NCCB Administrative Committee, for approval.

The Committee also recommended to the National Conference of Catholic Bishops that the ecumenical rite of marriage, entitled *A Christian Celebration of Marriage: An Ecumenical Liturgy* and proposed by the North American Consultation on Common Texts (CCT), be approved for liturgical use in the dioceses of the United States. They also provided input into the response of the Liturgy Committee to the proposed *Criteria for the Use of General Absolution* being prepared by the NCCB Committee on Canonical Affairs.

Five action items dealt with the approval of the *Book of Blessings* for use in the dioceses of the United States: 1) the ICEL Translation of *De Benedictionibus;* 2) the proposed USA additions to the *Book of Blessings;* 3) the proposed Table of Contents and ordering of the USA edition; 4) a collection of blessings and prayers for use in the Catholic home, tentatively entitled *Household Blessings and Prayers;* and 5) decisions concerning the publication of *Household Blessings and Prayers*. Each of these items was approved by the Committee for submission to the NCCB Administrative Committee.

In an open discussion of current or future projects of the Committee, the following matters were discussed: 1) revised edition of *Guidelines for Diocesan Liturgical Commissions/Offices of Worship* (due by late 1987); 2) current legislation regarding women/girls as altar servers; 3) training of liturgical ministers, with particular emphasis on the question of the institution of lectors and acolytes; 4) training of those who lead liturgical worship (priests, deacons, and lay leaders of prayer at Sunday worship in the absence of a priest) and continuing formation of those ministers; 5) "devotional" aspects of the liturgy, particularly dealing with the signs of reverence made in the liturgy, including the leaders' sense of reverence, postures and gestures, along with music and the environment for worship (the Committee asked that a statement dealing with the question of reverence be commissioned); 6) efforts to study the celebration of the Pentecost vigil in order to strengthen and encourage its use; 7) investigation of the liturgical processes by which people are returning to the practice of faith in the Church.

The Committee also discussed whether *Eucharistic Prayer A* might be re-introduced to the members of the National Conference of Catholic Bishops, and whether changes might be suggested in the particular law of the dioceses of the USA regarding postures at Mass (*General Instruction of the Roman Missal*, no. 21).

The next meeting of members, consultants, and advisors will take placer on June 7-9, 1988. Future meetings of the bishop members and consultants are set for November 15, 1987 and March 21, 1988.

Decree on Plenary Indulgences Granted for the Marian Year

On June 30, 1987 the National Conference of Catholic Bishops received the decree of the Sacred Apostolic Peniteniary concerning indulgences which are granted during the Marian Year. The following is an unofficial translation of the decree.

Sacred Apostolic Penitentiary

DECREE

The Plenary Indulgences Granted for the Marian Year

The most Blessed Virgin Mary is the Mother of God and Mother of the Church. Indeed she is the mother of us all. "Having entered deeply into the history of salvation, Mary in a way unites and re-echoes in her person the most important teachings of the faith" (*Lumen Gentium,* 65). And "when she is the subject of preaching and devotion, she calls believers to her Son, to his sacrifice, and to love of the Father" (*ibid.*). Indeed, "in a most special way and above all other persons she is the divine Redeemer's generous associate, and in a thoroughly unique way she has worked together with him to restore the supernatural life of souls" (*Lumen Gentium,* 61).

As the second millenium of the birth of our Savior approaches, the Church, the universal community of believers, turns to its divine Redeemer as well as to his Mother. In doing this the Church reflects upon Mary's presence in its midst and her readiness to offer assistance in the many and complex issues of our age which affect individuals, families, and nations (see, *Redemptoris Mater,* 52). Being aware of all such issues, the Supreme Pontiff, John Paul II, spurred on by his own devotion to Mary and carrying out his office as Vicar of Christ, by reason of which there is incumbent upon him a "daily and insistent care for all the churches" (2 Corinthians 11:28), recently announced to the Christian faithful a Marian Year to extend from Pentecost, 1987, until the Solemnity of the Assumption of the Blessed Virgin Mary, 1988. The year is to be celebrated with devout participation and should produce both growth in the virtues and advancement in spiritual health.

At the wedding in Cana of Galilee Mary addressed a message to the servants and through them all of us: "Do whatever he tells you" (John 2:5). Since there is need for that same message to ring out today, there is special advantage in having the faithful feel themselves urged with renewed fervor during the course of the Marian year to carry out various works of piety, mercy, and penance. And among such works there are those which have a special import, and to these, by ancient tradition, the Church attaches an indulgence.

In order to obtain an indulgence, the fervor of love for God and neighbor is required. And when it has been obtained, it is right to believe that, in gratitude for the goodness of God, our affections will be more ready to do good and avoid sin. For our Lord Jesus Christ recommends and demands such affections from his followers in every time and place.

The Church in its role as "the minister of redemption dispenses and applies with authority the treasury of the satisfying works of Christ and the saints" (Canon 992, CIC). By means of this present decree the Sacred Penitentiary, in virtue of its special apostolic mandate concerning the treasury of the Church, grants a plenary indulgence to be gained by all the Christian faithful for the following works. The usual conditions are to be correctly fulfilled, i.e., sacramental confession, eucharistic communion, and prayer for the Pope's intentions. This is being done so that the faithful may more richly share in the fruits of the Marian Year in purifying their consciences, in thoroughly changing their ways, and in increasing their love of God and neighbor.

(1) On the opening and closing day of the Marian Year when they devoutly assist at a sacred function connected with the Marian Year in their own parish church, in any Marian shrine, or sacred place;

(2) On solemnities and liturgical feasts of Mary, on any Saturday or other specific day on which one solemnly celebrates some "mystery" or "title" of Mary when they devoutly participate in a rite celebrated in honor of the Blessed Virgin Mary in the parish church, a Marian shrine, or in another sacred place;

(3) On each day of the Marian Year when they make a pilgrimage with a group to the sanctuaries of Our Lady designated for the diocese by the bishop and there participate in liturgical rites (among which the holy Mass has an absolutely singular excellence), in a communal penitential celebration, in the recitation of the holy rosary, or when they carry out another pious exercise in honor of the Blessed Virgin Mary;

(4) On each day of the Marian Year when they devoutly visit, even individually, the Basilica of Saint Mary Major in Rome and participate there in a liturgical function or at least stop for some time in devout prayer;

(5) When they piously receive the Papal Blessing, given by a bishop, even by means of radio or television. The Apostolic Penitentiary grants to bishops the faculty of giving the Papal Blessing with the attached plenary indulgence twice during the Marian Year, according to the established rite (see *Ceremoniale Episcoporum* 1122-1126) on the occasion of some Marian solemnity, or some diocesan pilgrimage. This is in addition to the three other occasions on which they can impart the blessing according to the general law.

It is opportune to note that according to the current norms the gift of the plenary indulgence may be obtained only once a day and the indulgence may always be applied to the dead by means of suffrage (see *Enchiridion Indulgentiarum,* Norms 4 and 24). The Apostolic Penitentiary takes this occasion to call attention to Norm 27 of the same *Enchiridion,* in virtue of which "confessors are able to commute either the prescribed work or the conditions which, by reason of a legitimate impediment, they are not able to carry out", and Norm 28, in virtue of which "Ordinaries or Hierarchs of the place are able . . . to grant the faithful, over whom they exercise lawful authority and who live in places where they cannot in any way or only with some difficulty go to confession and communion, a plenary indulgence without actual confession and communion. In such circumstances they must be contrite of heart and intend to receive these sacraments as soon as they can." Finally, the Apostolic Penitentiary strongly recommends as being very much in harmony with the Marian Year, the recitation of the rosary of the Blessed Virgin Mary, especially by families. For the faithful of the Eastern rites, it strongly recommends the corresponding prayer established by the Patriarchs. When such is done in a church or oratory, or carried out in a communal form, there is also attached a plenary indulgence (*Enchiridion* 48).

Anything to the contrary not withstanding.

Given in Rome, from the Sacred Penitentiary, Saturday, 2 May 1987.

+ Aloysius Cardinal Dadaglio
Major Penitentiary

+ Aloysius de Magistris
Regent

Prayer of Pope John Paul II for the Marian Year

The following prayer was composed by His Holiness Pope John Paul II for use during the Marian Year.

1. Mother of the Redeemer,
   in this year dedicated to you,
   with great joy we call you blessed.
   In order to carry out his providential plan of salvation,
   God the Father chose you before the creation of the world.
   You believed in his love and obeyed his word.

The Son of God desired you for his Mother
when he became man to save the human race.
You received him with ready obedience and undivided heart.
The Holy Spirit loved you as his mystical spouse
and he filled you with singular gifts.
You allowed yourself to be led
by his hidden and powerful action.

2. On the eve of the third Christian Millennium,
we entrust to you the Church
which acknowledges you and invokes you as Mother.
On earth you preceded the Church in the pilgrimage of faith:
comfort her in her difficulties and trails,
and make her always the sign and instrument
of intimate union with God
and of the unity of the whole human race.

3. To you, Mother of Christians,
we entrust in a special way
the peoples who are celebrating,
during this Marian Year,
the sixth Centenary or the Millennium
of their acceptance of the Gospel.
Their long history is profoundly marked by devotion to you.
Turn towards them your loving glance;
give strength to those who are suffering for the faith.

4. To you, Mother of the human family and of the nations,
we confidently entrust the whole of humanity,
with its hopes and fears.
Do not let it lack the light of true wisdom.
Guide its steps in the ways of peace.
Enable all to meet Christ,
the way and the truth and the life.
Sustain us, O Virgin Mary, on our journey of faith
and obtain for us the grace of eternal salvation.
O clement, O loving, O sweet Mother of God
and our Mother, Mary!

1987 National Meeting of Diocesan Liturgical Commissions

The National Meeting of Diocesan Liturgical Commissions and Offices of Worship will be held in Breckenridge, Colorado, October 5-8, 1987. The meeting is cosponsored by the Bishops' Committee and the Federation of Diocesan Liturgical Commissions. The Archdiocese of Denver and the other dioceses of Colorado, Wyoming, Arizona, New Mexico, Oklahoma and Texas are serving as hosts.

The conference has as its theme "Rites of Death andDying" and will feature as speakers: Reverend Lawrence Boadt, CSP, Washington Theological Union; Dr. Mary Dombeck, University of Rochester; Reverend Richard Rutherford, CSC, University of Portland; and Dr. Alan Wolfelt, Director, The Center for Loss and Life Transition, Fort Collins, CO.

The liturgical commissions and offices of worship of the dioceses of the United States meet each year to reflect upon an aspect of the renewed liturgy of the Church and to surface areas of possible collaboration. The 1987 meeting will be especially important since the members of the National Conference of Catholic Bishops approved the final translation of *Pastoral Care of the Sick: Rites of Anointing and Viaticum* in 1982 and the revised translation of *Order of Christian Funerals* in November 1985.

For a registration form and/or additional information, contact: Office of Liturgy, Archdiocese of Denver, 200 Josephine Street, Denver, CO 80206. Tel. 303/388-4411.

In Memoriam: Sister Maria Fidelis Burdick, CSJ

Sister Maria Fidelis Burdick, C.S.J., an artist who was known for her outstanding work in church renovation and liturgical book design, was called to the Lord Jesus on June 10, 1987.

Born in Brooklyn on June 21, 1928, and baptized Marie Harriet, Sister Maria Fedelis was educated at St. Anselm's School, Fontbonne Hall, and St. Joseph's College for Women in Brooklyn, and at Mt. St. Vincent's College, New Rochelle, New York, where she received the degree, Bachelor of Fine Arts.

In 1950, she entered the Congregation of the Sisters of Saint Joseph of Brentwood, New York, taking the name Maria Fidelis in honor of Our Lady's faithfulness as she persevered in prayer with the Apostles before the coming of the Holy Spirit on Pentecost. She received a Master of Fine Arts degree from The Catholic University of America, Washington, D.C.

Sister Maria Fidelis served as a member of the Art and Architecture Commission of the Diocese of Brooklyn from 1968 until 1979. In 1975 she established CSJ Design Service to assist her own Congregation and the dioceses of Brooklyn and Rockville Centre in their projects of church renovation.

From 1976 until her death, Sister Maria Fidelis was closely associated with the International Commission on English in the Liturgy (ICEL). As a member of ICEL's Presentation of Texts Subcommittee, she served as an advisor on book design and layout. Maria was responsible for the design of *The Roman Pontifical*, which was published in 1978 at the Vatican. She also designed *Pastoral Care of the Sick: Rites of Anointing and Viaticum, Rite of Christian Initiation of Adults, Order of Christian Funerals,* and a number of ICEL's consultation books. For the Bishops' Committee on the Liturgy, Maria designed the *Dedication of a Church and an Altar,* which was published by the United States Catholic Conference in 1978.

To all her work she brought not only her professional sense of design and fine arts, but also her dedication to beauty in the liturgy. A gentle woman of prayer and generosity, she was deeply committed to Christ and the Church both as a religious woman and a woman of the Church.

The Funeral Mass for Sister Maria Fidelis Burdick was celebrated at the Sacred Heart Chapel of the Motherhouse of the Congregation of the Sisters of Saint Joseph at Brentwood, New York on the evening of June 12, 1987. May she rest in peace.

> All-powerful God
> we pray for our sister Maria,
> who responded to the call of Christ
> and pursued wholeheartedly the ways of perfect love.
>
> Grant that she may rejoice
> on that day when your glory will be revealed
> and in company with all her brothers and sisters
> share for ever the happiness of your kingdom.
>
> We ask this through Christ our Lord.
>
> Amen.

Regional Workshops on the *Rite of Christian Initiation of Adults*

In a letter sent to all bishops in the United States on May 15, 1987, the Most Reverend Joseph P. Delaney, Bishop of Fort Worth and Chairman of the Bishops' Committee on the Liturgy, announced the recent work of the Liturgy Committee in implementing the National Plan for the Implementation of the *Rite of Christian Initiation of Adults,* approved by the members of the National Conference of Catholic Bishops at their November 1986 plenary assembly, in preparation for the mandatory effective date of the final text of the *Rite of Christian Initiation of Adults* on February 21, 1988.

The Liturgy Committee, through its Christian Initiation Subcommittee, is preparing a *Pastoral Companion to the Rite of Christian Initiation of Adults,* which will provide a commentary on all the rites and an outline of the catechetical components of the various periods of the catechumenate, and address the questions of ministries, the Christian initiation of children of catechetical age, several canonical matters, and related topics.

The Committee is also planning a series of six (6) regional workshops on the new ritual book. The workshops will be under the direction of the Bishops' Committee on the Liturgy and are intended for bishops and *diocesan leadership* in the areas of liturgy, religious education, continuing education of clergy, evangelization and the catechumenate. Because accommodations for the six workshops limit the total participation to a little more than 1,000 persons, each diocese is asked to plan for a maximum of four or five diocesan staff persons plus the bishop(s), if possible, to attend a workshop.

Meeting dates and sites have been chosen for the workshops (all beginning on Monday evening and concluding at noon on Thursday):

November 2-5, 1987	— Oakland, CA
November 9-12, 1987	— Holyoke, MA
November 30-December 3, 1987	— Dayton, OH
December 7-10, 1987	— Phoenix, AZ
December 7-10, 1987	— Joliet, IL
January 11-14, 1988	— Baton Rouge, LA

The purpose of each workshop is to review the rites, including the American additions approved in November 1986, present various models for imparting the catechetical components of the catechumenate, sensitize the participants to the need for discerning the readiness of candidates for the sacraments, discuss strategies for effective programs of evangelization, explore pressing canonical issues affecting the preparation of catechumens and candidates for reception, correct faulty pastoral practices which may have arisen, and provide practical assistance in the preparation of future diocesan workshops on the catechumenate and the rites, which are being planned for many dioceses in late 1987 and early 1988.

Liturgical Books for the Papal Visit

Over the past eight months the Secretariat of the Bishops' Committee on the Liturgy has been actively involved with the diocesan liturgical coordinators in the preparations for the liturgical celebrations of the second pastoral visit of his Holiness Pope John Paul II, September 1987. The staff of the Secretariat has met several times with those who are responsible for the liturgical celebrations in each of the dioceses that the Holy Father will visit.

The primary responsibility of the Secretariat has been the preparation of the special books that will be used for the Masses and other liturgical celebrations. Three books have been edited for the papal visit and are now being printed: *Sacramentary, Lectionary,* and *Book of Celebrations and Blessings.* The Sacramentary (256 pp.) contains the complete text of the ten Masses the Holy Father will celebrate. It also includes presidential chants and other liturgical music for the Pope. The prefaces have been printed in sense lines as an aid to singing. The *Sacramentary* will be bound in white leather with gold stamping on the cover and gilt edges on the pages. The cover and the designs throughout the book are the work of the Reverend Rod Tesseire Stephens.

The *Lectionary* contains all the Scripture readings for the Masses and other services. The readings are in sense lines as an aid to proclamation. The binding of the *Lectionary* is similar to that of the *Sacramentary.* The third book for the papal visit is the *Book of Celebrations and Blessings.* This book is approximately 100 pages long and contains the various services for the reception of the Holy Father in the cathedrals and churches he will visit, as well as the other prayers and blessings that he will use throughout his visit.

The books are being printed in a special limited edition for the use of the dioceses the Pope will visit. No additional copies will be available. Special thanks are due to Mr. Robert Cavelero, president of the Catholic Book Publishing Company, and his family who are graciously producing these fine books as a gift to the Holy Father and the Church in the United States of America. Additional thanks are due to Mr. Michael Buono of the staff of The Catholic Book Publishing Company for his invaluable assistance in this project.

In Memoriam: Father Secondo Mazzarello, Sch. P.

While recovering from an illness, Father Secondo Mazzarello, secretary of the Center for Liturgical Action (C.A.L.) in Rome and the director of the review, *Liturgia,* went out for his customary walk on the afternoon of January 27, 1987 and never returned. He is presumed dead although his body has not been recovered.

Father Mazzarello was born on February 4, 1912 at Mornese, Italy. At the age of 15 he entered the Novitiate of the Poor Clerics Regular of the Mother of God of the Pius Schools (Scolopi or Piarist Fathers). He made his solemn profession in 1933 and was ordained to the priesthood in the following year. Over the many years of his priesthood he fulfilled various teaching and administrative assignments in his religious community. He also taught liturgy in the seminaries of Verona and Treviso and was the pastor of a small parish. He served as a consultor to the Consilium for the Implementation of the Constitution on the Sacred Liturgy and also translated many of the revised liturgical rites into Italian, most notably, the Liturgy of the Hours. In 1969 he was appointed secretary of C.A.L., succeeding Monsignor Virgilio Noe who became the secretary of the Congregation for Divine Worship. He served that same Congregation as a consultor. Father Mazzarello was noted for his hard work in preparing for the annual liturgical weeks of C.A.L. and for his fine work manifested in the publications of C.A.L. In addition to editing *Liturgia,* he also authored or edited over 53 liturgical publications.

Father Mazzarello's death will be sorely felt by the Center for Liturgical Action and the Church in Italy.

> Lord God,
> You chose our brother Secondo to serve your people
>   as a priest
> and to share the joys and burdens of their lives.
> Look with mercy on him
> and give him the reward of his labors,
> the fullness of life promised to those who
>   preached your holy Gospel.
>
> We ask this through Christ our Lord.
>
> Amen.

Liturgical Programs/Conferences

North American Forum on the Catechumenate

The first convocation of the North American Forum on the Catechumenate will be held September 10-13, 1987, at the Shoreham Hotel, Washington, DC. The theme of the convocation is "The Church Reborn." Speakers include: Bishop Kenneth Untener, Mary Ann Simcoe, Reverend Patrick Brennan, Mary Ellen Cohn, Robert Rambusch, Reverend Ronald Lewinski, Reverend James Dunning, Reverend James Provost, Reverend James Lopresti, John Butler, Sue Buttino, Christopher Walker, Reverend Eugene LaVerdierer, Sister Catherine Dooley, Reverend Timothy O'Connell, Reverend Aidan Kavanaugh, Maureen Kelly, Jerry Ryle, John Butler, Francoise Darcy-Berube, Karen Hinman, Reverend Jaime Lara, Reverend Thomas Caroluzza, Doris Donnelly, Reverend Richard Fragomeni, Emilie Griffin, Sister Marguerite Stapleton, Reverend Gorman Sullivan, Reverend Richard Rohr, Reverend Patrick Carroll, Joanne McCoy, Sister Margaret Kelleher.

For further information contact: Time Consultants, 650 Ritchie Highway, Severna Park, MD 21146. Telephone: 301/647-8145.

SWLC Competition for Hymn Texts

The Southwest Liturgical Conference is sponsoring a competition for Spanish texts for hymns or songs for liturgical celebrations. Specific types of texts are being sought. The winning texts will be offered next year for a composition competition. The competition closes November 1, 1987. Winners will be announced at the January 1988 Study Week in Corpus Christi, Texas.

For more information, write to: Mary McLarry, Office of Worship, Diocese of Fort Worth, 800 West Loop 820 South, Fort Worth, TX 76108.

BISHOPS' COMMITTEE ON THE LITURGY

NEWSLETTER

NATIONAL CONFERENCE OF CATHOLIC BISHOPS

1987
VOLUME XXIII
AUGUST

Jubilate Deo, Second Typical Edition

By a decree dated November 22, 1986, the Congregation for Divine Worship has issued the second typical edition of *Jubilate Deo* (88 pp.), a book containing common Gregorian chants for the assembly.

Jubilate Deo is divided into two sections. The first, *Cantus Missae,* includes chants for the Latin texts of the introductory rites, the liturgy of the word, the eucharistic prayer, the rite of communion, and the concluding rites of the Mass. The second part, *Cantus Varii,* contains the text and music of the most commonly sung hymns, Marian antiphons, and canticles.

Copies of *Jubilate Deo* may be ordered directly from: Libreria Editrice Vaticana, 00120-Vatican City State, Europe.

Pope John Paul II's Address to the Plenaria of the Congregation for Divine Worship

On Friday, May 22, 1987 Pope John Paul II received in audience the participants in the general session ("plenaria") of the Congregation for Divine Worship. In the course of the audience, the Holy Father addressed the members of the Congregation, alluding to several projects which are hearing completion, such as the second typical edition of the Rite of Marriage, *the second typical edition of the ordination rites, and a proposed directory for Sunday celebrations in the absence of a priest. The following is the text of that address.*

1. I am happy to receive you on the occasion of your plenary assembly. The report which you have presented shows that the work of this department has been intense since your last general session in October 1985. Certain projects have been completed while others are still continuing.

I shall mention only the new official text of the Ritual of Marriage and of the Ritual of Ordinations; the preparation of a complete collection of the Roman Ritual which marks the completion of the revision of that of 1614 in accordance with the directives of the conciliar constitution *Sacrosanctum Concilium.* I am thinking as well of the Roman Martyrology which it was necessary to revise with a concern for historical accuracy; far from weakening devotion to the saints, this contributes to its increase among the Christian people. I also mention the preparation in progress of a biblical and patristic supplement to the Liturgy of the Hours. Finally, I am happy that the publication of a collection of Masses in honor of the Blessed Virgin Mary has preceded the opening of the Marian Year by several months.

2. Besides the liturgical texts, there is the broader and equally important problem of the adaptation of the liturgy. According to the instructions of the Council, the liturgy must remain alive without, however, allowing itself to be modelled according to the pleasure of each person's imagination. This is the goal of the directions prepared by your Congregation for the inculturation of the liturgy in the mentalities and traditions of various peoples and, furthermore, for the adaptation of liturgical celebrations for youth. Yes, it is necessary to seek the active participation rightly demanded by the Council, with the understanding that it is not a question of aiming merely at a type of exterior activity nor a mere expression on the level of the senses, but of intimate participation in the mystery of Christ, who calls us to follow him in his total obedience to the Father and in the gift which he makes of himself for our salvation and the salvation of the world.

During your meeting you have mainly examined questions concerning the Sunday celebration in places where a priest cannot be present, Holy Week, and artistic programs presented in places of worship.

1312 MASSACHUSETTS AVENUE, N.W. • WASHINGTON, D.C. 20005

Lack of priests

3. How is the Lord's Day to be celebrated in a Christian community deprived of a priest? This has long been a frequent situation in mission countries; it is a situation which many countries with a long Christian tradition are now experiencing as a result of the decline in the number of priests. This absence is not to be accepted with resignation, because the presence of the priest is necessary for the maintenance and the development of local Christian communities. The calling forth of vocations in these communities must remain a primary concern. The situation must be faced, however, and the best provisions must be made for the spiritual welfare of the faithful. Now one of the essential points of reference for Christians from which they draw both light and strength has been, since the beginning, the Sunday assembly, the gathering of the faithful in one place to celebrate the risen Lord. This can only be done fully in the celebration of the Eucharistic sacrifice, which is the memorial of the death and the resurrection of Christ in praise, thanksgiving and supplication.

The faithful who, due to the lack of a priest, cannot participate in a parish Mass, must nevertheless be able to gather together in prayer of praise and supplication, in listening to the Word of God and, if possible, in the communion of the Eucharistic Bread consecrated during an earlier Mass. This type of celebration does not replace the Mass but must cause one to desire it all the more. It is, for a small community of the faithful, a means, although imperfect, of preserving in a concrete manner its cohesion and vitality; it maintains from Sunday to Sunday its bonds with the whole Church which God does not cease to gather and which offers to him, from east to west, everywhere in the world a perfect offering (cf. the third Eucharist Prayer).

4. Another matter has occupied your attention: Holy Week. It was more than thirty years ago that first the Easter Vigil, and then later the whole of Holy Week was restored in the Roman Church. This restoration was enthusiastically received at that time.

Today it is good to weigh the situations, to evaluate the low level of interest or participation that may exist in certain regions, the difficulties which remain or have arisen regarding certain points, and to recall the importance of that great week in which the entire Church celebrates the paschal mystery. "Just as Sunday constitutes the culmination of the week, so does the solemnity of Easter constitute the culmination of the liturgical year" (*General Norms for the Liturgical Year and the Calendar*, n. 18). In following the Lord step by step from his messianic entry into Jerusalem on Palm Sunday until he is taken down from the cross on the evening of Good Friday, the Church journeys towards the holy night in which the Lord arose and which must be considered as the mother of all the holy vigils (*ibid.*, n. 21).

This means that a preparation is necessary throughout Lent in common prayer, in hearing the Word of God and in the practice of penance. This demands especially that pastors have a vigilant concern for preparing hearts for the meeting with Christ the Savior by a suitable catechesis and, in the first place, by the Sunday homilies. They should arrange convenient times for individual confession and for community penitential celebrations with personal confession and absolution, and for preparing other dignified and prayerful celebrations as well.

5. Finally, you have examined the problem of concerts and other artistic presentations in places of worship. It is true that our churches have for a very long time played an important role in the cultural life of cities and towns. Is not the church the house of the People of God? Has it not been in the churches that this people has had its first aesthetic experiences in seeing the beauty of the building, its mosaics, paintings, statues, or sacred objects; in hearing the organ music or the singing of the choir; in attending liturgical celebrations which draw it above itself and cause it to enter into the heart of Mystery?

The House of God

For this is indeed the primordial character of the church. It is the house of God; it is a sacred place because of the dedication or solemn blessing which has consecrated it to God. The church is the place where the Lord dwells in the midst of his people and where the people come together to worship and pray. This is why every measure must be taken to respect the sacred character of the church.

Outside of liturgical celebrations there can be a place for religious music in the form of a concert. This can be an occasion offered to Christians who are no longer practicing their faith, or even to non-Christians who are seeking God, to have access to a true religious experience, beyond a simple aesthetic emotion. The presence of the pastor is thus desirable to show how this spiritual presentation is fitting and to ensure respect for the holy place. In this manner, the church will remain, even through artistic presentations with no liturgical connection, the place where one can discover the presence of the living God, the source of all beauty.

Here, dear brothers and all of you who participate either daily or occasionally in the work of the Congregation for Divine Worship, are some thoughts which your work calls to my mind. I thank you for contributing, in an outstanding way, in the universal Church and in cooperation with the Successor of Peter, to the development of the liturgy and thus to the quality of prayer and to the theological life of the People of God. As I encourage you to continue your work with the necessary theological sensitivity, sense of the Church, and wisdom, I bless you with all my heart.

In Memoriam: Dr. Ralph A. Keifer

Dr. Ralph Keifer, well-known in North America as a speaker and writer on liturgical topics, died on Sunday, July 5, 1987. Dr. Keifer, who served on the staff of ICEL from 1971 to 1973, had been seriously ill for several months.

Born in England in 1940, Ralph Keifer came to the United States with his family as a child. He did his undergraduate studies at Providence College in Rhode Island and was graduated in 1963. After studies at the University of Notre Dame, he was awarded a doctorate in Liturgical Studies in 1972. Soon afterwards he came to ICEL, where he served as general editor and, from 1972 to 1973, as acting executive secretary. Dr. Keifer's principal work at ICEL was overseeing the preparation of the Roman Missal, which was issued to the conferences of bishops in its final "white book") translation in 1973. Dr. Keifer was also involved in the initial stages of the work on The Liturgy of the Hours.

Ralph Keifer returned to academic life in 1973 as a member of the faculty of St. Mary's Seminary and University in Baltimore, Maryland. In 1976 he began his association with the Catholic Theological Union in Chicago, where he held the position of full professor in the Word and Worship department at the time of his death. For a number of years he taught also in the Summer Graduate Program in Liturgical Studies at Notre Dame.

A gifted writer, Dr. Keifer was the author of several books, including *The Mass in Time of Doubt, The Meaning of the Mass for Catholics Today,* published in 1983, and was the editor of *The Catholic Liturgy Book,* published in 1975. He also wrote nearly fifty articles. Many of these articles appeared in *Worship.* Others were published in *Commonweal, New Catholic World, Studia Liturgica,* and *Pastoral Music.* For a number of years Dr. Keifer served on the editorial board of *Worship.*

Ralph Keifer is survived by two daughters and a son.

The Funeral Mass was celebrated at St. Giles Church, Oak Park, Illinois, on July 9.

> Into your hands, O Lord,
> we humbly entrust our brother Ralph.
> In this life you embraced him with your tender love;
> deliver him now from every evil
> and bid him enter eternal rest.
>
> The old order has passed away:
> welcome him then into paradise,
> where there will be no sorrow, no weeping nor pain,
> but the fullness of peace and joy
> with your Son and the Holy Spirit
> for ever and ever.
>
> Amen.

Frederick R. McManus, *Thirty Years of Liturgical Renewal: Statements of the Bishops' Committee on the Liturgy*

The Secretariat of the Bishops' Committee on the Liturgy is pleased to announce the imminent publication of *Thirty Years of Liturgical Renewal: Statements of the Bishops' Committee on the Liturgy,* edited with an introduction and commentaries by Monsignor Frederick R. McManus. The book traces the role of the American bishops in the liturgical movement in the United States from the establishment of the Bishops' Commission on the Liturgical Apostolate in 1958 and the Bishops' Committee on the Liturgy in 1966 until the present. *Thirty Years of Liturgical Renewal* contains statements and other documents of the Bishops' Committee on the Liturgy.

Father McManus, who is Ordinary Professor of Canon Law at The Catholic University of America in Washington, DC, comes to the task with the highest qualifications. He served as the Executive Director of the Liturgy Secretariat from 1965 until 1975. From 1959 until 1962, and again from 1964 until 1965, he was president of The Liturgical Conference. And from 1979 until 1981 he was president of the Societas Liturgica.

Father McManus' involvement with the Constitution on the Liturgy and the postconciliar liturgical reform is well-known. He served as a consultant to the Pontifical Preparatory Commission on the Sacred Liturgy for the Second Vatican Council from 1960 until 1962 and as peritus at the Council from 1962 until 1965. He also served as a consultant to the Consilium for the Implementation of the Constitution on the Liturgy, 1964-1970, consultant to the Pontifical Commission for the revision of the Code of Canon Law, 1967-1983, and consultant to the Secretariat for Promoting Christian Unity since 1979.

Besides being a consultant to the Bishops' Committee on the Liturgy (since 1975), Father McManus has also been a member of the Advisory Committee of the International Commission on English in the Liturgy since ICEL's foundation in 1964. Respected internationally as a liturgist and canonist, he has received a number of honorary degrees and awards in recognition of his contributions to the disciplines of liturgy, canon law, and education, including the Pax Christi Award of St. John's University, Collegeville (1964), the Gerald Ellard Award of the New English Liturgical Conference (1976), the Role of Law Award of the Canon Law Society of America (1973), the Michael Mathis Award of the University of Notre Dame (1976), the Berakah Award of the North American Academy of Liturgy (1979), and the Presidential Award of the National Catholic Educational Association (1983). In 1970 he was named an Honorary Archimandrite of Jerusalem and in 1980 Pope John Paul II named him a Prelate of Honor.

Father McManus has written extensively. Editor of *The Jurist* since 1959, he has written a number of books on the liturgy and many articles in such journals as *Studia Liturgica, The Jurist, Concilium, Liturgy, Worship, Chicago Studies, Pastoral Music,* and *The New Catholic Encyclopedia.*

Thirty Years of Liturgical Renewal is a major contribution to the history of liturgical progress in the United States. In the book Father McManus sketches the history of the American bishops' role in liturgical renewal, offers commentary on a number of early and later statements of the Bishops' Committee on the Liturgy, and situates these documents in their historical context.

Thirty Years of Liturgical Renewal: Statements of the Bishops' Committee on the Liturgy (Publication No. 154-7; Price: $16.95) will be sent to all Standing Order Service subscribers. Additional copies will be available at the end of November and may be ordered from: USCC Office of Publishing and Promotion Services, 1312 Massachusetts Avenue NW, Washington, DC 20005. For telephone orders, call: 1-800-235-USCC.

Liturgical Studies: Institut de Liturgia de Barcelona

The Institut de Liturgia de Barcelona (Spain) is an academic institution of higher studies canonically established by the Congregation for Catholic Education and incorporated by the same Congregation into the Faculty of Theology of Catalonia by decree of 15 August 1986. The Institute, which began teaching in 1964 and is connected to the activities of the Centro de Pastoral Liturgica de Barcelona, is the only academic institution for liturgical studies in Spain. It grants the canonical degrees of the licentiate and the doctorate in theology with specialization in liturgical studies as well as a Diploma in Liturgical Studies.

For more information on academic requirements, courses, and tuition, write to: Director del Institut de Liturgia, Facultat de Teologia de Catalunya, C/Diputación 231, 08007-Barcelona, España; or: Director del Institut de Liturgia, Centre de Pastoral Litúrgica, C/Rivadeneyra 6,7º, 08002-Barcelona, España.

BISHOPS' COMMITTEE ON THE LITURGY
NEWSLETTER
NATIONAL CONFERENCE OF CATHOLIC BISHOPS

**1987
VOLUME XXIII
SEPTEMBER/
OCTOBER**

Notice Concerning Regional Workshops on the *Rite of Christian Initiation of Adults*

Because of an insufficient number of registrants, two of the regional workshops on the *Rite of Christian Initiation of Adults,* being hosted by the Bishops' Committee on the Liturgy in collaboration with the North American Forum on the Catechumenate, have had to be cancelled: those in Phoenix, AZ, and Joliet, IL (both originally scheduled to be held from December 7-10).

The few persons who registered for those two workshops have been notified in order that they might be assisted in attending one of the other four workshops, namely, those in Oakland, CA(November 2-5), Holyoke, MA (November 9-12), Dayton, OH (November 30-December 3), and Baton Rouge, LA (January 11-14, 1988).

Inclusive Language: Pastoral Letter of Archbishop Roger M. Mahony

In his recent pastoral letter, Acknowledging Women's Role and Appreciating Their Gifts, *the Most Reverend Roger M. Mahony, Archbishop of Los Angeles, addressed the matter of inclusive language in the liturgy. Following are excerpts from the pastoral letter. (For the complete text, see* Origins, *Volume 17, Number 11 [August 27, 1987], pp. 165, 167-170).*

It should be noted that English liturgical texts prepared and approved since around 1977 have consistently been "inclusive" in their language. Furthermore, the English translation of The Roman Missal *(Sacramentary), approved in 1974 by the National Conference of Catholic Bishops (and other English-language conferences of bishops), is now being revised. It is hoped that the revised translation will be submitted to the conferences in 1991.*

As a body we need to recognize that cultural changes have brought both society and Church to a new recognition of the equality of men and women, and that this recognition must find new expression in our ecclesial life.

Furthermore, there are a number of positive steps we can take right away to acknowledge the presence of women and to recognize their gifts to the entire church community. Although there is much to be said about this subject, let me, at this time, address two concrete areas where we can make immediate progress.

1. *Inclusive Language.* One area of much concern in the Church today has to do with language, particularly what has come to be called "exclusive" or "sexist" language. It is now more commonly recognized that terms such as *man* and *mankind, brothers* and *brethren* and the preferred pronouns *he, his, him,* even if used with the intention of including both male and female persons, have the opposite effect. This usage makes many women feel excluded.

Raising this issue often causes irritation in both women and men who are of the mind that the reference to both men and women in the term *man* is obvious or that the reference to both male and female in the term *he* is implied. Some are inclined to trivialize the issue because, in their minds, these are "only words."

The seriousness of the issue, however, is more obvious when we consider that while we human beings shape language, it is also true that language shapes us. When people at prayer and worship are addressed as "brethren" and hear that the Gospel is good news and glad tidings for "men of good will" or that the Son of God came from heaven "for us men and for our salvation," more and more women feel themselves excluded.

1312 MASSACHUSETTS AVENUE, N.W. • WASHINGTON, D.C. 20005

More deeply, some women actually wonder whether the fullness of salvation is really theirs if the language does not include them.

To realize that our use of language is having an alienating effect on women calls for deep reflection and commitment to new ways of thinking, writing, speaking, teaching and preaching. Because clarity is desired in writing and speech, then we should name as specifically as possible those to whom we speak and simply say what we mean. For example, in giving a homily, priests are not speaking to our brothers only. Since they are speaking to our brother and sisters, they should indicate this. And if God in Jesus Christ came down from heaven, not just for "us men" but for us, all of us, then perhaps we need to find ways of expressing this great mystery in word and in worship.

One must keep in mind that such masculine words and phrasing are a proper translation from the Latin original texts and were never meant to be exclusive. I am hopeful that our National Conference of Catholic Bishops will continue to work closely with the International Commission on English in the Liturgy to give us newer language which is clearly inclusive.

Helpful changes have already been made in this regard. For example, in the institution narrative which forms the heart of the Eucharistic Prayer, the cup once offered "for you and for all men" is now offered "for you and for all." The revised translation of the New Testament of the New American Bible will give us God's message in more clearly inclusive language. But it is my hope that all of the Church's official prayer books, liturgical books and rituals will be reviewed with the goal of maximizing inclusive language.

A much more complex issue is the way we speak about God. On this point, it may be useful to remember that our language about God always falls short of naming the fullness of the divine mystery. We sometimes create an anthropomorphic view of God by implying that God is, in essence, male.

But the nature of God is always more than we could ask or imagine. In using the pronoun *he* in speaking about and writing about God, we must recognize that God is neither male nor female. Rather God is above, or beyond, our categories of masculine and feminine.

We know, however, from the tradition of the Jews, our forebears in faith, and from our own Christian tradition that God often is spoken of and imagined in male categories. But this does not mean that there is no place in the tradition or in contemporary life for a sense of the feminine in God. In fact, several Old Testament examples point to this "feminine side" of God: "Can a mother forget her infant, be without tenderness for the child of her womb? Even though she forget, I will never forget you" (Is. 49:15); "I have stilled and quieted my soul like a weaned child. Like a weaned child on its mother's lap, (so is my soul within me)" (Ps. 131:2).

Some of the great mystics within the Church had a deep sense of this other dimension. Jesus himself in the Gospels communicates the never-ending and persistent mercy of God in images both male and female. Jesus' relationship to God as "Son of the Father" is complemented by other images. One example of this is the parable of the shepherd who abandons the flock of sheep to seek and find the lost little one. Precisely the same message is communicated in the parable of the woman who searches the whole house, top to bottom, seeking a precious lost coin. We need to recover this inclusive sense of God's love and mercy communicated in both Scripture and tradition.

In one of his early encyclical letters, *Rich in Mercy,* Pope John Paul II devotes several pages to the image and notion of "mercy" in the Old Testament. One of the footnotes of that section of the encyclical describes the two words used in the Old Testament to denote mercy, *hesed* and *rahamim,* which speak to the feminine and masculine qualities of God's mercy.

In speaking, writing, teaching and preaching we need to develop increased sensitivity to women. The good news is for all people a word of healing, grace and freedom. Our language must be more inclusive in order to communicate more effectively this saving message. Further, our ways of speaking to and about God must both respect our tradition's rich and authentic teaching about the God of Jesus Christ as well as recognize that the name of God, neither male nor female, is above every other name.

Our Holy Father himself notes the feminine dimension of salvation in the person of Mary:

> "This Marian dimension of Christian life takes on special importance in relation to women and their status. In fact, femininity has a unique relationship with the mother of the Redeemer . . . (T)he figure of Mary of Nazareth sheds light on womanhood as such by the very fact that God, in the sublime event of the incarnation of his Son, entrusted himself to

the ministry, the free and active ministry of a woman. It can thus be said that women, by looking to Mary, find in her the secret of living their femininity with dignity and of achieving their own true advancement" ("Mother of the Redeemer" [*Redemptoris Mater*], 46).

A concern for inclusive language, then, does not seek just to handle a difficult problem which has arisen in the American context. It gives us an opportunity to care for the justice with which women are incorporated into the general linguistic culture, and it offers us a richer view of human life and of the nature of God.

Guidelines for the Concelebration of the Eucharist

On 23 September 1987 the Administrative Committee of the National Conference of Catholic Bishops approved a revised edition of the Guidelines for the Concelebration of the Eucharist *which first appeared in 1978 in* Study Text 5: Eucharistic Concelebration. *The purpose of these guidelines is to assist dioceses to establish their own norms for concelebration. Should a diocese wish further assistance, especially in the case of very large concelebrated Masses, the Bishops' Committee on the Liturgy stands ready to offer its advice.*

Permission to reprint these guidelines must be sought in writing from the Bishops' Committee on the Liturgy, 1312 Massachusetts Avenue NW, Washington, DC 20005.

Introduction

The following guidelines are provided to highlight the significance of concelebration of the eucharist as a sign of unity and Church order. As a unique collegial act of the Church at prayer, the concelebrated eucharist should be neither abused nor ignored. What is important for members of the liturgical assembly applies as well to bishops and priests who concelebrate: no one in the eucharist is required to say every word, perform every gesture, ritualize every action. The eucharist, whether ritually concelebrated or not, is a collegial act which depends on the authentic collaboration of all the ministers and the assembly presided over by the bishop or one of the presbyters.

The proper and effective celebration of the Eucharist always requires preparation according to the principles laid down in the General Instruction of the Roman Missal (= GIRM), no. 73.* Planning is especially necessary for all concelebrations of the Eucharist. Therefore, the norms laid down in the General Instruction of the Roman Missal, nos. 153-208, should be followed carefully. The following additional guidelines and procedures were approved by the Bishops' Committee on the Liturgy on 23 March 1987 and by the Administrative Committee of the National Conference of Catholic Bishops on 23 September 1987. These guidelines are meant to assist in the preparation and in the actual concelebration of the Eucharist.

Regulation of Concelebration

1. In accord with the law, the bishop possesses the right to regulate the discipline for concelebration in his diocese, even in churches and oratories of exempt religious (see GIRM 155). Accordingly, the bishop may establish diocesan guidelines regarding the aptness of concelebration, its advisability on certain occasions, the number of concelebrants, and the physical arrangements of his cathedral and parish churches for concelebration.

Aptness of Concelebration

2. "Concelebration is a sign and a strengthening of the fraternal bond of priests and of the whole community, because this manner of celebrating the sacrifice in which all share consciously, actively, and in the way proper to each is a clearer portrayal of the whole community acting together and is the preeminent manifestation of the Church in the unity of sacrifice and priesthood and in the single giving of thanks around the one altar" (Declaration *In celebratione Missae*, 7 August 1972, no. 1).

3. In particular cases, the decision to permit concelebration of the Eucharist should be based on whether or not the unity of the Church is more clearly manifested and whether or not the concelebration can take place

---

*Unless otherwise noted, all citations in these *Guidelines* are from *Documents on the Liturgy, 1963-1979: Conciliar, Papal, and Curial Texts* (Collegeville, MN: The Liturgical Press, 1982).

with "propriety and genuine reverence" (*In celebratione Missae,* no. 3a).

Advisability of Concelebration

4. Besides those instances when the *Rite of Concelebration* prescribes it, the General Instruction of the Roman Missal indicates other occasions when concelebration is permitted (no. 153). Concelebration is also recommended at those times when it is appropriate for the priests of diocese to concelebrate with their own bishop or when priests gather with their bishop on the occasion of a retreat or a meeting with the bishop.

5. At other times, the diocesan bishop should judge whether concelebration is advisable or opportune. For example, according to diocesan guidelines, the bishop should judge whether concelebration is opportune at diocesan, regional, or national meetings or conventions which take place within the diocese. At times it may be necessary for the bishop to issue norms or guidelines to cover specific local situations.

Number of Concelebrants

6. The bishop may regulate the number of concelebrants, if the dignity of the rite demands it (*Rite of Concelebration,* 7 March 1965, Introduction, no. 3). The number of concelebrants at a specific celebration is dependent on the pastoral considerations indicated above (no. 3-4), as well as on the space available in the presbyterium and around the altar (*Rite of Concelebration,* no. 4).

7. Great numbers of concelebrants, such as at regional or national meetings or conventions, may have a deleterious pastoral effect and may even hinder a sense of the unity of the gathered assembly. In such cases, it may be appropriate to designate a specific number of concelebrants. Priests chosen to concelebrate should be truly representative of the larger group. Such a limitation on the number of concelebrants should be understood as a pastoral response to the ritual problems which may occur because of the great number of priests who may be present rather than as an attempt at exclusion. Pastoral sensitivity toward all members of the assembly should be exercised in planning the Eucharist on such occasions.

8. In those cases when the number of concelebrants is limited for legitimate reasons, those in charge of planning should provide opportunities for the non-concelebrating priests to celebrate the Eucharist at another time each day of the convention or meeting.

Physical Arrangements

9. Concelebrants should be seated together as a group. They should not be intermingled with the assembly nor should anyone be seated between the concelebrants and the altar. If the space in the presbyterium is not large enough to accommodate the concelebrants appropriately, they may be seated in another area which physically and visually unites them with the liturgical action.

10. The position of the concelebrants should not obscure the fact that only one bishop or one presbyter presides over the whole celebration. Furthermore, the position of the concelebrants should not usurp the positions nor limit the functioning of other liturgical ministers nor block the view of the assembly. These same concerns apply to those situations when the Eucharist is concelebrated in a setting other than a church or chapel.

Vesture

11. The color and form of the vestments and their difference from everyday clothing call attention to the liturgical role of the concelebrants. Vestments are part of the ritual experience and the festive character of a liturgical celebration.

12. The guidelines for liturgical vestments for concelebration are clearly spelled out in the General Instruction of the Roman Missal (no. 161; see also Bishops' Committee on the Liturgy, *Environment and Art in Catholic Worship,* nos. 93-94).

13. In addition to the vestments indicated in the General Instruction, the chasuble-alb is approved for use by concelebrants in the dioceses of the United States (see *Newsletter of the Bishops' Committee on the Liturgy,* XIII [May-June 1977] 69 and XIV [April-May 1978] 116). If the chasuble-alb is used, the stole worn over it should be the color indicated for the Mass which is to be celebrated, if this is possible. The principal celebrant, however, is to wear the alb, stole, and chasuble.

14. Priests may not concelebrate in ordinary clerical garb or by wearing the stole over the cassock or street

clothing. Nor may priests of religious institutes concelebrate merely by placing a stole over the monastic cowl or habit (see the Instruction of the Congregation for Divine Worship *Liturgicae instaurationes*, "On the Orderly Carrying out of the Constitution on the Liturgy," 5 September 1970, no. 8c).

15. If chasubles are worn by all the concelebrants, they should be simpler in their decoration than that of the principal celebrant. If a sufficient number of chasubles is not available, and in order to avoid the impression of two classes of concelebrants, it may be preferable for all the concelebrants to be vested in albs and stoles.

Reverence to the Altar

16. As the concelebrants approach the altar during the entrance procession, they reverence it with a deep bow. If the Blessed Sacrament is directly behind the altar, a genuflection is made instead of a bow. If the Blessed Sacrament is located to the side or is not directly in view, only the altar is reverenced. After each concelebrant has reverenced the altar, he kisses it and goes directly to his seat.

Preparation of the Altar and the Gifts

17. "The rites for the preparation of the gifts are carried out by the principal celebrant; the other concelebrants remain at their places" (GIRM 166). However, the deacon assists the principal celebrant at the altar. The gifts of bread and wine are brought in procession and are placed on the altar in the usual way (see GIRM 49-53). When there are to be great numbers of communicants and all the ciboria cannot be conveniently placed on the altar, some of the concelebrants may hold the ciboria in their hands during the eucharistic prayer.

Approach to the Altar

18. The concelebrants approach the altar for the eucharistic prayer after the principal concelebrant has concluded the prayer over the gifts. If there is a great number of concelebrants, only those who will proclaim an individual part of the eucharistic prayer should be invited to stand with the principal celebrant at the altar.

Choice of Eucharistic Prayer

19. The eucharistic prayer should be chosen prior to the celebration, either from among Eucharistic Prayers I-IV of the Roman Missal (Sacramentary) or from the Eucharistic Prayers for Masses of Reconciliation I-II (for the latter see *Eucharistic Prayers for Masses of Reconciliation,* Introduction, no. 5; Sacramentary, Appendix VI). However, in the case of Masses with children, "in view of the psychology of children it seems better to refrain from concelebration . . ." (see *Eucharistic Prayers for Masses with Children,* Introduction, no. 22; Sacramentary, Appendix VI).

20. If they are to be prayed by designated concelebrants, the intercessions should be assigned prior to the beginning of the celebration. Whenever possible the intercessions should be recited from memory. In any case, cards or booklets containing the eucharistic prayer should be provided especially to those concelebrants who will read one or more of the intercessions. In this way, the movement of the Sacramentary on the altar from one concelebrant to another will be avoided.

21. The intercessions are said with hands extended. Careful attention should be given to the manner in which the intercessions are divided (see GIRM 171-191). The principal celebrant may also say the intercessions himself.

Singing of the Eucharistic Prayer

22. Singing the eucharistic prayer is a very solemn form of its proclamation. However, the eucharistic prayer should not be sung unless the principal concelebrant and the concelebrants are able to sing it well.

Proclamation of the Eucharistic Prayer

23. When it is not sung, the eucharistic prayer should be proclaimed by the principal celebrant in a loud and clear voice, while the concelebrating priests recite the epiclesis, words of institution, anamnesis, and post-consecratory epiclesis inaudibly. The concelebrants listen in silence during the postsanctus and the intercessions. Recitation from memory by the concelebrants is to be preferred to reading from cards or books. If the latter are used, the concelebrants should never rest them upon the altar.

Deacons and Other Ministers

24. When neither a deacon nor other ministers assist in a concelebrated Mass, their functions are to be carried out by one or more of the concelebrants (see GIRM 160). However, every effort should be made to provide a deacon and other ministers so that the various ministerial roles are always respected.

Gesture at the Epiclesis

25. The concelebrants hold their hands (or at least their right hand) outstretched toward the offerings, with the palm(s) facing down, in the traditional epicletic gesture during the epiclesis of the eucharistic prayer (GIRM 174a, 180a, 184a, 188a). (Note the variation in Eucharistic Prayer I.)

Gestures at the Institution Narrative

26. During the institution narrative, each concelebrant may extend the right hand, with the palm facing to the side, toward the bread and the chalice. Unlike the gesture at the epiclesis, this gesture is optional and may be omitted (GIRM 174c, 180c, 184c, 188c). However, a decision should be made before the celebration begins as to whether or not this gesture will be made.

27. All bow profoundly when the celebrant genuflects after the consecration of the bread and after the consecration of the wine.

Gestures during the Anamnesis and Epiclesis

28. The concelebrants hold their hands outstretched during the anamnesis and the post-consecratory epiclesis.

Doxology of the Eucharistic Prayer

29. During the final doxology of the eucharistic prayer only the principal concelebrant elevates the paten with the consecrated bread, while the deacon raises the chalice. The concelebrants do not elevate other chalices, ciboria, etc. If no deacon is present, one of the concelebrants may elevate the chalice.

30. All the concelebrants may join in the singing or recitation of the doxology or it may be sung or recited by the principal celebrant alone. The procedure to be followed should be decided before the celebration begins.

The Lord's Prayer

31. The principal celebrant, "with hands joined, introduces the Lord's Prayer; with hands outstretched, he then says [or sings] this prayer itself with the other concelebrants and the congregation" (GIRM 192). According to custom, the concelebrants may also hold their hands outstretched during the singing or recitation of the Lord's Prayer.

Prayers during the Communion Rite

32. The prayers of the communion rite are said by the principal celebrant alone. They may not be distributed for recitation by the concelebrants. Nor may they be recited by the concelebrants together with the principal celebrant (GIRM 193).

Sign of Peace

33. The sign of peace should not be overextended, thus delaying the rite of breaking the bread (see GIRM 56b and 194; see also Bishops' Committee on the Liturgy, *The Sign of Peace* [Washington, DC: USCC, 1977]).

Breaking of the Bread

34. The Lamb of God begins only after the sign of peace is completed. During this litany the deacon (or, in his absence, one of the concelebrants) assists the principal celebrant in the breaking of the bread and the pouring of the wine (see *This Holy and Living Sacrifice: Directory for the Celebration and Reception of Communion under Both Kinds*, 43).

35. At least some of the eucharistic bread should be broken for the concelebrants and the people. There is no

reason that the concelebrants should each receive a half of a large host; rather, large altar breads that can be broken into many pieces should be used.

36. All present are to receive the Lord's Body from the bread consecrated at the same Mass (see *Constitution on the Sacred Liturgy* 55; GIRM 56h; Instruction *Eucharisticum mysterium,* 25 May 1967, no. 31). It is never permitted, however, to distribute communion to the concelebrants from the Sacrament consecrated at another Mass and reserved in the tabernacle.

37. The deacon distributes the hosts to the concelebrating priests after the breaking of the bread without saying the formula *The body of Christ.* If there is a great number of concelebrants, they may receive the host and drink from the chalice while communion is being distributed to the faithful. In this case, the concelebrants may receive the host from a paten held by the deacon or one of the concelebrants; or the paten may be passed from one to another; or it may be left on the altar for each concelebrant to take as he approaches to receive from the cup (see GIRM 205).

Invitation to Communion

38. Only the principal celebrant shows the host to the people when he proclaims, *This is the Lamb of God . . .* Concelebrants do not elevate their hosts; rather they reverently hold the consecrated bread in the right hand with the left hand under it.

Communion from the Cup

39. Communion from the cup may be received in either of the following manners: the concelebrants approach the altar to receive from the cup; or the deacon may offer the cup to each concelebrant without saying the formula *The blood of Christ* (GIRM 201).

40. All in the assembly may receive communion under both kinds (see *This Holy and Living Sacrifice,* 20-21). The number of ordinary ministers for communion (and, if necessary, special ministers of holy communion), as well as the location of the communion stations, is to be determined beforehand. Deacons, when present, are to be ministers of the cup.

Ablutions

41. After communion, the deacon cleanses the vessels at the side table or, after the Mass has concluded, in the sacristy. In the latter case, the deacon covers the vessels and leaves them on a corporal on the side table to be washed after Mass (GIRM 138).

Reverence to the Altar

42. Before leaving, the principal celebrant reverences the altar in the customary manner. The concelebrants, however, do not kiss the altar (see GIRM 208).

Bishops' Committee on the Liturgy
National Conference of Catholic Bishops
September 1987

Newsletter Subscription Renewals

Computerized renewal notices will be sent to all subscribers to the Bishops' Committee on the Liturgy *Newsletter* in November. Subscribers are asked to return the completed renewal forms with their payment before December 18, 1987. (Subscriptions which have not been renewed by the time the January 1988 *Newsletter* goes to press will be placed on an inactive list and reinstated once payment is received.) The single subscription prices for 1988 will remain $8.00 domestic mail and $10.00 foreign airmail. Bulk rates will also remain at their current pricing.

In order that subscribers' accounts may be properly credited, the instructions accompanying the renewal forms should be followed. The "renewal coupon" portion of the invoice must be included with payment.

Coupon and payment should be returned in the self-mailer envelope which has been provided. This envelope is preaddressed for direct mail deposit to the bank. Payment should not be sent to the Liturgy Secretariat, since this needlessly slows down the renewal process.

Subscribers who have not received a renewal form by November 30, 1987 should contact the Liturgy Secretariat and a duplicate invoice will be sent. (*Newsletter* recipients whose subscription number is 205990, 205995, or 205999 are receiving *gratis* copies. Therefore, they will receive no renewal invoice.)

The Liturgy Secretariat expresses its thanks to all subscribers for their cooperation in the renewal process.

NCCB Administrative Committee Decisions

The Administrative Committee of the National Conference of Catholic Bishops met in Washington, DC, on September 22-24, 1987, at which time the members approved the following action items submitted by the Bishops' Committee on the Liturgy: (1) placing on the agenda of the plenary assembly of the National Conference of Catholic Bishops in November 1987 the request to raise the rank of Our Lady of Guadalupe (December 12) from an obligatory memorial to a feast in the Proper Calendar for the Dioceses of the United States of America; (2) approval of *El Bendicional,* the provisional Spanish translation of *De Benedictionibus,* for use *ad interim* in the dioceses of the United States of America where the liturgy is celebrated in Spanish; (3) approval of Pima-Papago (O'odham ha nioki) as a liturgical language; (4) approval of *Guidelines for the Concelebration of the Eucharist* for publication; (5) approval of the *Translation for Early Youth* of the American Bible Society for use in the proposed *Lectionary for Masses with Children*; (6) placing on the agenda of the November 1987 plenary assembly of the NCCB the request to approve for liturgical use *A Christian Celebration of Marriage - An Ecumenical Liturgy* (North American Consultation on Common Texts).

Solemnities of Saint Joseph and the Annunciation in 1989

Following is a translation of the notice of the Congregation for Divine Worship regarding the Liturgical Calendar for 1989 and dealing with two impeded solemnities which occur in that year. The notice appeared on page 397 of the June 1987 issue of Notitiae and was signed by the Most Reverend Virgilio Noè, Titular Archbishop of Voncaria and Secretary of the Congregation.

In 1989 the solemnity of Saint Joseph, Husband of Mary (March 19) falls on the same day as Passion (Palm) Sunday and the solemnity of the Annunciation of the Lord (March 25) occurs on Holy Saturday. These two conflicts in the calendar are resolved in the following manner:

1. Celebration of the solemnity of Saint Joseph, Husband of Mary

According to the *General Norms for the Liturgical Year and the Calendar,* no. 60, the solemnity of Saint Joseph, Husband of Mary, is anticipated on Saturday, March 18. But, wherever this solemnity is not observed as a holyday of obligation, it may be transferred by the conference of bishops to another day outside Lent, according to no. 56 of the *General Norms.*

2. Celebration of the solemnity of the Annunciation of the Lord

The solemnity of the Annunciation of the Lord will be celebrated on April 3, the Monday after the Second Sunday of Easter. Henceforth whenever this solemnity falls on some day in Holy Week, it will always be transferred to the Monday after the Second Sunday of Easter.

BISHOPS' COMMITTEE ON THE LITURGY
NEWSLETTER
NATIONAL CONFERENCE OF CATHOLIC BISHOPS

**1987
VOLUME XXIII
NOVEMBER**

Confirmation of *El Bendicional*

On October 27, 1987 the National Conference of Catholic Bishops received the decree of the Congregation for Divine Worship, dated October 16, 1987, confirming the decision of the Administrative Committee of the NCCB to approve the Spanish version of *De Benedictionibus* for use in the United States of America. The following is an unofficial English translation of that decree.

Prot. N. 1188/87

At the request of His Excellency John L. May, Archbishop of St. Louis and President of the National Conference of Catholic Bishops, on September 30, 1987, and in virtue of the faculty granted to this Congregation by the Supreme Pontiff, Pope John Paul II, we gladly conceed that, in the dioceses of the United States of America where Spanish is spoken, the Spanish text of *De Benedictionibus* may be used, as published in the volume titled *El Benedicional*, and already confirmed by this Dicastery on May 7, 1986 (Prot. N. 338/86).

In the printed text mention should be made of the confirmation granted by the Apostolic See. Two copies of printed text should be sent to this Congregation.

Anything to the contrary notwithstanding.

From the Congregation for Divine Worship, 16 October 1987.

> \+ Paul Augustin Cardinal Mayer
> Prefect
>
> \+ Virgilio Noè
> Titular Archbishop of Voncaria
> Secretary

Address of Bishop Joseph P. Delaney to the National Meeting of Diocesan Liturgical Commissions

On Monday, October 8, 1987, the Most Reverend Joseph P. Delaney, Bishop of Fort Worth and Chairman of the Bishops' Committee on the Liturgy, reported on the activities of the Committee to the delegates attending the annual National Meeting of Diocesan Liturgical Commissions. Sponsored by the Bishops' Committee on the Liturgy and the Federation of Diocesan Liturgical Commissions, the meeting took place at Breckenridge, Colorado and was hosted by the Archdiocese of Denver and the dioceses of Region 10. The following is the full text of Bishop Delaney's report to the delegates.

For nearly twenty years the Bishops' Committee on the Liturgy and the Federation of Diocesan Liturgical Commissions have cosponsored the annual National Meeting of Diocesan Liturgical Commissions of the United States. These meetings could never have been possible without the active cooperation of the host diocese and region. This year we are fortunate that the Archdiocese of Denver and Region 10 have enabled us to gather in the beautiful setting of the Rocky Mountains, a place I personally enjoy through hiking and camping. I am grateful to Archbishop Stafford for the welcome he has given to us all in this archdiocese. The mountains have always been a symbol of God's majesty and total otherness or transcendence. It is fitting that our purpose in these next days—to discuss and consider the Church's rites of death and dying—can be enhanced through the reminder which the mountains give us of God's transcendence and our ultimate hope of living in that same splendor with God.

This last year has been a busy one for the Bishops' Committee on the Liturgy, a year of transition, and of trying to play catch-up with an agenda which never seems to decrease in the number of items we are asked to consider. While some of this information may be familiar to you, I think it important nevertheless in making this report to highlight a few of the topics with which the Committee is grappling.

First of all, there have been Committee and staff changes. After Archbishop Daniel Pilarczyk was elected Vice President of the National Conference of Catholic Bishops in November 1986, I was elected to fill out his term until November 1987. At that time a new election for Liturgy Committee chairman will take place. On January 1, 1987 Msgr. Alan F. Detscher was appointed to work full-time as an associate director of the Liturgy Secretariat, while Father Ron Krisman went on half-time in order to fulfill his other duties as Conference Relocation Director.

Staff changes notwithstanding, the work of the bishops' conference goes on at its own, very often hectic, pace. In collaboration with the ten dioceses to be visited by His Holiness Pope John Paul II, the liturgy staff was given the responsibility to oversee the production of liturgical books for use during the papal visit. A time-consuming task in which the entire staff of the Secretariat was engaged, the work of the Committee nevertheless continued, as any of the bishop-members or consultants and advisors can tell you. The Marian Year also became a responsibility of our staff in Washington. I am happy to say that the materials produced for both the Papal Visit and the Marian Year have proved useful. With regard to the Papal Visit, I should like to take this opportunity publicly to thank The Catholic Book Publishing Company of New York for the gift of their time, resources, and energy in the production of three special liturgical books for use by the Holy Father during his visit to the Church in our country. The special *Sacramentary, Lectionary,* and *Book of Celebrations and Blessings* are fine examples of the quality and artistry necessary for the celebration of Christian worship.

In highlighting the work of the Committee over the last year I would like to single out a few projects with which you are no doubt familiar.

Late last year a *Task Group on Sunday Celebrations in the Absence of a Priest* was formed by the Liturgy Committee. Bishop Michael Sheehan of Lubbock chairs the task group. You have participated in a survey the purpose of which was to determine the frequency of such celebrations in America, the style and structure of such celebrations, and the projected needs of parishes in which the celebration of the Eucharist is becoming frequently less possible. The purpose of the task group will be to prepare a directory based on that now being prepared by the Congregation for Divine Worship. The Directory will give additional guidelines and liturgical texts to be used in Sunday celebrations without a priest. The time-line for this project is based on the issuance of the Roman Directory.

Another of the new projects of the Committee is the preparation of *God's Mercy Endures For Ever: Guidelines on the Presentation of Jews and Judaism in Catholic Preaching.* Already in a third draft, *God's Mercy Endures For Ever* has received the input of Catholic and Jewish liturgical and biblical scholars. It is our hope that these guidelines, when approved, will assist in the continued implementation of the Council's landmark document *Nostra Aetate.*

The Bishops' Committee on the Liturgy continues to work on the thorny but important issue of inclusive language in the liturgy, especially in biblical texts used in worship. A *Joint Committee on Inclusive Language* was established by the NCCB Committees on Doctrine and Liturgy under the chairmanship of Bishop Paul Waldschmidt of Portland (Oregon) with members from both Committees. It is staffed by Father Michael Buckley, S.J., and Father Gurrieri. The joint committee or task group is currently analysing the criteria or principles of inclusive language used in the liturgical books of other Churches with a view toward establishing criteria for the use of the members of the National Conference of Catholic Bishops.

I have mentioned only three of the new projects in which our Committee is presently engaged. However, work continues in the several other subcommittees established for specific purposes. The Black Liturgy Subcommittee has prepared *In Spirit and in Truth: Black Catholic Reflections on the Order of Mass,* a document, we hope, which will assist predominantly Black parishes in the process of liturgical inculturation. Another of the subcommittee's projects is the eventual issuance of a pastoral-theological statement by the Bishops' Committee on the Liturgy entitled *Black Americans and Catholic Worship.* The purpose of this more theoretical statement will be to move the same process of inculturation forward.

The Hispanic Liturgy Subcommittee, having conducted a national survey concerning current Spanish language translations of the Missal (*Consulta sobre el Misal Romano en Espanol*), is now working toward the preparation of a *Hispanic Sacramentary* for use in the dioceses of the United States. The Hispanic Sacramentary will eventually incorporate the new international translation of the Order of Mass and eucharistic prayers.

Our Christian Initiation Subcommittee has worked long and hard to prepare additional rites and prayers to be included in the *Rite of Christian Initiation of Adults*. As you know, the National Conference of Catholic Bishops approved these rites and the ICEL "White Book" in November 1986. The decree of confirmation by the Apostolic See, however, has not been received. While the mandatory date of implementation (First Sunday of Lent, 1988) probably cannot be maintained, it is our hope that, once confirmed, the ritual will be quickly published. (I should add that our Committee is grateful to the publishers of liturgical books for their patience and forebearance!) The national workshops planned by the subcommittee and to be implemented by the North American Forum on the Catechumenate and the Bishops' Committee on the Liturgy will nevertheless take place as scheduled. These workshops, together with the publication of the *Pastoral Companion to the Rite of Christian Initiation of Adults* will prove useful in the implementation the catechumenate in the United States.

The Lectionary Subcommittee, dormant for a while, has now begun the work of preparing the second typical edition of *The Lectionary for Mass* using the revised translation of the New American Bible. Current plans call for the publication of the Lectionary in conjunction with the revised translation of *The Roman Missal,* now being prepared by the International Commission on English in the Liturgy.

It was the hope of the Liturgy Committee to bring the *Book of Blessings* before the Administrative Committee of the National Conference of Catholic Bishops in September for approval and eventual submission to the Holy See for confirmation. Besides the ICEL provisional English translation of *De Benedictionibus* (which has been completed), the Blessings Subcommittee over the last three years prepared additional rites of blessing for use in the United States. These additional blessings and occasional services, based on your response to a survey conducted in 1984, are to be incorporated into the body of the *Book of Blessings*. The Subcommittee also prepared a book for use in the home, *Household Blessings and Prayers,* a volume based on the *Book of Blessings,* but with a very different approach. While these books are ready to be submitted to the bishops for their approval, the press of preparations for the papal visit prevented us from submitting them in September. It is our hope now to submit them to the bishops in March 1988.

I would like to report on one more project, the *Lectionary for Masses with Children.* As a consequence of a resolution approved by the members of the Federation of Diocesan Liturgical Commissions in Buffalo in 1982, a joint task group was established to prepare a lectionary for use in Masses with children. The pericopes of the lectionary are nearly complete and a decision has been made to use the new Translation for Early Youth of the American Bible Society by the members of the NCCB Administrative Committee.

Finally, I must report to you on the status of the *Order of Christian Funerals,* the subject of this National Meeting. As you know the National Conference of Catholic Bishops approved the *Order of Christian Funerals* in November 1985. Within the same period some nine other English-speaking conferences of bishops approved the new translation. The *Order of Christian Funerals* is a model liturgical book for many reasons: the beauty of its translated and original texts; the pastoral suitability of the new texts and rites; the pastoral utility of the format and layout of the various liturgical rites contained in the ritual. The *Order of Christian Funerals* truly expresses the Church's prayer for the dead and its ministry of consolation to the bereaved. The International Commission on English in the Liturgy is to be congratulated for the care and sensitivity with which it prepared this first of the revised rituals.

Unfortunately, I cannot report to you that the *Order of Christian Funerals* is ready for publication. While the Congregation for Divine Worship did issue a decree of confirmation in the early part of the summer, a number of modifications were requested in the ritual book which the leadership of the Conference is discussing with the Congregation. It is unfortunate that, after two years, we are not yet able to use this ritual in our liturgical celebrations for the dead. However, I am hopeful that these difficulties will soon be resolved.

1987 marks an anniversary for the Bishops' Committee on the Liturgy. Thirty years ago, in response to the liturgical reforms initiated by Pope Pius XII, the American bishops voted to establish the *Bishops' Commission on the Liturgical Apostolate,* a commission whose purpose was to assist the bishops in the implementation of liturgical reforms. In 1966, with the canonical establishment of the National Conference of Catholic Bishops, the Commission was replaced by the Bishops' Committee on the Liturgy. To mark the past three decades of liturgical progress, the Bishops' Committee on the Liturgy asked Msgr. Frederick R. McManus, the first executive director of the Commission (and later of the Committee), to write a history of the work of the of Commission and Committee, including a number of the statements issued since the foundation of both bodies. *Thirty Years of Liturgical Renewal: Statements of the Bishops' Committee on the Liturgy* will soon be published by the United States Catholic Conference's Office of Publishing and Promotion Services. As Cardinal Dearden states in the preface, this is not a complete history of liturgical renewal in the last thirty years, but rather a view of that history from the perspective of the bishops and their contribution to liturgical reform and renewal both before and after the Second Vatican Council. The Committee is grateful to Msgr. McManus for having prepared this book of over five hundred pages. Fred brings his own historical insight and liturgical acumen to bear upon the actions of the Committee. He speaks as one "who was there," for indeed he was—at the Council, at the birth of the Commission, and in the formative years of the Bishops' Committee on the Liturgy.

Thirty years is not a long time in the history of any institution. However, the last thirty years in the history of the Church in the United States has been a period of growth and renewal precisely because of the commitment of American Catholics to the reforms instituted by Vatican II and because of the love and excitement American Catholics bring to the worship due to God. Our commitment to liturgical renewal as bishops and diocesan liturgical commissions must remain strong and unstinting. Our work has only just begun.

Confirmation of Pima-Papago as a Liturgical Language

On October 27, 1987 the National Conference of Catholic Bishops received the decree of the Congregation for Divine Worship, dated October 16, 1987, confirming the decision of the Administrative Committee of the NCCB to approve the Pima-Papago language for use in the liturgy in the dioceses of the United States of America. The following is an unofficial English translation of that decree.

Prot. N. 1188/87

At the request of His Excellency John L. May, Archbishop of Saint Louis and President of the National Conference of Catholic Bishops, on September 30, 1987, and in virtue of the faculty granted to this Congregation by the Supreme Pontiff, Pope John Paul II, we gladly confirm the decision of that same Conference of Bishops, by which the Pima-Papago language may be introduced into liturgical celebrations for the faithful of that language in the United States, according to the norms of the letter *Decem iam annos*, 5 June 1976 (*Notitiae* XII, 1976, 300-302).

Anything to the contrary notwithstanding.

From the Congregation for Divine Worship, 16 October 1987.

+ Paul Augustin Cardinal Mayer
Prefect

+ Virgilio Noè
Titular Archbishop of Voncaria
Secretary

Election of Chairman

The National Conference of Catholic Bishops, at its November 16-19, 1987 meeting, elected the Most Reverend Joseph P. Delaney, Bishop of Fort Worth, to a full term (1987-1990) as the Chairman of the Bishops' Committee on the Liturgy. Bishop Delaney served as the Chairman of the Liturgy Committee for the past year, completing the unexpired term of Archbishop Daniel E. Pilarczyk who was elected Vice President of the Conference in November of 1986.

BISHOPS' COMMITTEE ON THE LITURGY
NEWSLETTER
NATIONAL CONFERENCE OF CATHOLIC BISHOPS

**1987
VOLUME XXIII
DECEMBER**

Feast of Our Lady of Guadalupe

On November 18, 1987, the National Conference of Catholic Bishops unanimously approved a proposal to raise the rank of Our Lady of Guadalupe (December 12) from an obligatory memorial to a feast in the Proper Calendar for the Dioceses of the United States of America. At the same time the Conference approved proper Mass texts for the new feast. Apart from the Opening Prayer, which was approved in November 1973 (and confirmed by the Apostolic See on February 4, 1974 [Prot. N. CD 1762/73]) and is found in present editions of the Sacramentary, the new texts are based on those found in *Misal Romano*, approved by the Mexican Bishops' Conference for use in the dioceses of Mexico. (The Bishops' Committee on the Liturgy is preparing proper texts for the Liturgy of the Hours.) The NCCB has requested the Apostolic See's confirmation of its decrees concerning Our Lady of Guadalupe.

Ecumenical Rite of Marriage Approved by NCCB

On Thursday, November 19, 1987 the members of the National Conference of Catholic Bishops approved the use of *A Christian Celebration of Marriage: An Ecumenical Liturgy* in the dioceses of the United States of America in the celebration of a marriage between a Roman Catholic and another Christian. The text was approved by a two-thirds majority of the *de iure* members of the Conference. If confirmed by the Apostolic See, the new rite will be inserted as a separate chapter into the *Rite of Marriage*.

A Christian Celebration of Marriage: An Ecumenical Liturgy was prepared by the North American Consultation on Common Texts (CCT), an ecumenical board representing the major Churches of Canada and the United States which prepares liturgical texts for common use by the member Churches. The CCT has also issued *Ecumenical Services of Prayer* and *A Common Lectionary*. The CCT also participates in the international English Language Liturgical Consultation (ELLC), the successor of the International Consultation on English Texts (ICET), which prepared the common liturgical texts used in the eucharistic liturgy (e.g., Kyrie, Gloria, Sanctus, etc.) and the Divine Office (Benedictus, Magnificat, etc.).

Prior to its presentation to the members of the National Conference of Catholic Bishops, the new marriage rite was submitted to the CCT member Churches for review and comment. The rite had been reviewed not only by the Bishops' Committee on the Liturgy but also by the Bishops' Committee for Ecumenical and Interreligious Affairs and the Bishops' Committee for Canonical Affairs. The edition approved by the NCCB incorporates further elements requested by the three committees.

The bishops have also adapted the ecumenical rite of marriage in several ways. Besides those already provided in the CCT rite, the bishops have inserted into the final version various other options and alternatives drawn from the Roman *Rite of Marriage*, viz., alternative nuptial blessings, readings from the Roman marriage lectionary, etc. For pastoral reasons, the bishops also decided that this rite may not be used within the celebration of the Eucharist.

Collection of Masses of the Blessed Virgin Mary Authorized

In a letter dated October 14, 1987, addressed to Archbishop John L. May, President of the National Conference of Catholic Bishops, the Congregation for Divine Worship has indicated that the English translation of twelve Mass formularies excerpted from the *Collection of Masses of the Blessed Virgin Mary*

1312 MASSACHUSETTS AVENUE, N.W. • WASHINGTON, D.C. 20005

may be used in the interim until the translation of the remaining thirty-four Mass formularies is completed. Cardinal Mayer noted in the letter that the decree of confirmation can only be issued once the entire *Collection* is presented to the Apostolic See. However, he indicated that the Congregation willingly grants "permission for the use of these twelve Mass formularies until further provision is made"(Prot. N. 1176/87).

The twelve Mass formularies of the *Collection of Masses of the Blessed Virgin Mary* are now being prepared for publication by The Catholic Book Publishing Company (New York). [For a description of the *Collection*, see *Newsletter*, April 1987, page 13.]

Liturgy Committee Meeting in Washington, DC

The bishop members and consultants of the Bishops' Committee on the Liturgy met in Washington, DC, on November 15, 1987 at the Capital Hilton Hotel on the eve of of the plenary assembly of the National Conference of Catholic Bishops. During the course of the meeting the Committee reviewed the modifications submitted by various bishops concerning the Committee's two action items scheduled for presentation to the bishops: Our Lady of Guadalupe and the ecumenical Rite of Marriage. The Committee also reviewed the current status of the *Order of Christian Funerals* and the *Rite of Christian Initiation of Adults*.

Among the other projects, the members and consultants briefly reviewed the progress of the following: *God's Mercy Endures For Ever: Guidelines on the Presentation of Jews and Judaism in Catholic Preaching*; initial results of the national survey on "Sunday Celebrations in the Absence of a Priest"; the use of the revised New Testament of the New American Bible in liturgical books; the use of the *Collection of Masses of the Blessed Virgin Mary*.

The Committee also reviewed *varia* or proposals submitted by various bishops, notably the following: special ministers of Communion; the "back-to-back" celebration of a Sunday and a holy day of obligation; inclusive language; lay preaching; Communion under both kinds. The Committee also heard reports from the following subcommittees and task groups: Black Liturgy Subcommittee, Hispanic Liturgy Subcommittee, Lectionary Subcommittee, Christian Initiation Subcommittee, Task Group for the Lectionary for Masses with Children, Blessings Subcommittee, and the Task Group on Sunday Worship in the Absence of a Priest.

The next meeting of the members and consultants of the Committee will take place in Washington on March 21, 1988.

Hispanic Liturgy Subcommittee Meeting in Mexico City

The Hispanic Liturgy Subcommittee of the Bishops' Committee on the Liturgy met in Mexico City on October 19, 1987 in connection with a regular meeting of the Instituto de Liturgia Hispana. The Most Reverend Ricardo Ramirez, Bishop of Las Cruces, chaired the meeting.

The subcommittee discussed at length the preparation of an American edition of the Sacramentary in Spanish ("Hispanic Sacramentary"). Apart from the Order of Mass and eucharistic prayers, it has been decided to use the Mexican translation of the prayers of the *Roman Missal*. This decision was based on the results of a national consultation (see *Newsletter*, January 1987, pp. 1-2). Work is now proceeding on a proper calendar and the actual preparation of the texts.

The weekday edition of the *Leccionario* is in the final stages of preparation and should be available soon. Once this volume is published, discussion will focus on the preparation of the third volume of the *Leccionario*.

Further work of the subcommittee will include a study of bilingual rituals and an evaluation of the proposed American blessings for Spanish translation and eventual inclusion into a future U.S. edition of *El Bendicional*.

Black Liturgy Subcommittee Meeting in Washington, DC

The Black Liturgy Subcommittee of the Bishops' Committee on the Liturgy met at Saint Joseph

Seminary in Washington, DC on October 26-27, 1987. Bishop Wilton Gregory, chairman of the subcommittee, reported that the Bishops' Committee on the Liturgy had approved for publication the draft of *In Spirit and Truth: Black Catholic Reflections on the Order of Mass*. This document presents the options contained in the *Sacramentary* with a special view towards the needs of Black Catholic parishes. *In Spirit and Truth* offers guidelines to assist parishes in the full and proper use of the options contained in the Missal and will also be of value to the Church as a whole.

The subcommittee also discussed a second document which is envisioned as a complement to *In Spirit and Truth*, entitled *Catholic Worship and Black Americans* (CWBA). This more theoretical document addresses the question of inculturation and provides a rationale and background for Black liturgical styles and traditions which have entered into the worship life of Black Catholic parishes. The subcommittee studied the results of a wide consultation on the draft. *Catholic Worship and Black Americans* is now being revised in the light of the many positive suggestions and comments received during the consultation period. The subcommittee hopes that CWBA can be submitted for the Liturgy Committee review and approval at its Spring meeting in 1988.

In Memoriam: Niels Krogh Rasmussen, O.P.

On August 29, 1987 the world of liturgical scholarship suffered a great loss through the sudden death of the Reverend Niels K. Rasmussen, OP, at the University of Notre Dame in South Bend, Indiana. At the time of his death he was 52 years old.

Father Rasmussen was born and raised in Denmark. During his student years he became a Roman Catholic and later joined the Dominican Order in the Paris Province. Early in his career he became a student of the renowned liturgist Pierre-Marie Gy, OP, who until recently was Director of the Institut Supérieur de Liturgie at the Institut Catholique de Paris. Niels studied paleography at the Ecole National des Chartes, hagiography and codicology at the Ecole Pratique des Hautes Etudes, and liturgy at the Institut Catholique de Paris. From this last institution he received the doctorate on January 28, 1978, with the defense of his dissertation, "Les pontificaux du haut moyen age." This study dealt with the evolution of pontificals of the ninth and tenth centuries.

His teaching career in liturgy began in 1968 and included the following institutions: University of Aarhus (Denmark), Institut Catholique de Paris, La Salle College (Philadelphia), St. John's University (Collegeville), The Catholic University of America, and finally the University of Notre Dame where he was granted tenure in 1985. From that time until his death he was the coordinator of the Ph.D. Program in Liturgical Studies at Notre Dame.

His writings were extensive and scholarly, often bridging the fields of theology and medieval history. Some of his latest publications showed his interest in and deep knowledge of Renaissance and Baroque liturgies. Perhaps he will be most remembered for his English translation and revision of Cyrille Vogel's major work in French which serves as a brilliant introduction to medieval liturgy: *Medieval Liturgy: An Introduction to the Sources* (translated and revised by William Storey and Niels Rasmussen; Washington, DC: The Pastoral Press, 1986).

Niels Rasmussen was known and respected as a liturgical scholar not only in the United States but throughout the world. Many will be comforted by the words of his mentor, Father Gy, preaching at a eucharist offered for Niels in Paris shortly after his death: "Perhaps we can ask Jesus that the secret of those last moments of the earthly life of Niels might be in some way assumed into the agony of Gethsemani and be saved by it."

> Lord our God,
> you are always faithful and quick to show mercy.
> Our brother Niels
> was suddenly and cruelly taken from us.
> Come swiftly to his aid,
> have mercy on him,
> and comfort his family and friends
> by the power and protection of the cross.
> We ask this through Christ our Lord.
> Amen.

Liturgical Colors

From time to time the Secretariat receives requests for a clarification concerning the liturgical colors of vestments for various feasts and seasons, especially with regard to the use of blue vestments during the season of Advent. Blue is approved or used by other Churches, for example, the Evangelical Lutheran Church in America. The *Manual on the Liturgy* of the *Lutheran Book of Worship* states the following: "The traditional color of Advent is purple, the royal color of the coming King. The preferred color in the *Lutheran Book of Worship,* however, is blue, which has a precedent in the Swedish Church and in the Mozarabic rite" (page 22). Blue is also commonly used for Advent and other times by many Anglican and Episcopalian parishes.

According to the current usage of the Roman Rite in the United States, only those colors mentioned in the General Instruction of the Roman Missal (no. 308) and in the Appendix to the General Instruction of the Roman Missal (no. 308) have been approved by the National Conference of Catholic Bishops: (1) *white* for the offices and Masses of the Easter and Christmas seasons, feasts and memorials of the Lord (other than of his passion), feasts and memorials of Mary, the angels, saints who were not martyrs, All Saints, John the Baptist (June 24), John the Evangelist (December 27), Chair of St. Peter (February 22), Conversion of St. Paul (January 25); in the United States white may also be used for offices and Masses for the dead; (2) *red* for Passion (Palm) Sunday, Good Friday, Pentecost, celebrations of the Lord's passion, birthday feasts of the apostles and evangelists, celebrations of the martyrs; (3) *green* for the offices and Masses of Ordinary Time; (4) *violet* for the offices and Masses of the seasons of Advent and Lent, and for the dead; (5) *black* (as well as violet and white) may be used for the offices and Masses for the dead; (6) *rose* may be used on *Gaudete* Sunday (Third Sunday of Advent) and on *Laetare* Sunday (Fourth Sunday of Lent).

The General Instruction also states: "On solemn occasions more precious vestments may be used, even if not of the color of the day" (GIRM, no. 309). The design and use of fabrics and materials in such "precious vestments" are left to the creativity of artists. The General Instruction also states the following with regard to other celebrations: "Ritual Masses are celebrated in their proper color, in white, or in a festive color; Masses for various needs and occasions are celebrated in the color proper to the day or the season or in violet if they bear a penitential character, for example, ritual Masses nos. 23, 28, and 40; votive Masses are celebrated in the color suited to the Mass itself or in the color proper to the day or season" (GIRM, no. 310).

Although GIRM, no. 308, also states that with regard to liturgical colors "the conference of bishops may choose and propose to the Apostolic See adaptations suited to the needs and cultures of peoples," until the present the National Conference of Catholic Bishops has chosen only to propose and approve the use of white for funeral offices and Masses. This choice was accepted by the Apostolic See in January 1971 when the *Rite of Funerals* was confirmed.

For the present the NCCB has neither proposed nor approved the use of blue either for the season of Advent or for memorials and feasts of Mary, nor any other color. The Bishops' Committee on the Liturgy reviewed this matter several years ago. However, because of increasing discussion of the use of blue, the Bishops' Committee on the Liturgy will give further consideration to the question.

Order of Crowning an Image of the Blessed Virgin Mary Published

Order of Crowning an Image of the Blessed Virgin Mary has recently been published by the Office of Publishing and Promotion Services of the United States Catholic Conference. The booklet contains the provisional English translation of *Ordo Coronandi Imaginem Beatae Mariae Virginis,* promulgated by the Congregation for the Sacraments and Divine Worship on March 25, 1981. [For more information concerning the *Order of Crowning,* see *Newsletter*, August 1986, pp. 29-31, October 1986, p. 39-40, June/July 1987, p. 21.] Containing 36 pages, it is priced at $6.95 per copy, before discounts.

To order a copy of *Order of Crowning an Image of the Blessed Virgin Mary* (Publication no. 167-9), write to the Office of Publishing and Promotion Services, United States Catholic Conference, 1312 Massachusetts Avenue NW, Washington, DC 20005-4105. Telephone (toll-free): 1-800-235-USCC.

BISHOPS' COMMITTEE ON THE LITURGY
NEWSLETTER

NATIONAL CONFERENCE OF CATHOLIC BISHOPS

1988
VOLUME XXIV
JANUARY

Concerts in Churches

On December 9, 1987, the National Conference of Catholic Bishops received a circular letter of the Congregation for Divine Worship, dated November 5, 1987, addressing the matter of musical concerts in churches. The letter was sent in the English version which is presented below, accompanied by an introductory letter in Latin, an unofficial English translation of which precedes the circular letter.

Congregation for Divine Worship
Prot. N. 1251/87

Rome, 5 November 1987

Your Excellency:

It gives me great pleasure to send you the document attached to this letter, prepared by this Dicastery.

The growing admission of musical concerts into churches seems to respond to the necessity among the people of today to unite at one time the demands of the nature of art and culture together with those demands that are spiritual. On the other hand, however, this fact exhibits negative aspects which cannot be ignored.

The attached document, which the Congregation for Divine Worship submits to the attention of the conferences of bishops and—through them—to the attention of national commissions on liturgy and sacred art, sets forth elements for an appropriate reflection, one that ought to be made upon this question: namely, the primary necessity of preserving the sacred character of each building destined for divine worship, as well as the opportunity of bringing into use to a greater extent the patrimony of musical art that has accompanied at different times liturgical celebrations and the religious devotions of the Christian people.

In the light of such elements it is obvious that some consequences for these concerts in churches should be carried into practice, a special attention being given to the norm of canon 1210 of the new Code of Canon Law which governs the matter.

The Congregation for Divine Worship hopes that in the future—because of a common pastoral effort—churches at all times and not only during celebrations of the sacred liturgy, will retain their properly sacred character completely and that the treasury of sacred and secular music which takes its origin both in the Church and for the Church, might both continue to fulfill the office of promoting the Christian faith and foster the values of authentic human culture.

On this occasion, therefore, and with sentiments of deep respect, I remain

Devotedly yours in the Lord,

+ Paul Augustin Cardinal Mayer, OSB
Prefect

+ Virgil Noè
Titular Archbishop of Voncaria
Secretary

Concerts in Churches

I. Music in Churches Other Than During Liturgical Celebrations

1. The interest shown in music is one of the marks of contemporary culture. The ease with which it is possible to listen at home to classical works, by means of radio, records, cassettes and television, has in no way diminished the pleasure of attending live concerts, but on the contrary has actually enhanced it. This is encouraging, because music and song contribute to elevating the human spirit.

The increase in the number of concerts in general has in some countries given rise to a more frequent use

1312 MASSACHUSETTS AVENUE, N.W. • WASHINGTON, D.C. 20005

of churches for such events. Various reasons are given for this: local needs, where for example it is not easy to find suitable places; acoustical considerations, for which churches are often ideal; aesthetic reasons, namely the desire to perform in beautiful surroundings; reasons of fittingness, that is to present the works in the settings for which they were originally written; purely practical reasons, for example facilities for organ recitals: in a word, churches are considered to be in many ways apt places for holding a concert.

2. Alongside this contemporary development a new situation has arisen in the church. The *Scholae cantorum* have not had frequent occasion to execute their traditional repertory of sacred polyphonic music within the context of a liturgical celebration.

For this reason, the initiative has been taken to perform this sacred music in church in the form of a concert. The same has happened with Gregorian Chant, which has come to form part of concert programmes both inside and outside of church.

Another important factor emerges from the so called "spiritual concerts", so termed because the music performed in them can be considered as religious, because of the theme chosen, or on account of the nature of the texts set to music, or because of the venue for the performance.

Such events are in some cases accompanied by readings, prayers and moments of silence. Given such features they can almost be compared to a "devotional exercise".

3. The increased numbers of concerts held in churches has given rise to doubts in the minds of pastors and rectors of churches as to the extent to which such events are really necessary.

A general opening of churches for concerts could give rise to complaints by a number of the faithful, yet on the other hand an outright refusal could lead to some misunderstanding.

Firstly it is necessary to consider the significance and purpose of a Christian church. For this, the Congregation for Divine Worship considers it opportune to propose to the Episcopal Conferences, and in so far as it concerns them, to the national Commissions of Liturgy and Music, some observations and interpretations of the canonical norms concerning the use of churches for various kinds of music: music and song, music of religious inspiration and music of non-religious character.

4. At this juncture it is necessary to re-read recent documents which treat of the subject, in particular the Constitution on the Liturgy *Sacrosanctum Concilium,* the Instruction *Musicam sacram* of March 5, 1967, the Instruction *Liturgicae Instaurationes* of September 5, 1970, in addition to the prescriptions of the Code of Canon Law, can. 1210, 1213 and 1222.

In this present letter the primary concern is with musical performances outside of the celebration of the liturgy.

The Congregation for Divine Worship wishes in this way to help individual bishops to make valid pastoral decisions, bearing in mind the socio-cultural situation of the area.

II. Points for Consideration

The character and purpose of churches

5. According to tradition as expressed in the Rite for the Dedication of a Church and Altar, churches are primarily places where the people of God gather, and are "made one as the Father, the Son and the Holy Spirit are one, and are the Church, the temple of God built with living stones, in which the Father is worshiped in spirit and in truth". Rightly so, from ancient times the name "church" has been extended to the building in which the Christian community unites to hear the word of God, to pray together, to receive the sacraments, to celebrate the Eucharist and to prolong its celebration in the adoration of the Blessed Sacrament (Cf. Order of the Dedication of Church, ch. II, 1)

Churches, however, cannot be considered simply as public places for any kind of meeting. They are sacred places, that is, "set apart" in a permanent way for Divine Worship by their dedication and blessing.

As visible constructions, churches are signs of the pilgrim Church on earth; they are images that proclaim the heavenly Jerusalem, places in which are actualized the mystery of the communion between man and God. Both in urban areas and in the countryside, the church remains the house of God, and the sign of His dwelling among men. It remains a sacred place, even when no liturgical celebration is taking place.

In a society disturbed by noise, especially in the big cities, churches are also an oasis where men gather, in silence and in prayer, to seek peace of soul and the light of faith.

That will only be possible in so far as churches maintain their specific identity. When churches are used for ends other than those for which they were built, their role as a sign of the Christian mystery is put at risk, with more or less serious harm to the teaching of the faith and to the sensitivity of the People of God, according to the Lord's words: "My house is a house of prayer" (Lk 19, 46).

Importance of Sacred Music

6. Sacred music, whether vocal or instrumental, is of importance. Music is sacred "insofar as it is composed for the celebration of divine worship and possesses integrity of form" (*Musicam sacram* n. 4a). The church considers it a "treasure of inestimable value, greater even than that of any other art", recognizing that is has a "ministerial function in the service of the Lord" (Cf. SC n. 112); and recommending that is be "preserved and fostered with great care" (SC n. 114).

Any performance of sacred music which takes place during a celebration, should be fully in harmony with that celebration. This often means that musical compositions which date from a period when the active participation of the faithful was not emphasized as the source of the authentic Christian spirit (SC n. 14; Pius X *Tra le sollecitudini*) are no longer to be considered suitable for inclusion within liturgical celebrations.

Analogous changes of perception and awareness have occurred in other areas involving the artistic aspect of Divine Worship: for example, the sanctuary has been restructured, with the president's chair, the ambo and the altar "versus populum". Such changes have not been made in a spirit of disregard for the past, but have been deemed necessary in the pursuit of an end of greater importance, namely the active participation of the faithful. The limitation which such changes impose on certain musical works can be overcome by arranging for their performance outside the context of liturgical celebration in a concert of sacred music.

Organ

7. The performance of purely instrumental pieces on the organ during liturgical celebrations today is limited. In the past the organ took the place of the active participation of the faithful, and reduced the people to the role of "silent and inert spectators" of the celebration (Pius XI, *Divini cultus*, n. 9).

It is legitimate for the organ to accompany and sustain the singing either of the assembly or the choir within the celebration. On the other hand, the organ must never be used to accompany the Prayers or chants of the celebrant nor the readings proclaimed by the reader or the deacon.

In accordance with tradition, the organ should remain silent during penitential seasons (Lent and Holy Week), during Advent and the Liturgy for the Dead. When, however, there is real pastoral need, the organ can be used to support the singing.

It is fitting that the organ be played before and after a celebration as a preparation and conclusion of the celebration.

It is of considerable importance that in all churches, and especially those of some importance, there should be trained musicians and instruments of good quality. Care should be given to the maintenance of organs and respect shown towards their historical character both in form and tone.

III. Practical Directives

8. The regulation of the use of churches is stipulated by canon 1210 of the Code of Canon Law:

"In a sacred place only those things are to be permitted which serve to exercise or promote worship, piety and religion. Anything out of harmony with the holiness of the place is forbidden. The Ordinary may, however, for individual cases, permit other uses, provided they are not contrary to the sacred character of the place".

The principle that the use of the church must not offend the sacredness of the place determines the criteria by which the doors of a church may be opened to a concert of sacred or religious music, as also the concomitant exclusion of every other type of music. The most beautiful symphonic music, for example, is not in itself of religious character. The definition of sacred or religious music depends explicitly on the original intended use of the musical pieces or songs, and likewise on their content. It is not legitimate to provide for the execution in the church of music which is not of religious inspiration and which was composed with a view to performance in a certain precise secular context, irrespective of whether the music would be judged classical or contemporary, of high quality or of a popular nature. On the one hand such performances would not respect the sacred character of the church, and on the other would result in the music being performed in an unfitting context.

It pertains to the ecclesiastical authority to exercise without constraint its governance of sacred places (Cf. canon 1213), and hence to regulate the use of churches in such a way as to safeguard their sacred character.

9. Sacred music, that is to say music which was composed for the liturgy, but which for various reasons can no longer be performed during a liturgical celebration, and religious music, that is to say, music inspired by the text of sacred scripture or the liturgy and which has reference to God, the Blessed Virgin Mary, to the Saints or to the Church may both find a place in the church building, but outside liturgical celebration. The playing of the organ or other musical performance, whether vocal or instrumental, may "serve to promote piety or religion". In particular they may:

a. prepare for the major liturgical Feasts, or lend to these a more festive character beyond the moment of actual celebration;

b. bring out the particular character of the different liturgical seasons;

c. create in churches a setting of beauty conducive to meditation, so as to arouse even in those who are distant from the Church an openess to spiritual values;

d. create a context which favors and makes accessible the proclamation of God's Word, as for example, a sustained reading of the Gospel;

e. keep alive the treasures of Church music which must not be lost; musical pieces and songs composed for the liturgy but which cannot in any way be conveniently incorporated into liturgical celebrations in modern times; spiritual music, such as Oratorios and religious Cantatas which can still serve as vehicles for spiritual communication;

f. assist visitors and tourists to grasp more fully the sacred character of a church, by means of organ concerts at prearranged times.

10. When the proposal is made that there should be a concert in a church, the ordinary is to grant the permission "per modum actus". These concerts should be occasional events. This excludes permission for a series of concerts, for example in the case of a Festival or a cycle of concerts.

When the Ordinary considers it to be necessary, he can, in the conditions foreseen in the Code of Canon Law, can. 1222 para. 2 designate a church that is no longer used for divine service, to be an "auditorium" for the performance of sacred or religious music, and also of music not specifically religious but in keeping with the character of the place.

In this task the bishop should be assisted by the Diocesan Commission for Liturgy and Sacred Music.

In order that the sacred character of a church be conserved in the matter of concerts, the Ordinary can specify that:

a. Requests are to be made in writing, in good time, indicating the date and time of the proposed concert, the programme giving the works and the names of the composers.

b. After having received the authorization of the Ordinary, the rectors and parish priests of the churches should arrange details with the choir and orchestra so that the requisite norms are observed.

c. Entrance to the church must be without payment and open to all.

d. The performers and the audience must be dressed in a manner which is fitting to the sacred character of the place.

e. The musicians and the singers should not be placed in the sanctuary. The greatest respect is to be shown to the altar, the president's chair and the ambo.

f. The Blessed Sacrament should be, as far as possible, reserved in a side chapel or in another safe and suitably adorned place (Cf. C.I.C., can. 938, par. 4).

g. The concert should be presented or introduced not only with historical or technical details, but also in a way that fosters a deeper understanding and an interior participation on the part of the listeners.

h. The organizer of the concert will declare in writing that he accepts legal responsibility for expenses involved, for leaving the church in order and for any possible damage incurred.

11. The above practical directives should be of assistance to the bishops and rectors of churches in their pastoral responsibility to maintain the sacred character of their churches, designed for sacred celebrations, prayer and silence.

Such indications should not be interpreted as a lack of interest in the art of music.

The treasury of sacred music is a witness to the way in which the Christian faith promotes culture.

By underlining the true value of sacred or religious music, Christian musicians and members of "Scholae Cantorum" should feel that they are being encouraged to continue this tradition and to keep it alive for the service of the faith, as expressed by the Second Vatican Council in its message to artists:

"Do not hesitate to put your talent at the service of the divine truth. The world in which we live has need of beauty in order not to lose hope. Beauty, like truth, fills the heart with joy. And this, thanks to your hands" (Cf. Second Vatican Council, Message to Artists, 8 December 1965).

BISHOPS' COMMITTEE ON THE LITURGY
NEWSLETTER
NATIONAL CONFERENCE OF CATHOLIC BISHOPS

1988
VOLUME XXIV
FEBRUARY

Liturgical Renewal and the Papal Visit

The following remarks concerning the liturgical celebrations of the September 1987 Papal Visit to the United States were made by the Most Reverend John L. May, Archbishop of Saint Louis and President of the National Conference of Catholic Bishops/United States Catholic Conference to the plenary assembly of the National Conference of Catholic Bishops on November 16, 1987.

From my perspective, the most wonderful moments [of the papal visit] were the times of prayer, specifically the liturgies he [Pope John Paul II] celebrated throughout the 10 days he was with us. If there is one aspect of post-conciliar American experience where we have grown, it is the liturgical renewal. For 10 days in September, American Catholics joined the Holy Father from Miami to Detroit, in fields in Miami and Monterey, in New Orleans and San Antonio, in the great arenas of Los Angeles, Phoenix, San Francisco and Detroit, in lifting their minds, hearts and voices to the Almighty in that chorus of praise and thanksgiving which is the eucharist. It may be that too much attention was given by commentators to the cost and design of altars and not enough to the faith of those great choirs of faithful who assembled with the successor of Peter to celebrate the eucharist with that simple majesty which is the American liturgical experience. Pope John Paul II saw once again a Church which is alive because of how it prays as Church.

Feast of Our Lady of Guadalupe and New Liturgical Texts

On February 1, 1988 the National Conference of Catholic Bishops received the decree of the Congregation for Divine Worship, dated January 8, 1988, confirming the decision of the National Conference of Catholic Bishops to raise the celebration of Our Lady of Guadalupe (December 12) to the rank of a feast in the proper calendar of the dioceses of the United States of America. The letter also confirmed the new proper Mass texts approved by the NCCB in November 1987. (Proper texts for the Liturgy of the Hours are being prepared for submission to the National Conference of Catholic Bishops later this year.) The following is an unofficial English translation of that decree along with the newly confirmed liturgical texts.

Prot. N. 1341/87

At the request of His Excellency John L. May, Archbishop of St. Louis and President of the National Conference of Catholic Bishops, on November 20, 1987, and in virtue of the faculty granted to this Congregation by the Supreme Pontiff, Pope John Paul II, we concede that the celebration of the Blessed Virgin Mary under the title "Our Lady of Guadalupe" may be incorporated into the proper calendar of the dioceses of the United States of America, with December 12 each year to be denoted with the rank of *feast*.

In addition we approve, that is, confirm the English language text of the Mass of Our Lady of Guadalupe, as it is appears on the attached copy.

In the printed text mention should be made of the confirmation granted by the Apostolic See. Moreover, two copies of the printed text should be sent to this Congregation.

Anything to the contrary notwithstanding.

From the Congregation for Divine Worship, 8 January 1988, during the Marian Year.

+ Paul Augustin Cardinal Mayer, OSB
Prefect

+ Virgil Noè
Titular Archbishop of Voncaria
Secretary

1312 MASSACHUSETTS AVENUE, N.W. • WASHINGTON, D.C. 20005

December 12   **OUR LADY OF GUADALUPE**   **Feast**

Entrance Antiphon

A great sign appeared in the sky, a woman clothed with the sun, with the moon under her feet, and on her head a crown of twelve stars.

(Revelation 12:1)

Opening Prayer

God of power and mercy,
you blessed the Americas at Tepeyac
with the presence of the Virgin Mary of Guadalupe.
May her prayers help all men and women
to accept each other as brothers and sisters.
Through your justice present in our hearts
may your peace reign in the world.

We ask this through our Lord Jesus Christ, your Son,
who lives and reigns with you and the Holy Spirit,
one God, for ever and ever. (Amen.)

Lectionary Readings

Any readings from the *Lectionary for Mass,* nos. 707-712, may be used. Especially appropriate are Zec 2:14-17 (707.11) or Rv 11:19; 12:1-6.10 (708.2) and Lk 1:39-47 (712.4).

Prayer Over the Gifts

Lord,
accept the gifts we present to you
on this feast of Our Lady of Guadalupe,
and grant that this sacrifice
will strengthen us to fulfill your commandments
as true sons and daughters of the Virgin Mary.

We ask this through Christ our Lord. (Amen.)

Preface of the Blessed Virgin Mary I or II (P 56 or P 57)

Communion Antiphon

The Lord has cast down the mighty from their thrones, and has lifted up the lowly.

(Luke 1:52)

or:

God has not acted thus for any other nation; to no other people has he shown his love so clearly.

(See Psalm 147:20)

Prayer After Communion

Lord,
may the Body and Blood of your Son,
which we receive in this sacrament,
reconcile us always in your love.
May we who rejoice in the holy Mother of Guadalupe
live united and at peace in this world
until the day of the Lord dawns in glory.

We ask through Christ our Lord. (Amen.)

Authentic Interpretations of Law Affecting Liturgical Practices

The Pontifical Commission for the Authentic Interpretation of the Code of Canon Law has replied to several *dubia* (doubts) proposed in its plenary meetings during the past three years. At least four of these replies relate to canonical legislation affecting liturgical practices.

In all cases Pope John Paul II was informed of the decisions of the Pontifical Commission during audiences granted to Rosalio Cardinal Castillo Lara and Msgr. Giuliano Harranz, the Commission's President and Secretary, respectively. The dates of the decisions of the Commission along with the dates of the audiences with Pope John Paul II, at which he ordered the publication of these decisions, are noted after the responses of the Pontifical Commission. The comments which follow the decisions are supplied by the NCCB Liturgy Secretariat.

Communion More than Once a Day

Q. Whether, according to Canon 917, a member of the faithful who has already received the Holy Eucharist can on the same day receive it only one more time or as many times as he or she participates in a eucharistic celebration.

R. In the affirmative to the first part; in the negative to the second. (Decision made on 26 June 1984; publication ordered by Pope John Paul II on 11 July 1984.)

Comment: Canon 917 as translated by the Canon Law Society of America, states, "A person who has received the Most Holy Eucharist may receive it again on the same day only during the celebration of the Eucharist in which the person participates, with due regard for the prescription of canon 921, par. 2." The authentic interpretation of the Pontifical Commission makes it clear that at only *one other* celebration at which a person *participates* on a given day may he or she receive Communion. Nevertheless, a person who has already received Communion once (or even twice) on the same day is urged to receive agan in the form of Viaticum if he or she comes to be in danger of death (canon 921, par. 2).

The Ordinary Who Prescribes the Disposition of Offerings from Second Masses

Q. Whether the Ordinary mentioned in canon 951, par. 1, is to be understood as the Ordinary of the place where the Mass is celebrated, or the proper Ordinary of the celebrant.

R. In the negative to the first part; in the affirmative to the second, except in the case of parish priests (pastors) and parochial vicars, for whom the Ordinary is the local Ordinary. (Decision made on 20 February 1987; publication ordered by Pope John Paul II on 23 April 1987.)

Comment: Canon 951, par. 1, states, "A priest who celebrates Mass more than once on the same day may apply the individual Mass for the intention from which the offering is made, but with the law that, except on Christmas, he may retain the offering for only one Mass, giving the other offerings to purposes prescribed by the *ordinary,* except for some recompense by reason of an extrinsic title" (emphasis added). The authentic interpretation of the Pontifical Commission makes it clear that the *ordinary* being referred to is usually one's *proper* ordinary. An exception is provided in the case of a priest who is serving as a pastor or associate pastor. In that case, the ordinary being referred to is the priest's *local ordinary,* that is, the diocesan bishop, his vicar(s) general and episcopal vicars, and those equated in the law to the diocesan bishop, namely, a territorial prelate, territorial abbot, apostolic vicar, apostolic prefect, or apostolic administrator.

Dispensation from the Law regarding the Homilist at Mass

Q. Whether the diocesan bishop can dispense from the norm of canon 767, par. 1, which reserves the homily to a priest or deacon.

R. In the negative. (Decision made on 26 May 1987; publication ordered by Pope John Paul II on 20 June 1987.)

Comment: Canon 767, par. 1, states, "Among the forms of preaching the homily is preeminent; it is a part of the liturgy itself and is reserved to a priest or to a deacon; in the homily the mysteries of faith and the norms of Christian living are to be expounded from the sacred text throughout the course of the liturgical year." The authentic interpretation of the Pontifical Commission states that the diocesan bishop is unable to dispense from the requirement that the homily in the liturgy be reserved to a priest or deacon.

The Role of Special Ministers of the Eucharist

Q. Whether the special minister of Holy Communion deputed according to canon 910, par. 2, and 230, par. 3, is able to exercise his or her suppletory ministry even when there are present in the church ordinary ministers, even if they are not participating in the eucharistic celebration, and provided that these ordinary ministers are in no way impeded.

R. Negative. (Decision made on 20 February 1987, with publication by the Congregation for Sacraments ordered by Pope John Paul II on 15 June 1987.)

Comment: This reply indicates that when ordinary ministers (bishops, priests, deacons) are present during a eucharistic celebration, whether they are participating in it or not, and are not prevented from doing so, they are to assist in the distribution of Communion. Accordingly, if the ordinary ministers are in sufficient number, special ministers of the Eucharist are not allowed to distribute Communion at that eucharistic celebration.

Causes which might prevent an ordinary minister from assisting with Communion would include infirmity or physical disability, and participation in some other ministry while the Eucharist is being celebrated.

Funerals on Holy Thursday and during the Paschal Triduum

From time to time the Secretariat of the Bishops' Committee on the Liturgy receives requests for a clarification and/or a change of discipline regarding the celebration of funeral Masses on Holy Thursday and during the Paschal Triduum. This matter is treated in no. 336 of the *General Instruction of the Roman Missal* (1975 edition): "The funeral Mass has first place among the Masses for the dead and may be celebrated on any day except solemnities that are days of obligation, Holy Thursday, the Easter Triduum, and the Sundays of Advent, Lent and the Easter season."

In 1974 *Notitiae,* the publication of the Congregation for Divine Worship, included the following response to the question whether a funeral Mass can be celebrated on Holy Thursday morning and during the Easter Triduum. "Reply: No. The directives of the Roman Missal apply. On Holy Thursday morning as a rule the chrism Mass is celebrated. In addition to the evening Mass of the Lord's Supper 'the local Ordinary may permit another Mass to be celebrated in churches and public or semipublic oratories in the evening or, in the case of genuine necessity, even in the morning, but exclusively for those who cannot in any way take part in the evening Mass' (*Sacramentary,* p. 135). Other eucharistic celebrations on Holy Thursday are entirely forbidden. On Good Friday 'according to the Church's ancient tradition, the sacraments are not celebrated' (*Sacramentary,* p. 140). 'On Holy Saturday the Church waits at the Lord's tomb, . . . and the sacrifice of the Mass is not celebrated' (*Sacramentary,* p. 167). In the case of Easter Sunday, the *General Instruction of the Roman Missal,* no. 336 (quoted above) forbids a funeral Mass, since this is a solemnity that is of obligation."

This is not a new law which has appeared subsequent to the liturgical reforms of the Second Vatican Council. The Church's tradition which underlies this practice is long-standing and of great force. Many Catholics, however, are not aware of this legislation until they happen to have a loved one die during Holy Week. In such situations the Church's legislation might appear to some as depriving them of the Church's full ministry to the bereaved. It is important, therefore, to explain to the family the reasons why a funeral Mass cannot be celebrated and that in the funeral liturgy only the liturgy of the eucharist will be omitted. Further, arrangements should be made for the celebration of the Eucharist for the deceased at the earliest date permitted by the liturgical calendar. The funeral Mass texts may be used for this celebration.

A funeral celebrated on Holy Thursday morning or during the Easter Triduum takes the following form: rites at the door of the church, procession, opening prayer, liturgy of the word (as at a funeral Mass), homily, general intercessions, Lord's Prayer, final commendation (as at a funeral Mass), procession from the church (see *Order of Christian Funerals,* Funeral Liturgy Outside Mass, nos. 183-203).

BISHOPS' COMMITTEE ON THE LITURGY
NEWSLETTER

NATIONAL CONFERENCE OF CATHOLIC BISHOPS

**1988
VOLUME XXIV
MARCH**

Rite of Christian Initiation of Adults: Confirmation, Publication, Implementation

On March 7, 1988 the National Conference of Catholic Bishops received the decree of the Congregation for Divine Worship, dated February 19, 1988, confirming the November 1986 decision of the NCCB to approve the final ("white book") translation of the *Rite of Christian Initiation of Adults* (*RCIA*) for use in the dioceses of the United States of America. The translation was produced by the International Commission on English in the Liturgy (ICEL) on behalf of its member and associate member conferences of bishops.

Likewise, the Congregation confirmed the decisions of the NCCB regarding various ritual elements of the *RCIA* which conferences of bishops have the competency to determine by reason of no. 33 (Latin edition, no. 65) of the rite. The Congregation also confirmed several newly-composed individual texts, six (6) complete rites to be incorporated at specified places into the ritual book: an optional parish rite of sending catechumens to the bishop for the celebration of the Rite of Election, an optional Rite of Election of Children of Catechetical Age, and four (4) optional rites which may be celebrated with baptized but previously uncatechized adults who are preparing for confirmation and/or the eucharist or for reception into the full communion of the Catholic Church.

Finally, the Congregation granted conditional confirmation of three (3) new chapters ("combined rites" for celebrations with catechumens and already baptized candidates for the sacraments and/or reception) and requested that they appear in an Appendix after Parts I and II. Accordingly, preparation for publication of the edition of the *Rite of Christian Initiation of Adults* as it was approved by the National Conference of Catholic Bishops and confirmed by the Congregation for Divine Worship for use in the Dioceses of the United States of America has now commenced.

After consultation with the publishers of liturgical books and the Chairman of the Bishops' Committee on the Liturgy, July 1, 1988 has been established as the new publication release date, while September 1, 1988 has been chosen as the new mandatory effective date of implementation of the *Rite of Christian Initiation of Adults* in the dioceses of the United States of America. However, it should be noted that the ritual may be implemented before September 1st, immediately upon publication.

The following is an unofficial English translation of the decree of the Congregation for Divine Worship.

Congregation for Divine Worship

Prot. N. 1192/86

At the request of His Excellency John L. May, Archbishop of St. Louis and President of the National Conference of Catholic Bishops, on November 21, 1986, and in virtue of the faculty granted to this Congregation by the Supreme Pontiff, Pope John Paul II, we gladly approve, that is, confirm the English translation of the *Rite of Christian Initiation of Adults,* prepared by the mixed commission for English-speaking countries, as it appears in the appended copy.

In the publication of this text mention should be made of the confirmation granted by the Apostolic See. Two copies of the printed text should be sent to this Congregation.

Anything to the contrary notwithstanding.

1312 MASSACHUSETTS AVENUE, N.W. ● WASHINGTON, D.C. 20005

From the Congregation for Divine Worship, 19 February 1988.

+ Paul Augustin Cardinal Mayer, OSB
Prefect

+ Virgilio Noè
Titular Archbishop of Voncaria
Secretary

Circular Letter Concerning the Preparation and Celebration of the Easter Feasts

A circular letter issued by the Congregation for Divine Worship, Prot. N. 120/88, dated January 16, 1988, with the title *Paschalis sollemnitatis,*" On the Preparation and Celebration of the Easter Feasts," was sent to the presidents of conferences of bishops throughout the world. A copy of the letter has been sent to each bishop and diocesan liturgical commission/liturgical office. The English text of the circular letter will be published by the Publishing Services of the United States Catholic Conference at a later date.

The letter treats the seasons of Lent and Easter and gives special emphasis to Holy Week and the Easter Triduum. While affirming that in many parts of the world the rites of the Easter Triduum are properly celebrated and the faithful participate in them with "great spiritual gain," the Congregation for Divine Worship indicates some of the problems that have arisen in certain areas regarding the celebration of the Triduum. "The very concept of the Vigil has almost come to be forgotten in some places with the result that it is celebrated as if it were an evening Mass, in the same way and at the same time as the Mass celebrated on Saturday evening in anticipation of the Sunday" (no. 3). [See *Newsletter,* February 1986, p. 8 and February 1987, p. 5 for a discussion of the time of the Easter Vigil.] The letter goes on to state: "Without any doubt one of the principal reasons for this state of affairs is the inadequate formation given to the clergy and the faithful regarding the paschal mystery as the center of the liturgical year and of Christian life" (no. 3). "With these points in mind, the Congregation for Divine Worship, after due consideration, thinks that it is a fitting moment to recall certain elements, doctrinal and pastoral, and various norms which have already been published concerning Holy Week" (no. 5). "It is the aim of this document that the great mystery of our Redemption be celebrated in the best possible way so that the faithful may participate in it with ever greater spiritual advantage" (see no. 5).

The letter is divided into the following sections: I. Lenten Season: The Rite of Christian Initiation; Celebrations during the Lenten Season; Particular details concerning the days of Lent; II. Holy Week: Passion (Palm) Sunday; Chrism Mass; Penitential Celebrations in Lent; III. The Easter Triduum in General; IV. Holy Thursday Evening Mass of the Lord's Supper; V. Good Friday; VI. Holy Saturday; VII. Easter Sunday of the Lord's Resurrection: The Easter Vigil: Meaning of the nocturnal character of the Vigil, Structure of the Vigil and significance of its elements and parts, Pastoral Considerations; Easter Day; VIII. Easter Time.

For the most part the circular letter repeats the instructions of the various liturgical documents and books which touch on the celebration of Lent, Holy Week, the Easter Triduum and Easter (see no. 5). The letter serves as a reminder of the structure and content of the celebrations. Those responsible for the planning and celebration of the Easter mysteries should review the texts of the various rites with a copy of the circular letter in hand.

International Commission on English in the Liturgy

The International Commission on English in the Liturgy (ICEL) recently reported on its activities in its *Newsletter* Vol. 14 (July-December 1987), No. 2. ICEL is now engaged in the major project of revising the English translation of the *Roman Missal* (*Sacramentary*). Work is progressing on the revision of the 1324 presidential prayers contained in the Missal. Nearly all of the formularies for the Sundays and weekdays of the Proper of Seasons have been revised or are in an advanced draft stage. During this year work will begin on the Sanctoral, Commons, Ritual Masses, and Prayers for Various Needs and Occasions. In addition, fifty examples of newly composed alternative opening prayers related to the *Lectionary for Mass* have been examined by the ICEL Advisory Committee. It is hoped that approximately three hundred original texts will be prepared for the revised Missal. A more detailed progress report on the revision of the *Roman Missal* has been prepared by ICEL which carefully explains and gives examples of how the prayers of the Missal are being revised. This report will be sent to all bishops and liturgical commissions/liturgy offices in the United States.

ICEL has recently published the provisional ("green book") translation of the Roman *Book of Blessings.* The book contains 41 chapters (511 pages) plus a selection of Latin texts for comparison with the English translation (28 pages). Copies were sent to the member and associate member conferences of bishops of ICEL. [In the United States copies have been sent to bishops and liturgical commissions/liturgy offices. The Bishops' Committee on the Liturgy will ask the Administrative Committee of the National Conference of Catholic Bishops to approve the text *ad interim.* If approved by the Administrative Committee, the *Book of Blessings* must also be confirmed by the Congregation for Divine Worship.]

Work is near completion on the English translation of the *Ceremonial of Bishops,* and the English version should be available near the end of the year.

The *ICEL Newsletter* also contains the latest revision of the English translation of the *Eucharistic Prayer of Hippolytus* along with an extensive commentary on the changes that have been made and the reasons for these changes. The English translation of this ancient anaphora was first published in 1983 and the present revision was made on the basis of the comments received during the period of consultation with episcopal conferences, liturgical commissions and other experts.

Days of Remembrance of the Victims of the Holocaust

The Congress of the United States has declared April 10-17, 1988 as National Days of Remembrance of Victims of the Holocaust (*Shoah*). This period corresponds to the Jewish observance of *Yom Hashoah* on April 14. Catholics should recall the victims of the Holocaust and pray for them and their families in the general intercessions during this week. The spirit of such prayer is well expressed in a letter of Pope John Paul II, dated August 8, 1987, to Archbishop May, president of the National Conference of Catholic Bishops:

> With our hearts filled with unyielding hope, we Christians approach with immense respect the terrifying experience of the extermination, the *Shoah*, suffered by the Jews during the Second World War, and we seek to grasp its most authentic, specific and universal meaning. Before the vivid memory of the extermination . . . it is not possible for anyone to pass by with indifference.

> Reflection upon the *Shoah* shows us to what terrible consequences the lack of faith in God and a contempt for humanity created in his image can lead. There is no doubt that the sufferings endured by the Jews . . . are today a warning, a witness and a silent cry before all peoples and all nations . . . and also for the Catholic Church a motive of sincere sorrow, especially when one thinks of the indifference and sometimes resentment which, in particular historical circumstances, have divided Jews and Christians.

Sample Intercessions

For the victims of the Holocaust, their families, and all our Jewish brothers and sisters, that the violence and hatred they experienced may never again be repeated, we pray to the Lord.

For the Church, that the Holocaust may be a reminder to us that we can never be indifferent to the sufferings of others, we pray to the Lord.

For our Jewish brothers and sisters, that their confidence in the face of long-suffering may spur us on to a greater faith and trust in God, we pray to the Lord.

Abbreviated Versions of Morning and Evening Prayer

Two publishers have recently produced abbreviated versions of Morning and Evening Prayer from the Liturgy of the Hours. Collins Liturgical Publications has published *A Shorter Morning and Evening Prayer*, and The Catholic Book Publishing Company has published *A Shorter Christian Prayer*. In addition to Morning and Evening Prayer from the four week cycle of the Psalter, both books contain Night Prayer, excerpts from the Proper of Seasons, propers for solemnities and feasts of the Lord, the Office for the Dead, and the Common of the Blessed Virgin for use on feasts of Mary and Saturdays.

These editions are approved for use in the United States and contain the approved texts. They are suitable for use by those not bound to the complete office or for those who are traveling. The books, which are printed on bible paper, easily fit into a pocket or purse.

A Shorter Morning and Evening Prayer is published by Collins Liturgical Publications, San Francisco, CA, and costs $8.95. *A Shorter Christian Prayer* is published by The Catholic Book Publishing Co., New York, NY, and costs $6.95.

Collection of Masses of the Blessed Virgin Mary

Twelve Masses from the *Collection of Masses of the Blessed Virgin Mary* have been published by The Catholic Book Publishing Company, New York, NY. The book is similar in appearance to the Sacramentary of the same publisher and is bound with a blue hard cover. The Collection is divided into two volumes bound as one: Volume 1 contains the Mass formularies and Volume 2 contains the Lectionary texts. When the complete *Collection of Masses* is published, the two volumes will be bound separately. [For additional information on the *Collection*, see *Newsletter*, April 1987, page 13 and December 1987, pages 45-46.]

Collection of Masses of the Blessed Virgin Mary, is published by The Catholic Book Publishing Company, New York, NY, and costs $14.95.

In Spirit and Truth

In Spirit and Truth: Black Catholic Reflections on the Order of Mass is a document that was prepared by the Black Liturgy Subcommittee of the Bishops' Committee on the Liturgy. *In Spirit and Truth* is part of a two-fold project of the Black Liturgy Subcommittee on the theology, nature, and manner of celebration of the liturgy in Black or predominantly Black parishes. *In Spirit and Truth* is a reflection on the *Order of Mass* and the options it contains, done by Black Catholics for Black Catholics. Special attention is given to the liturgical practices of Black Catholic churches in relation to the *Order of Mass*. Although written for Black communities, this document will be of assistance to any parish wishing to reflect on the options contained in the eucharistic liturgy.

In Spirit and Truth: Black Catholic Reflections on the Order of Mass is published by USCC Publications Services: Pub. No. 198-9, $3.95 a single copy (usual discounts available).

Thirty Years of Liturgical Renewal

Thirty Years of Liturgical Renewal: Statements of the Bishops' Committee on the Liturgy is a collection of statements produced by the Bishops' Committee on the Liturgy from the years 1957 through 1985. The book was edited by Rev. Msgr. Frederick R. McManus, who served as the first Director of the Secretariat of the Bishops' Committee on the Liturgy from 1965-1975 and and is a permanent Staff Consultant to the Liturgy Secretariat. Msgr. McManus introduces each of the thirty-seven statements and gives the background and purpose of each statement. This book serves as a fine overview of liturgical renewal in the United States of America and should be read by any serious student of the liturgical reform.

Thirty Years of Liturgical Renewal: Statements of the Bishops' Committee on the Liturgy, (279 pp.), ed. by Frederick R. McManus, is available from USCC Publishing Services: Pub. No. 154-7, $16.96 a single copy (usual discounts apply).

BISHOPS' COMMITTEE ON THE LITURGY
NEWSLETTER
NATIONAL CONFERENCE OF CATHOLIC BISHOPS

**1988
VOLUME XXIV
APRIL**

Saint Lawrence Ruiz and companions, martyrs (September 28)

The Congregation for Divine Worship, in a decree (Prot. 1215/87) dated March 22, 1988, has informed the Chairman of the Bishops' Committee on the Liturgy that Pope John Paul II has approved the inclusion of Saint Lawrence Ruiz and companions, martyrs, in the Roman Calendar as an optional memorial. Saint Lawrence and his companions suffered martyrdom in Nagasaki, Japan in the seventeenth century. The new memorial is placed in the calendar after Wenceslaus, martyr, which occurs on the same day.
The following is a unofficial translation of the decree:

Prot. 1215/87

DECREE

During the 17th century in the city of Nagasaki in Japan sixteen martyrs of Christ shed their blood out of love for him. This was a group of martyrs, including both Europeans and Asians, who, in various times and circumstances, spread the Christian faith in the Philippine Islands, Formosa, and Japan, thus wonderfully showing the universality of the Christian religion. Through the example of their lives and their deaths these dauntless missionaries also sowed the seed for the future of the Church.

The list of these martyrs is as follows: Dominic Ibañez de Erquicia, presbyter; James Kyushei Gorobioye Tomonaga, presbyter; Luke Alonso, presbyter; Hyacinth Ansalone, presbyter; Thomas Hioji Rokuzayemon Nishi, presbyter; Anthony Gonzalez, presbyter; William Courtet, presbyter; Michael de Aozaraza, presbyter; Vincent Schiwozuka, presbyter; Francis Shoyemon, religious; Matthew Kohioye, religious; Madeline of Nagasaki, virgin; Marina of Omura, virgin; Lawrence Ruiz, husband and father; Michael Kurobioye, layman; Lazarus of Kyoto, layman.

During his pastoral visit to the peoples of the Far East, Pope John Paul II, on 18 February 1981 at a Mass in Luneta Park, Manila beatified the holy martyrs Lawrence Ruiz and companions. On Sunday 18 October 1987 at a Mass in St. Peter's square he entered the names of these same martyrs into the catalog of saints.

In a letter of 21 October 1987 the Philippine conference of bishops requested that the celebration of the martyrs Lawrence Ruiz and companions be entered in the General Roman Calendar. Accordingly, by decision of Pope John Paul II this celebration is entered in the General Roman Calendar on 28 September with the rank of optional memorial.

Therefore this new memorial shall be included in all ordos for the celebration of Mass and the liturgy of the hours, and in future liturgical books to be published under the care of the conferences of bishops.

All things to the contrary notwithstanding.

Office of the Congregation for Divine Worship, 22 March 1988.

Paul Augustin Cardinal Mayer, OSB
Prefect

+ Virgilio Noè
Secretary

1312 MASSACHUSETTS AVENUE, N.W. ● WASHINGTON, D.C. 20005

Declaration on Eucharistic Prayers and Liturgical Experimentation

On March 21, 1988, the Congregation for Divine Worship issued a Declaration on Eucharistic Prayers and Liturgical Experimentation (Declaratio circa Preces eucharisticas et experimenta liturgica). The Declaration reaffirms the directives of the 1973 Circular Letter Eucharistiae participationem and of the 1970 Instruction Liturgicae instaurationes. The following is an unofficial translation of the Declaration:

Prot. 430/88

DECLARATION ON EUCHARISTIC PRAYERS AND LITURGICAL EXPERIMENTATION

In view of certain initiatives taking place in the celebration of the liturgy, the Congregation for Divine Worship deems it necessary to repeat some already-established norms that are still in force regarding eucharistic prayers and liturgical experiments. The issue involves matters about which it is necessary "to ensure that the entire Body of the Church may be able to move ahead single-mindedly and with the unity of charity . . . because the link between liturgy and faith is so close that service to the one redounds to the other."[1]

I. As to the use of eucharistic prayers, the Congregation considers it necessary to issue the following reminders, taken chiefly from the Circular Letter *Eucharistiae participationem.*

1. In addition to the four Eucharistic Prayers contained in the Roman Missal, the Congregation for Divine Worship has, in the course of time, approved other eucharistic prayers, either for universal use—the Eucharistic Prayers for Masses of Reconciliation, or for use by certain nations or regions—the Eucharistic Prayers for Masses with Children; other eucharistic prayers have, in special circumstances, been granted upon petition by the conference of bishops. The Congregation has also approved prefaces besides those contained in the Roman Missal.

2. The use of these eucharistic prayers and prefaces is restricted to those to whom they have been granted and within the time or the place specified in the concession. "It is unlawful to use any other eucharistic prayer that is composed without leave of the Apostolic See or that does not have its approval."[2]

3. "Moved by a pastoral love for unity, the Apostolic See reserves to itself the right to regulate a matter so important as the discipline of the eucharistic prayers. The Apostolic See will not refuse to consider lawful needs within the Roman Rite and will accord every consideration to the petitions submitted by the conferences of bishops for the possible composition in special circumstances of a new eucharistic prayer and its introduction into the liturgy. The Apostolic See will set forth the norms to be observed in each case."[3]

II. As to liturgical experiments, the Congregation for Divine Worship in the Instruction *Liturgicae instaurationes* has declared the following points, which remain in force.

1. "Any liturgical experimentation that may seem necessary or advantageous receives authorization from this Congregation alone, in writing, with norms clearly set out, and subject to the responsibility of the competent local authority."[4]

2. "All earlier permissions for experimentation with the Mass, granted in view of the liturgical reform as it was in progress, are to be considered no longer in effect. Since publication of the *Missale Romanum* the norms and forms of eucharistic celebration are those given in the General Instruction and the Order of Mass."[5]

3. "The conferences of bishops are to draw up in detail any adaptations envisioned in the liturgical books and submit them for confirmation to the Apostolic See."[6]

4. When, in keeping with the provisions of the Constitution *Sacrosanctum Concilium,* no. 40, changes in the structure of rites or in the order of parts set forth in the liturgical books are involved, or any departure from the usual, or the introduction of new texts, a point-by point outline is to be submitted to the Apostolic See by the conference of bishops prior to the beginning of any kind of experiment. While awaiting the response of the Apostolic See, no one, not even a priest, may put the petitioned adaptations into use or on his own add, remove, or change anything in the liturgy.[7]

5. "Such a procedure is called for and demanded by both the Constitution *Sacrosanctum Concilium* and the importance of the issue."[8] The Congregation for Divine Worship is going to publish

guidelines on the adaptations to the culture and traditions of peoples that are provided for in the Constitution *Sacrosanctum Concilium,* nos. 37-40.

* * * *

"The conferences of bishops and the bishops individually are urgently requested that by using compelling reasons they lead priests to respect the one practice of the Roman Church: this course will be a service to the good of the Church itself and to the correct carrying out of the liturgical celebration."[9] It is the responsibility of bishops to oversee, promote, and safeguard liturgical life, and to correct abuses; it is also their responsibility to explain to their people the theological basis for the discipline of the sacraments and of the entire liturgy.[10]

Office of the Congregation for Divine Worship, 21 March 1988.

Paul Augustin Cardinal Mayer, OSB
Prefect

+ Virgilio Noe
Titular Archbishop of Voncaria
Secretary

Notes

1. SC Divine Worship, Instruction (Third) *Liturgicae instaurationes,* On the orderly carrying out of the Constitution on the Liturgy, 5 September 1970: AAS 62 (1970), 694; Eng. tr. DOL 52, no. 511.

2. SC Divine Worshiop, Circular Letter *Eucharistiae participationem,* 27 April 1973, no. 6: AAS (1973), 342; Eng. tr., DOL 248, no. 1980.

3. *Ibid.*

4. SC Divine Worship, Instruction (Third) *Liturgicae instaurationes,* On the orderly carrying out of the Constitution on the Liturgy, 5 September 1970: AAS 62 (1970), 703; Eng. tr. DOL 52, no. 530.

5. *Ibid.*

6. *Ibid.*

7. SC Divine Worship, Instruction (Third) *Liturgicae instaurationes,* On the orderly carrying out of the Constitution on the Liturgy, 5 September 1970, no. 12: AAS 62 (1970), 703; Eng. tr. DOL 52, no. 530. Vatican Council II, Constitution on the Liturgy *Sacrosanctum Concilium,* no. 22, 3: Eng. tr., DOL 1, no. 22.

8. SC Divine Worship, Instruction (Third) *Liturgicae instaurationes,* On the orderly carrying out of the Constitution on the Liturgy, 5 September 1970, no. 12: AAS 62 (1970), 703; Eng. tr. DOL 52, no. 530.

9. SC Divine Worship, Circular Letter *Eucharistiae participationem,* 27 April 1973, no. 6: AAS (1973), 342; Eng. tr., DOL 248, no. 1980.

10. See Vatican Council II, Decree on the Pastoral Office of Bishops *Christus Dominus,* no. 15: DOL 7, no. 194. See also the Extraordinary Synod of Bishops, 1985, Final Report.

In Memoriam: Archbishop Guilford Young, 1916-1988

The Most Reverend Guilford C. Young, Archbishop of Hobart, Australia, one of the founding bishops of the International Commission on English in the Liturgy, died on March 16 following emergency cardiac surgery. Archbishop Young was born in Sandgate, Brisbane (Queensland, Australia), on November 10, 1916. He studied for the priesthood at the Propaganda Fidei College in Rome and was ordained in 1938. While in the seminary he became interested in the European liturgical movement and began to read widely on liturgical topics. He served in the Apostolic Delegation in Sydney and later taught theology in the major seminary at Brisbane. At the age of 31 he was ordained to the episcopacy. His first appointment was as the auxiliary bishop of Canberra-Goulburn. In 1955 he became the Archbishop of Hobart (Tasmania) after having briefly served as the coadjutor Archbishop of that diocese. He was a strong champion of liturgical reform and renewal and served as a member of the Consilium for the Implementation of the Constitution on the Sacred Liturgy. Archbishop Young was knighted by Queen Elizabeth II in 1978. During the first session of the Second Vatican Council, Archbishop Young participated in the early conversations among English-speaking bishops, including Archbishop Paul Hallinan, the first Chairman of the Bishops' Committee on the Liturgy, about the possibility of common English liturgical texts. He liked to recall that ICEL was really born during the second session of the Council when he, Archbishop Francis Grimshaw, and Archbishop Denis Hurley met at St. Josaphat's altar in Saint Peter's. This meeting took place on

October 11, 1963 and six days later the first meeting of what was later to be called the International Committee on English in the Liturgy was held. Monsignor Frederick McManus and Father Godfrey Diekmann, OSB attended this meeting. Archbishop Young served on the Episcopal Board of ICEL from 1963 until 1976. His memory is held dear by many American bishops and liturgists who knew him well.

> O God,
> from the ranks of your priests
> you chose your servant Guilford
> to fulfill the office of bishop.
>
> Grant that he may share
> in the eternal fellowship of those priests
> who, faithful to the teachings of the apostles,
> dwell in your heavenly kingdom.
>
> We ask this through Christ our Lord.
> Amen.

Meeting of the Bishops' Committee on the Liturgy, March 21, 1988

The Bishops' Committee on the Liturgy met in Washington, DC, on March 21, 1988. The Committee reviewed the plans and programs for the present year in preparation for its examination of the proposed plans and programs for 1989. Most of the programs of 1988 will be carried over into 1989. Work will continue on the preparation of the *Hispanic-American Sacramentary.*

In addition to the ongoing work of the Secretariat—which includes the publication of the *Newsletter,* the preparation of liturgical books for publication, and the review of participation aids and materials—work will begin or continue on the following projects: Sunday Worship in the Absence a Priest—preparation and publication of guidelines and a ritual; *Guidelines on Presiding in the Liturgy; Pastoral Companion to the Rite of Christian Initiation of Adults*—preparation, publication, and implementation; *Guidelines on Posture and Gesture at Mass and Other Liturgical Celebrations;* National Workshop on the *Ceremonial of Bishops* for diocesan masters of ceremonies, bishops, cathedral personnel, et al.; participation in liturgical-ecumenical consultations, such as the North American Consultation on Common Texts (CCT), the English Language Liturgical Consultation (ELLC), North American Academy of Liturgy, Consultation on Church Union Worship Commission, the Worship Commission of the National Council of the Churches of Christ.

The Secretariat will also be involved in the publication and/or implementation of the following in 1989: *Rite of Christian Initiation of Adults; Order of Christian Funerals; Book of Blessings; Catholic Household Blessings and Prayers; Collection of Masses of the Blessed Virgin Mary; Lectionary for Children; Ceremonial of Bishops; Enchiridion (Handbook) of Indulgences; Roman Missal,* revised edition; *Hispanic-American Sacramentary;* the Spanish translation of the new American blessings; *Solemn Exposition of the Eucharist; Study Texts:* No. 13: *Blessings in the Life of the Church* and No. 14: *Holy Week and the Easter Triduum.*

The Liturgy Committee approved the proposed plans and programs for 1989, which also must be approved by the plenary assembly of the National Conference of Catholic Bishops.

The Committee examined latest draft of *God's Mercy Endures For Ever: Guidelines on the Presentation of Jews and Judaism in Catholic Preaching* and a first draft of the proper office for the feast of Our Lady of Guadalupe.

Work continues on the second edition of the *Lectionary for Mass* which will use the revised New Testament of the *New American Bible* (NAB). The texts are being reviewed by the editorial board of the NAB and the Lectionary Subcommittee.

The Liturgy Committee reviewed *Guidelines on Lay Preaching* and the section on the liturgical preparation and celebration of marriage in the proposed *Marriage Handbook.* Both these documents are being prepared by the Committee on Pastoral Research and Practices.

Bishop Sheehan reported on the work of the Task Group on Sunday Worship in the Absence of a Priest. A summary of the survey conducted by the Task Group has been sent to all the bishops. Work is continuing on a statement and rite that is to be issued when the proposed Roman directory on this subject is published.

The next meeting of the members and advisors of the Bishops' Committee on the Liturgy will take place in Dallas, Texas on June 7-9, 1988.

BISHOPS' COMMITTEE ON THE LITURGY

NEWSLETTER

NATIONAL CONFERENCE OF CATHOLIC BISHOPS

1988
VOLUME XXIV
MAY-JUNE

John Paul II: Address to U.S. Bishops on the Call to Prayer

On Friday, June 10, Pope John Paul II received in audience the bishops from the ecclesiastical provinces of Baltimore, Washington, Atlanta, and Miami who were making their "ad limina Apostolorum" visits to the Holy See. In the course of the audience the Holy Father spoke of the Church's call to prayer and the relationship of prayer to Christian service. Following are excerpts from the address.

We have all meditated on the words of Jesus: "Pray constantly for the strength . . . to stand secure before the Son of Man" (Lk 21:36). And today we accept once again the call to prayer as it comes to each of us and to the whole Church from Christ himself. The call to prayer places all the Church's activity in perspective. In 1976, in addressing the Call to Action meeting in Detroit, Paul VI stated that "in the tradition of the Church any call to action is first of all a call of prayer." These words are indeed more relevant today than ever before. They are a challenge to the Church in the United States and throughout the world.

The universal Church of Christ, and therefore each particular Church, exists in order to pray. In prayer the human person expresses his or her nature; the community expresses its vocation; the Church reaches out to God. In prayer the Church attains fellowship with the Father and with his Son, Jesus Christ (cf. 1 Jn 1:3). In prayer the Church expresses her Trinitarian life because she directs herself to the Father, undergoes the action of the Holy Spirit, and lives fully her relationship with Christ. Indeed she experiences herself as the body of Christ, as the mystical Christ.

The Church meets Christ in prayer at the core of her being. It is in this way that she finds the complete relevance of his teaching and takes on his mentality. By fostering an interpersonal relationship with Christ, the Church actuates to the full the personal dignity of her members. In prayer the Church concentrates on Christ; she possesses him, savors his friendship, and is therefore in a position to communicate him. Without prayer all this would be lacking and she would have nothing to offer to the world. But by exercising faith, hope, and charity in prayer, her power to communicate Christ is reinforced.

Prayer is the goal of all catechesis in the Church, because it is a means of union with God. Through prayer the Church expresses the supremacy of God and fulfills the first and greatest commandment of love.

Everything human is profoundly affected by prayer. Human work is revolutionized by prayer, uplifted to its highest level. Prayer is the source of the full humanization of work. In prayer the value of work is understood, for we grasp the fact that we are truly collaborators of God in the transformation and elevation of the world. Prayer is the consecration of this collaboration. At the same time it is the means through which we face the problems of life and in which all pastoral endeavors are conceived and nurtured.

The call to prayer must precede the call to action, but the call to action must truly accompany the call to prayer. The Church finds in prayer the root of all her social action—the power to motivate it and the power to sustain it. In prayer we discover the needs of our brothers and sisters and make them our own, because in prayer we discover that their needs are the needs of Christ. All social consciousness is nurtured and evaluated in prayer. In the words of Jesus, justice and mercy are among "the weightier matters of the law" (Mt 23:23). The Church's struggle for justice and her pursuit of mercy will succeed only if the Holy Spirit gives her the gift of perseverance in attaining them. This gift must be sought in prayer . . .

In the life of the Church today we frequently perceive that the gift of prayer is linked to the word of God. A renewal in discovering the sacred Scriptures has brought forth the fruits of prayer. God's word, embraced and meditated on, has the power to bring human hearts into ever greater communion with the most Holy Trinity. Over and over again this has taken place in the Church in our day. The benefits received through

1312 MASSACHUSETTS AVENUE, N.W. ● WASHINGTON, D.C. 20005

prayer linked to the word of God call forth in all of us a further response of prayer—the prayer of praise and thanksgiving.

The Word of God generates prayer in the whole community. At the same time it is in prayer that the Word of God is understood, applied, and lived. For all of us who are ministers of the Gospel, with the pastoral responsibility of announcing the message in season and out of season and of scrutinizing the reality of daily life in the light of God's holy word, prayer is the context in which we prepare the proclamation of faith. All evangelization is prepared in prayer; in prayer it is first applied to ourselves; in prayer it is then offered to the world.

Each local Church is true to itself to the extent that it is a praying community with all the consequent dynamism that prayer stirs up within it. The universal Church is never more herself than when she faithfully reflects the image of the praying Christ: the Son who in prayer directs his whole being to his Father and consecrates himself for the sake of his brethren "that they may be consecrated in truth" (Jn 17:19).

For this reason, dear brothers in the episcopate, I wish to encourage you in all your efforts to teach people to pray. It is part of the apostolic Church to transmit the teaching of Jesus to each generation, to offer faithfully to each local Church the response of Jesus to the request: "Teach us to pray" (Lk 11:1). I assure you of my solidarity and of the solidarity of the whole Church in your efforts to preach the importance of daily prayer and to give the example of prayer. From the words of Jesus we know that where two or three are gathered in his name, there he is in their midst (cf. Mt 18:20). And we know that in every local Church gathered in prayer around a bishop there dwells the incomparable beauty of the whole Catholic Church as the faithful image of the praying Christ . . .

Prayer reaches a level of special dignity and efficacy for the community in the sacred liturgy of the Church and particularly in eucharistic worship, which is the source and summit of Christian living. In this regard the eucharistic celebration of the Sunday is of immense importance for your local Churches and for their vitality.

Five years ago, in speaking at some length about this matter, I mentioned that "throughout the United States there has been a superb history of eucharistic participation by the people, and for this we must all thank God" ("Ad limina" address of July 9, 1983). The time is ripe to renew gratitude to God for this great gift and to reinforce this splendid tradition of American Catholics. On that occasion I also mentioned: "All the striving of the laity to consecrate the secular field of activity to God finds inspiration and magnificent confirmation in the eucharistic sacrifice. Participating in the Eucharist is only a small portion of the laity's week, but the total effectiveness of their lives and all Christian renewal depends on it: the primary and indispensable source of the true Christian spirit!" (*ibid.*).

In their Sunday eucharistic assembly the Father repeatedly glorifies the resurrection of his Son Jesus Christ by accepting his sacrifice offered for the whole Church. He confirms the paschal character of the Church. The hour of Sunday eucharistic worship is a powerful expression of the Christocentric nature of the community, which Christ offers to his Father as a gift. And as he offers his Church to his Father, Christ himself convokes his Church for her mission: her mission, above all of love and praise, to be able to say: "By your gift I will utter praise in the vast assembly" (Ps 22:26).

At the same time that the Church is summoned to praise, she is summoned to service in fraternal charity and in justice, mercy and peace. In the very act of convoking his Church to service, Christ consecrates this service, renders it fruitful and offers it in the spirit to his Father. This service to which the Church is called is the service of evangelization and human advancement in all their vital aspects. It is service in the name of Christ and of his mercy, in the name of him who said: "My heart is moved with pity for the crowd" (Mt 15:32).

There are many other aspects of prayer, both private and liturgical, that deserve reflection. There are many other dimensions of the call to prayer that the Church would like to emphasize. I wish at this time, however, to allude only to two realities which the Church must constantly face and which she can face adequately only in prayer. They are suffering and sin.

It is in her prayer that the Church understands and copes with suffering; she reacts to it as Jesus did in the garden: "In his anguish he prayed with all the greater intensity" (Lk 22:44). Before the mystery of suffering, the Church is still unable to modify the advice of St. James or to improve on it: "Is anyone among you suffering? He should pray" (Jas 15:13). Combined with all her efforts to alleviate human suffering—which she must multiply until the end of time—the Church's definitive response to suffering is found only in prayer.

The other reality to which the Church responds in prayer is sin. In prayer the Church braces herself to engage in paschal conflict with sin and with the devil. In prayer she asks pardon for sin; in prayer she implores mercy for sinners; and in prayer she extols the power of the Lamb of God who takes away the sins of the world. The Church's response to sin is to praise salvation and the superabundance of the grace of Jesus Christ, the Savior of the world. "To him who loves us and freed us from our sins by his own blood . . . be glory and power forever and ever" (Rev 1:5-6).

Profoundly convinced of the power of prayer and humbly committed to it in our lives, let us, dear brothers, confidently proclaim throughout the Church the call to prayer. At stake is the Church's need to be herself, the Church of prayer, for the glory of the Father. The Holy Spirit will assist us, and the merits of Christ's paschal mystery will supply for our human weaknesses.

The example of Mary, the mother of Jesus, as a model of prayer, is a source of confidence and trust for all of us. As we ourselves look to her, we know that her example sustains our clergy, religious and laity. We know that her generosity is a legacy for the whole Church to proclaim and imitate.

Finally, in the words of Paul, I ask you all: "Pray for me that God may put his word on my lips, that I may courageously make known the mystery of the Gospel . . . Pray that I may have courage to proclaim it as I ought . . . Grace be with all who love our Lord Jesus Christ with unfailing love" (Eph 6:19-20, 24).

June Meeting of the Bishops' Committee on the Liturgy

The annual meeting of the members, consultants, and advisors of the Bishops' Committee on the Liturgy took place in Irving, Texas, from June 7-9, 1988. During the course of the meeting the Committee reviewed the progress of several projects and received reports from its subcommittees.

The Liturgy Committee approved the final draft of *God's Mercy Endures For Ever: Guidelines on the Presentation of Jews and Judaism in Catholic Preaching* and asked that it be placed on the agenda of the Administrative Committee of the National Conference of Catholic Bishops in September 1988. *God's Mercy* gives guidelines to assist the homilist in presenting Judaism and the Jewish people in such a way that the Scriptures are put in their proper context and anti-Semitism is avoided. *God's Mercy* is the result of extensive consultation with scholars of both the Catholic and Jewish faiths and with the cooperation of the Bishops' Committee on Ecumenical and Interreligious Affairs.

Proposed texts for Morning Prayer, Evening Prayer, and the Office of Readings for the feast of Our Lady of Guadalupe were approved by the members of the Committee. The texts are an adaptation of the Mexican office for the feast. The new office will be submitted to the Administrative Committee for approval and for the subsequent confirmation of the Apostolic See.

Several calendar questions were considered: a) Philippine Duschesne will soon be canonized, and the Committee voted that her commemoration should be included in the proper calendar for the United States as an optional memorial on November 17; b) Lawrence Ruiz and Companions have been placed on the universal calendar as an optional memorial on September 28. The English translation of the proper opening prayer is now being prepared by the International Commission on English in the Liturgy and will be submitted for approval when it is ready; c) The optional memorial of Jane Frances de Chantal (December 12) is presently not celebrated, since the feast of Our Lady of Guadalupe takes precedence; the Committee approved the request of the Visitation nuns of the United States that the optional memorial be transferred to August 18 in order that it might be celebrated in the United States; d) Junipero Serra will soon be beatified; the Committee approved the request that his commemoration be placed on the proper calendar for the United States with the rank of optional memorial; e) Katherine Drexel will also be beatified in the near future; the Committee agreed that her feast should appear on the proper calendar for the United States as an optional memorial. All the above calendar decisions are subject to the approval of the National Conference of Catholic Bishops and the confirmation of the Apostolic See.

The Liturgy Committee reviewed the texts for two Masses: one for the Bicentennial of the Establishment of the U.S. Hierarchy (1989), and the other for the Fifth Centenary of the Evangelization of the Americas (1992).-The liturgical texts were carefully reviewed, and as a result of the comments made during the meeting, the texts will undergo revision and then be submitted to the Liturgy Committee at its meeting in November.

The question of additional eucharistic prayers for use in the United States was throughly discussed by the members, consultants, and advisors of the Liturgy Committee. The Committee was unanimous that more eucharistic prayers are needed. Many suggestions were made relative to the type and content of such prayers. It was agreed that a consultation book should be prepared which would present the eucharistic prayers approved for the United States as well as those approved for other countries. The book will also present the results of the ICEL consultation on the Order of Mass and that which was done by the Bishops' Committee on the Liturgy and the Federation of Diocesan Liturgical Commissions under the title, *The Mystery of Faith*. It is hoped that the consultation book will be ready by November.

Father Ron Krisman gave a report on the progress of the commentary on the *Rite of Christian Initiation of Adults*, entitled *Pastoral Companion to the Rite of Christian Initiation of Adults*. Almost all the chapters have been completed, and the various drafts for the individual chapters are in the process of being edited. The *Pastoral Companion* is addressed to those on the parish level who have the responsibility for the catechumenate and the various liturgical celebrations of the RCIA. As the title indicates, the book is meant to be of concrete pastoral assistance. The present plan calls for the publication of the book by the end of this year.

Father John Gurrieri reported on the work of the International Commission on English in the Liturgy and on its recent *Progress Report on The Roman Missal*. He noted that the staff of the Liturgy Secretariat participates in several of the ICEL subcommittees and knows well the work that is presently being done on the Missal and other rites. The *Progress Report* has been sent to all bishops, liturgical commissions/offices, and consultants. The purpose of the book is to explain the process used for the revision of the prayers of the Missal and to point out some of the difficulties of translating the texts into English. It was noted that the Missal will be published in two volumes: Volume I will be for Sundays, solemnities, and major feasts, and Volume II will be for weekdays and other occasions. The first volume should be ready by 1991-1992, and the second volume shortly thereafter. Bishop Delaney will ask that the *Progress Report* be placed the agenda of the November meeting of the National Conference of Catholic Bishops. He also proposed that a letter be sent to the International Commission on English in the Liturgy which would express support for its goals and projects and thank the ICEL Secretariat staff for its dedication and fine work. This proposal was unanimously approved by the members of the Liturgy Committee.

Bishop Ricardo Ramirez reported on the work of the Hispanic Liturgy Subcommittee and especially on the proposed Hispanic Sacramentary. Two editors have been appointed and have begun the process of preparing the book. Texts from the *Sacramentary* that exist only in English are in the process of being translated. The title of the Missal for use in the dioceses of the United States will be *Sacramentario* in order to clearly relate it to the American title for the Missal: *Sacramentary*.

The Committee agreed to propose the First Sunday of Advent in 1989 as the date of implementation of the "texto unico" of the Order of Mass in Spanish. The members of the National Conference of Catholic Bishops have already approved this text of the Order of Mass and confirmation has been given by the Apostolic See. Implementation of the new Spanish text of the Order of Mass will be preceded by adequate catechesis.

There was an initial discussion on gestures and postures in worship, and a document will be prepared for further discussion on the subject. The Liturgy Committee also discussed liturgical colors and decided that an article should be prepared for publication in the *Newsletter* which would address some of the questions which have been raised about violet and blue.

Monsignor Alan Detscher reported on the progress of the *Lectionary for Masses with Children* and the second edition of the *Lectionary for Mass*. The American Bible Society's translation of the Scriptures for young people, which is proposed for use in the *Lectionary for Masses with Children*, is well advanced. The New Testament is already finished and the Old Testament will be completed next year. The introduction to the children's lectionary and the introductions to the various sections of it are in draft form. The editorial work on the second edition of the *Lectionary for Mass* is on schedule. Both lectionaries should be published in 1991-1992.

Father Ron Krisman gave a report on the work of the task group on Sunday Worship in the Absence of the Priest. A statement has been drafted which will accompany the forthcoming Roman directory on this subject, and liturgical texts also have been prepared. The task group intends to continue to refine these texts. However, publication will depend on the publication of the proposed Roman directory. The Liturgy Committee asked that the results of the survey which was conducted by the task group be shared with the bishops and diocesan liturgical commissions/offices.

Brief reports were given on the status of the *Order of Christian Funerals* and the *Ecumenical Marriage Rite*. Mention was made that the English translation of the Roman *Book of Blessings* and the supplementary American blessings have be sent to the Congregation for Divine Worship for confirmation. *Catholic Household Blessings and Prayers,* which was approved by the Administrative Committee in March, is in the process of publication by the USCC Office of Publishing and Promotion Services. The book is expected to be ready in the fall of this year.

Fathers Michael Spillane and Richard Ward gave a report on the Federation of Diocesan Liturgical Commissions. The October 10-13 National Meeting will take place in San Diego, CA and will have as its theme: Liturgy and Social Justice. Next year's meeting will be in Pittsburg, PA, and will mark the twentieth anniversary of the founding of the Federation of Diocesan Liturgical Commissions. The theme of that meeting will be: Full, Active, and Conscious Participation. Fathers Ward and Spillane encouraged the payment of dues to the Federation since it is one of the Federation's main sources of revenue. They also noted with concern that there seems to be less of an emphasis on diocesan liturgical offices and, in some cases, offices have been closed or reduced to part-time status. Revised guidelines for diocesan liturgical commissions/offices will be submitted to the Bishops' Committee on the Liturgy for approval and publication.

Father Juan Sosa reported on the activities of the Instituto de Liturgia Hispana (Institute for Hispanic Liturgy). There will be a Fourth National Conference on Hispanic Liturgy in San Jose, CA from October 27-30. The Institute continues to function well, but needs financial support in order to continue its work in the future.

The meeting ended with a brief report on the activities of the Secretariat and with an expression of thanks by Bishop Delaney to all who were present. The bishop members and consultants of the Liturgy Committee will meet on November 13, and the next annual meeting of the members, consultants, and advisors will take place from June 13-15, 1989, at a place to be determined.

Rite of Christian Initiation of Adults

The *Rite of Christian Initiation of Adults* will be available after July 1st from bookstores in editions by four publishers:

Catholic Book Publishing Company -	Minister's edition, $17.95 Study edition, $7.95
The Liturgical Press -	Minister's edition, $19.95 Study edition, $8.95
Liturgy Training Publications -	Minister's edition, $15.00 Study edition, $8.00
USCC Publishing Service -	Minister's edition, $19.95 Study edition, $8.95.

The use of the *Rite of Christian Initiation of Adults* is mandatory beginning on September 1, 1988.

Pueblo Publishing Company will publish a revised edition of its *Rites of the Catholic Church* (Volume I a) which will contain the *Rite of Christian Initiation of Adults,* the *Rite of Baptism for Children,* and the *Rite of Confirmation.*

The Federation of Diocesan Liturgical Commissions has several publications related to the *Rite of Christian Initiation of Adults: An Introduction to the Rite of Christian Initiation of Adults* (No. 464, 20¢/set—minimum of 100 sets)—a series of three brochures on the rites suitable for parish distribution; *The Rite of Christian Initiation of Adults: Liturgical Commentary* (No. 462, $11.25); *RCIA Scrolls:* Lord's Prayer (No. 469A), Apostles' Creed (No. 469B), Nicene Creed (469C). The scrolls are $1.25 each (minimum order of 10 scrolls).

The revised editions of two publications prepared by the Bishops' Committee on the Liturgy will be of great value to those who wish to know more about the *Rite of Christian Initiation of Adults: Study Text 10: Christian Initiation of Adults: A Commentary* (Pub. No. 934-3, $6.95); and *Liturgy Documentary Series 4: Christian Initiation of Adults* (Pub. No. 895-9, $4.50). The revised versions of these texts will be available in

September from the USCC Office of Publishing and Promotion Services, 1312 Massachusetts Avenue, NW, Washington, DC 20005.

Work is continuing on the *Pastoral Companion to the Rite of Christian Initiation of Adults*. The *Pastoral Companion* is a commentary and pastoral aid which is intended to assist ministers and others involved in the use of the RCIA to use it to the greatest pastoral advantage. The publication date for the *Pastoral Companion* is set for the end of this year, and it will be available from the USCC Office of Publishing and Promotion Services.

Interim Approval for the *Book of Blessings*

The Administrative Committee of the National Conference of Catholic Bishops, at its March 21, 1988 meeting in Washington, DC, approved three books concerned with blessings: *Book of Blessings* (the ICEL provisional "green book" translation), a collection of 46 new American blessings and occasional services, and *Catholic Household Blessings and Prayers* (a prayer book for use in the home).

Book of Blessings

The *Book of Blessings* is the ICEL translation of the portion of the *Roman Ritual* containing blessings: *De Benedictionibus,* published in Latin in 1984. The ICEL translation of this book contains 511 pages and is divided into five parts:

Part I: Blessings Directly Pertaining to Persons
      Chapters 1-7
Part II: Blessings Related to Buildings and to Various Forms of Human Activity
      Chapters 8-24
Part III: Blessings of Objects that Are Designed or Erected for Use in Churches, Either in the Liturgy or in Popular Devotions
      Chapters 25-35
Part IV: Blessings of Articles Meant to Foster the Devotion of the Christian People
      Chapters 36-39
Part V: Blessings for Various Needs and Occasions
      Chapters 40-41

The *Book of Blessings* has been sent to the Congregation for Divine Worship for confirmation. Once the text has been confirmed, the publication and implementation dates will be set.

Book of Blessings: New Blessings

The Administrative Committee approved 46 new blessings as well as their insertion into the appropriate sections of the English translation of the *Book of Blessings*. The list of these new American blessings which follows will serve to indicate their variety and pastoral utility.

Blessings Directly Pertaining to Persons

Order for the Blessing of Parents before Childbirth
Order for the Blessing of Parents after a Miscarriage
Order for the Blessing of Parents and an Adopted Child
Order of Blessing on the Occasion of a Birthday
Order for the Blessing of a Person Suffering from Addiction or Substance Abuse
Order for the Blessing of a Victim of Crime or Oppression
Order for the Blessing of Catechists
Blessings of Catechumens
Order for the Blessing of Students and Teachers
Prayers for Meetings
Order for the Blessing of Ecumenical Groups
Prayers for Interfaith Gatherings

Blessings Related to Buildings and to Various Forms of Human Activity

Order for the Blessing of a Parish Hall or Catechetical Center

Order for the Blessing of Boats and Fishing Gear
Order for the Blessing of Seeds at Planting Time
Order for the Blessing of an Athletic Event

Blessings of Objects That Are Designed or Erected for Use in Churches, Either in the Liturgy or in Popular Devotions

Order for the Blessing of a Repository for the Holy Oils
Order for the Blessing of a Chalice and Paten
Blessing of Hymnals and Service Books

Blessings Related to Feasts and Seasons

Order for the Blessing of an Advent Wreath
Order for the Blessing of a Christmas Manger or Nativity Scene
Order for the Blessing of a Christmas Tree
Order for the Proclamation of the Birth of Christ
Order for the Blessing of Homes During the Christmas and Easter Seasons
Order for the Proclamation of the Date of Easter on Epiphany
Order for the Blessing of Throats on the Feast of Saint Blase
Order for the Blessing and Distribution of Ashes
Order for the Blessing of Saint Joseph's Table
Order for the Reception of the Holy Oils
Order for the Blessing of Food for the First Meal of Easter
Order for the Blessing of Mothers on Mother's Day
Order for the Blessing of Fathers on Father's Day
Order for Visiting a Cemetery on All Souls Day, Memorial Day, or on the Anniversary of Death or Burial
Order for the Blessing of Food for Thanksgiving Day
Order for the Blessing of Foods and Other Elements Related to Religious Devotions

Blessings for Various Needs and Occasions

Order for the Installation of a Pastor
Order for the Blessing of Those Who Exercise Pastoral Service
Order for the Blessing of Readers
Order for the Blessing of Altar Servers, Sacristans, Musicians, and Ushers
Order for the Commissioning of Special Ministers of Holy Communion
Order for the Blessing of a Parish Council
Order for the Blessing of Officers of Parish Societies
Order for the Welcome of New Parishioners
Order for the Blessing of a Departing Parishioner
Order for the Blessing of Those Receiving Ecclesiastical Honors
Prayer on the Occasion of the Inauguration of a Public Official

Appendix

Solemn Blessings and Prayers over the People

When confirmation has been received from the Apostolic See, these blessings will be inserted in the appropriate chapters of the *Book of Blessings,* and will be published as an integral part of it.

Catholic Household Blessings and Prayers

This book is intended for family use and complements the official liturgical books. Arrangements have been made for its publication and work has already begun with the publisher, the United States Catholic Conference Office of Publishing Services. The book is divided into five parts:

Part I: The Daily Blessings
Blessings for daily activities from rising in the morning to retiring at night.
Part II: Days and Seasons
Blessings for the seasons and feasts of the liturgical year.
Part III: Times in Life: Blessings of Family Members

Blessings and prayers for various occasions in lives of family members, and resources for the celebration of the sacraments.

Part IV: Blessings for Various Times and Places

Blessings for activities, objects, and times in a persons life.

Part V: Common Prayers

Prayers of intercession, praise and thanksgiving, litanies, psalms and canticles, prayers before the eucharist, to Mary, invocations, baptismal promises and creeds, prayers in other languages, Morning and Evening Prayer.

Appendix: Calendar

The Bishops' Committee on the Liturgy expects that this book will be published by the end of the year.

Leccionario, Edicion Hispanoamericana, Ferial (Volume II)

The second volume of the *Leccionario, Edicion Hispanoamericana* has been published by the Northeast Hispanic Catholic Center of New York. The *Leccionario,* which contains the *Biblia Latinoamerica* translation and other texts prepared by the Comisión Episcopal Española de Liturgia, is the official Spanish-language *Lectionary for Mass* approved for use in the dioceses of the United States. Volume I, *Domingos y Solemnidades,* which contains the readings for Sundays, solemnities, and feasts, was published originally in 1982 (see *Newsletter,* Vol. XVIII, March 1982, p. 12). This second volume, *Ferial,* contains the readings, psalms, gospel acclamations for weekday celebrations. (An eventual third volume will contain the readings for ritual and votive Masses and Masses for various needs and occasions.) Volume I has been corrected and revised and is available in a new third edition. For copies, write to: Northeast Hispanic Catholic Center, Inc., 1011 First Avenue, New York, NY 10022. Price: $98.00 each volume.

National Workshop on the *Ceremonial of Bishops*

The Bishops' Committee on the Liturgy, at its March meeting, approved a proposal for a national workshop on the revised *Ceremonial of Bishops,* which is expected to be published in its English translation by the end of this year. The *Ceremonial of Bishops* is not a liturgical book in the sense of a collection of prayer texts, but rather is a collection of the rubrics which govern the liturgical celebrations in which the bishop takes part. This workshop will be held in the fall of 1989 in California, and is intended for all those who are responsible for the preparation and celebration of episcopal ceremonies: bishops, masters of ceremonies, cathedral personnel, musicians, diocesan liturgy office personnel, etc. Further details will be announced in the *Newsletter.*

Messale Ambrosiano, New Edition

In 1986 the Archdiocese of Milan (Italy) published a second edition of the *Messale Ambrosiano.* This edition is based on the Latin *Missale Ambrosianum* of 1980, which updated the first Italian edition of the Missal of 1976 (see *Newsletter,* Vol. XIII, January 1977).

Like the previous edition, this new edition consists of two beautifully bound volumes with gold stamping and edges and with color reprints of artwork taken from the ancient liturgical books of the Ambrosian Rite. The changes in this edition include the introduction of additions from the second edition of the Italian *Messale Romano,* (Roman Rite), e.g., additional greetings, third forms of the penitential rite, invitatories to the Lord's Prayer, and the eucharistic prayers of reconciliation. The forms of the penitential rite and preparation of the gifts proper to the Ambrosian Rite are now given the first place in the text and the Roman forms are given second. The Ambrosian positions for the Creed (immediately before the prayer over the gifts) and the sign of peace (immediately after the general intercessions) are now established as the primary places for these elements of the liturgy, although the sign of peace may be given, as in the Roman Rite, during the communion rite.

The *Messale Ambrosiano* is available from the Centro Ambrosiano di Documentazione e Studi Religiosi, Piazza Fontana 2, 20122 Milan, Italy, for approximately $230.00.

Hand missals for Sundays and Weekdays are also available from Edizioni Piemme, S.p.A., Via del Carmine, 5, 15033 Casale Monferrato (AL), Italy: *Messale Ambrosiano Festivo* - 30,000 lire; *Messale Ambrosiano Quotidiano* (2 vols.) - 70,000 lire.

NEWSLETTER

BISHOPS' COMMITTEE ON THE LITURGY

NATIONAL CONFERENCE OF CATHOLIC BISHOPS

1988
VOLUME XXIV
JULY/AUGUST

John Cardinal Dearden

His Eminence John Cardinal Dearden, former Archbishop of Detroit, died on August 1, 1988, at the age of 80. Cardinal Dearden was born on October 15, 1907, in Valley Falls, RI. He attended Catholic elementary and high schools in Cleveland, as well as Saint Mary's Seminary. He began his theological studies in 1929 at the North American College in Rome, and was ordained to the priesthood in 1932. After receiving a doctorate in theology from the Gregorian University, he served as a philosophy professor and as the rector of Saint Mary's Seminary in Cleveland. Pope Pius XII nominated him as Coadjutor Bishop of Pittsburg in 1948, and he later became the Ordinary of that diocese. In 1958 he was appointed Archbishop of Detroit. Pope Paul VI named him a Cardinal in 1969.

Although he submitted his resignation as the Archbishop of Detroit in 1980, Cardinal Dearden continued to remain active up until his death. He will be remembered as the first president of the National Conference of Catholic Bishops. He served a six year term in this office and was responsible for guiding the formative years of the NCCB. Archbishop John May, president of the National Conference of Catholic Bishops, recently said that Cardinal Dearden was "in many ways the key figure in helping the Church in this country to implement the reforms of the Second Vatican Council and in guiding the bishops' conferences to the role they currently play in the life of the Church."

Cardinal Dearden had the special distinction of being the first chairman of the Bishops' Committee on the Liturgy. He also assisted the Liturgy Committee as a consultant until the time of his death. During the past twenty-three years his knowledge and wisdom have been invaluable in assisting the Bishops' Committee on the Liturgy in its work. Cardinal Dearden also served as a member of the Congregation for the Sacraments. He was a wise and gentle man who will be greatly missed.

> O God,
> from the ranks of your priests
> you chose your servant John
> to fulfill the office of bishop.
> Grant that he may share
> in the eternal fellowship of those priests
> who, faithful to the teachings of the apostles,
> dwell in your heavenly kingdom.
>
> We ask this through Christ our Lord.

Directory for Sunday Celebrations in the Absence of a Priest

On June 1, 1988, His Eminence Paul Augustin Cardinal Mayer, OSB, Prefect of the Congregation for Divine Worship, sent the presidents of National Liturgical Commissions copies of the recently approved Directory for Sunday Celebrations in the Absence of a Priest *(Directorium de Celebrationibus Dominicalibus Absente Presbytero). The Directory was published in Latin and Italian and is now being translated into English. Cardinal Mayer noted in his cover letter that the Directory was examined by the members of the Congregation for Divine Worship at the plenary session of the Congregation in 1987 and was approved for publication by Pope John Paul II on May 21, 1988. In the summary which follows, the*

1312 MASSACHUSETTS AVENUE, N.W. • WASHINGTON, D.C. 20005

The Directory for Sunday Celebrations in the Absence of a Priest is a brief document, consisting of an introduction and three chapters: Chapter 1 - Sunday and Its Observance; Chapter 2 - Conditions for Having Sunday Celebrations in the Absence of a Priest; Chapter 3 - The Celebration.

The Congregation explains that the Directory is the result of the convergence of various factors: a) it is not always possible, in every place, to have a full celebration of Sunday, i.e., with the Eucharist; b) many episcopal conferences have asked the Congregation for Divine Worship for guidelines regarding these cases; c) the Holy See and individual bishops have been concerned about this important question for some time. The Directory has profited from the concerns and experience of those who have had to face the reality of an insufficient number of priests to celebrate the Eucharist on each Sunday in every community.

The fundamental principle that underlies the Directory is the desire to insure that there be a Christian celebration of Sunday in each community. Without forgetting that the Mass remains the proper celebration of Sunday, the Directory speaks of those elements which are essential to a Sunday celebration when Mass cannot be celebrated.

The introduction of the Directory briefly presents the *de facto* situation in which it is not always possible to celebrate the Eucharist for every Catholic community that desires it each Sunday.

The first chapter (nos. 8-17) is dedicated to the meaning of Sunday and takes its starting point from no. 106 of the *Constitution on the Sacred Liturgy* of the Second Vatican Council:

> By a tradition handed down by the apostles and having its origin from the very day of Christ's resurrection, the Church celebrates the paschal mystery every eighth day, which, with good reason, bears the name of the Lord's Day or Sunday. For on this day Christ's faithful must gather together so that, by hearing the word of God and taking part in the eucharist, they may call to mind the passion, the resurrection, and the glorification of the Lord Jesus and may thank God, who "has begotten them again unto a living hope through the resurrection of Jesus Christ from the dead" (1 Pt 1:3). Hence the Lord's Day is the first holyday of all and should be proposed to the devotion of the faithful and taught to them in such a way that it may become in fact a day of joy and of freedom from work. Other celebrations, unless they be truly of greatest importance, shall not have precedence over the Sunday, the foundation and core of the whole liturgical year.

Numerous citations are also given from the Fathers of the Church on the meaning and importance of Sunday. This chapter, in effect, is a synthesis of the Church's understanding of the nature and purpose of Sunday and the divine command to worship on the Day of the Lord.

The second chapter (nos. 18-34) is the most important part of the document, for it indicates the conditions upon which a decision can be made to have Sunday celebrations in the absence of a priest. The Directory recommends that, whenever possible, the faithful should go to a neighboring church for Mass if it is not possible to have Sunday Mass in their own church (18). When this cannot be done, at least there should be a celebration of the Word of God which, circumstances permitting, may be followed by the distribution of Holy Communion. It is also appropriate, on occasion, that the Sunday celebration be united to the celebration of the sacraments or sacramentals (19-20).

The Directory states that Sunday celebrations in the absence of a priest should not be held in places where Mass has been celebrated the previous evening, even when this has been done in another language. It is also noted that Sunday celebrations in the absence of a priest should not be repeated on any given Sunday (21).

There should be no confusion in the mind of the faithful between these celebrations and the celebration of the Eucharist; rather such celebrations in the absence of a priest should lead them to a greater desire for the eucharist and help them to make a better preparation for the eucharistic celebration (22).

The faithful are encouraged to pray for vocations to the priesthood so that in the future there will be sufficient priests for the celebration of Mass on Sunday (23).

The diocesan bishop, after consulting with the council of priests, is to establish regulations for Sunday celebrations in the absence of a priest. All such celebrations must be approved by the bishop and be under the supervision of a pastor (24). Before he establishes the practice of permitting these celebrations, the bishop must first consider other alternatives, such as having other priests or religious without pastoral responsibilities assist in the parish, or having the people go to other churches or parishes for Mass (25).

The bishop, by means of a delegate or a special commission, should see that the celebrations are properly conducted and that those who lead them are properly prepared. He should also insure that there has been sufficient catechesis on the reasons for Sunday celebrations in the absence of a priest and that the Eucharist is celebrated in the parish with some frequency (26).

The pastor has the responsibility to prepare for these celebrations, to celebrate the sacraments, especially Penance, and to provide the Eucharist which will be distributed to the people (27-28).

Sunday celebrations may be led by deacons (29) or by suitably prepared lay persons (29-30).

When it is not possible to have a Sunday celebration, the Directory encourages individuals to spend some time in prayer on Sunday either alone, with their family, or with a group of families (32).

Another alternative suggested by the Directory is the celebration of Morning or Evening Prayer from the *Liturgy of the Hours*. The readings appointed for Mass may be inserted into either of these hours of the Divine Office, and Holy Communion may also be distributed at the conclusion of Morning or Evening Prayer (33).

The third chapter explains the structure of a celebration of the Word and the distribution of Holy Communion. It says that in no case should there be a presentation (and preparation) of the gifts or the proclamation of the eucharistic prayer (35). [This does not exclude the taking up of a collection.]

The Opening Prayer and Prayer after Communion are taken from the Sacramentary, and the readings are taken from the *Lectionary for Mass* (36).

When a deacon presides at a Sunday celebration in the absence of a priest, he uses all the texts and gestures appropriate to his ministry. He vests in the usual vestments (including the dalmatic, if desired) and presides from the presidential chair (38). A lay person uses the forms of greeting and blessing proper to lay ministers (39) and wears the vesture approved by the bishop. A lay person who presides does not use the presidential chair and is seated outside the presbyterium (40). The roles of reader, cantor, etc., are distributed among suitable persons (40).

The conference of bishops may determine the actual rites and texts to be used for Sunday celebrations in the absence of a priest according to the following structure:

> Introductory Rites
> Liturgy of the Word
> Thanksgiving
> Rite of Communion
> Concluding Rites

[The Bishops' Committee on the Liturgy is in the process of preparing both a ritual for Sunday celebrations in the absence of a priest and a statement on the subject (see below).]

The Directory does not indicate the content of the Introductory Rites and says only that the *Lectionary for Mass* is used for the Liturgy of the Word.

The Thanksgiving takes one of the following forms:

a) After the General Intercessions or after the distribution of Holy Communion, the leader invites all to give thanks, and a psalm (e.g., 100, 113, 118, 136, 147, or 150), a hymn or canticle (e.g., Glory to God or Magnificat), or a litany that is then sung or recited by all.

b) Alternatively, before the Lord's Prayer the leader places the eucharist on the altar and all kneel before the sacrament and sing or recite a hymn, psalm, or litany.

The Thanksgiving is not to take the form of a eucharistic prayer. The prefaces and eucharistic prayers of the Sacramentary are not to be used (45).

The Communion Rite follows the form given in the *Roman Ritual: Holy Communion and Worship of the Eucharist Outside Mass* (46).

The Eucharist to be distributed during the service is to have been consecrated that day and brought to the church before the service, or is that which was reserved after the previous Mass celebrated in the church. The Eucharist is taken from the tabernacle and placed on the altar before the Lord's Prayer (47).

The Lord's Prayer is always sung or recited, even when Holy Communion is not distributed (48).

The celebration may conclude with announcements before the dismissal (49).

Consultation Concerning Sunday and Weekday Worship in the Absence of a Priest

On April 8, 1988, the Most Reverend Joseph P. Delaney, Bishop of Fort Worth and Chairman of the Bishops' Committee on the Liturgy, sent the members of the National Conference of Catholic Bishops the results of a national consultation concerning Sunday (and weekday) worship in the absence of a priest which was conducted between July and December 1987.

The survey was designed to provide input to the Liturgy Committee's Task Group on Sunday Worship in the Absence of a Priest, established in April 1987. It requested information regarding the liturgical rites presently used for those occasions on which a parish/mission community gathers for Sunday (and/or weekday) worship in the absence of a priest, those who serve as leaders of prayer in the absence of a priest, and the number of parishes/missions in each arch/diocese which are under the pastoral care of a deacon, a lay person, or a religious sister or brother.

The response to the questionnaire was most gratifying. Responses were received from 167 of 174 dioceses. Each diocesan bishop had been asked to respond personally or through a member of the diocesan staff. Respondents included: 53 diocesan bishops, 27 chancellors, 8 vicars general, 43 directors or coordinators of the diocesan Office of Worship or Liturgical Commission, 9 vice-chancellors or assistant chancellors, 7 directors of clergy personnel or vicars for priests, 3 moderators of the curia, 2 episcopal vicars, 2 directors of Offices of Lay Ministries, 7 administrative assistants or secretaries to the Bishop, 6 persons who had other diocesan positions.

The Task Group continues to develop two projects which will eventually be presented to the members of the National Conference of Catholic Bishops: 1) a three-chapter ritual which will contain morning and evening prayer from the *Liturgy of the Hours,* the order for a Liturgy of the Word, and the order for the Sunday (or weekday) Liturgy of the Word with the rite of Holy Communion outside Mass (Chapter 1 of *Holy Communion and Worship of the Eucharist outside Mass*); and 2) a statement of the Liturgy Committee concerning the proper and dignified celebration of Sunday and weekday worship in the absence of a priest. These projects are scheduled for completion in early 1989.

Below are the results of the national survey dealing with the question of Sunday (and weekday) worship in the absence of a priest:

1. Seventy dioceses presently have parishes/missions which are under the administration of a deacon, a lay person, or a religious sister or brother; 97 dioceses do not. The number of such parishes/missions is 193, and a total of 201 persons are involved. (The number does not add up to "193" since some persons administer more than one parish or mission, and some parishes/missions or groupings of them are administered by a team.) These persons are: 40 deacons, 125 women religious, 8 men religious (brothers), 14 laywomen, 14 laymen.

2. Thirty-one of the dioceses which have parishes/missions under the administration of deacons, men and women religious, or laypersons had Sunday worship in the absence of a priest within the past year; 39 dioceses did not. The number of these parishes/missions which have had Sunday worship in the absence of a priest within the past year according to various frequencies were noted: 14 parishes/missions had one celebration, 52 parishes/missions had occasional celebrations, 5 parishes/missions had monthly celebrations, 9 parishes/missions had bimonthly celebrations, and 15 parishes/missions had more frequent celebrations.

3. Forty-nine dioceses reported that there were parishes with a priest as pastor or administrator which needed occasionally to have Sunday worship in the absence of a priest within the past year. The number of such parishes and the frequency of the celebrations were: 74 parishes had one celebration, 128 parishes had occasional celebrations, 13 parishes had monthly celebrations, 9 parishes had bimonthly celebrations, and 30 parishes had celebrations more than twice a month.

4. Those authorized to serve as the leaders of prayer at these Sunday celebrations in the absence of a priest in the 51 different dioceses which had responded "YES" to nos. 2 or 3 are: 16 deacon-administrators of parishes/missions, 58 women religious-administrators, 5 men religious-administrators, 3 laywomen-

administrators, 4 laymen-administrators; and 153 other deacons, 81 other women religious, 6 other men religious (brothers), 93 other laywomen, and 90 other laymen.

5. The ritual used at most of these Sunday celebrations was a Liturgy of the Word using all the appointed readings from the *Lectionary for Mass,* followed by the Rite of Holy Communion from *Holy Communion and Worship of the Eucharist outside Mass* (50 dioceses). Four dioceses reported the use of the Rite of Holy Communion from *Holy Communion and Worship of the Eucharist outside Mass* with no expanded Liturgy of the Word; 3 dioceses had some use of Morning (or Evening) Prayer from *The Liturgy of the Hours,* followed by the Rite of Holy Communion from *Holy Communion and Worship of the Eucharist outside Mass;* one diocese reported the use of a Liturgy of the Word using all the appointed readings from the *Lectionary for Mass,* without being followed by the distribution of Holy Communion; and ten used another Order of Worship (four dioceses were using the *Ritual for Lay Presiders,* published by the Western Liturgical Conference of Canada, while the other six dioceses had prepared their own liturgical materials). No diocese was using Morning (or Evening) Prayer from *The Liturgy of the Hours,* without being followed by the distribution of Holy Communion.

6. One hundred and thirty-seven dioceses reported weekday celebrations of Holy Communion outside Mass in the absence of a priest within the past year. The individual responses from these 137 dioceses reflected a wide degree of variation in practice, from one (1) parish to all the parishes of the diocese. Most stated that the usual frequency is "occasional," but several also noted weekly ("on the pastor's day off") or even daily celebrations in some parishes/missions without a resident priest. A large number of dioceses stated that these liturgies are often celebrated in parishes during priest conferences and retreats. Needless to say, completely accurate data regarding this matter could not be supplied by most diocesan respondents.

The rites used in each diocese at these weekday celebrations were: 121 dioceses - a Liturgy of the Word using the appointed readings of the day from the *Lectionary for Mass,* followed by the Rite of Holy Communion from *Holy Communion and Worship of the Eucharist outside Mass;* 33 dioceses - The Rite of Holy Communion from *Holy Communion and Worship of the Eucharist outside Mass* with no additions; 15 dioceses - Morning (or Evening) Prayer from *The Liturgy of the Hours,* followed by the Rite of Holy Communion from *Holy Communion and Worship of the Eucharist outside Mass;* 6 dioceses - Morning (or Evening) Prayer from *The Liturgy of the Hours,* without being followed by the distribution of Holy Communion; 3 dioceses - a Liturgy of the Word using the appointed readings for the day from the *Lectionary for Mass,* without being followed by the distribution of Holy Communion; 16 dioceses - another Order of Worship (most often mentioned was the *Ritual for Lay Presiders,* published by the Western Liturgical Conference of Canada).

7. In the 51 dioceses having Sunday celebrations in the absence of a priest, the leaders of prayer at those liturgies in 47 of the dioceses have been authorized to preach. These ministers usually were deacons and the administrators of parishes/missions.

8. In the 137 dioceses having weekday celebrations in the absence of a priest, the leaders of prayer at those liturgies in 68 of the dioceses have been authorized to preach. Again most were deacons and the administrators of parishes/missions. Five respondents said that the pastor gives the authorization to preach. Several others noted that those authorized to serve as leaders of prayer at these liturgies also have authorization to preach.

9. Seventeen dioceses have established their own guidelines, norms, or directives for the training of leaders of prayer for Sunday (and/or weekday) worship in the absence of a priest. These arch/dioceses are: Albany, Archdiocese for Military Services, Burlington, Gaylord, Helena, Jackson, La Crosse, Las Cruces, Little Rock, Milwaukee, Nashville, New Ulm, Portland in Oregon, Salina, San Diego, Shreveport, Wheeling-Charleston.

10. Nine dioceses have established a commissioning service for leaders of prayer for Sunday (and/or weekday) worship in the absence of a priest. These arch/dioceses are: Baltimore, Helena, Jackson, La Crosse, Las Cruces, Little Rock, New Orleans, Salina, Sioux Falls.

11. Twenty dioceses have prepared orders of worship, or other liturgical materials to supplement *Holy Communion and Worship of the Eucharist outside Mass* and to be used by leaders of prayer for Sunday (and/or weekday) worship in the absence of a priest. These arch/dioceses are: Albany, Alexandria, Bismarck, Cheyenne, Cincinnati, Des Moines, Fairbanks, Fort Worth, Gaylord, Las Cruces, Little Rock, Nashville, Paterson, Portland, Portland in Oregon, Rochester, Salina, Shreveport, Syracuse, Wheeling-Charleston.

12. Finally, respondents in 91 of the 116 arch/dioceses not presently faced with the need to have Sunday worship in the absence of a priest foresee a day on which such might be necessary. Twenty-one (21) respondents could give no estimate of when this might be necessary in the dioceses in which they minister. Fourteen (14) stated that it would occur in 10 or more years, while twenty-seven (27) said that it would occur in about five years. The remaining 29 respondents gave a variety of responses, all under five years: "soon," "1," "1-2," "3-4," "a few years."

Confirmation of the *National Statutes for the Catechumenate*

On July 13, 1988, the Most Reverend John L. May, Archbishop of Saint Louis and President of the National Conference of Catholic Bishops, received the letter of the Congregation for Divine Worship, dated 26 June 1988 (Prot. No. 1191/86), confirming the decision of the NCCB on 11 November 1986 to approve the *National Statutes for the Catechumenate*.

The text of the *National Statutes* appears in all the published US editions of the *Rite of Christian Initiation of Adults* (Appendix III). In confirming the Statutes, the Congregation for Divine Worship asked that a slight modification be made in the wording of norm 17. The emended and confirmed text now reads:

17) Baptism by immersion is the fuller and more expressive sign of the sacrament and, therefore, provision should be made for its more frequent use in the baptism of adults. The provision of the *Rite of Christian Initiation of Adults* for partial immersion, namely, immersion of the candidate's head, should be taken into account.

It should also be noted that norm 20 in the published National Statutes contains a typographical error in some ritual editions. The internal reference in that norm should read "nos. 331-332," *not* "nos. 307-308."

Second printings of the *Rite of Christian Initiation of Adults* will contain the corrected wording of statute 17 of the *National Statutes,* together with the notification of the date of confirmation by the Congregation for Divine Worship.

The Liturgy at which the Bishop Presides

On February 12, 1988, Pope John Paul II addressed a group of Italian bishops who had just completed a course of studies on liturgical renewal which was sponsored by the Liturgical Commission of the Italian Episcopal Conference. The address was published in Italian in the March 1988 issue of Notitiae. *The following English translation was made by the Secretariat staff of the Bishops' Committee on the Liturgy.*

Venerable brothers in the episcopate:

Welcome! My cordial greetings to all. You are gathered in Rome to support the endeavors of the Liturgical Commission of the Italian Conference of Bishops, which has sponsored a course of renewal on the theme, "Celebrating Today." I rejoice with its organizers and with each one of you.

Without repeating the various points touched upon in the course of this week, I would like to emphasize both the importance of the liturgy at which the bishop presides as well as the importance of liturgy in his personal life.

1. The office of bishop as teacher, sanctifier, and pastor of his Church shines forth most clearly in a liturgy that he celebrates with his people (*Ceremonial of Bishops* [hereafter "CB"], no. 11). The Second Vatican Council has rightly emphasized this: "Therefore all should hold in great esteem the liturgical life of the diocese centered around the bishop, especially in his cathedral church; they must be convinced that the preeminent manifestation of the Church is present in the full, active participation of all God's holy people in these liturgical celebrations, especially in the same eucharist, in a single prayer, at one altar at which the bishops presides, surrounded by his college of priests and by his ministers (*Constitution on the Sacred Liturgy* [hereafter "CSL"], art. 41).

When the bishop celebrates in the midst of the people entrusted to him, it is the mystery itself of the Church which is manifested by means of the lawful celebration of the eucharist (CB, no. 7); he is the high priest of his people. "Through the preaching of the gospel and in the power of the Spirit the bishop calls men and women to faith or confirms them in the faith . . . " (CB, no. 6), and through the sacraments he sanctifies the faithful (see CB, no. 7). Thus it is necessary that the bishop be strongly convinced of the importance of such celebrations for the Christian life of his faithful. Such celebrations must be the model for the whole diocese.

2. For everything to result in manifesting both the unity of the local Church as well as the diversity of functions, it is important that the bishop be surrounded by priests, deacons, and other ministers, who are each to carry out their proper role.

The church where the bishop celebrates, in particular his cathedral church, ought to be a worthy and appropriate model and demonstrate "in an exemplary way to the other churches of the diocese that which is laid down in liturgical documents and books with regard to the arrangement and adornment of churches" (CB, no. 46).

It is important that the role of the schola and that of the organist be in harmony, that the accompanying hymns should be a true expression of the faith and conform to both liturgical rules and the norms of art, and that there be manifested that note of universality belonging to celebrations presided over by the bishop, which should allow for the participation of the people (CB, no. 40).

In order that each person should know what to do or to say, and that everything might be carried out with order, simplicity, and beauty, the presence of a master of ceremonies who is discrete and attentive to all things is indispensable (CB, nos. 34–35).

These are some directives, particularly intended for you, which are explained in more detail in the *Ceremonial of Bishops,* published in 1984. It contains all that is necessary to do during the liturgical year in order to obtain an episcopal liturgy that is simple and noble and, at the same time, full of pastoral efficacy and may serve as a model for all other celebrations.

3. All this is important, but to understand fully the value of the liturgy one needs to go into greater depth (see 1985 Extraordinary Synod of Bishops, Final Report).

In the first place, it is by means of the liturgy that one can be united to the mystery of salvation today. When the bishop offers the eucharistic sacrifice and celebrates the sacraments, he passes on that which he himself has received from the tradition that comes from the Lord (see 1 Corinthians 11:25), and he builds up the Church. This does not have its origin in the desire of the disciples, as if they decided to give the rites of the old covenant a new form. The Church has been created as a new people of God around the table of the Last Supper, as I emphasized in the letter *Dominicae Cenae* (see no. 4). It is continually founded upon the actions of Christ, accomplished in his name by ordained ministers: it is thus able to associate itself to the mystery of the death and resurrection of the Lord and to receive his life-giving Spirit.

For this reason the Second Vatican Council affirmed that "the liturgy is the summit towards which the activity of the Church is directed; at the same time it is the fount from which all the Church's power flows" (CSL, art. 10). This states the importance of the liturgical celebration, for it treats of expressing with words and gestures the extraordinary grace that is accomplished there: knowing and manifesting the gift of God, which is Christ himself.

The liturgical celebration is, in the second place, nourishment for an authentic Christian life, be it personal or communal. When we celebrate the liturgy, we participate in the mysteries of redemption, accomplished by our Lord, and we have communion with the life of the Father together with all our brothers and sisters who, like us, have been redeemed: we represent the universe reconciled with God. That which we celebrate in spirit and truth, we live, foretasting in the Spirit that which we will be for ever. When the liturgy is celebrated, the Church is revealed to itself, and each of us is likewise revealed to him or herself. These are moments of fullness and grace.

In order that a true experience of conversion to God can be realized, the celebration needs to be geared toward the whole person, not only to the intellect, but also to the senses. From this derives the place given to each element of beauty: song, music, light, and incense. From this also flows the necessity of a certain length of time for the celebration and for its well ordered internal structure.

4. Finally, the celebration gives rise to the mission of the Church and of each Christian.

This missionary dynamic does not come from the desire of men and women who decide to make themselves propagators of their faith. It is born of the Spirit, who pushes the Church to expand itself. It flows forth from faith in the love of God. The liturgical celebration is the moment in which Christians discover in Christ and in the Church the face of God and God's ineffable gift; it is the moment in which they discover that they are loved to the utmost. If the celebration will be such, witness and mission can be born from this certitude.

Let your manner of celebrating be the same as the expression of your faith. It will be for your faithful a witness and an example. Thus, in each one of your local Churches, there will be realized that which Saint Ignatius of Antioch desired for the Church of Philadelphia: "There is only one flesh of our Lord Jesus Christ and only one cup that unites us, just as there is only one bishop with the presbyterate and deacons. Thus all that you do, do it according to God" (Phil. 1).

With this hope, and to confirm the sentiments of fraternal communion which unite me to you and, through you, to the faithful of your Churches, I impart to you from the heart my blessing.

Liturgy Committee and Secretariat Publications in Progress

The following Secretariat and/or Committee publications are in various stages of preparation for eventual publication by the USCC Office of Publishing and Promotion Services in 1988:

1. Liturgical Calendar and Ordo 1990 for the Dioceses of the United States of America, the official liturgical calendar for the dioceses of the United States of America, published annually by the Bishops' Committee on the Liturgy.

2. *Liturgy Documentary Series 8: Order of Christian Funerals, Introduction and Pastoral Notes*, a compendium of documentation from the *Order of Christian Funerals* and related materials.

3. *Study Text 12: Order of Christian Funerals*, a commentary on the revised funeral rites especially written for pastors, other priests, deacons, lay ministers, liturgy planning teams, and discussion groups.

4. *Pastoral Companion to the Rite of Christian Initiation of Adults*, an extensive commentary on the *Rite of Christian Initiation of Adults*, the formational components of the catechumenate, the various liturgical rites, canonical questions, and other matters. The *Pastoral Companion* is being edited by Rev. Ronald F. Krisman and will include contributions by Father James Dunning, Mrs. Karen Hinman Powell, Sister Barbara O'Dea, DW, Father John Huels, OSM, Father Francis Sokol, Father James Lopresti, SJ, and Father Donald Neumann.

5. *Enchiridion of Indulgences*, the official English translation of the revised edition of the *Enchiridion Indulgentiarum: Normae et Concessiones* (third edition, May 1986).

6. *Guidelines on the Presentation of Jews and Judaism in Catholic Preaching* responds to the decrees of *Nostra aetate* and the 1985 *Notes on the Correct Way to Present the Jews and Judaism in Preaching and Catechesis of the Roman Catholic Church*. The *Guidelines*, a joint project of the Bishops' Committee on the Liturgy and the Bishops' Committee on Ecumenical and Interreligious Affairs, are meant to assist preachers, particularly in the preparation of the eucharistic homily.

7. *Guidelines on the Concelebration of the Eucharist*, a revision of the 1978 guidelines published by the Bishops' Committee on the Liturgy in *Study Text: Eucharistic Concelebration*. The revised guidelines have been published in the *Newsletter* of the Bishops' Committee on the Liturgy (Volume XXII, September/ October 1987) and will be incorporated into a revised edition of *Study Text 5*.

8. *Guidelines for Diocesan Liturgical Commissions and Offices of Worship*, a revised edition of the 1970 statement of the Bishops' Committee on the Liturgy.

9. *Solemn Exposition and Benediction of the Eucharist*, a ritual book, minister's and people's editions, meant to foster eucharistic devotion, especially extended periods of exposition and adoration of the Blessed Sacrament.

The actual publication dates of the above will be announced in future issues of the Bishops' Committee on the Liturgy *Newsletter*.

BISHOPS' COMMITTEE ON THE LITURGY
NEWSLETTER
NATIONAL CONFERENCE OF CATHOLIC BISHOPS

**1988
VOLUME XXIV
SEPTEMBER**

Congregation for Divine Worship

On June 28, 1988, Pope John Paul II issued the Apostolic Constitution on the Roman Curia, *Pastor Bonus,* which reforms the various congregations, secretariats, councils, and offices of the Roman Curia. Section III deals with the various Roman congregations. Of special interest to those involved with liturgy is the joining of the Congregation for Divine Worship to the Congregation for the Discipline of the Sacraments to form the new Congregation for Divine Worship and the Discipline of the Sacraments. [A brief history of the Congregation of Divine Worship and the Congregation for the Sacraments is given in the April/May 1984 issue of the Newsletter.]

Pastor Bonus lists the various responsibilities of the Congregation for Divine Worship and the Discipline of the Sacraments. Following is an unofficial translation provided by the Liturgy Secretariat:

Article 62

While safeguarding the competency of the Congregation for the Doctrine of the Faith, the Congregation [for Divine Worship and the Discipline of the Sacraments] is responsible for those things which pertain to the Apostolic See regarding the moderation and promotion of the sacred liturgy, especially the sacraments.

Article 63

It fosters and cares for the discipline of the sacraments, especially that which concerns their valid and licit celebration; moreover, it grants favors and dispensations in those areas to which the faculties of diocesan bishops do not extend.

Article 64

§1. The Congregation promotes pastoral liturgical action, especially that which pertains to the eucharistic celebration, by effective and suitable means; it assists diocesan bishops in order that the Christian faithful might actively participate in the sacred liturgy to a greater extent each day.

§2. It takes care of the preparation or emendation of liturgical texts; it reviews the particular calendars and the propers of Masses and Offices of particular Churches and Institutes, which enjoy this right.

§3. It reviews the versions of liturgical books and their adaptations legitimately prepared by conferences of bishops.

Article 65

It supports and has dealings with the commissions or institutes founded for the promotion of the liturgical apostolate, music, chant, or sacred art; it establishes according to the norms of law or reviews or approves the statutes of associations of this sort which exhibit an international character; moreover it fosters meetings from various regions to promote liturgical life.

Article 66

It attentively takes care to see that liturgical directives are exactly observed, that abuses are guarded against, and that when such are detected, they are rooted out.

Article 67

It is the function of this Congregation to determine the fact of the non-consummation of a marriage as well as the existence of a just cause for granting a dispensation. Accordingly, it receives all the acts of the case

1312 MASSACHUSETTS AVENUE, N.W. • WASHINGTON, D.C. 20005

along with the votum of the bishop and the observations of the defender of the bond and examines them in accord with its particular procedures and, if the case should so warrant, it submits a petition to the Supreme Pontiff for the requested dispensation.

Article 68

It is also competent in deciding cases concerning the nullity of sacred ordinations, according to the norm of law.

Article 69

The Congregation is competent regarding the veneration of sacred relics, the confirmation of heavenly patrons, and the granting of the title of "minor basilica."

Article 70

Beyond liturgical worship, the Congregation provides assistance to the bishops in order that the prayers and pious practices of the Christian people which are in complete harmony with the norms of the Church may be fostered and held in honor.

Paul Augustin Cardinal Mayer, OSB

On July 1, 1988, Pope John Paul II accepted the resignation of His Eminence Paul Augustin Cardinal Mayer, OSB, prefect of both the Congregation for Divine Worship and the Congregation for Sacraments, which had been presented in accord with canon 354 of the *Code of Canon Law* (dealing with resignation from ecclesiastical office due to advanced age).

Cardinal Mayer was born in Altoetting, Germany, in 1911, and was ordained to the priesthood as a member of the Benedictine Order in 1935. He was ordained to the episcopacy in 1972 and was given the personal title of archbishop.

Cardinal Mayer served as the Secretary to the Congregation for Religious and Secular Institutes before his appointment as the Pro-Prefect of the Congregation for Divine Worship and of the Congregation for Sacraments by Pope John Paul II in 1984. He was elevated to the College of Cardinals in 1985.

On July 9, 1988, Pope John Paul II appointed Cardinal Mayer president of the commission which had been established in accordance with the terms of the recent *motu proprio, Ecclesia Dei* (no. 6a and b), to collaborate with bishops, the departments of the Roman Curia, and all those concerned with facilitating full ecclesial communion with the priests, seminarians, religious communities and other individuals until now linked in various ways with the Fraternity founded by the now excommunicated Archbishop Marcel Lefebvre. Those who wish to remain united to the Successor of Peter will be allowed to preserve their spiritual and liturgical traditions.

The members, consultants, advisors, and Secretariat staff of the Bishops' Committee on the Liturgy thank Cardinal Mayer for his many years of dedicated service to the Church, its liturgy, and its sacraments.

Eduardo Cardinal Martinez Somalo

His Holiness Pope John Paul II appointed His Eminence Eduardo Martinez Somalo, 61, as the Prefect of the new Congregation for Divine Worship and the Discipline of the Sacraments on July 1, 1988. Cardinal Martinez Somalo replaces Cardinal Paul Augustin Mayer, who served as the prefect of the previously separate Congregation of Divine Worship and Congregation for the Sacraments.

Cardinal Martinez Somalo was born in Manos de Rio Tobia, Spain, in 1927. He studied at the Pontifical Gregorian University in Rome and was ordained to the priesthood in 1950. After a brief period of pastoral work in Spain, he returned to Rome and studied at the Pontifical Ecclesiastical Academy, the Vatican school for the diplomatic service. He was appointed as an attaché of the Secretary of State in 1956, and, the next year, became a professor at the Academy. After serving in several diplomatic posts under the Secretary of State, he was appointed the "sostituto" or assistant Secretary of State by Pope John Paul II. He was raised to the dignity of the College of Cardinals in June 1988 by Pope John Paul II and shortly thereafter was appointed Prefect of the Congregation for Divine Worship and the Discipline of the Sacraments.

The Bishops' Committee on the Liturgy extends to Cardinal Martinez Somalo its good wishes as he undertakes his new responsibilities.

FDLC Resolutions

The following Position Statements were adopted by the Diocesan Liturgical Commissions at the Annual National Meeting sponsored by the Bishops' Committee on the Liturgy and the Federation of Diocesan Liturgical Commissions in Breckenridge, Colorado, October 5-8, 1987; and are addressed to the Bishops' Committee on the Liturgy. The degree of commitment of the members to the statement is indicated in parentheses. The voting scale is graded from +3 (highest degree of commitment) to -3 (completely negative to the statement). A commitment of 1.5 is required for acceptance. The action taken by the Bishops' Committee on the Liturgy follows each statement.

Position Statement 1987 A (Degree of Commitment: 2.85): *Cremation*

It is the position of the delegates to the 1987 National Meeting of Diocesan Liturgical Commissions that:

the Bishops' Committee on the Liturgy and the Federation of Diocesan Liturgical Commissions begin a process of research and study on cremation leading to the formulation of catechesis and guidelines for our constituencies, paying particular attention to pastoral questions surrounding cremation and to liturgical concerns which arise when cremation takes place prior to the Funeral Mass.

We request that a time-line and procedures for implementation of this resolution be set by the Federation of Diocesan Liturgical Commissions Board of Directors at the January, 1988 Board Meeting.

The BCL Secretariat will begin discussions with the FDLC in addressing the above questions on cremation.

Position Statement 1987 E (Degree of Commitment: 1.93): *Rites of Committal*

It is the position of the delegates to the 1987 National Meeting of Diocesan Liturgical Commissions that:

the Bishops' Committee on the Liturgy, diocesan worship offices, liturgical commissions, and ministers to the bereaved emphasize in all catechetical material and commentary, and communicate to funeral directors, cemetery administrators and cemetery associations that the *Order of Christian Funerals* presumes the actual graveside, and not chapels and false settings, as the ordinary place for final committal rites, and burial or entombment as an integral part of the rite.

We request that a time-line and procedures for implementation of this resolution be set by the Federation of Diocesan Liturgical Commissions Board of Directors at the January, 1988 Board Meeting.

This is addressed in Study Text 12: Order of Christian Funerals *which will be available as soon as the* Order of Christian Funerals *has been published. Father John A. Gurrieri, Executive Director of the Liturgy Secretariat, will address the question when he speaks at the annual meeting of the National Association of Catholic Cemetery Directors to be held in Chicago later this year. The Secretariat staff continues discussion on this matter with the FDLC.*

Liturgical Color for Advent

The December 1987 edition of the *Newsletter* contained a clarification on liturgical colors in response to the many questions that come to the Secretariat regarding the use of blue vestments during Advent. At the end of that article it was noted: "For the present the National Conference of Catholic Bishops has neither proposed nor approved the use of blue either for the season of Advent or for memorials and feasts of Mary, nor any other color. The Bishops' Committee on the Liturgy reviewed this matter several years ago. However, because of the increasing discussion of the use of blue, the Bishops' Committee on the Liturgy will give further consideration to the question."

Subsequently the Liturgy Committee discussed the use of blue for Advent at its June meeting in Irving, Texas (see May/June 1988 *Newsletter,* page 20). The Committee declined to propose to the NCCB any change in the present liturgical color sequence for the United States. However, it did recommend that the following observations be made.

The present order of colors for the various seasons and celebrations of the liturgical year represents a gradual development which was not complete until the end of the medieval period. In the East, the Churches never developed a color sequence, and even today there is a great variety of colors in use. The Eastern

Churches generally make a distinction between bright and dark colors, but allow the priest to choose the actual color that will be used for a particular occasion. The first sequence of colors in the West was apparently based on that which was used in the Latin Church of the Holy Sepulchre at Jerusalem during the twelfth century. However, when the Western Church began to establish color sequences for feasts and seasons, there remained a great deal of variety. Black, violet (purple), and blue were all seen to be various shades of the same color and were often used interchangeably. The inventories of vestments which were prepared at the beginning of the English Reformation provide us with information on the vast assortment of colors and hues that were used for liturgical vesture in England. It is only in the post-Tridentine liturgical books that one finds a defined sequence of liturgical colors for use throughout the Latin Church.

The official color for the seasons of Advent and Lent is *violet*. This color, which is often called purple, has a variety of shades ranging from blue-violet to red-violet. The shade that is traditionally known as "Roman purple" is actually a red-purple. Elsewhere in Europe, violet tended to be more blue-purple than the Roman color. This difference is partially attributable to the variations in violet dyes obtained from shellfish in various regions of Europe.

Those who have proposed the use of *blue* for Advent have done so in order to distinguish between the Advent season and the specifically penitential season of Lent. The same effect can be achieved by following the official color sequence of the Church, which requires the use of violet for Advent and Lent, while taking advantage of the varying shades which exist for violet. Hence, the bluer hues of violet might be used for Advent and the redder shades for Lent. Light blue vestments are not authorized for use in the United States.

New Publications

Several new liturgical publications are available from Liturgy Training Publications of the Archdiocese of Chicago:

At Home with the Word - 1989 edition - contains the Sunday readings for cycle C along with a reflection. $2.25.

A Workbook for Lectors and Gospel Readers 1989 - readings for the Sundays, holy days, vigil Masses, Easter Triduum of cycle C. Also contains aids for public reading and commentaries on the readings. $6.50.

Sourcebook for Sundays and Seasons 1989 by Peter Scagnelli - a planning guide based on the Sacramentary, Lectionary and other liturgical books. This book will be helpful to ministers and liturgical committees. $4.50

Parish Weddings by Austin Fleming - aid to the planning of good wedding liturgies. $3.25

Parish Funerals - this is a handbook for clergy, funeral directors, liturgical committees and musicians on the new Order of Christian Funerals. $3.25.

Guide for Sponsors - revised edition of the popular 1980 guide which is addressed to the sponsor who will participate in the Rite of Christian Initiation of Adults. $3.25.

How to Form a Parish Liturgy Board - a step-by-step approach for creating or renewing a parish liturgy committee. $6.95

An Advent Source Book by Thomas O'Gorman - readings, prayers, poetry, hymns, etc. A resource for homilists and musicians that is also suitable for private prayer and meditation. $12.95.

An Easter Source Book: The Fifty Days by Gabe Huck, Gail Ramshaw and Gordon Lathrop - scripture readings, prayers, poetry and prose, hymns and homilies for each day of the Easter season. $12.95.

Handbook for Cantors by Diana Kodner Sotak - treats the role and functions of the cantor and how to sing. $3.25.

The above publications are available, with quantity discounts, from: Liturgy Training Publications, 1800 North Hermitage Avenue, Chicago, IL 60622-1101. Telephone: 312/486-7008.

BISHOPS' COMMITTEE ON THE LITURGY

NEWSLETTER

NATIONAL CONFERENCE OF CATHOLIC BISHOPS

1988
VOLUME XXIV
OCTOBER

Father Gurrieri Completes Term as Executive Director

Reverend John A. Gurrieri, Executive Director of the Secretariat of the Bishops' Committee on the Liturgy for the past seven years, will leave his position on December 1, 1988. Father Gurrieri joined the staff of the Secretariat of the Bishops' Committee on the Liturgy in 1978 as Associate Director and was appointed Executive Director of the Secretariat in December 1981. After having completed studies at Cathedral College of the Immaculate Conception (Brooklyn) and St. Mary's Seminary and University (Baltimore), Father Gurrieri was ordained a priest of the Diocese of Brooklyn on May 27, 1967. He pursued graduate studies in religious education at Fordham University and studied liturgy and sacramental theology at the Institut Superieur de Liturgie in Paris, where he received the S.T.L. for his dissertation, *Enlightenment: Baptismal Rites of the Oriental Churches*. Prior to his appointment to the Secretariat he served as one of its consultants. He is a member of the Advisory Committee of the International Commission on English in the Liturgy and of ICEL's Original Texts Subcommittee.

Father Gurrieri served as a member of the Board of Directors of the Federation of Diocesan Liturgical Commissions. Presently he is a member of North American Academy of Liturgy, the Societas Liturgica, The Liturgical Conference, The Canon Law Society of America, and a member of the Board of the North American Consultation on Common Texts (CCT). From 1980-1985 Father Gurrieri was Lecturer in the Graduate Liturgical Studies Program at The Catholic University of America. Previously he taught at the Seminary of the Immaculate Conception, Huntington, NY. He has written numerous publications for the Bishops' Committee on the Liturgy, among which are *Study Text IV: Rite of Penance*, *Study Text V: Eucharistic Concelebration*, *Study Text VI: The Deacon*, and *Holy Days in the United States*. He has contributed essays to several books and has published articles in the *New Catholic Encyclopedia*, *Worship*, *Liturgy*, *Pastoral Music*, *The Jurist*, *Espace*, and several other journals.

Father Gurrieri will take a sabbatical at the Institute for Ecumenical and Cultural Research at Saint John's University, Collegeville, MN, where he hopes to finish his doctoral dissertation. He will then begin work in the Archdiocese of Los Angeles, where he will assist in on-going liturgical renewal and implementation on both the archdiocesan and university levels.

In announcing Father Gurrieri's departure from the staff to the National Conference of Catholic Bishops, Monsignor Daniel F. Hoye, General Secretary of the NCCB, said: "Father Gurrieri for the past decade has ably fulfilled a key position in the Conference staff, for nothing is more integral or important in the life of the Church than worship. He has with great skill assisted the bishops and the diocesan liturgical commissions in implementing the directives of the Holy See concerning the liturgy of the Church, and we are all in debt to this talented and gifted priest."

The members, advisors, consultants, and staff of the Bishops' Committee on the Liturgy echo Monsignor Hoye's words and express their thanks to Father Gurrieri for his dedicated service to the liturgical life of the Church in this country.

Father Krisman Appointed Executive Director

Monsignor Hoye has announced that the Reverend Ronald F. Krisman, Associate Director of the Secretariat of the Bishops' Committee on the Liturgy, has been appointed as the new Executive Director of the Liturgy Secretariat, effective December 1, 1988. Father Krisman, a priest of the Diocese of Lubbock, was ordained to the priesthood in 1973. He received the S.T.M. in theology from Woodstock College and

1312 MASSACHUSETTS AVENUE, N.W. • WASHINGTON, D.C. 20005

the bachelor's degree in music, with specialization in organ performance, composition, and church music, from Manhattanville College in Purchase, NY.

Father Krisman has served as a member of the board of directors of the Federation of Diocesan Liturgical Commissions, as treasurer of the FDLC, and as the chairman of its Music Committee. He has also been a member of the Music Subcommittee of the Bishops' Committee on the Liturgy and the Music Subcommittee of the International Commission on English in the Liturgy.

Father Krisman, after serving in several positions in the Diocese of Amarillo, was appointed Associate Director of the Secretariat of the Bishops' Committee on the Liturgy in January of 1982. For the past two years he has had the additional responsibility of coordinating the move to the Conference's new headquarters near Catholic University. The members, advisors, consultants and staff of the Bishops' Committee on the Liturgy extend their congratulations to Father Krisman, and look forward to his new role as Executive Director of the Liturgy Secretariat.

Catholic Household Blessings and Prayers

Catholic Household Blessings and Prayers (CHBP), which was approved by the Administrative Committee of the National Conference of Catholic Bishops in March 1988, is being published by USCC Publishing Services and will be available in November (see Newsletter, Volume XXIV, May/June 1988, pages 22-24).

Handsomely bound and beautifully illustrated, *Catholic Household Blessings and Prayers* contains prayers and blessings to mark the rhythms of daily life: joys and sorrows, daily routines, and the cycle of the Church's liturgical year. A hardcover book containing approximately 400 pages, CHBP is divided into five parts: I. *The Daily Blessings*, II. *Days and Seasons*, III. *Times in Life: Blessings of Family Members*, IV. *Blessings for Various Times and Places*, V. *Common Prayers*. The introduction provides detailed instructions for individual and family or small group use.

Catholic Household Blessings and Prayers sells for $18.95. Discounts are available for Standing Order Service members (40%), Parishes (20%), Dioceses, Seminaries and Religious Orders (30%) and Trade Accounts (40%). The book will make a fine Christmas gift for a family or for individuals.

In the Foreword, the Bishops' Committee on the Liturgy sets the tone of the book and explains its purpose:

> Since the promulgation of the *Constitution on the Sacred Liturgy* of the Second Vatican Council, all of us have experienced the first steps toward a renewal of the liturgy of the Church. We see clearly now that this liturgical renewal cannot be a matter of texts and rubrics only; the heart of this renewal is prayer. And the key to renewing the prayer of the Sunday assembly is enkindling a love for and practice of prayer in the hearts of those who make up the Church. Prayer must happen in the "little churches"—the households, the families—if the Sunday assembly is to become a community of prayer. The Council taught that the liturgy "is the primary and indispensable source from which the faithful are to derive the true Christian spirit" (*Constitution on the Sacred Liturgy*, 14). How can that spirit come to fill and give shape to our lives unless it is there in the prayers of individuals and families?
>
> In 1984, a *Book of Blessings* was published by the Vatican Congregation for Divine Worship. It includes many texts for blessings that are to be used by both clergy and laity and suggests that the local Church adapt and expand these rites. We have accepted this invitation to provide a book of blessings and prayers for all Catholics in the United States. In doing so, we have sought ways in which our Church's liturgy can become a strong and constant source of the "true Christian spirit" for clergy and laity alike.
>
> And so, this book is devoted to that "bond of prayer" that joins the prayer of the Sunday assembly to the daily prayers of every Catholic, the bond between Roman Catholics of all descriptions, and our bond to other Christians and, in many ways, to Jews from whom we have learned so much of our prayer.
>
> We hope that this book will find a place in every Catholic household—but not a place to rest. This book and the family's Bible, side by side, should become worn out with use. Along with other signs—the cross, holy water, blessed candles—the presence of the Bible and this book of prayers

expresses a way of life. This Catholic way—a way of daily justice, of service, and of care that is found around the family table and around the world's wide table—is our baptismal charge. It is the garment we put on at baptism; we are clothed with Christ.

From one generation to the next, we must learn, hold dear, and hand on the words and gestures, the songs and Scriptures of our faith. At the altar on Sunday, at table and at bedside all week, we learn throughout our lives who we are: the Body of Christ.

We address a special word to parents. Some of you grew up with such words and ways of prayer. Some did not. All of us, whatever our background, are still learning to pray, still learning to be Christians. Take this book, then, and search through it. Learn well, for your own sake, some of its daily prayers, some of its blessings for ordinary and special times. Begin to pray beside your children even when they are very young. Pray in your own words, by all means, but pray especially the words of the Church. Pray because you yourself need to pray. Then, as your children grow, invite them into this prayer. Bless them each night. Pray at table with them each evening. Let them hear you singing the songs of faith and reading the holy Scriptures. Let them know that fasting and almsgiving, care for the poor and the sick, and daily intercession for justice and for peace are what you hold most dear.

To all Catholics we say: take time with these pages. Come to know the strength of the texts they hold. Find those prayers and rites that can be celebrated in your life and in your home. Wear this book out with use until you know much of it by heart.

Newsletter Subscription Renewals

Computerized renewal notices will be sent to all subscribers to the Bishops' Committee on the Liturgy *Newsletter* in November. Subscribers are asked to return the completed renewal forms with their payment before December 20, 1988. (Subscriptions which have not been renewed by the time the January 1989 *Newsletter* goes to press will be placed on an inactive list and reinstated once payment is received.) Because of increases in printing and mailing costs during the past two years, the single subscription prices for 1989 will be raised to $9.00 domestic mail and $11.00 foreign airmail. Bulk rates will be raised 5 percent over the 1988 pricing.

In order that subscribers' accounts may be properly credited, the instructions accompanying the renewal forms should be followed. The "renewal coupon" portion of the invoice must be included with payment. Coupon and payment should be returned in the self-mailer envelope which has been provided. This envelope is preaddressed for direct mail deposit to the bank. Payment should not be sent to the Liturgy Secretariat, since this needlessly slows down the renewal process.

Subscribers who have not received a renewal form by November 30, 1988 should contact the Liturgy Secretariat and a duplicate invoice will be sent. (*Newsletter* recipients whose subscription number is 205990, 205995, or 205999 are receiving *gratis* copies. Therefore, they will receive no renewal invoice.)

The Liturgy Secretariat expresses its thanks to all subscribers for their cooperation in the renewal process.

New Publications of the Liturgy Committee and Secretariat

The Office of Publishing and Promotion Services of the United States Catholic Conference will soon make available several new publications prepared by the Bishops' Committee on the Liturgy and its Secretariat.

In cooperation with the Bishops' Committee on Ecumenical and Interreligious Affairs, and the active participation of a number of Catholic and Jewish biblical and liturgical scholars, including the Anti-Defamation League of B'nai B'rith, the Bishops' Committee on the Liturgy has prepared a statement which concerns preaching and worship in the context of Catholic-Jewish relations. *God's Mercy Endures For Ever: Guidelines on the Presentation of Jews and Judaism in Catholic Preaching* responds to the 1985 *Notes on the Correct Presentation of Jews and Judaism in Catholic Preaching and Catechesis,* issued by the Holy See's Commission for Religious Relations with the Jews. The new statement will be available in late January 1989. Publication number: 247-0. Price: $2.45.

On June 2, 1988, the Congregation for Divine Worship issued a *Directorium de celebrationibus dominicalibus absente presbytero* in Latin and Italian. At the request of the Bishops' Committee on the Liturgy and several other English-speaking conferences of bishops, the International Commission on English in the Liturgy has prepared an English translation, *Directory for Sunday Celebrations in the Absence of a Priest.* (For information on other aspects of this question and how it is being addressed by the Bishops' Committee on the Liturgy, see *Newsletter,* June/July 1988, pages 25-30.) This *Directory* is presently being prepared for publication by the USCC Office of Publishing and Promotion Services and will be available in late November 1988. Publication number: 251-9. Price: $1.95.

In 1970 the Bishops' Committee on the Liturgy issued *The Diocesan Liturgical Commission,* a document meant to assist dioceses in the establishment of liturgical commissions, music commissions and commissions for art and architecture. With the collaboration of the Federation of Diocesan Liturgical Commissions, the Secretariat of the Bishops' Committee on the Liturgy has prepared *Promoting Liturgical Renewal: Guidelines for Diocesan Liturgical Commissions and Offices of Worship,* a completely new document to replace the 1970 statement. Twenty-five years after the promulgation of *Sacrosanctum Concilium* liturgical commissions and offices of worship remain important diocesan structures to continue the liturgical renewal and reform desired by the Second Vatican Council. *Promoting Liturgical Renewal* will be available from the USCC Office of Publishing and Promotion Services in early December 1988. Publication number: 250-0. Price: $1.95.

To place your advance order for these publications, call 1-800-235-USCC (8722), or mail your order to: United States Catholic Conference, Office of Publishing and Promotion Services, 1312 Massachusetts Avenue, NW, Washington, DC 20005.

September Administrative Committee Meeting

The Administrative Committee of the National Conference of Catholic Bishops met on September 13-15, 1988, at which time it considered several proposals of the Bishops' Committee on the Liturgy. It approved the request to include a presentation on the revision of *The Roman Missal* at the November plenary meeting of the NCCB. Representatives of the International Commission on English in the Liturgy will report on the progress of the revision of the English translation of the Missal and will respond to the questions of the bishops.

The Administrative Committee approved the First Sunday of Advent, December 3, 1989, as the implementation date for the "texto unico" of the Order of Mass in Spanish. The Spanish edition of the *Sacramentary (Sacramentario),* for use in the dioceses of the United States of America, will use this version of the Order of Mass. The preparation of the *Sacramentario* has already begun and should be completed by mid-1990.

The Administrative Committee also authorized the publication of *God's Mercy Endures For Ever: Guidelines on the Presentation of Jews and Judaism in Catholic Preaching,* a statement of the Bishops' Committee on the Liturgy prepared in response to the 1985 *Notes on the Correct Presentation of Jews and Judaism in Catholic Preaching and Catechesis,* issued by the Holy See's Commission for Religious Relations with the Jews. It is meant to assist Catholic preachers to present Jews and Judaism correctly throughout the liturgical year. *God's Mercy* was prepared in collaboration with the Bishops' Committee for Ecumenical and Interreligious Affairs and Catholic and Jewish scholars. The statement will be published by USCC Publishing Services.

Finally, the Administrative Committee agreed to place the following items on the agenda of the November plenary meeting of the National Conference of Catholic Bishops: new English liturgical texts for the Office of Readings, Morning Prayer, and Evening Prayer of the *Liturgy of the Hours* for the feast of Our Lady of Guadalupe (12 December); English and Spanish versions of the Mass for the Bicentennial of the Establishment of the U.S. Hierarchy; English and Spanish versions of the Mass for the Fifth Centenary of the Evangelization of the Americas; liturgical calendar questions regarding Saint Rose Philippine Duchesne, Saint Jane Frances de Chantal, Blessed Junipero Serra, and Venerable Katharine Drexel. The Liturgy Committee will propose that Saint Rose Philippine Duchesne be commemorated as an optional memorial on November 18. Since the feast of our Lady of Guadalupe has prevented the liturgical celebration of the commemoration of Saint Jane Frances de Chantal on December 12, the Liturgy Committee has agreed to propose the transfer of her memorial to August 18 with the rank of an optional memorial. The Bishops' Committee on the Liturgy will also propose that Blessed Junipero Serra and Venerable Katharine Drexel, who will be beatified in late November, both be commemorated in the proper calendar for the dioceses of the United States with the rank of optional memorials.

BISHOPS' COMMITTEE ON THE LITURGY
NEWSLETTER
NATIONAL CONFERENCE OF CATHOLIC BISHOPS

1988
VOLUME XXIV
NOVEMBER

November Plenary Assembly of the NCCB

The National Conference of Catholic Bishops gathered in plenary assembly, November 14-17, in Washington, DC. The Bishops' Committee on the Liturgy presented seven action items for the consideration of the bishops. All the action items were approved by the required two-thirds majority of the *de iure* members of the episcopal conference and must now be confirmed by the Apostolic See.

Proper texts were approved for insertion into the *Liturgy of the Hours* for use on the feast of Our Lady of Guadalupe (December 12). These include new proper texts for the Office of Readings, Morning Prayer, and Evening Prayer. The new office is a translation of the Spanish text used in Mexico and has been adapted for use in the United States. Those who celebrate the Divine Office in Spanish may use the Mexican propers.

The bishops approved English and Spanish versions of a Mass in Celebration of the 200th Anniversary of the Establishment of the Hierarchy in the United States of America. The Mass contains the entrance antiphon, opening prayer, readings, prayer over the gifts, preface, communion antiphon, and prayer after communion. The new Mass will be used in November 1989, when the National Conference of Catholic Bishops gathers in Baltimore for the bicentennial commemoration of the appointment of John Carroll as the first bishop of the United States. The Mass may also be used in local celebrations of the event and eventually will be inserted into the *Sacramentary* as a Mass for the Church in the United States of America.

The bishops also approved English and Spanish versions of a Mass in Celebration of the Fifth Centenary of the Evangelization of the Americas. The Mass contains the entrance antiphon, opening prayer, readings, prayer over the gifts, preface, communion antiphon, prayer after communion, and solemn blessing. Prepared at the request of the NCCB Ad Hoc Committee for the Observance of the Fifth Centenary of the Evangelization of the Americas, this Mass text will be available for use during the 1992 celebration of the fifth centenary.

The bishops also approved four changes in the Proper Calendar for the Dioceses of the United States of America.

A commemoration of Saint Rose Philippine Duchesne, virgin, is to be inserted in the calendar on November 18 with the rank of an optional memorial. Saint Rose Philippine was born on August 29, 1769 in Grenoble, France. She came to the United States in 1818 and founded the first American house of the Religious of the Sacred Heart of Jesus. Especially noteworthy is the fact that she opened the first American free school west of the Mississippi. At the age of 71 she began a school for Indians at Sugar Creek, Missouri. Her biographers have stressed her courage in frontier conditions, her singlemindedness in pursuing her dream of serving Native Americans, her self-acceptance, and her contemplative presence which was so evident that the Indians called her "the woman who prays always." She was beatified in 1940 and canonized on July 3, 1988. Although the optional memorial of the Dedication of the Churches of Saints Peter and Paul is observed on the same day, either that optional memorial or the optional memorial of Saint Rose Philippine may be observed. The opening prayer has already been confirmed by the Apostolic See for the Religious of the Sacred Heart. It may be used for Mass and for the Liturgy of the Hours.

> Gracious God,
> you filled the heart of Philippine Duchesne
> with charity and missionary zeal,
> and gave her the desire
> to make you known among all peoples.

Fill us, who honor her memory today,
with that same love and zeal
to extend your kingdom to the ends of the earth.

We ask this through our Lord Jesus Christ, your Son,
who lives and reigns with you and the Holy Spirit,
one God, for ever and ever.

The National Conference of Catholic Bishops approved the inclusion of the optional memorial of Saint Jane Frances de Chantal, religious, on August 18, in the Proper Calendar for the Dioceses of the United States of America. The General Roman Calendar includes the commemoration of Saint Jane Frances on December 12; however, in the United States this optional memorial has been impeded for two decades by the obligatory memorial of Our Lady of Guadalupe (which is now a feast). The Superiors of the Visitation Monasteries in the United States requested that her commemoration be moved to a day when it could be celebrated, and they suggested the date of August 18 as a possible alternative. The bishops approved the transfer of Saint Jane Frances de Chantel's commemoration to August 18 and the its rank remains that of an optional memorial.

The bishops approved the insertion of the commemoration of Blessed Junipero Serra in the Proper Calendar for the Dioceses of the United States of America, on the date to be determined by the Apostolic See, with the rank of an optional memorial. Fray Junipero Serra was responsible in a large part for the foundation and spread of the Church on the West Coast of our country while it was still Spanish territory. He was beatified by Pope John Paul II on September 25, 1988.

The bishops also approved the optional memorial of Blessed Katharine Drexel for inclusion in the Proper Calendar for the Dioceses of the United States of America on March 3. Blessed Katharine came from a prominent Philadelphia family. She dedicated her life to the evangelization of Black and Native American peoples and founded religious communities for this purpose. She was beatified by Pope John Paul II on November 20, 1988.

1988 National Meeting of Diocesan Liturgical Commissions

The annual National Meeting of Diocesan Liturgical Commissions, sponsored by the Federation of Diocesan Liturgical Commissions and the Bishops' Committee on the Liturgy, held in San Diego, CA, from October 10-13, drew about 250 participants, including liturgical commission delegates from 12 regions throughout the United States.

Speakers at the National Meeting said that the liturgy, which is an experience of the kingdom of God, calls the assembly to work for peace and justice throughout the world. Developing the theme of the annual meeting, "Liturgy and Social Justice: Celebrating Rites—Proclaiming Rights," speakers noted that eucharistic celebrations, to which all people are invited, unite congregations in the challenge to break down divisive barriers in society: racism, sexism, classism, ageism, nationalism and chauvinism.

At the opening session, a homily by Archbishop Raymond G. Hunthausen of Seattle stated, "It is impossible to worship God in good conscience and ignore our clear responsibilities to work at building up that kingdom." Archbishop Hunthausen was unable to attend the meeting due to poor weather conditions in Seattle, and his homily had to be read to the assembly. Citing Pope John Paul's encyclical *On Social Concerns,* Archbishop Hunthausen stressed the importance of giving "preference to the poor"—those who are hungry, homeless, "without medical care, and above all, those without hope of a better future." The liturgy "gives a glimpse of what the kingdom (of God) could be like" and invites the assembly to overcome its inertia and improve existing social and economic structures by combating "militarism, the arms race, sickness, poverty, hatred and oppression of every sort," the archbishop said.

Sister Thea Bowman, a Franciscan Sister of Perpetual Adoration and a faculty member at the Institute of Black Catholic Studies at Xavier University in New Orleans, gave a fine presentation which incorporated Black spirituals, gospel music, and Black preaching. She emphasized that the Creed underscores the equality of all people and calls the faithful to protect and defend life. "Having shared our belief, are we willing to offer bread and wine in union with our brothers and sisters in Russia, Cuba and South Africa?" Receiving the Eucharist is "our communion with Jesus, Jesus with the Father and our communion with each other." Sister Bowman reminded her audience that justice, which includes eliminating child abuse and spouse abuse, should be preached from the pulpit. "If you don't want to talk about justice, call it love." She exhorted her listeners to be intolerant of racism and to use their "spiritual, social, economic and political power" to work for justice. At the conclusion of her presentation, Sister Bowman urged a daily examination of the participants' commitment to "help someone overcome oppression" by sheltering the homeless, teaching the illiterate and listening to people who hurt.

Father J. Bryan Hehir, U.S. Catholic Conference counselor for social policy, noted that the Second Vatican Council's document on the Church in the Modern World, *Gaudium et Spes,* places "social ministry at the heart of the life of the Church" but that it has been difficult to forge that link between liturgy and social action. Father Hehir said the Church in the United States is a microcosm of society that is "faced with creating a common vision out of voices, faces, races and cultures." "Those who gather on Sunday morning should get some sense of how they should be the Church in a thousand places this week. . . and make decisions about how to raise their kids, do their jobs and vote," he said.

Father Jose Rubio of the Diocese of San Jose spoke on the need for liturgy to preserve the cultural identity of ethnic groups, which he called necessary for the Church's survival among these groups. In particular, he pointed out that certain Hispanic ceremonies can be used while preserving the unity of the Roman Rite. Effective use of cultural adaptations to the liturgy requires dialogue between the clergy and members of the ethnic community, he added.

Resolutions of the Federation of Diocesan Liturgical Commissions

The following Position Statements were adopted by the Diocesan Liturgical Commissions at the Annual National Meeting sponsored by the Bishops' Committee on the Liturgy and the Federation of Diocesan Liturgical Commissions in San Diego, California, October 10-13, 1988. The degree of commitment of the members to the statement is indicated in parentheses. The voting scale is graded from +3 (highest degree of commitment) to -3 (completely negative to the statement). A commitment of 1.5 is required for acceptance. Those resolutions addressed to the Bishops' Committee on the Liturgy (BCL) will be considered by the Liturgy Committee at its next meeting.

Catechesis on the Relationship Between Liturgy and Social Justice
P. S. 1988 A

It is the position of the delegates to the 1988 National Meeting of Diocesan Liturgical Commissions that the Board of Directors of the FDLC request and assist the BCL in publishing an appropriate document developing a catechesis on how the liturgical rites inherently articulate a spirituality of Social Justice.

We request that a time-line and procedure for implementation of this resolution be set by the FDLC Board of Directors at the January 1989 Board Meeting. (Passed + 2.0)

Primacy of the Sunday Lectionary
P. S. 1988 B

It is the position of the delegates to the 1988 National Meeting of Diocesan Liturgical Commissions that the Eucharist and Liturgical Year Committee of the FDLC develop guidelines in collaboration with other national organizations, suggesting how special themes and causes may be appropriately included in the Sunday liturgy while maintaining the primacy of the Sunday lectionary.

We request that a time-line and procedure for implementation of this resolution be set by the FDLC Board of Directors at the January 1989 Board Meeting. (Passed + 1.67)

Guidelines for Liturgical Personnel
P. S. 1988 C

It is the position of the delegates to the 1988 National Meeting of Diocesan Liturgical Commissions that the Ministry Committee of the FDLC in dialogue with the National Association of Church Personnel Administrators (NACPA) formulate national guidelines that incorporate criteria for just employment agreements, including job descriptions, just salary/benefit ranges, and recourses for grievances for diocesan and parochial liturgical personnel.

We request that a time-line and procedure for implementation of this resolution be set by the FDLC Board of Directors at the January 1989 Board Meeting. (Passed + 2.34)

Importance of Diocesan Worship and/or Liturgical Commissions
P. S. 1988 D

It is the position of the delegates to the 1988 National Meeting of Diocesan Liturgical Commissions that the FDLC Board of Directors in collaboration with the BCL encourage all diocesan bishops to initiate or to continue to support the establishment and maintaining of active, adequately staffed and funded Worship Offices and Diocesan Liturgical Commissions which can stand, in their own right, as a viable means of encouragement, direction and support for the liturgical life of the entire diocese and all the faithful.

We request that a time-line and procedure for implementation of this resolution be set by the FDLC Board of Directors at the January 1989 Board Meeting. (Passed + 2.94)

Two resolutions of immediate concern were also passed by the delegates:

Tridentine Mass
R.I.C. 1988 E

Whereas in July 1988, *Ecclesia Dei* asked for a "wider and more liberal use of the 1984 Indult for the use of the Tridentine Liturgy;

Whereas in light of the concessions which have been made, confusion has followed:

The delegates to the 1988 National Meeting of the Diocesan Liturgical Commissions are resolved that the ecclesiological dimensions and pastoral implications of these concessions are a matter of significant and immediate concern to them. They urge that the BCL Secretariat communicate this concern to the appropriate authorities so that they may give this matter serious consideration in the near future. (Passed + 2.97)

The Reverend John A. Gurrieri
R.I.C. 1988 F

Whereas Reverend John A. Gurrieri has served the BCL for the past ten years;

Whereas he has served the FDLC and its members in innumerable ways;

Whereas he has always been a friend of the FDLC;

Whereas he has modeled for us a love of the Lord and a love of the liturgy;

It is our immediate concern that the delegates to the 1988 National Meeting of Diocesan Liturgical Commissions express their gratitude and love to Rev. John A. Gurrieri for a "job well done" and a wish for "God's speed" to where ever his journey leads him. (Passed by acclamation)

Clarification on Sprinkling with Holy Water and Incensation

The following clarification appeared in the July 1988 issue of Notitiae *(No. 264, page 476).*

Question: How are the rubrics of the Missal concerning sprinkling with holy water and incensation to be understood? Since these actions are optional (*ad libitum*), is there not an inclination to interpret that which is optional as exceptional or superfluous?

Response: In regard to the sprinkling with holy water, the Missal maintains it as optional for all Sunday Masses, and no longer as in the past only for use at the principal Mass. The sprinkling takes the place of the penitential rite.

In regard to incensation, the General Instruction of the Roman Missal states: "The use of incense is optional in any form of Mass" (no. 235). The phrase ought to be understood in its entirety: *optional* signifies that incensation is not obligatory, but *in any form of Mass* means that incensation is not reserved to that which in the past was called the "solemn Mass" with a deacon and subdeacon.

The optional aspect of sprinkling and incensation is, therefore, not to be understood as restrictive, but goes together with an enlargement of the possibilities offered for the use of these symbolic actions.

After a period marked by an inflation of the word to the detriment of signs, it is good to rediscover the importance of symbolic actions in the liturgy. The *Ceremonial of Bishops* can be a guide in this sense (see *Ceremonial of Bishops,* ch. 3, "The Cathedral Church;" for incensation, see nos. 89-98; for sprinkling, see nos. 110-114).

BISHOPS' COMMITTEE ON THE LITURGY
NEWSLETTER

NATIONAL CONFERENCE OF CATHOLIC BISHOPS

**1988
VOLUME XXIV
DECEMBER**

Reverend Kenneth F. Jenkins Named BCL Associate Director

On December 14, 1988, Monsignor Daniel F. Hoye, General Secretary of the National Conference of Catholic Bishops, announced that he had appointed the Reverend Kenneth Frank Jenkins, a priest of the Diocese of San Bernardino, as an Associate Director of the Secretariat of the Bishops' Committee on the Liturgy.

Born in Santa Rosa, California, Father Jenkins was ordained for the Diocese of San Bernardino on January 25, 1980. He studied at the Saint Meinrad School of Theology in Indiana, from which he was granted the Master of Divinity degree in 1980. Before pursuing studies for the priesthood, he received the Bachelor of Arts degree in Ancient Civilizations and the Masters in Business Administration from the University of California in Riverside in 1973, and 1975, respectively. Subsequent to his ordination he was awarded in August 1980 the Master of Arts degree in Theology (Liturgical Studies) from the University of Notre Dame.

Currently Father Jenkins serves as Director of the Diocesan Office of Worship, and as Administrative Assistant to the Bishop, Director of the Office of Continuing Education for Clergy and Religious, Vicar to Priests in Special Works, and Episcopal Master of Ceremonies. Since July, 1980, he has served as chair of the diocesan liturgical commission.

Additional responsibilities which Father Jenkins has fulfilled include serving as Secretary-Treasurer of the diocesan Presbyteral Council, chairman of the San Bernardino Diocesan Tenth Anniversary Committee, coordinator of the past two diocesan Convocations of Priests, chairman of the Ministries Subcommittee for the Los Angeles Coliseum Papal Mass in September 1987, member of the Liturgy and Music Committee for several Los Angeles Religious Education Congresses, and member of the Diocesan Council on Economic Affairs. In addition he is an associate of the North American Academy of Liturgy and of the Notre Dame Center for Pastoral Liturgy.

Father Jenkins will assume his new position in Washington, DC, on January 23, 1989.

Twenty-Fifth Anniversary of the Constitution on the Liturgy

The twenty-fifth anniversary of the promulgation by Pope Paul VI of the Constitution on the Sacred Liturgy, *Sacrosanctum concilium,* was observed on December 4, 1988. As the first document of the Second Vatican Ecumenical Council and in conjunction with the Dogmatic Constitution on the Church, *Lumen Gentium,* and the Pastoral Constitution on the Church in the Modern World, *Gaudium et spes,* the liturgical constitution has been responsible for a profound transformation in the life of the Church.

In observance of this significant anniversary, Georgetown University, Washington, DC, on December 2-4, 1988, hosted an invitational Colloquium on Liturgical Renewal: 1963-1988. Sponsored by the centers for liturgy in the United States—The Corpus Christi Center for Liturgy, The Georgetown Center for Liturgy, Spirituality, and the Arts, The Loyola Pastoral Institute, and The Notre Dame Center for Pastoral Liturgy—the Colloquium centered around nine addresses, which presented reflections on a study of the worship attitudes and practices of 15 English-speaking parishes in various portions of the United States. The speakers drew out inferences contained in the study from the viewpoints of sociology (Dr. William McCready), ritual studies (Dr. Ronald Grimes), the theology of grace (Rev. Roger Haight, SJ), Christology (Rev. Gerard Sloyan), ecclesiology (Dr. Monika Hellwig), symbol and the hidden languages of liturgy (Dr. Don Saliers), liturgical history (Rev. Aidan Kavanagh, OSB), liturgical theology (Rev. John Baldovin, SJ), and "liturgical futurology" (Sr. Kathleen Hughes, RSCJ). The Colloquium eucharist was celebrated by Bishop Joseph P. Delaney, Chairman of the Bishops' Committee on the Liturgy.

The proceedings of this invitational colloquium will be published at a future date.

1312 MASSACHUSETTS AVENUE, N.W. ● WASHINGTON, D.C. 20005

Promoting Liturgical Renewal

In 1970 the Bishops' Committee on the Liturgy published *The Diocesan Liturgical Commission: Documentation, Proposed Goals, and Present Projects*. Eventually this statement was allowed to go out of print since its contents had become somewhat dated over the course of 15 years. A few years ago the Liturgy Secretariat, in cooperation with the Federation of Diocesan Liturgical Commissions, began to prepare a revised set of guidelines for liturgical commissions and offices of worship. The revision, entitled *Promoting Liturgical Renewal: Guidelines for Diocesan Liturgical Commissions and Offices of Worship*, has recently been published by the USCC Office of Publishing and Promotion Services. It should be of great assistance to those seeking to establish or renew diocesan liturgical commissions and/or offices of worship.

Promoting Liturgical Renewal contains sections on: Liturgy in the Life of the Church; The Role of the Bishop in Worship; Liturgical Co-Workers with the Bishop; The Local Structures Which Support the Bishop's Role; and Models of Organization for Diocesan Liturgical Structures. The respective functions of national liturgical organizations (the Federation of Diocesan Liturgical Commissions, and the Bishops' Committee on the Liturgy) and international ones (the International Commission on English in the Liturgy and the Congregation for Divine Worship and the Discipline of the Sacraments) are also presented.

Promoting Liturgical Renewal (Publication No. 250-0) is available from the Office of Publishing and Promotion Services, United States Catholic Conference, 1312 Massachusetts Avenue, NW, Washington, DC 20005 for $1.95 per copy. The usual bulk order, parish, and diocesan discounts are available. For telephone orders, please call (toll free) 1-800-235-USCC.

National and International Liturgical Organizations

Inquiries directed at the Secretariat of the Bishops' Committee on the Liturgy often reveal a lack of knowledge about the functions and respective competencies of the Bishops' Committee on the Liturgy, the Federation of Diocesan Liturgical Commissions, the International Commission on English in the Liturgy, and the Congregation for Divine Worship and the Discipline of the Sacraments. The following paragraphs, taken from *Promoting Liturgical Renewal*, spell out the roles of each of these organizations.

Bishops Committee on the Liturgy

The Bishops' Committee on the Liturgy (BCL) is a standing committee of the National Conference of Catholic Bishops (NCCB) with a history dating back to November 1958. Originally, this committee was called the "Bishops' Committee on the Liturgical Apostolate," a title derived from the 1947 encyclical *On the Sacred Liturgy (Mediator Dei)*, which refers to the task of diocesan commissions as promoting "the liturgical apostolate." In 1967, following a general pattern for designating both standing and ad hoc bodies of the NCCB, the title was changed to "Bishops' Committee on the Liturgy." The Second Vatican Council's *Constitution on the Sacred Liturgy* more clearly defined the work of this group. The Committee, assisted by a Secretariat in Washington, DC, is composed of seven member bishops, various consultant bishops, and ten advisors (lay, religious, and priests).

The functions of the BCL are to: contribute to the preparation of appropriate liturgical rites, texts, and books; assist bishops individually and collegially in implementing the official norms and directives of the Holy See and of the NCCB; and assist the bishops in the development of liturgical catechesis and the continued liturgical renewal of priests, deacons, religious men and women, and the laity of the Church.

The BCL publishes a *Newsletter,* which gives liturgical directives, notices, activities, and so forth. Although primarily intended for the bishops of the United States and their diocesan liturgy personnel, the publication enjoys a much broader circulation since it is a valuable source of current liturgical information as well as a practical liturgical tool. In addition, the BCL Secretariat distributes various documents to diocesan liturgical commissions and offices.

Federation of Diocesan Liturgical Commissions

The Federation of Diocesan Liturgical Commissions (FDLC), first convened in 1969 by the Secretariat of the Bishops' Committee on the Liturgy, is a national organization of diocesan liturgical commissions or their equivalent structures in the United States and its territories.

The purposes of the organization are to: foster and coordinate the work of diocesan liturgical personnel;

commission, gather, and dispense informational materials that will aid diocesan liturgy personnel in their work; serve the Bishops' Committee on the Liturgy in an advisory capacity; bring to the Bishops' Committee on the Liturgy the insights arising from pastoral experience; encourage, promote, and facilitate the legitimate adaptation of liturgical rites in the light of experiences in the United States; and be a medium through which diocesan liturgy personnel may contribute responsibly and effectively to articulating the voice of clergy, religious, and laity in the development of liturgy.

Participants at the annual National Meeting of Diocesan Liturgical Commissions, co-sponsored by the FDLC and the Bishops' Committee on the Liturgy, profit from formal presentations, specialized workshops and interest sessions, and dialogue with one another. In such a way, diocesan liturgy personnel become acquainted with approaches for possible use when they return home and are afforded an opportunity to meet persons from other dioceses who are willing to share experiences and projects. In the meeting's business sessions, members of the FDLC are able to vote on liturgical priorities that are presented for consideration to the Bishops' Committee on the Liturgy or are acted upon by the Federation itself or its member dioceses.

The International Commission on English in the Liturgy

The International Commission on English in the Liturgy (ICEL) was established in 1963, during the Second Vatican Council, by the principal conferences of bishops from English-speaking countries. The primary program of ICEL is the translation into English of the official Latin texts of the Roman liturgy. This program also includes auxiliary undertakings: commentaries or notes on texts, liturgical documentation, commissioning of musical settings for ICEL texts, subsidiary catechetical materials, and so forth. Another responsibility is the composition of original liturgical texts.

The governing body of ICEL is an Episcopal Board consisting of eleven bishops, designated by the constituent episcopal conferences. Serving as a consultative and coordinating body, the ICEL Advisory Committee consists of experts in various disciplines who advise the Episcopal Board, formulate ICEL programs and policies, and oversee the work of those undertaking various projects.

The actual authority to approve texts for liturgical use resides in the individual episcopal conferences themselves, each for its own territory. This approbation is, in turn, subject to confirmation by the Holy See.

The Congregation for Divine Worship and the Discipline of the Sacraments

In May 1969, Pope Paul VI divided the Sacred Congregation of Rites into two distinct congregations (i.e., the Congregation for Divine Worship and the Congregation for the Causes of Saints). The first incorporated the Consilium for the Implementation of the Constitution on the Sacred Liturgy, which continued as a particular commission within the Congregation until its work of revising the Roman liturgical books was completed.

In 1975, Pope Paul VI established a new congregation (i.e., the Sacred Congregation for the Sacraments and Divine Worship) to take the place of the Congregation of the Sacraments (created by Pope Pius X in 1908) and the Congregation for Divine Worship.

In 1984, Pope John Paul II divided the former congregation into the Congregation for the Sacraments and the Congregation for Divine Worship, and in 1988, he reunited these two congregations under the title of Congregation for Divine Worship and the Discipline of the Sacraments.

The Congregation for Divine Worship and the Discipline of the Sacraments is responsible for the pastoral, spiritual, canonical, and disciplinary dimensions of the sacraments and other liturgical rites of the Church. This congregation also publishes *Notitiae*, a monthly journal containing short articles on liturgical renewal and reports on the liturgical activities of episcopal conferences and national liturgical commissions.

Both the International Commission on English in the Liturgy and the Congregation for Divine Worship and the Discipline of the Sacraments exist to help the episcopal conferences and the local Churches to celebrate the liturgy of the Church in spirit and in truth.

Workshop on the Ceremonial of Bishops

The May/June 1988 issue of the *Newsletter* (page 24) noted that the Bishops' Committee on the Liturgy had approved a proposal for a national workshop on the revised *Ceremonial of Bishops,* which is due to be published in English during the early part of 1989.

The workshop will take place in San Francisco at Saint Mary's Cathedral, from Thursday evening, November 30, until 1:00 p.m. on Sunday, December 3, 1989. It is intended to serve as an introduction to the provisions of the *Ceremonial* for those who are actively involved in the planning and execution of liturgical celebrations at which the bishop presides: bishops, masters of ceremonies, cathedral personnel, musicians, diocesan liturgy office personnel, etc.

A tentative listing of topics to be discussed includes: Episcopal Liturgy as a Theological *Locus* for Ecclesiology; An Overview of Papal and Episcopal Ceremonials: How We Have Gotten to Where We Are Today; The Role of the Bishop as Celebrant among His People, and Those Who Assist Him; Selected Chapters from the *Ceremonial of Bishops:* The Stational Mass and Ordinations; The *Ceremonial of Bishops* and Its Relation to Other Liturgical Books: Pastoral Applications; The Church at Prayer: Going beyond Rubrics to the Heart of the Church's Worship.

In addition to these major presentations, there will be workshops and special interest sessions covering the following: rites of initiation; installations and funerals of bishops; confirmation; the role and presence of bishops at liturgical celebrations; the role of the deacon and the master of ceremonies; interrelation of the office of worship and the cathedral staff; Chrism Mass; architectural elements of the cathedral; bishops; masters of ceremonies and secretaries to the bishop; cathedral rectors; musicians; diocesan offices of worship/liturgical commissions.

Further information will be provided in upcoming issues of the *Newsletter*. Those interested in attending the workshop are asked to reserve these dates in their calendars.

Southwest Liturgical Conference 1989 Study Week

The Southwest Liturgical Conference, which comprises the dioceses of the states of Arizona, Colorado, New Mexico, Oklahoma, Texas, Utah, and Wyoming, will hold its 27th annual study week at the Oklahoma City Archdiocesan Pastoral Center on January 16-19, 1989. The theme of the conference is "Let the Children Come to Me," with a focus on children, faith, and worship.

Major topics and speakers will include: "Faith Development in the Child," the keynote address by the Reverend Robert Hater: "Sacraments and Initiation for the Child," Reverend Frank Sokol; "Faith Formation in the Family: Liturgy and Learning," Gerard Baumbach; "Scripture and the Child," Mary Catherine Berglund; "Music for Children," Lee Gwozdz; and "Worship and the Child," Elizabeth McMahon Jeep.

A variety of workshops of special interest are planned for preachers, musicians, liturgy planners, catechists, and others. There will also be a number of sessions showcasing music for children.

For additional information, contact: SWLC Study Week, Office of Worship and Spiritual Life, P.O. Box 32180, Oklahoma City, OK 73123. Telephone: (405) 721-5651.

Resources

Sunday: The Original Feast Day: Pastoral letter of the Most Reverend Joseph A. Fiorenza, Bishop of Galveston-Houston, on the Sunday Eucharist. Available in English, Spanish and Vietnamese: study guide available in English and Spanish. Cost: $2.00 per copy. Study guide: $1.00. Write: Office of Worship, Diocese of Galveston-Houston, 1700 San Jacinto, Houston, TX 77002. Telephone: 713/659-5461.

BISHOPS' COMMITTEE ON THE LITURGY
NEWSLETTER
NATIONAL CONFERENCE OF CATHOLIC BISHOPS

1989
VOLUME XXV
JANUARY

Address of Pope John Paul II to the Members and Consultants of the Congregation for Divine Worship

On Friday, December 2, 1989, Pope John Paul II received in special audience the participants attending the advisory meeting ("Consulta") of the Congregation for Divine Worship. Following is the text of his address on that occasion.

1. I am happy to meet you, superiors, officials, consultors and experts of the Congregation for Divine Worship, assembled for the advisory meeting.

I greet all present, particularly Cardinal Eduardo Martinez Somalo; I thank him for the words he has addressed to me, and I cordially wish him every success in the office of Prefect of your Congregation, which I have recently entrusted to him.

The meeting is held on the occasion of the 25th anniversary of the publication of the Constitution *Sacrosanctum Concilium* which actually took place on 4 December 1963. This document marks a milestone in the history of the Church, rediscovering the profound Christian tradition in the liturgical field. True, there have been unlawful interpretations, but it is indisputable that its beneficial influence has stimulated a new impetus in community prayer. The fruits which it has given to the Church are many. This is not the time to enumerate them; God willing, I will do so soon in a commemorative document.

2. The twenty-five years which separate us from that day tell us that the situation in the Church, and also in society, has been subjected to change. New generations have arrived, and they are now taking on their responsibilities even in the field of liturgical apostolate. This involves the necessity to evaluate the Church's liturgy more and more deeply, and above all to live it and make it lived according to the spirit and the letter, genuinely interpreted, of the important Conciliar document.

The work which now occupies you is to put into practice its profound statements, when it says that the liturgy is the most important manifestation of the life of the Church (see *Sacrosanctum Concilium*, 2, 26, 41). If, as the Constitution *Lumen Gentium* recalls, this is "the people brought together by the unity of the Father, Son and Holy Spirit," then the liturgy also must express this trinitarian energy in an intense way.

The liturgy lives by drawing from this source: in fact, in it is celebrated the paschal mystery of Christ, ever present and working in the center of all liturgical actions. It celebrates the praises of, and gives thanks to, the "'fountain-like' love" of the Father (see *Ad Gentes*, 2). In it also the Church invokes the Holy Spirit because she wishes to express her awareness of not acting according to human capacity but of doing what only God's grace can do.

3. To arrive at the spiritual depth of the liturgical celebration, it requires the "theological, historical, spiritual, pastoral and juridical" formation of which *Sacrosanctum Concilium* speaks in no. 16. It is what the Constitution *Pastor Bonus* established by reuniting in one single Congregation all the activity proper to the sanctifying office. It states: "Without prejudice to the competence of the Congregation for the Doctrine of the Faith, the Congregation is concerned with everything pertaining to the Apostolic See as regards the regulation and promotion of the sacred liturgy, in the first place, of the sacraments" (*Pastor Bonus*, art. 62), and "it promotes and defends the rules" connected with them (art. 63).

It is not a question of two different things, the liturgy on the one hand and the sacraments on the other, but of one single reality, the liturgy of the Church; within this the sacraments, of which the Eucharist is fundamental, have their place. Indeed, it is in the sacraments that the work of redemption is especially perpetuated and participated in by all the members of the Mystical Body, to the glory of God and the salvation of the world.

1312 MASSACHUSETTS AVENUE, N.W. • WASHINGTON, D.C. 20005

Thus, in the Roman Curia and in all the particular Churches there opens up a more organic view of the sanctifying office. It will be the Church's concern to make a creative effort in all the areas mentioned to ensure that this desire expressed in the Constitution *Pastor Bonus* may be realized effectively. As *Sacrosanctum Concilium* has already stated, and the 1985 Synod of Bishops reaffirmed, "in order that the liturgy may be able to produce its full effects it is necessary that the faithful come to it with proper dispositions, that their minds be attuned to their voices, and that they cooperate with heavenly grace lest they receive it in vain. Pastors of souls must, therefore, realize that when the liturgy is celebrated, something more is required than the laws governing valid and lawful celebration. It is their duty also to ensure that the faithful take part, fully aware of what they are doing, actively engaged in the rite and enriched by it" (*Sacrosanctum Concilium*, 11).

4. The reference which is made to pastors in this Conciliar text introduces a particularly important aspect, namely that of assisting diocesan bishops so that they may guide their faithful to participate more and more actively and spiritually in the sacred liturgy (see *Pastor Bonus*, art. 64, 1). The restoration to the bishop's authority of the power and office of regulating the liturgy in his own particular Church: this was one of the great achievements of *Sacrosanctum Concilium* (see arts. 22.1, 41).

The Congregation, as an organ of the Petrine ministry, has the task of serving ecclesial communion between the Church of Rome and the local Churches throughout the world. In this matter also it is necessary to study attentively the ways of personal collaboration and of seeking the spiritual and pastoral needs which appear in the whole Church.

On all sides, the liturgical reform has caused a great and generous commitment. It must be continued, maintained and, when necessary, purified. Here also the presence of the Congregation will prove useful as a means of liaison and help which does not suppress, but throws into greater relief, the original characteristics of each body.

To you, who have a role of primary importance in this mission, I wish success in your work.

For my part, I accompany you with my special interest and my constant prayer. May the Apostolic Blessing, which I now cordially impart to all of you, sustain you.

New Committee Member and Advisors

The Most Reverend Joseph P. Delaney, Chairman of the Bishops' Committee on the Liturgy, recently made three appointments to the Committee. The Most Reverend Charles J. Chaput, OFM Cap, ordained as Bishop of Rapid City this past summer, was appointed as the seventh member of the Committee. This position had been vacant for the past year.

Newly appointed as advisors to the Committee were: Sister Jennifer Glen, CCVI, instructor in liturgical studies at Saint Mary's Seminary in Houston and a doctoral candidate in the Liturgical Studies Program at the Catholic University of America; and Reverend John Huels, OSM, professor of canon law at the Catholic Theological Union in Chicago and a specialist in liturgical and sacramental law.

Sister Rosa Maria Icaza, CCVI, member of the pastoral team of the Mexican American Cultural Center in San Antonio, TX, was recently elected president of the Institute for Hispanic Liturgy. By virtue of that position, she will serve as an *ex-officio* advisor to the Bishops' Committee on the Liturgy, replacing Father Juan Sosa of Miami. Sr. Icaza also serves as a member of the Hispanic Liturgy Subcommittee.

Advisors who have served on the Liturgy Committee during the past year but whose appointments were not previously announced in the *Newsletter* are: Sister Nancy Swift, RCE, professor of liturgy at Saint John's Seminary, Brighton, MA, and previously associated with the Woodstock Center for Religion and Worship; Reverend Douglas Ferraro, Director of the Office for Liturgy and Worship of the Archdiocese of Los Angeles; and Reverend Andrew Ciferni, O Praem, instructor in liturgical studies at The Catholic University of America, Washington, DC, who serves as an *ex-officio* advisor to the Liturgy Committee as the representative of the Conference of Major Superiors of Men Religious.

Continuing to serve as advisors to the Committee are: Reverend William M. Cieslak, OFM Cap, Franciscan School of Theology, Berkeley, CA; Sister Kathleen Loewen, OP, Director of the Office of Worship, Archdiocese of Milwaukee; Reverend Michael Spillane, Executive Secretary of the Federation of Diocesan Liturgical Commissions; and Reverend Richard E. Ward, Chairman of the Board of Directors of the FDLC.

Liturgy Committee members are: Bishops Joseph P. Delaney, Patrick R. Cooney, Wilton D. Gregory, Ricardo Ramirez, CSB, Michael J. Sheehan, and Richard J. Sklba. Episcopal consultants are: His Eminence Joseph Cardinal Bernardin (member, Congregation for Divine Worship and the Discipline of the Sacraments); Most Reverend Daniel E. Pilarczyk (U.S. representative on the ICEL Episcopal Board), Most Reverend John J. Snyder, and Most Reverend John F. Whealon (chairman, Lectionary Subcommittee).

November 1988 Meeting of the Bishops' Committee on the Liturgy

The NCCB Liturgy Committee met in Washington, DC, on November 13, 1988. In addition to reviewing the seven liturgical action items on the agenda of the NCCB Plenary Meeting [see *Newsletter,* November 1988, pp. 41-42.] the members also approved the agenda for the Workshop and Presentation on the *Progress Report on the Revision of the Roman Missal,* which was conducted on Tuesday, November 15, 1988.

These matters were also discussed: 1) the North American Consultation on Common Text's *A Celebration of Baptism: An Ecumenical Liturgy;* 2) Liturgical Texts: Memorial of St. Lawrence Ruiz and companions, martyrs (approved for submission to the NCCB Administrative Committee in March); 3) *Criteria for the Evaluation of Inclusive Language in Scripture Translations Destined for Use in the Liturgy,* drafted by the Joint Committee (Liturgy and Doctrine) on Inclusive Language; 4) the FDLC Resolutions from the October 1988 National Meeting of Diocesan Liturgical Commissions in San Diego; 5) Lakota as a Liturgical Language; 6) Proposed National Guidelines on Cremation and Catholic Burial Practices (a task force will be established in June to begin studying these various matters).

Reports were received on several projects: *Lectionary for Mass,* second edition; *Catholic Worship and Black Americans,* a proposed statement of the Black Liturgy Subcommittee; the proposed statement of the Bishops' Committee on the Liturgy on, and the ritual for, Sunday Celebrations in the Absence of a Priest; and the *Lectionary for Masses with Children and for other Celebrations.* In addition Bishop Ramirez reported on the projects of the Hispanic Liturgy Subcommittee: 1) the Spanish *Sacramentario* for use in the dioceses of the United States; 2) bilingual editions of the rites of baptism and marriage; 3) *Order of Christian Funerals* in Spanish (possibly a bilingual edition); 4) Spanish edition of the American additions to the *Book of Blessings.*

The Liturgy Committee members, consultants and advisors of the will meet for their annual plenary meeting at Seton Hall University in South Orange, NJ, on June 13-15, 1989.

Twenty-fifth Anniversary of the International Commission on English in the Liturgy

A history-making occasion for the liturgical renewal in the English-speaking world occurred in Rome on October 17, 1963. On that day, representatives from several English-speaking conferences of bishops (including the late Archbishop Paul Hallinan of Atlanta) established the International Committee on English in the Liturgy. To mark the twenty-fifth anniversary of that event, Bishop Joseph P. Delaney, Chairman of the Bishops' Committee on the Liturgy, on December 12, 1988, sent the following letter of congratulations to Mr. John R. Page, Executive Secretary of the International Commission on English in the Liturgy.

As chairman of the Committee on Liturgy of the National Conference of Catholic Bishops, I am writing to congratulate the Episcopal Board, the Advisory Committee, the Subcommittees and the Secretariat staff of the International Commission on English in the Liturgy on the occasion of the twenty-fifth anniversary of ICEL's founding on October 17, 1963.

For one quarter of a century the International Commission on English in the Liturgy has given outstanding service to the world's English-speaking conferences of bishops in the preparation of translations and original English texts for use in the liturgy. And, as was admirably demonstrated during the workshop on the revision of the *Roman Missal,* presented by ICEL on November 15, 1988, to the members of the National Conference of Catholic Bishops of the United States of America, we have every expectation that ICEL's projects in the next several years will attain even greater heights of simplicity, beauty, and prayerfulness.

The members of the Bishops' Committee on the Liturgy unanimously join me in expressing their congratulations to the International Commission on English in the Liturgy for a job well done.

Activities of the Congregation for Divine Worship

On January 2, 1989, His Eminence Eduardo Cardinal Martinez, Prefect of the Congregation for Divine Worship and the Discipline of the Sacraments, wrote to the presidents of national liturgical commissions in order to indicate the present and future activities of the Congregation. Following is a brief summary of that letter.

Projects of the Congregation during the Past Year

• The preparation of the revised edition of the *Roman Martyrology* continues at a slow pace, since it involves a great deal of checking and comparing texts.

• The fifth volume of the *Liturgy of the Hours* is still under preparation. This volume will contain a two-year cycle of biblical and patristic readings as well as the psalm prayers which were mentioned in the General Instruction of the Liturgy of the Hours, but were not included in the original four volumes of the Divine Office.

• The Congregation approved the adaptations of the Order of Mass and the Roman Missal, proposed for use in the Dioceses of Zaire.

• The Congregation confirmed a revision of the Mozarabic Rite. This rite, one of the ancient Latin liturgies of the West, had become considerably latinized over the centuries. Its use has been limited to a chapel in the cathedral of Toledo and to several other churches. The revision restores this venerable rite to its ancient form.

• As a part of its on-going work, the Congregation has reviewed and confirmed the calendars and propers of particular Churches and religious families.

• Throughout the year the Congregation has welcomed to its offices numerous bishops from New Guinea, Uganda, Zaire, Kenya, Zambia, Canada, Mexico, the United States of America, Australia, New Zealand, England and Wales, the Netherlands, and Poland on the occasion of their "*Ad limina*" visits to the Apostolic See.

• The Congregation published the following documents: *Circular Letter on the Preparation and Celebration of the Paschal Feasts; Declaration on Eucharistic Prayers and Liturgical Experimentation; Directory for Sunday Celebrations in the Absence of a Priest.* These documents, along with commentaries, were published in *Notitiae,* the journal of the Congregation.

From November 29 through December 3, 1988, the Consultors of the Congregation met in Rome. During the course of the meeting there was a commemoration of the twenty-fifth anniversary of the promulgation of the Constitution on the Sacred Liturgy, *Sacrosanctum Concilium,* and a discussion of the Apostolic Constitution, *Pastor Bonus* [see *Newsletter,* September 1988, pages 33-34].

Future Projects of the Congregation

To be published in the future are: a document on liturgical adaptation; a *Directory on the Participation of Young People in the Liturgy;* a letter, pastoral in scope, intended as an aid to a re-reading of the *Roman Missal;* and a "General Instruction" for all the rites which comprise the *Roman Ritual.* The latter will be similar to the introductions to the *Roman Missal* and the *Liturgy of the Hours.*

Corrigendum

The edition of the *Directory for Sunday Celebrations in the Absence of a Priest* from the Congregation for Divine Worship which was published by the USCC Office of Publishing and Promotion Services (publication no. 251-9) contains an omission on page 10, at the end of no. 30, paragraph 1.

The text of that paragraph should read: "In the absence of both a priest and a deacon, the pastor is to appoint laypersons, who are to be entrusted with the care of these celebrations, namely, with leading the prayers, with the ministry of the word, and with giving holy communion."

Errata sheets will be enclosed with copies of the present printing of the *Directory,* and future printings will contain the corrected text.

BISHOPS' COMMITTEE ON THE LITURGY

NEWSLETTER

NATIONAL CONFERENCE OF CATHOLIC BISHOPS

1989
VOLUME XXV
FEBRUARY

Rereading the Constitution on the Liturgy

The twenty-fifth anniversary of the promulgation of the Constitution on the Sacred Liturgy *Sacrosanctum concilium* on 4 December 1963 provides a fitting occasion to reflect, in the next few issues of the *Newsletter,* on the some of the basic principles expressed in that charter for liturgical renewal. Many of these principles not only underlie the reforms experienced in the past two decades; they also embody the foundational ecclesiological and theological concepts that shaped the pastoral orientation of the Second Vatican Council.

The *Constitution on the Sacred Liturgy* presents the goals of the conciliar reform of the Church's liturgy:

> This Sacred Council has several aims in view: it desires to *impart* an ever increasing *vigor to the Christian life* of the faithful; to *adapt* more suitably *to the needs of our own times* those institutions that are subject to change; to foster whatever can *promote union among all who believe in Christ;* to strengthen whatever can help to *call the whole of humanity into the household of the Church.* The Council therefore sees particularly cogent reasons for undertaking the reform and promotion of the liturgy (art. 1).[1]

As the first document of the Second Vatican Ecumenical Council, the *Constitution on the Sacred Liturgy* had a two-fold function. In the particular it provided for the reform of the liturgical life of the Church. In the universal it introduced the framework of the conciliar reform that would be expressed in the subsequent documents promulgated by the Council. Thus the Conciliar Fathers declared in the Constitution that they desired to give vigor to the Christian life, adapt the Church and its institutions to the needs of our time, promote unity among all who believe in Christ, and call all people into the household of the Church. These general motives for reform take on flesh in the renewal of the liturgical life of the Church.

Looking back over the past twenty-five years it is clear that the Church in the United States today is vibrant and alive. Although there have been controversies, excesses, and even mistakes in the implementation of post-conciliar reforms, the Church continues to move ahead renewing ecclesial life. This vitality is most clearly experienced in the celebration of the reformed liturgical rites. The liturgy is again understood as a central part of the activity of the parish, the diocese, and of the whole Church. No longer are Catholics mere spectators at the Church's highest act of worship. They now actively participate along with the priest and the other ministers in the celebration of the eucharistic liturgy, the Mass. The eucharist has been restored to its ancient simplicity so that it is once again manifestly the prayer of the entire Body of Christ. Each person, by virtue of baptism, has a unique role in the celebration of the eucharist, participating by singing, praying, listening, and ultimately sharing in the Body and Blood of Christ. Eucharistic assemblies are alive, at least in those places where the liturgical reforms have been adequately explained, lovingly accepted, and fully implemented.

The liturgical reform has had a vast impact on the life of other Churches and ecclesial communities. In the past twenty-five years almost every major Christian denomination in the United States has undergone a renewal of its liturgical life. A careful examination of the resulting rites reveals that the principles of the *Constitution on the Liturgy* have influenced the shape of the vast majority of these reformed liturgies. Not only are they similar to one another; most also reflect various aspects of the Roman reform.

As Protestants, Lutherans, and Anglicans have begun to stress the importance of the weekly celebration of the eucharist, Catholics have stressed a renewed appreciation of the proclamation of the Word of God. All Churches and ecclesial communions that have initiated reforms have come to see that the proclamation of the Word of God and the celebration of the sacrament of the Eucharist are the norm for Sunday worship.

1312 MASSACHUSETTS AVENUE, N.W. • WASHINGTON, D.C. 20005

The liturgical year and calendar are virtually the same in every Church. The structure of the liturgy follows the same basic outline and often the same prayers are used. The eucharistic prayer of Hippolytus, for example, is the basis of at least one eucharistic prayer in each Church.

Probably the greatest ecumenical fruit of the liturgical reform and renewal is the lectionary. In the United States nearly every Church or ecclesial communion has adopted some form of the Roman lectionary, adapted, of course, to the particular needs and traditions of each Church. As Christians grow in sharing these common forms of prayer, they will also grow in a common understanding of the meaning of that prayer.

The renewal within the Church has led to an opening, an invitation, to those outside the Christian family. As forebears in the faith of Abraham and Moses, Jews are seen with a new closeness as Catholics recognize their Jewish roots. Elements of Christian prayer reflect the synagogue, the Jewish family table, and the Temple. The Church's liturgical reforms respect these Jewish origins of Christian worship.

In addition, the Church is now willing to accept into its worship elements from local cultures which are not contrary to the Christian faith. This is a return to the process whereby the Roman liturgy and the liturgies of the Churches of the East took on their distinctive characteristics. Thus, the liturgy is no longer a static and unchanging ceremony, rather it is a reflection, a mirror, of the life and the faith of the people who celebrate it.

Note

¹ Quotations from the *Constitution on the Liturgy* are taken from *Documents on the Liturgy, 1963-1979: Conciliar, Papal, and Curial Texts,* edited by the International Commission on English in the Liturgy, published by The Liturgical Press, Collegeville, MN, 1982. All rights reserved. Used with permission.

Ministries in the Church

On 30 December 1988 Pope John Paul II issued his post-synodal Apostolic Exhortation Christifideles Laici, *on the vocation and the mission of the lay faithful in the Church and in the world. The following excerpt deals with the distinction between ministries exercised by the ordained and by lay persons in the Church. The numbering of the paragraphs and footnotes corresponds to that of the full document. For the complete text of* Christifideles Laici, *see* Origins, *vol. 18, no. 35 (February 9, 1989), pp. 561-595.*

21. The Second Vatican Council speaks of the ministries and charisms as the gifts of the Holy Spirit which are given for the building up of the Body of Christ and for its mission of salvation in the world.⁶⁴ Indeed, the Church is directed and guided by the Holy Spirit, who lavishes diverse hierarchical and charismatic gifts on all the baptized, calling them to be, each in an individual way, active and coresponsible.

We now turn our thoughts to ministries and charisms as they directly relate to the lay faithful and to their participation in the life of Church-Communion. [. . .]

The Ministries Derived from Holy Orders

22. In a primary position in the Church are the ordained ministries, this is, the ministries that come from the sacrament of orders. In fact, with the mandate to make disciples of all nations (see Matthew 28:19), the Lord Jesus chose and constituted the apostles—the seed of the People of the New Covenant and origin of the hierarchy⁶⁵—to form and to rule the priestly people. The mission of the apostles, which the Lord Jesus continues to entrust to the pastors of his people, is a true service, significantly referred to in Sacred Scripture as *"diakonia,"* namely, service or ministry. The ministries receive the charism of the Holy Spirit from the Risen Christ, in uninterrupted succession from the apostles, through the sacrament of orders: from him they receive the authority and sacred power to serve the church, acting *in persona Christi Capitis* (in the person of Christ, the Head)⁶⁶ and to gather her in the Holy Spirit through the Gospel and the sacraments.

The ordained ministries, apart from the persons who receive them, are a grace for the entire Church. These ministries express and realize a participation in the priesthood of Jesus Christ that is different, not simply in degree but in essence, from the participation given to all the lay faithful through baptism and confirmation. On the other hand, the ministerial priesthood, as the Second Vatican Council recalls, essentially has the royal priesthood of all the faithful as its aim and is ordered to it.⁶⁷

For this reason, so as to assure and to increase communion in the Church, particularly in those places where there is a diversity and complementarity of ministries, pastors must always acknowledge that their ministry is fundamentally ordered to the service of the entire People of God (see Hebrews 5:1). The lay faithful, in turn, must acknowledge that the ministerial priesthood is totally necessary for their participation in the mission of the Church.[68]

The Ministries, Offices and Roles of the Lay Faithful

23. The Church's mission of salvation in the world is realized not only by the ministers in virtue of the sacrament of orders but also by all the lay faithful; indeed, because of their baptismal state and their specific vocation, in the measure proper to each person, the lay faithful participate in the priestly, prophetic and kingly mission of Christ.

The pastors, therefore, ought to acknowledge and foster the ministries, the offices and the roles of the lay faithful that find their foundation in the sacraments of baptism and confirmation, indeed, for a good many of them, in the sacrament of matrimony.

When necessity and expediency in the Church require it, the pastors, according to established norms from universal law, can entrust to the lay faithful certain offices and roles that are connected to their pastoral ministry but do not require the character of orders. The Code of Canon Law states: "When the necessity of the Church warrants it and when ministers are lacking, lay persons, even if they are not lectors or acolytes, can also supply for certain of their offices, namely, to exercise the ministry of the word, to preside over liturgical prayers, to confer baptism, and to distribute holy communion in accord with the prescriptions of the law."[69] However, *the exercise of such tasks does not make pastors of the lay faithful:* in fact, a person is not a minister simply in performing a task, but through sacramental ordination. Only the sacrament of orders gives the ordained minister a particular participation in the office of Christ, the Shepherd and Head, and in his Eternal Priesthood.[70] The task exercised in virtue of supply takes its legitimacy formally and immediately from the official deputation given by the pastors, as well as from its concrete exercise under the guidance of ecclesiastical authority.[71]

The recent Synodal Assembly has provided an extensive and meaningful overview of the situation in the Church on the ministries, offices and roles of the baptized. The Fathers have manifested a deep appreciation for the contribution of the lay faithful, both women and men, in the work of the apostolate, in evangelization, sanctification and the Christian animation of temporal affairs, as well as their generous willingness to supply in situations of emergency and chronic necessity.[72]

Following the liturgical renewal promoted by the Council, the lay faithful themselves have acquired a more lively awareness of the tasks that they fulfill in the liturgical assembly and its preparation, and have become more widely disposed to fulfill them: the liturgical celebration, in fact, is a sacred action not simply of the clergy, but of the entire assembly. It is, therefore, natural that the tasks not proper to the ordained ministers be fulfilled by the lay faithful.[73] In this way there is a natural transition from an effective involvement of the lay faithful in the liturgical action to that of announcing the word of God and pastoral care.[74]

In the same Synod Assembly, however, a critical judgment was voiced along with these positive elements, about a too-indiscriminate use of the word "ministry," the confusion and the equating of the common priesthood and the ministerial priesthood, the lack of observance of ecclesiastical laws and norms, the arbitrary interpretation of the concept of "supply," the tendency toward a "clericalization" of the lay faithful and the risk of creating, in reality, an ecclesial structure of parallel service to that founded on the sacrament of orders.

Precisely to overcome these dangers the Synod Fathers have insisted on the necessity to express with greater clarity, and with a more precise terminology[75] both the unity of the Church's mission in which all the baptized participate, and the substantial diversity of the ministry of pastors which is rooted in the sacrament of orders, all the while respecting the other ministries, offices and roles in the Church, which are rooted in the sacraments of baptism and confirmation.

In the first place, then, it is necessary that in acknowledging and in conferring various ministries, offices and roles on the lay faithful, the pastors exercise the maximum care to institute them on the basis of baptism in which these tasks are rooted. It is also necessary that pastors guard against a facile yet abusive recourse to a presumed "situation of emergency" or to "supply by necessity," where objectively this does not exist or where alternative possibilities could exist through better pastoral planning.

The various ministries, offices and roles that the lay faithful can legitimately fulfill in the liturgy, in the transmission of the faith, and in the pastoral structure of the Church, ought to be exercised in conformity to their specific lay vocation, which is different from that of the sacred ministry. [. . .]

In the course of Synod work the Fathers devoted much attention to the *lectorate* and the *acolytate*. While in the past these ministries existed in the Latin Church only as spiritual steps on route to the ordained ministry, with the *motu proprio* of Paul VI, *Ministeria Quaedam* (15 August 1972), they assumed an autonomy and stability, as well as a possibility of their being given to the lay faithful, albeit, only to men. This same fact is expressed in the new *Code of Canon Law*.[77] At this time the Synod Fathers expressed the desire that "the *motu proprio Ministeria Quaedam* be reconsidered, bearing in mind the present practice of local churches and above all indicating criteria which ought to be used in choosing those destined for each ministry."[78]

In this regard a Commission was established to respond to this desire voiced by the Synod Fathers, specifically to provide an in-depth study of the various theological, liturgical, juridical and pastoral considerations which are associated with the great increase today of the ministries entrusted to the lay faithful.

While the conclusions of the Commission's study are awaited, a more ordered and fruitful ecclesial practice of the ministries entrusted to the lay faithful can be achieved if all the particular Churches faithfully respect the above mentioned theological principles, especially the essential difference between the ministerial priesthood and the common priesthood, and the difference between the ministries derived from the sacrament of orders and those derived from the sacraments of baptism and confirmation.

Notes

[64] See Second Vatican Ecumenical Council, Dogmatic Constitution on the Church *Lumen Gentium*, 4.

[65] See Second Vatican Ecumenical Council, Decree on the Mission Activity of the Church *Ad Gentes*, 5.

[66] See Second Vatican Ecumenical Council, Decree on the Sacred Priesthood *Presbyterorum Ordinis*, 2; see Second Vatican Ecumenical Council, Dogmatic Constitution on the Church *Lumen Gentium*, 10.

[67] See Second Vatican Ecumenical Council, Dogmatic Constitution on the Church *Lumen Gentium*, 10.

[68] See John Paul II, Letter on Holy Thursday to all the Priests of the Church (9 April 1979), 3-4: *Insegnamenti*, II, 1 (1979), 844-847.

[69] *Code of Canon Law*, canon 230 §3.

[70] See Second Vatican Ecumenical Council, Decree on the Ministry and Life of Priests *Presbyterorum Ordinis*, 2 and 5.

[71] See Second Vatican Ecumenical Council, Decree on the Apostolate of Lay People *Apostolicam Actuositatem*, 24.

[72] The *Code of Canon Law* lists a series of roles and tasks proper to the sacred ministers, that nevertheless for special and grave circumstances, and concretely in areas which lack priests or deacons, can temporarily be exercised by the lay faithful, with previous juridic faculty and mandated by competent ecclesiastical authority: See canons 230 §3; 517 §2; 776; 861 §2; 910 §2; 943; 1112, etc.

[73] See Second Vatican Ecumenical Council, Constitution on the Sacred Liturgy *Sacrosanctum Concilium*, 28; *Code of Canon Law*, canon 230 §2 that states: "lay persons can fulfill the function of lector during the liturgical actions by temporary deputation; likewise all lay persons can fulfill the functions of commentator or cantor or other functions, in accord with the norm of law."

[74] The *Code of Canon Law* presents diverse roles and tasks that the lay faithful can fulfill in the organized structure of the Church: see canons 228; 229 §3; 317 §3; 463 §1, 5 and §2; 483; 494; 537; 759; 784, 785; 1282; 1421.

[75] See *Propositio 18*.

[77] See *Code of Canon Law*, canon 230 §1.

[78] *Propositio 18*.

God's Mercy Endures Forever

God's Mercy Endures Forever: Guidelines on the Presentation of Jews and Judaism in Catholic Preaching, the most recent statement of the Bishops' Committee on the Liturgy, has recently been published by the Office of Publishing and Promotion Services of the United States Catholic Conference. This document is the product of cooperation between Catholic and Jewish scholars and is a concrete application of the guidelines contained in the 1985 *Notes on the Correct Way to Present the Jews and Judaism in Preaching and Catechesis of the Roman Catholic Church* issued by the Vatican Commission for Religious Relations with the Jews.

God's Mercy Endures Forever includes chapters on: Jewish Roots of the Liturgy; Historical Perspectives and Contemporary Proclamation; Advent: The Relationship between the Scriptures; Lent: Controversies and Conflicts; Holy Week: The Passion Narratives; The Easter Season; Pastoral Activity during Holy Week and the Easter Season; Preaching throughout the Year; Suggested Reading. The statement should be studied by all those who have the responsibility for preaching the Word of God and planning liturgical celebrations.

God's Mercy Endures Forever (Publication No. 247-0) is available from the USCC Office of Publishing and Promotion Services, 1312 Massachusetts Avenue NW, Washington, DC 20005. Telephone (toll-free): 1-800-235-USCC. Cost: $2.45 per copy; the usual discounts apply.

BISHOPS' COMMITTEE ON THE LITURGY
NEWSLETTER

NATIONAL CONFERENCE OF CATHOLIC BISHOPS

**1989
VOLUME XXV
MARCH/APRIL**

Confirmation of Book of Blessings

On February 8, 1989 the National Conference of Catholic Bishops received the decree of the Congregation for Divine Worship, dated January 27, 1989, confirming the decision of the Administrative Committee of the NCCB to approve the English version of De Benedictionibus *and a supplementary collection of proper blessings for use in the dioceses of the United States of America. The following is an unofficial English translation of that decree.*

Prot. N. 699/88

At the request of His Excellency John L. May, Archbishop of St. Louis and President of the National Conference of Catholic Bishops, on January 19, 1989, and in virtue of the faculty granted to this Congregation by the Supreme Pontiff, Pope John Paul II, we gladly approve, that is, confirm *ad interim* the English text of *De Benedictionibus* (Green Book), as it appears in the appended copy.

In addition we gladly approve, that is, confirm the proper Supplement to this book, as it appears in the appended copy.

This decree, by which the requested confirmation is granted by the Apostolic See, is to be included in its entirety in the published text. Two copies of the printed text should be sent to this Congregation.

Anything to the contrary notwithstanding.

From the Congregation for Divine Worship, 27 January 1989.

+ Eduardo Cardinal Martinez
  Prefect

+ Virgilio Noe
  Titular Archbishop of Voncaria
  Secretary

Confirmation of Proper Texts for the *Liturgy of the Hours* on the Feast of Our Lady of Guadalupe

On February 8, 1989 the National Conference of Catholic Bishops received the decree of the Congregation for Divine Worship, dated January 20, 1989, confirming the decision of the National Conference of Catholic Bishops on November 15, 1988, to approve proper liturgical texts in English for use in the dioceses of the United States of America in celebrations of the Liturgy of the Hours *on the feast of Our Lady of Guadalupe (December 12). The following is an unofficial English translation of that decree.*

Prot. N. 1609/88

At the request of His Excellency John L. May, Archbishop of St. Louis and President of the National Conference of Catholic Bishops, on December 20, 1988, and in virtue of the faculty granted to this Congregation by the Supreme Pontiff, Pope John Paul II, we gladly approve, that is, confirm the English text of the *Liturgy of the Hours* in honor of the Blessed Virgin Mary, under the title "Our Lady of Guadalupe," as it appears in the appended copy.

1312 MASSACHUSETTS AVENUE, N.W. ● WASHINGTON, D.C. 20005

This decree, by which the requested confirmation is granted by the Apostolic See, is to be included in its entirety in the published text. Two copies of the printed text should be sent to this Congregation.

Anything to the contrary notwithstanding.

From the Congregation for Divine Worship, 20 January 1989.

+ Eduardo Cardinal Martinez
Prefect

+ Virgilio Noe
Titular Archbishop of Voncaria
Secretary

THE LITURGY OF THE HOURS
DIVINE OFFICE
[In the dioceses of the United States]

December 12   **OUR LADY OF GUADALUPE**   **Feast**

The shrine of Our Lady of Guadalupe, near Mexico City, is one of the most celebrated places of pilgrimage in North America. On December 9, 1531, the Blessed Virgin Mary appeared to an Indian convert, Juan Diego, at Tepeyac and left him with a picture of herself imprinted upon his cloak. Devotion to Mary under the title of "Our Lady of Guadalupe" has continually increased, and today she is the Patroness of the Americas. Because of the close link between the Church in Mexico and the Church in the United States this feast was also added to the proper calendar for the dioceses of the United States.

From the common of the Blessed Virgin Mary, 1326, except the following:

INVITATORY

Ant.   Come, let us worship Christ, the Son of Mary.

Invitatory psalm as in the Ordinary, page 648.

OFFICE OF READINGS

HYMN: *Lo, How a Rose E'er Blooming*

Text: Isaiah 11:1; *Es ist ein' Ros' entsprungen; Speier Gebetbuch,* 1599; Tr. Stanzas 1-2 by Theodore Baker, 1851-1934; Stanza 3, *The Hymnal,* 1940

Tune: ES IST EIN' ROS' ENTSPRUNGEN 7 6 7 6 6 7 6; *Geistliche Kirchengesang,* Cologne, 1599; Harm. by Michael Praetorius, 1571-1621

PSALMODY

Ant. 1   Mary received a blessing from the Lord and loving kindness from God her savior.

Psalms from the Common of the Blessed Virgin Mary, 1328.

Ant. 2   Arise, my beloved, my beautiful one, and come; fragrant flowers now appear upon the earth.

Ant. 3   Behold, my beloved comes to me, springing across the mountains, leaping across the hills.

Blessed are those who hear the word of God.
— And cherish it in their hearts.

FIRST READING: Isaiah 52:7,9-10; 54:10-15;55:3b,12b-13 (*Peace will be proclaimed over the mountains*)

RESPONSORY

Even though I walk in the dark valley, I fear no evil; you are at my side; for I am wretched and poor and my heart is pierced within me.

— As a mother comforts her child, so will I comfort you. The sun shall not harm you by day, nor the moon by night.

— As a mother comforts her child, so will I comfort you.

SECOND READING

From a report by Don Antonio Valeriano, a Native American author of the sixteenth century (*Nican Mopohua,* 12th ed., 3-19, 21)

The Voice of the Turtledove has been heard in our land

At daybreak one Saturday morning in 1531, a few days before the month of December, an Indian named Juan Diego was going from the village where he lived to Tlatelolco in order to take part in divine worship and listen to God's commandments. When he came near the hill called Tepeyac, dawn had already come, and Juan Diego heard someone calling him from the very top of the hill: "Juanito, Juan Dieguito."

He went up the hill and caught sight of a lady of unearthly grandeur whose clothing was as radiant as the sun. She said to him in words both gentle and courteous: "Juanito, the humblest of my children, know and understand that I am the ever virgin Mary, Mother of the true God through whom all things live. It is my ardent desire that a church be erected here so that in it I can show and bestow my love, compassion, help, and protection to all who inhabit this land and to those others who love me, that they might call upon and confide in me. Go to the Bishop of Mexico to make known to him what I greatly desire. Go and put all your efforts into this."

When Juan Diego arrived in the presence of the Bishop, Fray Juan de Zumarraga, a Franciscan, the latter did not seem to believe Juan Diego and answered:"Come another time, and I will listen at leisure."

Juan Diego returned to the hilltop where the Heavenly Lady was waiting, and he said to her: "My Lady, my maiden, I presented your message to the Bishop, but it seemed that he did not think it was the truth. For this reason I beg you to entrust your message to someone more illustrious who might convey it in order that they may believe it, for I am only an insignificant man."

She answered him: "Humblest of my sons, I ask that tomorrow you again go to see the bishop and tell him that I, the ever virgin holy Mary, Mother of God, am the one who personally sent you."

But on the following day, Sunday, the bishop again did not believe Juan Diego and told him that some sign was necessary so that he could believe that it was the Heavenly Lady herself who sent him. And then he dismissed Juan Diego.

On Monday Juan Diego did not return. His uncle, Juan Bernardino, became very ill, and at night asked Juan to go to Tlatelolco at daybreak to call a priest to hear his confession.

Juan Diego set out on Tuesday, but he went around the hill and passed on the other side, toward the east, so as to arrive quickly in Mexico City and to avoid being detained by the Heavenly Lady. But she came out to meet him on that side of the hill and said to him: "Listen and understand, my humblest son. There is nothing to frighten and distress you. Do not let your heart be troubled, and let nothing upset you. Is it not I, your Mother, who is here? Are you not under my protection? Are you not, fortunately, in my care? Do not let your uncle's illness distress you. It is certain that he has already been cured. Go up to the hilltop, my son, where you will find flowers of various kinds. Cut them, and bring them into my presence."

When Juan Diego reached the peak, he was astonished that so many Castillian roses had burst forth at a time when the frost was severe. He carried the roses in the folds of his *tilma* (mantle) to the Heavenly Lady. She said to him: "My son, this is the proof and the sign which you will bring to the Bishop so that he will see my will in it. You are my ambassador, very worthy of trust."

Juan Diego set out on his way, now content and sure of succeeding. On arriving in the bishop's presence, he told him: "My Lord, I did what you asked. The Heavenly Lady complied with your request and fulfilled it. She sent me to the hilltop to cut some Castillian roses and told me to bring them to you in person. And this I am doing, so that you can see in them the sign you seek in order to carry out her will. Here they are; receive them."

He immediately opened up his white mantle, and as all the different Castillian roses scattered to the ground, there was drawn on the cloak and suddenly appeared the precious image of the ever virgin Mary, Mother of God, in the same manner as it is today and is kept in her shrine of Tepeyac.

The whole city was stirred and came to see and admire her venerable image and to offer prayers to her; and following the command which the same Heavenly Lady gave to Juan Bernardino when she restored him to health, they called her by the name that she herself had used: "the ever virgin holy Mary of Guadalupe."

Alternative:

From the message of Pope Paul VI to the Mexican people (*L'Osservatore Romano*, 18 October 1970)

The best homage to Mary: loving God and neighbor

Beloved sons and daughters, we wish to unite our voice to that filial hymn which the Mexican people raise up today to the Mother of God. Devotion to the most holy Virgin of Guadalupe must be for all of you a constant and specific demand for authentic Christian renewal. The crown which she expects from all of you is not so much a material one as a precious spiritual crown, shaped by a profound love of Christ and a sincere love of all: the two commandments which sum up the gospel message. The same most holy Virgin, with her example, guides us on these two paths.

In the first place, she exhorts us to make Christ the center and summit of our whole Christian life. She remains hidden, with supreme humility, so that the image of her Son might appear to humanity with all its incomparable brightness. For this reason, true Marian devotion reaches its fullness and its most rightful expression when it is a path to the Lord and directs all its love toward him, just as Mary knew how to do, so as to intertwine in one and the same impulse the tenderness of a mother and the piety of a creature.

But in addition, and precisely because she loved Christ so dearly, our Mother fulfilled perfectly that second commandment which must be the norm of all human relations: the love of neighbor. How beautiful and delicate was the intervention of Mary at the wedding feast of Cana, when she moved her Son to accomplish the first miracle of turning the water into wine solely to help those young spouses! It is a complete sign of the constant love of the Virgin for humanity in need, and ought to be an example for all those who seek to be considered truly her sons and daughters.

Christians can do no less than to show solidarity in seeking a solution to the situation of those to whom the bread of culture has not yet come nor the opportunity of honorable and justly remunerated work. They cannot remain indifferent while new generations find no path for the realization of their legitimate aspirations, and while part of humanity continues to be placed at the margins of the advantages of civilization and progress. For this reason, on this celebrated feast, we urge you from our heart to give your Christian life a clear social sense—as the Council has asked—that you may always be in the front line in all efforts to attain progress, and in all the initiatives for improving the situation of those who suffer want. See in each person a brother or a sister—a brother or sister in Christ—in such a way that the love of God and the love of the neighbor become united in the same love, alive and operative, which is the only thing that can redeem the miseries of the world, renewing it in its most profound root, the human heart.

The person who has much should be conscious of his or her obligation to serve and contribute with generosity to the good of all. The person who has little or who has nothing should, with the help of a just society, make every effort at self-improvement and of going beyond self, and even in cooperating in the progress of those who suffer the same situation. And, all of you, feel the obligation to unite fraternally so as to help forge this new world for which the human race longs.

This is what the Virgin of Guadalupe asks of you today, this fidelity to the Gospel, of which she knew how to be the most eminent example.

Upon you, dearly beloved sons and daughters, we implore with confidence the maternal benevolence of the Mother of God and Mother of the Church, in order that she may continue to protect your nation and to direct and impel it more and more along the paths of progress, communal love, and of a peaceful life together.

RESPONSORY

You shall love the Lord, your God, with all your heart, with all your soul, and with all your mind. This is the greatest and first commandment. And the second is like it: You shall love your neighbor as yourself.

— You shall love your neighbor as yourself.

Whatever you do for the least of my brothers and sisters, you do for me.

— You shall love your neighbor as yourself.

HYMN *Te Deum,* page 651.

PRAYER *(as at Morning Prayer)*

MORNING PRAYER

HYMN: *Hail Blessed Virgin*

Text: Anthony G. Petti, 1971

Tune: AVE VERA VIRGINITAS, L M - Josquin des Pres, c. 1445-1521 (*Worship II,* No. 106)

PSALMODY

Ant. 1. Who is this that comes forth like the dawn, as beautiful as the moon, as resplendent as the sun?

Psalms and canticle from Sunday, Week I, 688.

Ant. 2. You are the glory of Jerusalem, the joy of Israel; you are the fairest honor of our race.

Ant. 3. O Virgin Mary, how great your cause for joy; God found you worthy to bear Christ our Savior.

READING: Zechariah 2: 14-17

RESPONSORY

I lift up my eyes toward the mountains, from where shall help come to me?

— I lift up my eyes toward the mountains, from where shall help come to me?

Lord, for you I rise early, give me a sign of your favor.

— From where shall help come to me?

Glory to the Father . . .

— I lift up my eyes . . .

CANTICLE OF ZECHARIAH

Ant. Go up onto a high mountain, Jerusalem, herald of good news! Say to the cities of Judah: Here is your God! Like a shepherd he feeds his flock.

INTERCESSIONS

Let us praise God our all powerful Father, and say:

Lord, Creator of life, hear us.

Blessed are you, Lord of the universe. In your great goodness you sent us the Mother of your Son,
— to call us to faith and make us members of your holy people.

We bless you, Lord, because you have hidden your message from those who are wise and prudent in the ways of this world,
— and have revealed it to the lowly and the poor.

You call us to be your worthy and trusted messengers,

— may we carry to all peoples and nations your words of love and peace.

By the presence of Mary, you made the desert bloom with flowers,

— may the Blessed Virgin Mary's love transform us into the image of Christ.

Make us attentive to the message of Our Lady of Guadalupe,

— so that we may deserve to meet Mary along the path of our lives.

Our Father . . .

PRAYER

God of power and mercy,
you blessed the Americas at Tepeyac
with the presence of the Virgin Mary of Guadalupe.
May her prayers help all men and women
to accept each other as brothers and sisters.
Through your justice present in your hearts
may your peace reign in the world.

We ask this through our Lord Jesus Christ, your Son,
who lives and reigns with you and the Holy Spirit,
one God, for ever and ever.

EVENING PRAYER

HYMN: *Mary, How Lovely the Light of Your Glory*

Text: Brian Foley, b. 1919

Tune: CHANCE, 11 10 11 10; Colin Mawby, b. 1936 © 1971, Faber Music Ltd., London

PSALMODY

Ant. 1.   I have consecrated this temple and my name shall dwell within it.

Psalms and canticle from the Common of the Blessed Virgin Mary, 1345.

Ant. 2.   Blessed are you, O Mary, from you has come the salvation of the world.

Ant. 3.   The Virgin Mary is exalted above all the choirs of angels.

READINGS: Revelation 21, 2-3

RESPONSORY

Her children rose up and they called her blessed.

— Her children rose up and they called her blessed.

She opened her lips with wisdom and her tongue spoke words of love.

— And they called her blessed.

Glory to the Father . . .

— Her children rose up and they called her blessed.

CANTICLE OF MARY

Ant.   Deep waters cannot quench love, nor floods sweep it away.

INTERCESSIONS

God sent us the Blessed Virgin Mary to console us in our sorrow and to lead us to himself. Let us confidently pray:

Grant us her love, help, and protection.

You made Mary the gate through which the true Light shone over the earth,
— by the light of her Son may the Church seek justice for the oppressed and peace for all people.

The image of the Mother and your Son was imprinted on the garment of the Indian Juan Diego with the features of his race,
— imprint within us Mary's virtues and her love for the poor and the defenseless.

Through Mary you changed barren Tepeyac into a fragrant garden of flowers,
— through her transform us, that we may grow fruitfully as true Christians.

In Juan Diego you give us an example of simplicity and humility,
— teach us constancy in suffering and fidelity to the Gospel.

You made the Virgin Mary the protector of all who call upon her and trust in her,
— may the light of her consolation shine on those who have departed from this life.

Our Father . . .

PRAYER (*as at Morning Prayer*)

Confirmation of Calendar Change and Additions

On February 8, 1989 the National Conference of Catholic Bishops received the decree of the Congregation for Divine Worship, dated January 20, 1989, confirming the NCCB approval of three additions to and one change of date in the Proper Calendar for the Dioceses of the United States. The following is an unofficial English translation of that decree.

Prot. N. 1609/88

At the request of His Excellency John L. May, Archbishop of St. Louis and President of the National Conference of Catholic Bishops, on December 20, 1988, and in virtue of the faculty granted to this Congregation by the Supreme Pontiff, Pope John Paul II, we gladly concede that the following celebrations may be inserted into the Proper Calendar for the Dioceses of the United States of America with the rank of *optional memorial:*

— Blessed Katharine Drexel, virgin — March 3
— Saint Jane Frances de Chantal, virgin — August 18
— Blessed Junipero Serra, priest — August 28
— Saint Rose Philippine Duchesne, virgin — November 18

Anything to the contrary notwithstanding.

From the Congregation for Divine Worship, 20 January 1989.

+ Eduardo Cardinal Martinez
Prefect

+ Virgilio Noe
Titular Archbishop of Voncaria
Secretary

Liturgical Programs/Conferences

Rensselaer Program of Church Music and Liturgy

The 30th annual summer session of the Rensselaer Program of Church Music and Liturgy at Saint Joseph College will be held June 20-August 3, 1989. Graduate and undergraduate sequences are offered. A three summer program leading to a Diploma in Pastoral Liturgy is also available. Tuition is $98 per undergraduate hour and $107 per graduate hour.

The music curriculum includes: Theory, Counterpoint, Composition, Conducting, Pedagogy, and Applied Music. The liturgical courses offered include: Rites of Initiation; Eucharist; Liturgical Year; Gesture and Movement; Liturgies for Children, Teens, and Families; Symbol, Ritual, and Celebration; and Music as Pastoral Prayer.

For further information and/or applications contact Rev. Lawrence Heiman, CPPS, Director of the Rensselaer Program of Church Music and Liturgy, Saint Joseph College, P.O. Box 815, Rensselaer, IN 47978. Telephone: 219/866-6272.

The Catholic University of America

"The Singing Role of the Celebrant," a music workshop for bishops, priests and deacons, will be offered at the Benjamin T. Rome School of Music, The Catholic University of America, June 5-7, 1989. The faculty includes: Frederick R. McManus; Garry B. Giroux; Mary Alice O'Connor, CSJ; and Theodore Marier. The registration is $50.

For more information contact: Committee of Priests' Music Workshop, The Benjamin T. Rome School of Music, The Catholic University of America, Washington, DC 20064. Telephone 202/635-5420.

Notre Dame Center for Pastoral Liturgy

The eighteenth annual conference of the Notre Dame Center for Pastoral Liturgy will be held at the University of Notre Dame, June 19-22, 1989. The topic of the conference is "Ritual and Pastoral Care: The Vital Connection." Major speakers include Elaine J. Ramshaw; Gilbert Ostdiek, OFM; and Paul J. Philibert, OP. Planned focus session speakers are Ronald J. Lewinski; Paul F.X. Covino; Arlene Bennett, RSM; Jennifer Glen, CCVI; Michael H. Marchal; and Fred Moleck.

For further information concerning the program and speaker topics contact the Notre Dame Center for Pastoral Liturgy, P.O. Box 81, Notre Dame, IN 46556. Telephone: 219/239-5435. For information on registration and accommodations contact the Center for Continuing Education, P.O. Box 1008, Notre Dame, IN 46556. Telephone 219/239-6691. A limited number of scholarships are available.

New York School of Liturgical Music

The tenth annual summer seminar sponsored by the New York School of Liturgical Music will be held June 26-29, 1989. "Psalms: Songs of Celebration" will be explored by this year's seminar personnel including: Abbot Martin Burne, Fred Moleck, Robert Hebble, Ronald MacDonald, Gail Archer, Alec Wyton, and Steve and Anthony Kirbos.

For further information and registration forms, write: The Registrar, New York School of Liturgical Music, 1011 First Avenue, New York, NY 10022. Telephone: 212-371-1000, ext. 2291 or 2292.

Detroit Conference on Liturgy

The ninth annual Detroit Conference on Liturgy, having as its theme "Inculturation and the Future of Worship," will be held at the Cobo Conference Center, Detroit, MI, August 7-10, 1989. Principal speakers will include John Baldovin, SJ; Barbara O'Dea, DW; Elaine Rendler; Arlene Bennett, RSM; Bishop Wilton Gregory; Robert Rambusch; Charles Gusmer; Mary Ellen Cohn; Arturo Banuelas; and Dom Anscar Chupungco, OSB.

For additional information contact: Department of Christian Worship, 305 Michigan Avenue, Detroit, MI 48226. Telephone: 313/237-5932.

BISHOPS' COMMITTEE ON THE LITURGY
NEWSLETTER
NATIONAL CONFERENCE OF CATHOLIC BISHOPS

1989
VOLUME XXV
MAY

New Address of the Liturgy Secretariat

On June 12, 1989, the Secretariat of the Bishops' Committee on the Liturgy and the other Secretariats, Departments and Offices of the National Conference of Catholic Bishops and the United States Catholic Conference are scheduled to relocate to the new NCCB/USCC headquarters building in northeast Washington, DC, near the campus of The Catholic University of America. Please note the new address, which is effective on June 12, 1989:

> Bishops' Committee on the Liturgy
> 3211 Fourth Street, NE
> Washington, DC 20017-1194

The Liturgy Secretariat's new telephone number will be: (202) 541-3060.

Rereading the Constitution on the Liturgy (art. 1-13)

In assessing the impact of the *Constitution on the Liturgy* (hereafter "CSL") during the past 25 years, one might take the approach of simply recalling the results of the reform: new liturgical books, the use of vernacular languages, a revised calendar, a restoration of ministerial roles, a renewed emphasis upon music and the other arts in worship. Such might be instructive of the breadth of the reform, but it risks mistaking "the trees" for "the forest." Reforming the liturgy had as its goal the "full, conscious, and active participation of the Christian faithful." Such involvement was to be the sacramental expression of the faithful's progressive incorporation into the death and resurrection of Christ, the life-giving source of the Church's identity and mission. A more helpful approach to taking stock of where the Church in the United States is with regard to its pastoral liturgical life is to begin with the foundational doctrine concerning the liturgy.

Articles 1-13 of the *Constitution* develop the ecclesiological and christological framework for a proper understanding of the nature of liturgy. They succinctly present the relationship between Christ and the Church as a reality which evokes faith and conversion, generates evangelization, and ultimately constitutes Christian worship. The goal of the conciliar reform of the liturgy was to highlight and strengthen this primary relationship.

So closely identified are Christ and the Church that CSL 2 employs several christological concepts to describe the Church: "it is of the essence of the Church to be both human and divine, visible yet endowed with invisible resources, eager to act yet intent on contemplation, present in the world, yet not at home in it."[1] This theological vision moves beyond neo-scholastic, juridical definitions. The Church is a living organism issued "from the side of Christ as he slept the sleep of death on the cross" (CSL 5). The Church not only celebrates the paschal mystery of Christ but lives it as well. The experience of living, dying and rising in Christ moves the Church beyond institutional realities into a worshiping body led by the Holy Spirit. This body has a mission, one with the mission of Christ, to reconcile the world to the Father. This mission in the broadest sense becomes the activity of all the baptized, those "plunged into the paschal mystery of Christ" (CSL 6).

An inadequate appreciation of the implications of this scripturally-based ecclesiology often leads to misunderstandings on many levels of the Church's life, most visibly when the Church gathers for liturgy. Too often liturgical tensions find their root cause, not in aberrant liturgical practices, but in a defective understanding of the nature of the Church. Parish liturgy committees and diocesan liturgical commissions can benefit from analyzing the effects that differing ecclesiologies have upon the continuing reform and promotion of the liturgy. Just as some have balked at a view of the Church as a pilgrim people embracing the mission of Christ, others have welcomed the concept yet pushed aside much of the Church's rich tradition by espousing an ecclesiology which emphasizes the parish community to the exclusion of the local and the universal Church. Neglecting the Church's comprehensive self-understanding will inevitably thwart the development of quality liturgical celebrations.

In the liturgy, especially the eucharist, the Church experiences its preeminent self-manifestation. On any level, whether that of a pontifical ceremony or a parish Mass, how a particular community views itself is revealed through the liturgy. Parishes that have invested in developing the importance of proclaiming Christ's victory over sin and death and are actively involved in the proclamation of the paschal mystery through prayer and action normally take seriously the mandate for quality liturgical celebrations. Reverence for the multifaceted dimensions of Christ's presence in the world and thus in the liturgy is revealed in both action and prayer.

Although Catholics have a fervent belief in the real presence of Christ in the eucharistic elements, the presence of Christ in the Church may not always be as firmly professed. CSL 7 speaks of the Church being permeated with Christ's presence, especially in its liturgical celebrations, manifested through the words of sacred Scripture, through the assembly gathered in prayer and song, through the person of the priest, and through the sacraments, especially the eucharist. (See also the *General Instruction of the Roman Missal* 7.) Efforts of parishes and dioceses to reinforce this christocentric liturgical orientation can be judged by their use of quality signs. Are the Scriptures proclaimed rather than simply read, and is the book that is used a nobly bound Lectionary? What does the design and placement of the presidential chair say about the role of the celebrant? Are baptism and other sacraments seen as communal or private celebrations? Is there respect for the role of the assembly? Although simple questions, the answers may reflect the degree to which a particular community recognizes the manifestations of Christ in the liturgy.

The *Constitution* speaks of the liturgy as being the action of Christ the High Priest. Yet this assertion is not meant to be limiting. Other scriptural images—such as, the Word made flesh, the Proclaimer of liberation to the poor, the Healer of wounded hearts, Medicine for the whole person, and the Mediator between heaven and earth—taken together present a broader image of Christ, human and divine. Thus, the liturgy, while being the activity of Christ the High Priest offering himself to the Father, is also the activity of Christ and his Church glorifying God and sanctifying people through the sacrifice of praise. The sacrificial prominence is not neglected but rather completed by viewing Christ's total mission, which becomes the mission of the Church. It is no wonder that the liturgy has such an all-encompassing effect on the Church.

Possibly the most quoted words of the *Constitution* are found in CSL 10: "The liturgy is the summit toward which the activity of the Church is directed; at the same time it is the fount from which all the Church's power flows... (It) moves the faithful, filled with 'the paschal sacraments,' to be 'one in holiness';... the renewal in the eucharist of the covenant between the Lord and his people draws the faithful into the compelling love of Christ and sets them on fire. From the liturgy, therefore, particularly the eucharist, grace is poured forth upon us as from a fountain; the liturgy is the source for achieving in the most effective way possible human sanctification and God's glorification, the end to which all the Church's other activities are directed."

These words find their realization when the liturgy is promoted as the meeting ground where the mission of Christ and the Church converge. The glorification of God and the sanctification of all people flow from the serious and deliberate effort to insure quality liturgical prayer. Reflecting upon the theological realities which ground all ecclesial celebrations can move those responsible for the liturgical life of a community from a preoccupation with, or even a neglect of, rubrics to an understanding of the foundation upon which the revised Roman rites rest. Then the words of the Fourth Gospel, to "worship in Spirit and in truth," will be realized in a comprehensive way in each community's liturgical life.

Note

1. Quotations from the *Constitution on the Liturgy* are taken from *Documents on the Liturgy, 1963-1979: Conciliar, Papal, and Curial Texts,* edited by the International Commission on English in the Liturgy, published by The Liturgical Press, Collegeville, MN, 1982. All rights reserved. Used with permission.

Communion Practices at Mass

Q. At a Mass with a congregation is it proper for the priest or another minister of the eucharist to distribute hosts which have been consecrated at a previous Mass? Is it proper for the celebrant to consecrate only one host, consume that host, and then distribute the reserved eucharist to the congregation? May concelebrants receive communion from previously consecrated hosts?

R. These questions deal with various practices concerning the distribution of holy communion at Mass using hosts consecrated at a previous celebration. The *Notre Dame Study of Catholic Parish Life*[1] reported that the faithful received holy communion from hosts consecrated at the same Mass at less than 20% of the Masses observed in the course of the study. The most frequent parochial practice observed was that both hosts consecrated at a Mass and those taken from the tabernacle were distributed to participants.

The normative liturgical practice should include the breaking of a large host during the fraction rite with distribution of the parts to at least some of those participating, the remainder receiving smaller hosts consecrated at that Mass.

The practice of consecrating a large number of hosts at one Mass for distribution at other Masses runs contrary to the nature of the faithful's participation in the eucharistic celebration. The full, conscious, and active participation of the faithful includes their reception of the eucharist consecrated at the Mass in which they are participating. The General Instruction of the Roman Missal (GIRM) 56 (h) states: "It is most desirable that the faithful receive the Lord's body from hosts consecrated at the same Mass and that, in the instances when it is permitted, they share in the chalice. Then even through the signs communion will stand out more clearly as a sharing in the sacrifice actually being celebrated."

This matter has been addressed in the encyclicals *Certiores effecti* (1591) of Pope Benedict XIV and *Mediator Dei* (1946) of Pope Pius XII, as well as in recent liturgical documents. *Mediator Dei* 118 quotes the forceful statement of Pope Benedict XIV which emphasizes the significance of the communicants' reception of hosts consecrated at the same Mass in which they participate.

> "Moreover, our predecessor of immortal memory, Benedict XIV, wishing to emphasize and throw fuller light upon the truth that the faithful by receiving the Holy Eucharist become partakers of the divine sacrifice itself, praises the devotion of those who, when attending Mass, not only elicit a desire to receive holy communion but also want to be nourished by hosts consecrated during the Mass, even though, as he himself states, they really and truly take part in the sacrifice should they receive a host which has been duly consecrated at a previous Mass. He writes as follows: 'And although in addition to those to whom the celebrant gives a portion of the Victim he himself has offered in the Mass, they also participate in the same sacrifice to whom a priest distributes the Blessed Sacrament that has been reserved; however, the Church has not for this reason ever forbidden, nor does she now forbid, a celebrant to satisfy the piety and just request of those of whom, when present at Mass, want to become partakers of the same sacrifice, because they likewise offer it after their own manner, nay more, she approves of it and desires that it should not be omitted and would reprehend those priests through whose fault and negligence this participation would be denied to the faithful.'"

The reservation of the eucharist is not maintained for the purpose of storing large quantities of consecrated hosts for use at subsequent Masses. Rather the eucharist is to be reserved in parish churches and oratories primarily for the administration of viaticum to the dying, and secondarily for giving communion—especially to the sick—outside Mass and for eucharistic adoration [cf. *Eucharisticum Mysterium* 49 (1967) and *Holy Communion and Worship of the Eucharist Outside Mass* 6]. There is no mention made in post-conciliar liturgical norms of reservation of the eucharist for distribution at later Masses.

Clearly, the practice of distributing reserved hosts on a regular basis at Mass is a practice which compromises the fullest understanding of the eucharist as the source of the Church's unity and jeopardizes the recognition of the role of all the baptized in the eucharistic celebration.

Another practice commonly observed is that of the celebrant breaking the host during the chanting of the Lamb of God and then at the appropriate time consuming the entire host himself. The eucharist by its nature is meant to be broken and distributed to those present. The GIRM 283 states that "the eucharistic bread should be made in such a way that... the priest is able actually to break the host into parts and distribute them to at least some of the faithful." Although small hosts may be used for some, or even most, of the individuals present, the action of breaking the bread and distributing its parts should not be neglected. As the GIRM 283 continues, "The action of the breaking of the bread, the simple term for the eucharist in apostolic times, will more clearly bring out the force and meaning of the sign of the unity of all in the one bread and of their charity, since the one bread is being distributed among the members of one family." Broken parts—and small hosts, if used—should be sufficient in quantity for the number of communicants at that Mass plus a small reserve for viaticum, for communion outside Mass, and for adoration.

It also is improper for the celebrant of a Mass with a congregation to consecrate only one host, consume that host and then distribute the reserved eucharist to the congregation. This practice is often observed at weekday Masses. The celebrant's host should always be broken and distributed to at least some of the faithful along with the distribution small hosts, if used, that have been consecrated at that Mass.

Concelebrants are always to receive communion consecrated at the Mass at which they concelebrate. In an October, 1981, private response the Sacred Congregation for Divine Worship and the Sacraments addressed the validity and lawfulness of concelebrants receiving hosts consecrated at a previous Mass in the following manner:

> "The concelebrated Mass in which some concelebrants, even the principal celebrant himself, receive for the priests' communion sacred Hosts from the tabernacle consecrated at an earlier Mass, is *certainly valid*, provided that they receive the Holy Blood consecrated in the Mass itself.
>
> However, such a manner of doing *is not licit*, since it is not performed according to the liturgical norms which ask that celebrants receive the Body of Christ consecrated in the Mass itself.
>
> In concrete cases when there could not be sufficient Hosts, it seems *not obligatory* to take Sacred Hosts from the tabernacle for the priest's communion, since a part of concelebrants can communicate by receiving only the Blood of Christ."

The response concluded by suggesting that sacristans should take care to provide sufficient hosts and wine for all who will receive holy communion. By careful observation over a few weeks, it is easy to determine the approximate number of communicants at each Mass. A sufficient number of hosts can then be consecrated at each Mass which will obviate the need to distribute communion from the tabernacle.

Note

1. Mark Searle and David C. Leege, *Notre Dame Study of Catholic Parish Life,* "The Celebration of Liturgy in the Parishes," Report No. 5, University of Notre Dame, August, 1985.

National Association of Pastoral Musicians National Convention

The biennial national convention of the National Association of Pastoral Musicians, having as its theme "How Can I Keep From Singing," will be held in Long Beach, CA, June 26-30, 1989. Major speakers include Michael Joncas, Doris Donnelly, Robert Hovda, Alice Parker, Joseph Gelineau and James Dunning. A special performance of the Durufle Requiem will be featured at the Garden Grove "Crystal Cathedral." For additional information contact: National Association of Pastoral Musicians, 225 Sheridan Street, NW, Washington, DC 20011. Telephone: 202/723-5800.

BISHOPS' COMMITTEE ON THE LITURGY
NEWSLETTER
NATIONAL CONFERENCE OF CATHOLIC BISHOPS

**1989
VOLUME XXV
JUNE/JULY**

Apostolic Letter *Quinto iam lustro expleto*

On Pentecost Sunday, May 14, 1989, the Apostolic See released the text of the apostolic letter of Pope John Paul II, Quinto iam lustro expleto, *dated December 4, 1988, the 25th anniversary of the promulgation of the Constitution on the Sacred Liturgy,* Sacrosanctum Concilium, *of the Second Vatican Ecumenical Council. The following excerpts highlight significant portions of the letter. The numbering of the paragraphs and footnotes corresponds to that of the complete document. The USCC Office of Publishing and Promotion Services has published the complete text of the apostolic letter (publication no. 286-1). It is also available in* Origins, *vol. 19, no. 2 (May 15, 1989), pp. 17-25.*

4. . . . An overall reform of the liturgy was in harmony with the general hope of the whole Church. In fact, the liturgical spirit had become more and more widespread together with the desire for an "active participation in the most holy mysteries and in the public and solemn prayer of the Church,"[14] and a wish to hear the word of God in more abundant measure. Together with the biblical renewal, the ecumenical movement, the missionary impetus and ecclesiological research, the reform of the liturgy was to contribute to the overall renewal of the Church . . .

(The reform) was undertaken in accordance with the conciliar principles of fidelity to tradition and openness to legitimate development,[17] and so it is possible to say that the reform of the liturgy is strictly traditional and in accordance with "the ancient usage of the holy Fathers."[18]

5. The guiding principles of the Constitution, which were the basis of the reform, remain fundamental in the task of leading the faithful to an active celebration of the mysteries, "the primary and indispensable source of the true Christian spirit."[19] Now that the greater part of the liturgical books have been published, translated and brought into use, it is still necessary to keep these principles constantly in mind and to build upon them.

6. The first principle is the re-enactment of the paschal mystery of Christ in the liturgy of the Church, based on the fact that "it was from the side of Christ as he slept upon the cross that there issued forth the sublime sacrament of the whole Church."[20] The whole of liturgical life gravitates about the eucharistic sacrifice and the other sacraments, in which we draw upon the living springs of salvation (cf. Is 12:3).[21] Hence we must have a sufficient awareness that through the "paschal mystery we have been buried with Christ in baptism, so that we may rise with him to a new life."[22] When the faithful participate in the eucharist, they must understand that truly "each time we offer this memorial sacrifice the work of our redemption is accomplished,"[23] and to this end bishops must carefully train the faithful to celebrate every Sunday the marvelous work that Christ has wrought in the mystery of his passover, in order that they likewise may proclaim it to the world.[24] In the hearts of all, bishops and faithful, Easter must regain its unique importance in the liturgical year, so that it really is the Feast of Feasts.

Since Christ's death on the cross and his resurrection constitute the content of the daily life of the Church[25] and the pledge of his eternal passover,[26] the liturgy has as its first task to lead us untiringly back to the Easter pilgrimage initiated by Christ, in which we accept death in order to enter into life.

7. In order to re-enact his paschal mystery, Christ is ever present in his Church, especially in liturgical celebrations.[27] Hence the liturgy is the privileged place for the encounter of Christians with God and the one whom he has sent, Jesus Christ (cf. Jn 17:3).

Christ is present in the Church assembled at prayer in his name. It is this fact which gives such a unique character to the Christian assembly . . .

Christ is present and acts in the person of the ordained minister who celebrates.[28] The priest is not merely entrusted with a function, but in virtue of the ordination received he has been consecrated to act "*in persona Christi.*" . . .

Christ is present in his word as proclaimed in the assembly and which, commented upon in the homily, is to be listened to in faith and assimilated in prayer. All this must derive from the dignity of the book and of the place appointed for the proclamation of the word of God, and from the attitude of the reader, based upon an awareness of the fact that the reader is the spokesman of God before his or her brothers and sisters.

Christ is present and acts by the power of the Holy Spirit in the sacraments and, in a special and pre-eminent fashion (*sublimiori modo*), in the Sacrifice of the Mass under the Eucharistic Species,[29] also when these are reserved in the tabernacle apart from the celebration with a view to communion of the sick and adoration by the faithful.[30] With regard to this real and mysterious presence, it is the duty of pastors to recall frequently in their catechetical instructions the teaching of the faith, a teaching that the faithful must live out and that theologians are called upon to expound. Faith in this presence of the Lord involves an outward sign of respect towards the church, the holy place in which God manifests himself in mystery (cf. Ex 3:5), especially during the celebration of the sacraments: holy things must always be treated in a holy manner.

8. The second principle is the presence of the word of God. The Constitution *Sacrosanctum Concilium* sets out likewise to restore a "more abundant reading from Holy Scripture, one more varied and more appropriate."[31] The basic reason for this restoration is expressed both in the Constitution on the Liturgy, namely, so that "the intimate link between rite and word" may be manifested,[32] and also in the Dogmatic Constitution on Divine Revelation, which teaches: "The Church has always venerated the divine Scriptures, just as she has venerated the very body of the Lord, never ceasing above all in the sacred liturgy to nourish herself on the bread of life at the table both of the word of God, and of the Body of Christ, and to minister it to the faithful."[33] Growth in liturgical life and consequently progress in Christian life cannot be achieved except by continually promoting among the faithful, and above all among priests, a "warm and living knowledge of Scripture."[34] The word of God is now better known in the Christian communities, but a true renewal sets further and ever new requirements: fidelity to the authentic meaning of the Scriptures which must never be lost from view, especially when the Scriptures are translated into different languages; the manner of proclaiming the word of God so that it may be perceived for what it is; the use of appropriate technical means, the interior disposition of the ministers of the word so that they carry out properly their function in the liturgical assembly;[35] careful preparation of the homily through study and meditation; effort on the part of the faithful to participate at the table of the word; a taste for prayer with the psalms; a desire to discover Christ—like the disciple at Emmaus—at the table of the word and the bread.[36]

9. Finally, the Council saw in the liturgy an epiphany of the Church: it is the Church at prayer. In celebrating divine worship the Church gives expression to what she is: one, holy, catholic and apostolic . . .

10. From these principles are derived certain norms and guidelines which must govern the renewal of liturgical life. While the reform of the liturgy desired by the Second Vatican Council can be considered already in progress, the pastoral promotion of the liturgy constitutes a permanent commitment to draw ever more abundantly from the riches of the liturgy that vital force which spreads from Christ to the members of his Body which is the Church.

Since the liturgy is the exercise of the priesthood of Christ, it is necessary to keep ever alive the affirmation of the disciple faced with the mysterious presence of Christ: "It is the Lord!" (Jn 21:7). Nothing of what we do in the liturgy can appear more important than what in an unseen but real manner Christ accomplishes by the power of his Spirit. A faith alive in charity, adoration, praise of the Father and silent contemplation will always be the prime objective of liturgical and sacramental pastoral care.

Since the liturgy is totally permeated by the word of God, any other word must be in harmony with it, above all in the homily but also in the various interventions of the minister and in the hymns which are sung. No other reading may supplant the Biblical word, and the words of men must be at the service of the word of God without obscuring it.

Since liturgical celebrations are not private acts but "celebrations of the Church, the 'sacrament of unity',"[45] their regulation is dependent solely upon the hierarchical authority of the Church.[46] The liturgy belongs to the whole body of the Church.[47] It is for this reason that it is not permitted to anyone, even the priest, or any group, to add, subtract or change anything whatsoever on their own initiative.[48] Fidelity to the rites and to the authentic texts of the liturgy is a requirement of the *lex orandi,* which must always be in conformity with the *lex credendi*. A lack of fidelity on this point may even affect the very validity of the sacraments.

Since it is a celebration of the Church, the liturgy requires the active, conscious and full participation of all, according to the diversity of orders and of office.[49] All, the ministers and the other faithful, in the accomplishment of their particular function, do that and only that which is proper to them.[50] It is for this reason that the Church gives preference to celebrations in common, when the nature of the rites implies this;[51] she encourages the formation of ministers, readers, cantors and commentators, who carry out a true liturgical ministry;[52] she has restored concelebration,[53] and she recommends the common celebration of the Liturgy of the Hours.[54]

Given that the liturgy is the school of the prayer of the Church, it has been considered good to introduce and develop the use of the vernacular—without diminishing the use of Latin, retained by the Council for the Latin Rite[55]—so that every individual can understand and proclaim in his or her mother tongue the wonders of God (cf. Acts 2:22). It has likewise been considered good to increase the number of prefaces and eucharistic prayers, so as to enrich the Church's treasury of prayer and an understanding of the mystery of Christ.

Since the liturgy has great pastoral value, the liturgical books have provided for a certain degree of adaptation to the assembly and to individuals, with the possibility of openness to the traditions and culture of different peoples.[56] The revision of the rites has sought a noble simplicity[57] and signs that are easily understood, but the desired simplicity must not degenerate into an impoverishment of the signs. On the contrary, the signs, above all the sacramental signs, must be easily grasped but carry the greatest possible expressiveness. Bread and wine, water and oil, and also incense, ashes, fire and flowers, and indeed almost all the elements of creation have their place in the liturgy as gifts to the Creator and as a contribution to the dignity and beauty of the celebration.

11. It must be recognized that the application of the liturgical reform has met with difficulties due especially to an unfavorable environment marked by a tendency to see religious practice as something of a private affair, by a certain rejection of institutions, by a decrease in the visibility of the Church in society, and by a calling into question of personal faith. It can also be supposed that the transition from simply being present, very often in a rather passive and silent way, to a fuller and more active participation has been for some people too demanding. Different and even contradictory reactions to the reform have resulted from this. Some have received the new books with a certain indifference, or without trying to understand or help others to understand the reasons for the changes; others, unfortunately, have turned back in a one-sided and exclusive way to the previous liturgical forms which some of them consider to be the sole guarantee of certainty in faith. Others have promoted outlandish innovations, departing from the norms issued by the authority of the Apostolic See or the bishops, thus disrupting the unity of the Church and the piety of the faithful, and even on occasion contradicting matters of faith.

12. This should not lead anyone to forget that the vast majority of the pastors and the Christian people have accepted the liturgical reform in a spirit of obedience and indeed joyful fervor.

For this we should give thanks to God for that movement of the Holy Spirit in the Church which the liturgical renewal represents;[58] for the fact that the table of the word of God is now abundantly furnished for all;[59] for the immense effort undertaken throughout the world to provide the Christian people with translations of the Bible, the Missal and other liturgical books; for the increased participation of the faithful by prayer and song, gesture and silence, in the Eucharist and the other sacraments; for the ministries exercised by lay people and the responsibilities that they have assumed in virtue of the common priesthood into which they have been initiated through baptism and confirmation; for the radiant vitality of so many Christian communities, a vitality drawn from the well-spring of the liturgy.

These are all reasons for holding fast to the teaching of the Constitution *Sacrosanctum Concilium* and to the reforms it has made possible . . .

13. Side by side with these benefits of the liturgical reform, one has to acknowledge with regret deviations of greater or lesser seriousness in its application.

On occasion there have been noted illicit omissions or additions, rites invented outside the framework of established norms; postures or songs which are not conducive to faith or to a sense of the sacred; abuses in the practice of general absolution; confusion between the ministerial priesthood, linked with ordination, and the common priesthood of the faithful, which has its foundation in baptism.

It cannot be tolerated that certain priests should take upon themselves the right to compose eucharistic prayers or to substitute profane readings for texts from sacred Scripture. Initiatives of this sort, far from being linked with the liturgical reform as such, or with the books which have issued from it, are in direct contradiction to it, disfigure it and deprive the Christian people of the genuine treasures of the liturgy of the Church.

It is for the bishops to root out such abuses, because the regulation of the liturgy depends on the bishop within the limits of the law[61] and because "the life in Christ of his faithful people in some sense is derived from and depends upon him."[62]

14. . . . The principles enunciated in (*Sacrosanctum Concilium*) are an orientation also for the future of the liturgy, in such a way that the liturgical reform may be ever better understood and implemented. "It is therefore necessary and urgent to actuate a new and intensive education in order to discover all the richness contained in the liturgy."[63]

The liturgy of the Church goes beyond the liturgical reform. We are not in the same situation as obtained in 1963: a generation of priests and of faithful which has not known the liturgical books prior to the reform now acts with responsibility in the Church and society. One cannot therefore continue to speak of change as it was spoken of at the time of the Constitution's publication; rather one has to speak of an ever deeper grasp of the liturgy of the Church, celebrated according to the current books and lived above all as a reality in the spiritual order.

15. The most urgent task is that of the biblical and liturgical formation of the people of God, both pastors and faithful. The Constitution had already stressed this: "there is no hope that this may come to pass unless pastors of souls themselves become imbued more deeply with the spirit and power of the liturgy so as to become masters of it."[64] This is a long-term program, which must begin in the seminaries and houses of formation[65] and continue throughout their priestly life.[66] A formation suited to their state is indispensable also for lay people,[67] especially since in many regions they are called upon to assume ever more important responsibilities in the community.

16. . . . There remains the considerable task of continuing to implant the liturgy in certain cultures, welcoming from them those expressions which are compatible with aspects of the true and authentic spirit of the liturgy, in respect for the substantial unity of the Roman Rite as expressed in the liturgical books.[69] The adaptation must take account of the fact that in the liturgy, and notably that of the sacraments, there is a part which is unchangeable, because it is of divine institution, and of which the Church is the guardian. There are also parts open to change, which the Church has the power and on occasion also the duty to adapt to the cultures of recently evangelized peoples.[70] This is not a new problem for the Church. Liturgical diversity can be a source of enrichment, but it can also provoke tensions, mutual misunderstandings and even divisions. In this field it is clear that diversity must not damage unity. It can only gain expression in fidelity to the common faith, to the sacramental signs that the Church has received from Christ and to hierarchical communion. Cultural adaptation also requires conversion of heart and even, where necessary, a breaking with ancestral customs incompatible with the Catholic faith. This demands a serious formation in theology, history and culture, as well as sound judgment in discerning what is necessary or useful and what is not useful or even dangerous to faith . . .

17. The effort towards liturgical renewal must furthermore respond to the needs of our time. The liturgy is not disincarnate.[72] In these twenty-five years new problems have arisen or have assumed new importance, for example: the exercise of a diaconate open to married men; liturgical tasks in celebrations which can be entrusted to lay people; liturgical celebrations for children, for young people and the handicapped; the procedures for the composition of liturgical texts appropriate to a particular country.

In the Constitution *Sacrosanctum Concilium* there is no reference to these problems, but the general principles are given which serve to coordinate and promote liturgical life . . .

21. In every diocese the bishop is the principle dispenser of the mysteries of God, and likewise the governor, promoter and guardian of the entire liturgical life of the Church entrusted to him.[90] When the bishop celebrates in the midst of his people, it is the very mystery of the Church which is manifested. Therefore it is necessary that the bishop should be strongly convinced of the importance of such celebrations for the Christian life of his faithful. Such celebrations should be models for the whole diocese.[91] Much still remains to be done to help priests and the faithful to grasp the meaning of the liturgical rites and texts, to develop the dignity and beauty of celebration and the places where they are held, and to promote, as the Fathers did, a "mystagogic catechesis" of the sacraments. In order to bring this task to a successful conclusion, the bishop

should set up one or more diocesan commissions which will help him to promote liturgical activity, music and sacred art in his diocese.[92] . . .

23. The time has come to renew that spirit which inspired the Church at the moment when the Constitution *Sacrosanctum Concilium* was prepared, discussed, voted upon and promulgated and when the first steps were taken to apply it. The seed was sown: it has known the rigors of winter, but the seed has sprouted, and become a tree. It is a matter of the organic growth of the tree becoming ever stronger the deeper it sinks its roots into the soil of tradition.[95] . . .

Notes

14. Pius X, Motu Proprio *Tra le sollecitudini dell'officio pastorale* (22 November 1903): *Pii X Pontificis Maximi Acta,* 1, p. 77.

17. Cf. Second Vatican Council, Constitution on the Sacred Liturgy *Sacrosanctum Concilium* [hereafter CSL], 23.

18. Cf. CSL 50; Roman Missal, Preface, 6.

19. CSL 14.

20. CSL 5; Roman Missal, The Easter Vigil: Prayer after the 7th Reading.

21. CSL 5-6. 47. 61. 102. 106-107.

22. Roman Missal, The Easter Virgil, Renewal of Baptismal Promises.

23. *Ibid.,* Evening Mass "In Cena Domini," Prayer over the Gifts.

24. Cf. *ibid.,* Preface of Sundays in Ordinary Time, 1.

25. Cf. Encyclical Letter *Redemptor Hominis* (4 March 1979), 7: *AAS* 71 (1979), pp. 268-270.

26. Cf. Letter *Dominicae Cenae* (24 February 1980), 4: *AAS* 72 (1980), p. 119-121.

27. Cf. CSL 7; cf. Paul VI, Encyclical Letter *Mysterium Fidei* (3 September 1965): *AAS* 57 (1965), pp. 762, 764.

28. Cf. Sacred Congregation of Rites, Instruction *Eucharisticum Mysterium* (25 May 1967), 9: *AAS* 59 (1967), p. 547.

29. Cf. Paul VI, Encyclical Letter *Mysterium Fidei* (3 September 1965): *AAS* 57 (1965), p. 763.

30. Cf. *ibid.,* pp. 769-771.

31. CSL 35.

32. *Ibid.*

33. Second Vatican Council, Constitution on Divine Revelation *Dei Verbum,* 21.

34. CSL 24.

35. Cf. Letter *Dominicae Cenae* (24 February 1980), 10: *AAS* 72 (1980), pp. 134-137.

36. Cf. Liturgy of the Hours, Monday of Week IV, Prayer at Evening Prayer.

45. CSL 26.

46. Cf. CSL 22 and 26.

47. Cf. CSL 26.

48. Cf. CSL 22.

49. Cf. CSL 26.

50. Cf. CSL 28.

51. Cf. CSL 27.

52. Cf. CSL 29.

53. Cf. CSL 57; cf. Sacred Congregation of Rites, General Decree *Ecclesiae Semper* (7 March 1965): *AAS* 57 (1965), pp. 410-412.

54. CSL 99.

55. CSL 36.

56. Cf. CSL 37-40.

57. Cf. CSL 34.

58. Cf. CSL 43.

59. Cf. Second Vatican Council, Dogmatic Constitution on Divine Revelation *Dei Verbum,* 21; CSL 51.

61. CSL 22, 1.

62. CSL 41.

63. Letter *Dominicae Cenae,* (24 February 1980): *ASS* 72 (1980), p. 133.

64. CSL 14.

65. Cf. Sacred Congregation of Rites, Instruction *Inter Oecumenici* (26 September 1964), 11-13: *AAS* 56 (1964), pp. 879-880; Sacred Congregation for Catholic Education, *Ratio Fundamentalis* on priestly formation (6 January 1970), cap. VIII: *ASS* 62 (1970), pp. 351-361; Instruction *In Ecclesiasticam Futurorum,* On Liturgical formation in Seminaries (3 June 1979), Rome 1979.

66. Cf. Sacred Congregation of Rites, Instruction *Inter Oecumenici* (26 September 1964), 14-17: *AAS* 56 (1964), pp. 880-881.

67. CSL 19.

69. Cf. CSL 37-40.

70. Cf. CSL 21.

72. Cf. Address to the Congress of Presidents and Secretaries of National Liturgical Commissions (27 October 1984), 2: *Insegnamenti,* VII, 2 (1984), p. 1051.

90. Cf. Second Vatican Council, Decree on the Bishops' Office in the Church *Christus Dominus,* 15.

91. Cf. Address to Italian Bishops attending a course of liturgical renewal (12 February 1988), 1: *L'Osservatore Romano* of 13 February 1988, p. 4.

92. Cf. CSL 45-46.

95. Cf. CSL 23.

Saints Lawrence Ruiz and Companions: Confirmation of Texts

On May 15, 1989 the National Conference of Catholic Bishops received the decree of the Congregation for Divine Worship and the Sacraments, dated April 27, 1989, confirming the decision of the Administrative Committee of the NCCB to approve *ad interim* the provisional English translation of proper liturgical texts for the optional memorial of Saints Lawrence Ruiz and companions, martyrs (September 28). The following is an unofficial English translation of that decree.

Prot. N. 207/89

At the request of His Excellency John L. May, Archbishop of Saint Louis and President of the National Conference of Catholic Bishops, on April 17, 1989, and in virtue of the faculty granted to this Congregation by the Supreme Pontiff, Pope John Paul II, we gladly approve, that is, confirm *ad interim* the English text of the collect and of the Liturgy of the Hours in honor of the holy martyrs Lawrence Ruiz and companions, as it appears in the appended copy.

This decree, by which the requested confirmation is granted by the Apostolic See, is to be included in its entirety in the published text. Two copies of the printed text should be sent to this Congregation.

Anything to the contrary notwithstanding.

From the Congregation for Divine Worship and the Sacraments, 27 April 1989.

+ Eduardo Cardinal Martinez
Prefect

+ Virgilio Noè
Titular Archbishop of Voncaria
Secretary

September 28 LAWRENCE RUIZ AND COMPANIONS, MARTYRS Optional Memorial

Common of Martyrs

Opening Prayer

Lord God,
in our service to you and to our neighbor
give us the patience of the holy martyrs,
Lawrence and his companions;
for those who suffer persecution for justice' sake
are blessed in the Kingdom of heaven.

We ask this through our Lord Jesus Christ, your Son,
who lives and reigns with you and the Holy Spirit,
one God, for ever and ever.

R. Amen.

Rereading the Constitution on the Liturgy (art. 14-19)

The present ongoing reform of the Roman liturgy did not begin with the Second Vatican Council. While some persons lacking an historical perspective may think that the decision to embark on a liturgical restoration appeared "out of the blue" during the first sessions of the Council, the facts reveal something quite different. Far from appearing suddenly, the renewal was the result of a gradual unfolding of a liturgical awakening that reached an apex in the promulgation of the Constitution on the Sacred Liturgy (CSL). Certainly that document was the profound leap in a pastoral, historical and theological development that had spanned the centuries following the Council of Trent. Intensive research and even the discovery of ancient documents by liturgical scholars during the later years of the nineteenth century brought into greater focus the fundamental liturgical principles which would be developed in the liturgical documents that preceded the Constitution.

The principle (CSL 14) that spiritual renewal flows from the "full, conscious, and active participation" of the Christian faithful in the Church's liturgy took on a more forceful meaning when such participation was put forth as the "aim to be considered before all else" in the reform and promotion of the liturgy. But this principle was not something new in the Church's teaching. Pope St. Pius X had encouraged participation as early as 1903 in his *motu proprio Tra Le Sollecitudini* on the restoration of Church music. He stated that the sanctity and dignity of the Church is expressed in the "active participation in the holy mysteries and in the public and solemn prayer of the Church."[1] The Encyclical Letter of Pope Pius XII, *Mediator Dei* (30 November 1947), emphasized the participatory nature of the liturgy when it stated that "the Christian community is in duty bound to participate in the liturgical rites according to their station."[2] Less than a decade later in response to multiple requests the Holy See restored the Holy Week rites and changed the times of their celebration from morning to evening so that the faithful could participate.[3] Finally, just preceding the Council the 1962 edition of the *Missale Romanum* took another step in encouraging active participation: it permitted the singing of vernacular hymns at low Masses, the assembly's joining in all the responses, the simultaneous reading of Scripture in the vernacular and Latin, and a simplification of rubrics as issued in the *New Rubrical Code* (25 July 1960) of Pope John XXIII.

Yet the binding force of the CSL required that a general restoration take place in which all rites and texts be composed so that "the Christian people, so far as possible, should be enabled to understand them with ease and to take part in them fully, actively, and as befits a community" (CSL 21).

The task of revising the liturgical books of the Roman Rite is now nearing its completion. But the reform of the liturgy was not initiated simply to remold rituals. It was to develop rituals and texts that would allow for the full participation of the people of God. That challenge remains. To celebrate these restored rites as they are intended is to engage fully those who form the liturgical assembly.

These revisions and the development of new prayer texts continue to enable the understanding and participation of the gathered community. Whether the celebration be the simplest of community gatherings for the Liturgy of the Hours or the most elaborate stational Mass, the full, conscious, and active participation, both internal and external (CSL 19), of all present must be the foremost consideration. Although great strides have been made in this respect, it is important that liturgical commissions, parish committees, and local ministers constantly keep this principle in the forefront of planning and celebration. Participation is not an end in itself. Rather it is from participation in the liturgy that the faithful "derive the true Christian spirit" leading to the renewal of the Church.

The CSL gives great attention to the liturgical instruction of the clergy. There is an implicit recognition that the success of the reform depends on those ordained ministers who lead public prayer and worship and are responsible for the spiritual formation of local communities. Seminaries and religious houses of formation are to have compulsory liturgical programs that go beyond academic course work. Liturgical formation is to be integral to spiritual formation.

Many seminaries continue to struggle with this directive because of the unavailability of liturgical experts, already overburdened academic schedules, and other demands on the curriculum. Yet if promotion of the liturgy is a prerequisite for the renewal of the Church and that renewal is most effected when the local Church gathers to hear the Scriptures proclaimed and to celebrate the Eucharist, then significant attention must be paid to ministerial formation. Not to do so is to short change both the ordained minister and the liturgical assembly, and to short circuit authentic renewal of the Church. Although much has been accomplished with regard to the liturgical formation of seminarians as well as with the continuing formation of the clergy, both efforts at formation continually need to be encouraged.

Yet the liturgical instruction and formation of the Christian laity should parallel that of the clergy. All should be led to a deeper appreciation of their role and mission in the Church and in the world which flows from baptism and confirmation. In addition ongoing formation for all who assume various ministries in the liturgy should incorporate an understanding of the theological, historical, spiritual, pastoral, and juridical dimensions of the liturgical life of the Church in order to provide for the fruitful participation of all the faithful.

Although much as been done to increase and encourage the full participation of the faithful since the promulgation of the reformed rites, studies indicate that participation of a high quality is less than uniform in the United States.[4] The high priority that the Constitution on the Liturgy gives to participation and liturgical formation holds the hope that the liturgy will become the vehicle for the spiritual formation and transformation of the Church which it is intended to be.

Notes

1. Pius X, motu proprio *Tra le sollecitudini dell'officio pastorale (Among the Cares of the Pastoral Office): Acta Pii X.*

2. See Pius XII, Encyclical Letter *Mediator Dei.* n. 5: *AAS* 39 (1947). Also compare nos. 78, 80, 82, 83, 88, 92, 104-106, 199.

3. See Sacred Congregation of Rites, Decree on the Restoration of the Holy Week Order, 16 November 1955.

4. See Mark Searle and David C. Leege, *The Notre Dame Study of Catholic Parish Life,* Report 5: "The Celebration of Liturgy in the Parishes," August, 1985; and Report 6, "Of Piety and Planning: Liturgy, the Parishioners, and the Professionals," December, 1985.

Activities of the Congregation for Divine Worship and the Sacraments

The January-February 1989 issue of Notitiae *(vol. XXV, nos. 270-271), the official journal of the Congregation for Divine Worship and the Sacraments, contained a report from Archbishop Virgilio Noè, Secretary of the Congregation, concerning several of the Congregation's projects. The report was given at the meeting of consultants and advisors to the Congregation, held in Rome on November 29-December 3, 1988.*

Rite of Marriage - The introduction of the *Rite of Marriage* has been revised and harmonized with the more recent documents of the Church on marriage. An additional chapter (Rite for Celebrating Marriage in the Presence of a Layperson) has been added; it is intended for those occasions, provided for in the law, when a lay minister may assist at a marriage and act as the Church's official witness. The lectionary has been enriched by additional biblical readings. The Order for Blessing a Married Couple on the Occasion of Their Wedding Anniversary has been inserted in the appendix of the rite, and it provides two forms for the renewal of marriage vows. Provisions for the blessing and exchange of rings and the blessing of the couple on wedding anniversaries is already found in the *Book of Blessings.* After final editorial work and approval of the Holy Father, the new edition of the *Rite of Marriage* should be published in the near future.

Rites of Ordination - A revision of the rites of ordination has been completed and has received the approval of the Congregation for the Doctrine of the Faith. The text was sent to the Holy Father at the end of June 1988 for his approval.

Fifth Volume of the *Liturgy of the Hours* - The readings have been chosen, and work has begun on the responsories and the psalm prayers. It will still be some time before this volume is ready for publication.

Exorcisms - The Congregation has completed a draft of this final portion of the *Roman Ritual* and has sent it to the Congregation for the Doctrine of the Faith for its review.

Passion - a new Latin edition of the Passion of the Lord, based on the Neo-Vulgate, is ready for publication. The edition will contain two melodies for the singing of the Passion.

Order for Holy Week - A simplified version of the Holy Week rites is being prepared for use in smaller churches where there are not sufficient musicians, ministers, etc., to carry out the complete rites.

BISHOPS' COMMITTEE ON THE LITURGY
NEWSLETTER

NATIONAL CONFERENCE OF CATHOLIC BISHOPS

**1989
VOLUME XXV
AUGUST**

Saint Andrew Dung-Lac, priest and martyr, and companions, martyrs (November 24)

The Congregation for Divine Worship and the Sacraments, in a decree (Prot. CD 154/89) dated June 1, 1989, has informed the President of the National Conference of Catholic Bishops that Pope John Paul II has approved the inclusion of Saint Andrew Dung-Lac and companions, martyrs, in the Roman Calendar as an obligatory memorial. Saint Andrew and his 116 companions suffered martyrdom in Vietnam in the eighteenth century.

The Congregation also sent the National Conference of Catholic Bishops the liturgical texts (in Latin), which consist of complete proper texts for use at Mass and an alternate reading and responsory for the Office of Readings in the Liturgy of the Hours. After these liturgical texts have been translated by the International Commission on English in the Liturgy they will be submitted to the National Conference of Catholic Bishops for approval and to the Congregation for Divine Worship and the Sacraments for confirmation.

The following is an unofficial translation of the decree prepared by the International Commission on English in the Liturgy:

Prot. CD 154/89

DECREE

The Church's missionary activity to all peoples derives from the command of its divine Founder, who sent the apostles into the whole world to preach the Gospel and to gather all peoples into the Church (see Vatican Council II, *Ad gentes,* no. 6). In this way the Church fulfills the divine intention of forming the entire human race into the one people of God, and it fulfills the plan of the Creator when all those who are reborn through the Holy Spirit and become sharers in the divine nature are enabled to say, "Our Father" (*ibid.,* no. 7).

In accord with the incarnational plan of salvation, newly established Christian communities, rooted in Christ and built up on the foundation of the apostles, take to themselves in a wonderful exchange all the riches of the nations which were given to Christ as an inheritance. From the customs and traditions of their own people, from their wisdom and learning, their arts and sciences, these communities borrow all that can contribute to glorifying the Creator, to revealing the grace of the Savior, or to guiding Christian life in right paths (*ibid.,* no. 22).

Through the missionary efforts of various religious families beginning in the sixteenth century and continuing in succeeding centuries the Vietnamese people heard the message of the Gospel, that God is the Father of all and that his only Son is the Savior of the world. This message was warmly welcomed by the people, who show a marked filial devotion toward the God of heaven, and among them the Gospel has reaped a joyous harvest.

But from the beginning acceptance of the Gospel has led to persecution as a supreme test of love for God the Father (see Vatican Council II, *Lumen gentium,* no. 42). Through its sons and daughters the Church of Vietnam has not been "ashamed of the scandal of the cross" (*Ad gentes,* no. 24). In the course of the sixteenth, seventeenth, and eighteenth centuries, with intermittent intervals of peace, many Christians of this Church received the gift of martyrdom, among them bishops, priests, men and women religious, catechists of both sexes, laymen and laywomen from various levels of society.

During solemn celebrations in Saint Peter's Square on 19 June 1988 the Supreme Pontiff John Paul II

3211 4TH STREET, N.E. ● WASHINGTON, D.C. 20017-1194

from the great number of Vietnamese martyrs entered 117 names into the catalogue of saints. Among these are included ninety-six Vietnamese, eleven missionaries born in Spain and belonging to the Province of the Holy Rosary of the Order of Preachers, and ten French missionaries belonging to the Paris Foreign Mission Society.

The liturgical celebration of holy martyrs manifests Christ's paschal mystery and presents to the faithful examples for them to imitate that are signs of the Church's holiness through the ages. To the number of saints, therefore, who by preaching the Gospel and shedding their blood have built up or illumined the Church on the various continents, it is right, as a way of bringing together the one family of Christ throughout the world, to add those who by their glorious martyrdom have consecrated the beginnings of the Catholic religion of Vietnam.

At the request of the Conference of Bishops of Vietnam, in their letter of 12 April 1989, that the celebration of the Holy Martyrs of Vietnam Andrew Dung-Lac, Priest, and his Companions be entered in the General Roman Calendar, the Supreme Pontiff John Paul II has decreed that this celebration be entered in the Roman Calendar and that the memory of the Martyrs of Vietnam be observed by all each year on 24 November with the rank of obligatory memorial.

Therefore the new memorial is to be entered in all ordos for the celebration of Mass and the Liturgy of the Hours and it is to be indicated in all the liturgical books to be published in the future under the supervision of the conferences of bishops.

All things to the contrary notwithstanding.

The Congregation for Divine Worship and the Discipline of the Sacraments, 1 June 1989.

> \+ Eduardo Cardinal Martinez
> Prefect
>
> \+ Lajos Kada
> Titular Archbishop of Tibica
> Secretary

June Meeting of the Committee on the Liturgy

The annual meeting of the members, consultants, advisors, and staff of the Committee on the Liturgy took place at Seton Hall University, South Orange, New Jersey, from June 14-15, 1989. During the course of the meeting the Committee reviewed the progress of several projects and received reports from its subcommittees.

The Committee took the following actions: 1) it reviewed the latest drafts of the general introduction and the brief introductions to the various parts of the *Lectionary for Masses with Children and for Other Celebrations* [these will be revised and re-presented to the Liturgy Committee in November]; 2) it approved for publication *Study Text 11: Order of Christian Funerals, A Commentary;* 3) it reviewed and approved the agenda and content for a workshop for new bishops at the November, 1989 meeting of the NCCB; 4) it gave general approval to the *Criteria for the Evaluation of Inclusive Language in Scripture Translations Destined for Use in the Liturgy,* drafted by the Joint Committee (Liturgy and Doctrine) on Inclusive Language; 5) it approved a survey/consultation instrument on new eucharistic prayers; 6) it established a task group to study questions regarding cremation and other funeral practices; 7) it discussed a varium regarding a scope and sequence chart for a three-year cycle of homilies based on the *Lectionary for Mass;* 8) it established a task group to work on guidelines for televised Masses; 9) it discussed problems concerning the reservation of the eucharist in small religious communities; 10) it approved a press release concerning the implementation date for the use of the common Spanish translation (*"texto unico"*) of the Order of Mass; 11) it established a procedure for the approval of liturgical texts in Spanish for the USA edition of the *Sacramentario;* 12) it discussed a *varium* regarding the washing of feet on Holy Thursday; 13) and it reviewed a proposed joint statement concerning conflicts in pastoral practice regarding confirmation of children and the *Rite of Christian Initiation of Adults.*

The Liturgy Committee also approved the following action items to be presented at the September meeting of the Administrative Committee: 1) Approval of Lakota as a liturgical language; 2) approval of liturgical texts in Spanish for the USA edition of the *Sacramentario;* 3) approval of *Gathered in Steadfast Faith: Statement of the Bishops' Committee on the Liturgy on Sunday Celebrations in the Absence of a*

Priest; 4) request that the *Order for Sunday Celebrations in the Absence of a Priest* be placed on the agenda of the November meeting of the NCCB; 5) request that a proposed change of date for the optional memorial of Blessed Junipero Serra from August 28 to July 1 be placed on the agenda of the November meeting of the NCCB; 6) approval of the ICEL provisional (green book) translation of the *Collection of Masses of the Blessed Virgin Mary.*

Monsignor Alan Detscher reported that the Lectionary Subcommittee is continuing its work on the preparation of the second edition of the *Lectionary for Mass.* The entire text (including the Old Testament) of the *New American Bible* is being edited for horizontal inclusive language; a new translation of the psalms is being prepared; the readings will be in sense lines; difficult Hebrew and Greek proper names will be syllabified for ease in pronunciation; references to the Jews (*hoi Ioudaioi*) will be clarified in accord with the principles of the Council for Religious Relations with the Jews (1974); the summaries of the readings will be printed before the introduction to the reading; the alleluia verse will be identified separately and be printed before the reference to the gospel; each of the Sunday cycles will be printed separately, that is, all of cycle A, followed by cycle B, then cycle C; a similar principle will be used for the weekday readings.

Bishop Ricardo Ramirez reported that the Hispanic Liturgy Subcommittee is working on the preparation of the Spanish translation of the *Sacramentary,* which will be called the *Sacramentario.* It is hoped that the book will be published in 1990. The "*texto unico*" of the Order of Mass in Spanish will be published before the First Sunday of Advent of this year. Future projects of the Hispanic Liturgy Subcommittee, in the order of priority, are: 1) *Order of Christian Funerals* in Spanish (and, possibly, in a bilingual edition); 2) *Order for Sunday Celebrations in the Absence of a Priest;* 3) bilingual editions of the marriage and baptismal rites; 4) Spanish translation of the USA edition of the *Rite of Christian Initiation of Adults;* 5) Spanish edition of the American additions to the Book of Blessings.

Bishop Wilton Gregory reported the progress of the Black Liturgy Subcommittee in developing its statement concerning Catholic worship and African-Americans. The initial draft has been completed and is being reviewed by subcommittee members and other experts.

Father Michael Spillane, Executive Secretary of the Federation of Diocesan Liturgical Commissions, reported that the Task Group on the Lectionary for Masses with Children continues its work on the *Lectionary for Masses with Children and for Other Celebrations.* The American Bible Society hopes to give final approval to its entire translation for early youth in March of 1990. However, the pericopes for the Lectionary should be ready by October of this year.

The Joint Committee (of the Committee on Doctrine and the Committee on the Liturgy) on Inclusive Language has submitted to the Committees on Liturgy and on Doctrine the latest draft of criteria to be used in the evaluation of inclusive language contained in biblical translations intended for use in the liturgy. The text is now being revised in light of the comments made by the two committees.

Father Kenneth Jenkins reported that preparations continue for the National Workshop on the *Ceremonial of Bishops* for bishops, cathedral rectors, episcopal masters of ceremonies, cathedral personnel, *et al.,* to be held in San Francisco on November 30-December 3, 1989. The schedule and proposed speakers were presented for the review of the committee.

Father Ronald Krisman reported that the final editorial work has been completed on the *Book of Blessings,* and the publication release date has been set for October 1, 1989. The *Order for the Solemn Exposition of the Holy Eucharist* has been completed and will be published in several months. Editorial work is nearing completion on the *Pastoral Companion to the Rite of Christian Initiation of Adults.*

Father Michael Spillane and Richard Ward (Chairman of the F.D.L.C. Board of Directors) reported that the Federation of Diocesan Liturgical Commissions continues to assist in the preparation of the *Lectionary for Masses with Children and for Other Celebrations.* It has consulted with the Bishops' Committee on the Liturgy concerning the possible re-publication of its catechetical materials on communion under both kinds. The Federation has encouraged the Liturgy Committee to form task groups to study televised Masses and Cremation and other funeral practices, respectively.

The meeting concluded with words of thanks from Bishop Delaney to all who were present. The bishop members and consultants of the Liturgy Committee will meet on November 4 in Baltimore, MD, and the next annual meeting of the members, consultants, and advisors will take place from June 16-18, 1990, at a place to be determined.

The Rite of Religious Profession

The revised edition of *The Rite of Religious Profession* containing all the changes mandated by the *Emendations in the Liturgical Books following upon the New Code of Canon Law* (Congregation for the Sacraments and Divine Worship, September 12, 1983), as well as the 1982 revised translation of the Introduction to the rite, has been recently published by the USCC Office of Publishing Services. The Rite of Religious Profession for Men and the Rite of Religious Profession for Women both include 1) the Norms for the Rite of Initiation into the Religious Life, 2) the Rite of Temporary Profession during Mass, 3) the Rite of Perpetual Profession during Mass, 4) the Rite of Renewal of Vows during Mass, and 5) Other Texts for the Rites of Religious Profession. An appendix contains a sample formula of profession and texts for the various Masses of religious profession. Copies may be ordered from the USCC Office of Publishing Services, 3211 Fourth Street, NE, Washington, DC 20017-1194, Publication No. 273-X, $11.95 per single copy (usual discounts apply).

National Workshop on the *Ceremonial of Bishops*

The National Workshop on the *Ceremonial of Bishops,* sponsored by the Bishops' Committee on the Liturgy, will be held from November 30-December 3, 1989 at the Cathedral of Saint Mary, San Francisco, CA. This workshop is intended for bishops, cathedral rectors, bishop's secretaries, masters of ceremonies, diocesan liturgical personnel, diocesan and cathedral musicians, and others involved with episcopal liturgies.

Major addresses will include "Episcopal Liturgy as a Theological Locus for Ecclesiology," "An Overview of the *Caeremoniale Episcoporum:* History and General Norms," "The Sacraments: The Paschal Presence of the Bishop," "The Stational Mass: From Refinements to Renewal," "Offices and Ministries in Episcopal Liturgy," and "The Church at Prayer: Going Beyond Rubrics to the Heart of the Church's Worship." Special interest sessions are planned to address selected sections of the *Ceremonial* as well as special ministries and relationships involved in the celebration of episcopal liturgies. These sessions include "General Norms," "The Cathedral," "Christian Initiation," "Confirmation," "Holy Orders," "The Cathedral Musician," "The Bishop's Office, the Office of Worship, and the Cathedral Staff: Working Relationships," "Those Who Assist the Bishops: The Role of Deacons and Master of Ceremonies," and "Special Days in the Life of a Bishop and Diocese."

Hotel accommodations will be provided by the nearby Cathedral Hill Hotel at a substantially reduced convention rate. American Airlines has been designated as the conference airline offering special discounts on all round trip fares when arranged through International Travel Advisers. The 24 hour a day reservation telephone number is 1-800/446-6000. The workshop registration fee will be $125 per person.

The *Ceremonial of Bishops* will be available in September, 1989 through The Liturgical Press, St. John's Abbey, Box 7500, Collegeville, MN 56321-9989, at the cost of $28.95 per copy. Advance orders are now being accepted.

For further workshop information and reservation materials please contact the Secretariat of the Bishops' Committee on the Liturgy, 3211 Fourth Street, NE, Washington, DC 20017. Telephone: 202/541-3060.

1989 National Meeting of Diocesan Liturgical Commissions

The Diocese of Pittsburgh and Region III will host the 1989 National Meeting of Diocesan Liturgical Commissions at The Westin William Penn Hotel in Pittsburgh, PA, from October 9-12. Addressing the theme "Active Participation: Neither Strangers Nor Spectators," major presenters will include Fred Molleck, Marchita Mauck, Irene Nowel, OSB, Mark Searle, and Archbishop Rembert Weakland, OSB. A variety of workshops concerning active participation are also being offered.

For further information contact the Registration Committee, 1989 FDLC National Meeting, 1607 Greentree Road, Pittsburgh, PA 15220.

BISHOPS' COMMITTEE ON THE LITURGY
NEWSLETTER

NATIONAL CONFERENCE OF CATHOLIC BISHOPS

**1989
VOLUME XXV
SEPTEMBER**

Confirmation of the *Order of Christian Funerals*

On June 29, 1987 the National Conference of Catholic Bishops received the decree of the Congregation for Divine Worship, dated April 29, 1897, confirming the decision of the NCCB to approve the revised translation of the *Ordo Exsequiarum* (*Order of Christian Funerals*) for use in dioceses in the United States of America. With the letter the Congregation included a "somewhat extensive list of modifications which [were] to be incorporated into the approved text." These modifications included altering selected ritual actions, retranslating, emending, and modifying various texts translated from the Latin, and reformulating several prayers composed in English and intended for pastoral situations not addressed in the Latin *editio typica* of the *Ordo Exsequiarum*.

In February 1989 the NCCB, along with other member conferences of bishops, requested the assistance of their joint commission, the International Commission on English in the Liturgy, in making the necessary modifications. In July these refinements were approved by the ICEL Episcopal Board and were forwarded to the NCCB Executive Committee, which subsequently approved the changes for inclusion in the USA edition of the *Order of Christian Funerals*.

The following is an unofficial English translation of the decree of confirmation issued by the Congregation for Divine Worship.

Prot. N. 1550/85

At the request of His Excellency James W. Malone, Bishop of Youngstown, and President of the National Conference of Catholic Bishops, in a letter dated 26 November 1985, and in virtue of the faculty granted to this Congregation by the Supreme Pontiff, Pope John Paul II, we gladly approve, that is confirm, the English text of the *Ordinis Exsequiarum,* prepared by the International Commission on English in the Liturgy, as it appears in the appended copy.

In the printed text mention should be made of the confirmation granted by the Apostolic See. Two copies of the printed text should be sent to this Congregation.

Anything to the contrary notwithstanding.

From the Congregation for Divine Worship, 29 April 1987.

+ Paul Augustin Cardinal Mayer, OSB
Prefect

+ Virgilio Noé
Titular Archbishop of Voncaria
Secretary

Effective Date for *Order of Christian Funerals:* All Souls Day, 1989

On the Solemnity of the Assumption, the Most Reverend John L. May, President of the National Conference of Catholic Bishops, issued the following decree declaring the *Order of Christian Funerals* to be the vernacular typical edition of the *Ordo Exsequiarum* for the dioceses of the United States of America. In this decree the date of mandatory use has been set for All Souls Day, November 2, 1989.

3211 4TH STREET, N.E. ● WASHINGTON, D.C. 20017

DECREE

In accord with the norms established by decree of the Sacred Congregation of Rites *Cum, nostra aetate* (27 January 1966), the Order of Christian Funerals is declared to be the vernacular typical edition of the *Ordo Exsequiarum* for the dioceses of the United States of America and may be published by authority of the National Conference of Catholic Bishops.

The *Order of Christian Funerals* was canonically approved by the National Conference of Catholic Bishops in plenary assembly on 14 November 1985 and was subsequently confirmed by the Apostolic See by decree of the Congregation for Divine Worship on 29 April 1987 (Prot. N. CD 1550/85).

On 1 October 1989 the *Order of Christian Funerals* may be published and used in funeral celebrations. From All Souls Day, 2 November 1989, its use is mandatory in the dioceses of the United States of America. From that date forward no other English version of these rites may be used.

Given at the General Secretariat of the National Conference of Catholic Bishops, Washington, DC, on 15 August 1989, the Solemnity of the Assumption.

> \+ John L. May
> Archbishop of Saint Louis
> President, National Conference of Catholic Bishops
>
> Robert N. Lynch
> General Secretary

Rereading the Constitution on the Liturgy (art. 20-24)

Inserted between the sections "The Promotion of Liturgical Instruction" and "The Reform of the Sacred Liturgy" is CSL 20, a two sentence article dealing with sacred rites and electronic communication. It states that transmission of liturgical celebrations must be marked by "discretion and dignity, under the leadership and direction of a competent person appointed for this office by the bishops." Certainly, in the years prior to the Council, broadcasts of major liturgical events by radio and, to a far lesser extent, television had aired throughout the United States. But these transmissions were more the exception than the rule. As bishops became aware of the potential of electronic media as a means of evangelization, education, and devotion, regularly scheduled liturgical broadcasts became more common.

Balancing liturgical norms and media production requirements continues to be problematic. While special liturgical events are often quite successful in this matter, regularly scheduled televised Masses often seem to neglect many liturgical imperatives. Because of production constraints, it is not uncommon that several Masses are videotaped one after the other. The liturgical calendar is ignored in order to fulfill a production schedule (e.g., Easter Masses taped during Lent). The congregation is often reduced to a handful of people where there is little or no participation, music of poor quality, and a severe restriction on the time available for the celebration.

Although electronic transmission of liturgical celebrations will never be able to substitute for one's actual presence at and participation in the liturgy, attention must nevertheless be given to the principles of the liturgical reform in celebrations which will be broadcast. Just as the Decree on the Means of Social Communication (*Inter Mirifica*), which was promulgated on the same day as the Constitution on the Sacred Liturgy (4 December 1963), encouraged the training of electronic communication experts, liturgical experts should be encouraged to lend their support and expertise to the preparation of these broadcasts in order to insure the finest quality liturgical expression.

In 1988 the Board of Directors of the Federation of Diocesan Liturgical Commissions asked the Bishops' Committee on the Liturgy to study the phenomenon of televised Masses. Their request has been accepted, and a Task Group will be appointed to develop guidelines for eventual publication. The age of electronic communication and transmission need not short change the profound possibilities of renewal inherent in the liturgical reform. Electronic transmission can be effectively used, and liturgical celebrations can be aired with "discretion and dignity" when the foundational principles of Catholic worship are respected.

The Reform of the Sacred Liturgy

The third section of Chapter 1 (CSL 21-40) legislates the norms for the liturgical reform. So that the Christian people "may more surely derive an abundance of graces from the liturgy" the Council fathers endorsed a general reform, not a piecemeal approach, or just a minor revision. While some elements of the liturgy are divinely instituted and unchangeable, many other elements were introduced into the liturgy over the centuries and are subject to change. These latter elements, the Council decreed, must in fact be changed if they are out of harmony with the nature of the liturgy or if they have lost their meaning. Several of these additions, such as multiple orations when saints shared the same day of the calendar, private preparatory prayers that individualized the liturgy, the precedence of saints' feasts over Sundays, multiplication of such gestures as the sign of the cross, and a general disengagement of those present through a lack of encouragement to participate, had come to obscure the "holy things they signify." And so there needed to be a stripping away of these accretions to allow the faithful to understand "with ease" the rites and texts being used and enable them to participate "fully, actively, and as befits a community" (CSL 21).

Those with responsibility for the restoration were identified by the Council Fathers. The Apostolic See retains ultimate authority for the regulation of the liturgy; territorial bodies of bishops and individual diocesan bishops share this responsibility within certain limits defined by law.

The involvement of the conferences of bishops has been and continues to be a significant instrument for renewal, restoration, and cultural adaptation of the liturgy. While the Apostolic See during the past 25 years has fulfilled in an admirable manner its mandate from the Council Fathers to prepare the revised liturgical books, the conferences of bishops have also exercised their authority over the preparation and approval of the vernacular translations of these books. In addition they have been authorized to determine those adaptations specifically allowed for in the books themselves and, at times, may even propose more substantial adaptations when these are judged necessary for the expression of their peoples' faith. In all cases, whether it be the preparation of liturgical texts by the Apostolic See or the translation and adaptation of rites by the conferences of bishops, no changes are to be introduced "unless the good of the Church genuinely and certainly requires them" (CSL 23). And all new liturgical forms should grow organically from existing ones, thus pointing out the need for thorough scholarship at every stage in the revision process.

Just as theological, historical, and pastoral research enabled the Concilium to restore the Church's liturgical rites to a more noble simplicity, so too today the same research should guide those responsible for proposing adaptations in the liturgical books. Similarly, most liturgical questions that are raised on a local level and not addressed directly in liturgical legislation can be resolved by a thorough understanding of the theological, historical and pastoral principles involved. In this way the Church's own liturgical tradition contributes to further developments.

One of the greatest successes of the liturgical renewal has been the restoration of the place of Scripture in the liturgy and in the lives of the faithful, as called for in CSL 24. Long after our present rites have undergone even further revision, the words "it is essential to promote that warm and living love for Scripture" will still be remembered. Each revised rite today incorporates Scripture, from the simplest blessing to the celebration of one of the sacraments. Unfortunately the appreciation of the role of Scripture in the actual celebration of these liturgical rites is at times sadly lacking. In celebrations of the anointing of the sick and of the reconciliation of individual penitents the proclamation of Scripture is still frequently omitted, manifesting a view of Scripture as "optional," with little appreciation of the power and importance of God's Word for those seeking consolation. Thus more attention should to be paid to the incorporation of Scripture in liturgical prayer so that the participants will be enriched by both word and sacrament.

In Memoriam: Reverend Eugene A. Walsh, SS, 1911-1989

After a long and distinguished career as priest, seminary professor/rector, and pastoral liturgist, Sulpician Father Eugene A. Walsh died of a heart attack in Hilo, Hawaii, on the Solemnity of the Assumption, August 15, 1989.

A native of Baltimore, MD, Father Walsh entered the Society of St. Sulpice and earned B.A. and M.A. degrees from The Catholic University of America before being ordained a priest on June 7, 1938. After several years teaching philosophy at St. Mary's Seminary (Baltimore) he returned to The Catholic University, where he was awarded an STD in 1949. From 1946 to 1968 Father Walsh taught philosophy of education, music, and theology at St. Mary's Seminary and served as choir master at the Basilica of the Assumption. From 1968 to 1971 he served as rector of The Theological College of The Catholic University of America (Washington, DC). There he assisted in the transformation of seminary life as directed by the decrees of the Second Vatican Council. He remained on the faculty there until 1985. During his later years he embarked upon a new career, devoting himself to the liturgical renewal through published articles, workshops, and study days in which he developed the practical aspects of prayer, liturgy, and worship. He also served as an advisor to the Bishops' Committee on the Liturgy.

Throughout his 51 years of ordained ministry, Father Walsh enriched thousands of lives through his patient direction and loving friendship and influenced the liturgical renewal of many dioceses and parishes in the English speaking world.

> God of endless ages,
> from one generation to the next
> you have been our refuge and strength.
> Before the mountains were born
> or earth came to be,
> you are God.
> Have mercy now on your servant Eugene
> whose long life was spent in your service.
> Give him a place in your kingdom,
> where hope is firm for all who love
> and rest is sure for all who serve.
>
> We ask this through Christ our Lord.

Publications

Order of Christian Funerals

Ritual editions of the Order of Christians Funerals will be available after October 1, 1989 from the following publishers at the listed prices.

Catholic Book Publishing Company -   Minister's edition $17.95
Minister's edition, leather bound with gold edges $23.95

The Liturgical Press -   Minister's edition $23.50
Vigil Service and Evening Prayer, Leader's edition $6.95

Liturgy Training Publications -   Minister's edition $18.00
Rite of Committal Minister's edition $14.00

Various participants' editions are also available from The Liturgical Press and Liturgy Training Publications. Complete study editions will be available after April 1, 1990.

Study Text 11: The Order of Christian Funerals will be published by the USCC Office of Publishing Services in the coming months.

Book of Blessings

The USA edition of the *Book of Blessings,* which contains over forty new American blessings in addition to those contained in the Latin edition, will be available on October 1, 1989. The mandatory date for the use of the *Book of Blessings* is the First Sunday of Advent, December 3, 1989.

The *Book of Blessings* will be available from the following publishers:

Catholic Book Publishing Company -   Minister's edition $26.95

The Liturgical Press -   Minister's edition $27.95

Study editions and excerpts from the *Book of Blessings* will be available at a future date.

Rite of Religious Profession

In addition to the edition published by the USCC Office of Publishing and Promotion Services, which was mentioned in the August 1989 issue of the Bishops' Committee on the Liturgy *Newsletter,* Liturgy Training Publications, Chicago, is also publishing a comb-bound, paperback edition of the *Rite of Religious Profession.* It features a pastoral introduction by Edward Foley, OFM Cap, and will cost $9.95.

BISHOPS' COMMITTEE ON THE LITURGY
NEWSLETTER

NATIONAL CONFERENCE OF CATHOLIC BISHOPS

1989
VOLUME XXV
OCTOBER/NOVEMBER

November Plenary Assembly of the NCCB

At the November 6-9, 1989, plenary assembly of the National Conference of Catholic Bishops, which was held in Baltimore, Maryland, the Bishops' Committee on the Liturgy presented three action items for the consideration of the bishops. All were approved by the required two-thirds majority vote of the de iure members of the NCCB and have been sent for the confirmation of the Apostolic See.

The bishops approved the request to change the date of the optional memorial of Blessed Junipero Serra from August 28 (the same date as is assigned by the *General Roman Calendar* for the obligatory memorial of Saint Augustine) to July 1 (the date Father Serra entered California in 1769) in the Proper Calendar for the dioceses of the United States. In addition, they approved the proposal that "*Ustedes*" be allowed in the published Spanish translations of the Scriptures and liturgical texts for use in the dioceses of the United States.

Finally, the bishops approved for liturgical use in the dioceses of the United States an *Order for Sunday Celebrations in the Absence of a Priest,* which includes Morning and Evening Prayer for Sundays and the Celebration of the Liturgy of the Word on Sundays, each of which may be concluded with the rite of holy communion. Five appendices complete the ritual and contain: sample general intercessions; various acts of thanksgiving; the opening prayers and prayers after communion for all Sundays, solemnities, and feasts of the Lord; additional prayers after communion from *Holy Communion and Worship of the Eucharist outside Mass;* blessings.

Effective Date for the *Texto unico:* December 3, 1989

The following press release on the "texto unico" *Spanish translation of the Order of Mass was released by the NCCB Liturgy Secretariat in November 1989. It emphasizes the importance of this new translation, which becomes effective in the dioceses of the United States on Sunday, November 3, 1989, the First Sunday of Advent.*

On November 11, 1986, the National Conference of Catholic Bishops approved the common (*"texto unico"*) Spanish translation of the Order of Mass, fourteen eucharistic prayers (including the five-fold "Swiss Synod" prayer), and several recent additions to the *Roman Missal.* This decision was confirmed by the Apostolic See by decree of the Congregation for Divine Worship (Prot. N. 899/87) on July 16, 1987. Subsequently a mandatory effective date for the use of this new translation was established for the dioceses of the United States of America: the First Sunday of Advent, December 3, 1989.

The publishers of missalettes and other participation aids have been notified of this decision and have incorporated the new texts for the Order of Mass into their issues for Advent 1989. In December 1989 The Catholic Book Publishing Company will publish an edition of the new Spanish version of the Order of Mass and eucharistic prayers for use until the new Spanish edition of the *Sacramentary (Sacramentario)* for the dioceses of the United States is published in the fall of 1990.

The *"texto unico"* of the Order of Mass provides a greater variety of optional texts for the greetings, penitential rites, invitations to the Lord's Prayer, etc., than had been previously available in Spanish. Those familiar with the English version of the *Roman Missal (Sacramentary)* are already aware of such a variety. The texts of the congregation remain basically the same. However, there will be some minor changes in the wording of the Gloria, Creed, and Lord's Prayer to which the congregation may take a few weeks to become accustomed.

3211 4th STREET N.E. ● WASHINGTON, D.C. 20017

The Bishops' Committee on the Liturgy is pleased that the Spanish-speaking Catholics of the United States will now have a translation of the Order of Mass which is common to all Spanish speaking countries, and next year will have a Spanish version of the *Sacramentary* which has been prepared and published specifically for their use.

Pastors of parishes where Spanish is used in the celebration of the Mass should provide the catechesis necessary for a fruitful reception of the new texts by their congregations well in advance of the First Sunday of Advent (December 3, 1989). The introduction of the new Spanish translation of the Order of Mass is an ideal opportunity for catechesis on the Mass as a whole, and not merely on the new texts, and for encouraging the full and active participation of the congregation in the liturgy as desired by the Second Vatican Council.

Address of Bishop Joseph P. Delaney

On Wednesday, October 11, 1989, the Most Reverend Joseph P. Delaney, Bishop of Fort Worth and Chairman of the Liturgy Committee of the National Conference of Catholic Bishops, reported on the activities of the Committee to the delegates and guests attending the annual National Meeting of Diocesan Liturgical Commissions in Pittsburgh, PA. The full text of Bishop Delaney's report follows.

May I begin by saying it is a pleasure to be with you once again. It is a special pleasure for me, since this meeting marks the twentieth anniversary of the first organizational meeting of the twenty-two delegates of the charter committee of the Federation of Diocesan Liturgical Commissions. The Bishops' Committee on the Liturgy is proud of its role in the birth of the Federation. On April 22, 1969, the Liturgy Committee sent a memorandum to the chairmen and secretaries of diocesan liturgical commissions who expressed interest in organizing a federation of commissions. The memorandum proposed a division of the United States into twelve regions from which two representatives were to be chosen in a ballot conducted by the Bishops' Committee on the Liturgy. The Liturgy Committee suggested that the new organization be considered a federation of diocesan commissions, a name that has remained to this day. Over the past twenty years the Federation has served the needs of the liturgical life of the Church in the United States. It has generally supported the work of the Bishops' Committee on the Liturgy, on occasion it has challenged some of the decisions of the BCL, but it has always been willing to do whatever is necessary to continue the work of liturgical reform and renewal. In the name of the past and present members, consultants, advisors, and secretariat staff of the Bishops' Committee on the Liturgy may I extend to all of you thanks for your continued dedication to the work of the Church and its liturgy and urge you to continue to foster that work in the days ahead.

You have received an information report on the activities of the Bishops' Committee on the Liturgy in your meeting packets, and I will not repeat its contents. However, I would like to highlight several items that may be of interest to you.

Order of Christian Funerals

After over four years of delays, the *Order of Christian Funerals* has finally been published by The Catholic Book Publishing Company, The Liturgical Press, and Liturgy Training Publications. The Liturgical Press is also publishing an excerpt from the *OCF* containing the Vigil for the Deceased and related materials, and Liturgy Training Publications is publishing the Committal Rite. Study editions of the *Order of Christian Funerals* will be available in April from the publishers. This new edition of the funeral rites represents the fruits of the ICEL revisions process and the labor of a large number of individuals. We all owe ICEL our thanks for the work which has been done under often trying circumstances. The *OCF* is a complete retranslation of the Latin text, along with newly composed prayers and copious pastoral and introductory notes. As is true for all the revised liturgical books, the Introduction and pastoral notes of the *Order of Christian Funerals* are extremely important and respond to expressed pastoral needs. The newly composed prayers are the result of the consultation the ICEL conducted with the various episcopal conferences and provide for such occasions as suicide, violent or accidental death and the death of an infant. Several new rites are provided for the period before the funeral, and there is a rite for a funeral outside Mass. The mandatory effective date for the use of the *Order of Christian Funerals* is November 2, 1989.

Book of Blessings

October also marks the publication of the English translation of the *Book of Blessings,* the last major portion of the *Roman Ritual* to be revised. In addition to the blessings contained in the Latin edition, the American edition of the *Book of Blessings* contains an additional 40 blessings proper to this country. Work began on the American blessings in 1985 with the formation of a subcommittee on blessings by the Bishops' Committee on the Liturgy. This subcommittee was also responsible for *Catholic Household Blessings and Prayers,* which contains simplified versions of many of the blessings contained in the minister's edition. I would like to take this opportunity to express my thanks to all those who assisted in the preparations of these two books, which are an important contribution to the prayer life of the Church in the United States. The *Book of Blessings* is being published by The Catholic Book Publishing Company and The Liturgical Press and should be available this week. The mandatory effective date for the use of the *Book of Blessings* is December 3, 1989, the First Sunday of Advent.

Revision of the Roman Missal

For several years the International Commission on English in the Liturgy has been engaged in revising the English translation of the *Roman Missal* or *Sacramentary,* as it is called in this country. ICEL hopes to have its work completed by 1992 for presentation to the English-speaking conferences of bishops. ICEL is in the process of preparing additional texts for a three-year cycle of opening prayers related to the readings, additional prefaces, alternative texts within the Order of Mass, and pastoral notes for each portion of the *Sacramentary.* Present plans call for the *Sacramentary* to be issued in two volumes: volume one will contain *Sundays, Solemnities and Feasts,* and volume two will contain the texts for *Weekdays and Other Occasions.* The two-volume arrangement is necessary because of the large number of new prayers and the other material that will be included in the *Sacramentary.* From the sample texts that have been distributed to the episcopal conferences, I can say that ICEL has done a fine job in revising its translations, and we all can look forward to this new English edition of the *Roman Missal.*

Lectionary for Mass

The Bishops' Committee on the Liturgy is in the process of preparing a second edition of the *Lectionary for Mass* based on the second Latin edition. This new edition will contain additional readings that were not included in the present edition. All the readings will be in sense lines and formatted for ease of proclamation. The *Revised New Testament of the New American Bible* is being used for this edition and, with the assistance of the editors of the *NAB* and the BCL Lectionary Subcommittee, changes are being made to insure the use of inclusive language. To this end the subcommittee is following the principles that have been enunciated by the Joint Committee (of the BCL and Doctrine Committee) on Inclusive Language in Biblical Translations. Every effort has been made to address each particular instance of exclusive language and, insofar as it is possible, inclusive language has been substituted. The use of inclusive language in the Scriptures is a complicated question, and not everyone will be satisfied. However, the Bishops' Committee on the Liturgy has attempted to address all the questions that have been raised and offer solutions that are biblically, doctrinally, and linguistically sound.

Lectionary for Children

Work on the *Lectionary for Masses with Children and Other Celebrations* is nearing completion, thanks to the active involvement of the Federation. The introductions to the various sections of the Lectionary are being revised and will be presented to the Bishops' Committee on the Liturgy in March. The Liturgy Committee has chosen to use the American Bible Society's *Translation for Early Youth* for the Lectionary. The Bible Society has prepared all the pericopes needed for the Lectionary, and we should be receiving the readings by the end of October. Since comments have been made about this translation at conferences on Children's liturgy and the so-called Rite of Christian Initiation for Children, I would like to make some clarifications. The American Bible Society has worked closely with the FDLC and the chairman of the BCL Subcommittee on the Lectionary, Archbishop John Whealon, on this new translation. The *Translation for Early Youth* is geared for 7-8 year old children in its choice of vocabulary, sentence structure, etc. It is not a paraphrase, but rather it is a fresh translation from the Greek and Hebrew Scriptures and is faithful to the original texts. Some of the critiques have been based on the recently published *Gospel of Luke,* e.g., the "woes" that follow the beatitudes. It has been said that such texts would frighten children, yet the argument is misplaced. The translation is accurate. To tone the passage down to such an extent that it looses its original meaning would not be faithful to the original text. The real argument is whether or not such passages should be read at Mass with children. This Lectionary is careful to avoid these passages. I would hope that these critics will be objective enough to wait for the publication of the final text.

Spanish Liturgical Texts

The Hispanic Liturgy Subcommittee of the Bishops' Committee on the Liturgy has completed the translation of the American prayers and texts that are not found in the Spanish *Misal Romano*. These texts have been approved by the Administrative Committee and will be sent to the Congregation for Divine Worship and the Discipline of the Sacraments for confirmation. We hope to be able to publish the first Spanish Sacramentary for the United States during the next year. The new Sacramentary will be called the *Sacramentario* and will be based on the Mexican *Misal Romano*. It will include the Masses and prayers proper to the United States, the patronal feast of each of the North, Central, and South American countries, and the common Spanish translation ("*texto unico*") of the Order of Mass. The Spanish *Order of Mass* will be published in December, 1989 by The Catholic Book Publishing Company and its use will be mandatory on December 3, the First Sunday of Advent, for all Masses celebrated in Spanish. The Congregation for Divine Worship and the Discipline of the Sacraments has recently asked episcopal conferences that use Spanish as a liturgical language if the plural person pronoun "*Ustedes*" rather than "*vosotros*" should be allowed in published liturgical texts. The Committee on the Liturgy will recommend to the bishops at their November meeting that Rome be requested to allow this usage which is common throughout our country. May I also take this opportunity to thank the members of the Hispanic Subcommittee and others who have assisted them in their work.

Task Forces

Each year the Liturgy Committee carefully examines the resolutions passed by the liturgical commissions at this National Meeting in order to respond to proposals addressed to it. In response to two resolutions of previous national meetings, the Bishops' Committee on the Liturgy has established two task forces: one will deal with the questions raised by cremation and other burial practices, and the other will deal with the questions raised by televised Masses. In regard to the latter, the Congregation for Divine Worship and the Discipline of the Sacraments has indicated that it too is investigating the question of televised Masses and has asked for our input. We look forward to honest and fruitful collaboration with the Congregation on this and other issues.

Future Directions

As we conclude our twenty-sixth year of the liturgical reform and renewal mandated by the Second Vatican Council, it becomes clearer that for liturgical renewal truly to work, to be effective, it must consist not merely in external changes, but in the internalization of the principles of the reform. Pope JohnPaul II made this abundantly clear in his apostolic letter on the occasion of the twenty-fifth anniversary of the promulgation of the Constitution on the Sacred Liturgy. There are those who have gone far beyond the conciliar reform to the point of creating their own liturgies with little relationship to the prayer of the Church; they need to reestablish their connection to the broader community of the local Church under the bishop and the universal Church. There are also those who refuse to accept the conciliar reform on the basis of a notion of tradition that stops with the Tridentine reform. These people, as Pope John Paul II notes, need to be catechized as to the nature of the liturgy and its proper place in the life of the Church and the individual.

Once again, congratulations on your twentieth anniversary and be assured of the commitment of the Bishops' Committee on the Liturgy to strong, vital, and active liturgical commissions and offices of worship in each diocese.

Rereading the Constitution on the Liturgy (art. 26-32)

The understanding that "liturgical services are not private functions, but are celebrations of the Church" in CSL 26 led the Church to rethink how rites can and should facilitate the common prayer of the faithful. In the decades just prior to the liturgical reforms, the manner in which the Church's liturgy was celebrated often gave the impression that worship was primarily a private action. While the priest "said" Mass, attentive to a missal containing rubrics for only the priest and other principal ministers, the congregation prayed private devotions and meditations that may have hoped to mirror the meaning of what the priest was doing. Altar servers assumed the role of the congregation by responding to prayers and reciting liturgical texts, while at more solemn gatherings the choir made the liturgical responses and provided other musical selections. Celebrating Mass was in practice the private action of the priest, rather than the celebration of the entire

Church. Even the terminology surrounding the liturgical celebrations supported this private view of worship, and on occasion can still be heard today. Priests speak of "offering *my* Mass" and people will acknowledge "*his* liturgy."

Despite the fact that the eucharistic celebration during this period of the Church's history was less oriented toward communal celebration than it is today, one should not overlook the fact that Catholics still enjoyed a rich communal prayer life, particularly in the United States. Novenas, devotions, and processions were the mainstay of the American Catholic spiritual diet. Parishioners prayed together, sang together, and celebrated their religious unity principally outside Mass. The thrust of the *Constitution on the Sacred Liturgy* was to reorient that communal prayer life back to the primary celebration of the eucharist as the *locus* of unity in Christ and in the Church. The challenge then became to transform the eucharistic celebration into a more authentic expression of communal prayer while at the same time preserving the personal orientation which is a component of all prayer.

Certainly in the United States where cultural attitudes of what has been called "fierce individualism" have overflowed into religious practice, people are more apt to view liturgical celebrations as a time of private prayer within the context of a gathering of the Church. The effort to row against that cultural tide has met with varying success. Many parishes have successfully catechized parishioners to the fuller meaning of the eucharistic gathering and have therefore encouraged a balanced horizontal and vertical theological relationship with regard to liturgical engagement. Not only do "servers, lectors, commentators, and members of the choir exercise a genuine liturgical function" (CSL 29), but the people have taken well to their external role of participating in "acclamations, responses, psalmody, antiphons, and songs, as well as by means of actions, gestures, and bodily attitudes" (CSL 30). Such participation reveals the richer reality that all contribute to the liturgy of the Church according to their office, ministry or role.

The desire ritually to express unity with one another has led to a common practice in the United States of holding hands during the Lord's Prayer. Whether people are comfortable or uncomfortable with this practice is a separate issue. The more significant liturgical concern seems to be that the desire to express unity is seen as separate from the assembly's corporate act of receiving communion. It is in the reception of communion that we are united in Christ and united in the Church. And our liturgical practice should support that reality. No doubt because of our previous religious practice, our cultural attitudes, and the profound experience of receiving communion, the tendency is to privatize the reception of communion to the point of jeopardizing the communal nature of the liturgy. A healthier balance between the personal and communal prayer needs to be developed through catechesis and ritual experience. In some local Churches, the diocesan bishop has asked that all remain standing throughout the reception of communion out of respect for those receiving communion. Once all have received communion, all may then kneel or sit in silence or possibly sing together a song of praise together, as the Order of Mass indicates. Whatever the liturgical action, a better balance between the personal and communal aspects of the liturgy needs to be embraced.

Fourth Sunday of Advent and Christmas in 1989

Several dioceses in the United States have already begun to address the scheduling of Masses on Sunday, December 24, and Monday, December 25, this year. The Liturgy Secretariat encourages all dioceses and parishes to consider thoughtfully recent trends in Christmas Mass scheduling and the serious challenge posed this year.

Christmas last fell on a Monday in 1978. Since that time it has become more and more the practice in the United States that Catholics celebrate Christmas by participating in one of the vigil Masses in their parish. This phenomenon has led to the multiplication of Masses on Christmas eve in an attempt to accommodate the large crowds. Although these crowds are indeed commendable, the resulting increase in the number of Christmas vigil masses should not compromise the importance of celebrating the paschal mystery on Sunday, "the original feast day" (CSL 106) when Christmas falls on the next day. As the *General Norms for the Liturgical Year and the Calendar* 5 states: "Because of its special importance, the Sunday celebration gives way only to solemnities or feasts of the Lord. The Sundays of the seasons of Advent, Lent, and Easter, however, take precedence over all solemnities and feasts of the Lord." Therefore, every attempt should be made to catechize the faithful as to the primary importance of Sunday and, in particular because of this year's calendar, the relationship between the Fourth Sunday of Advent and Christmas. It may be suggested that the faithful be encouraged to attend Mass on the morning of the Fourth Sunday of Advent and on

Christmas morning or on the vigil of the Fourth Sunday of Advent and the vigil of Christmas or the Mass at Midnight.

Parishes are encouraged to review the Mass schedules for the Fourth Sunday of Advent and Christmas and to keep in mind the potential strain on the clergy and other ministers which could result from inattention to liturgical principles and pastoral situations. It may be suggested that the number of vigil masses on both Saturday and Sunday be limited and that masses with low attendance be combined with other masses for this one occasion. Because of the limited time available to transform the worship environment, it is also suggested that decorations for Christmas reflect a spirit of "noble simplicity" emphasizing the primary Christian elements of the season.

The same suggestions are applicable for the following Sunday and Monday when the Church celebrates on Sunday, December 31, the Feast of the Holy Family and on Monday, January 1, the Solemnity of Mary, Mother of God.

Newsletter Subscription Renewals

Computerized renewal notices will be sent to all subscribers to the Bishops' Committee on the Liturgy *Newsletter* in late November or early December. Subscribers are asked to return the completed forms with their payment before December 23, 1989. (Subscriptions which have not been renewed by the time of the January 1990 *Newsletter* goes to press will be placed on an inactive list and reinstated once payment is received.) Subscriptions rates for 1990 remain the same as that of 1989. Single subscription prices are $9.00 domestic mail and $11.00 foreign mail. Bulk rates also will remain the same.

In order that subscribers' accounts may be properly credited, the instructions accompanying the renewal forms should be followed. The "renewal coupon" portion of the invoice must be included with payment. Coupon and payment should be returned in the self-mailer envelop which has been provided. This envelop is preaddressed for direct mail deposit to the bank. Payment should not be sent to the NCCB Secretariat for the Liturgy, since it needlessly slows down the renewal process.

Subscribers who have not received a renewal form by December 10, 1980 should contact the Liturgy Secretariat so that a duplicate invoice may be sent. (*Newsletter* recipients whose subscription number is 205990, 205995, or 205999 are receiving *gratis* copies. Therefore, they will receive no renewal invoice.)

The Liturgy Secretariat expresses its gratitude to all subscribers for their cooperation in the renewal process.

Book of Blessings: Seasonal Blessings

The publication of the *Book of Blessings* on October 1, 1989, provides a rich resource for the fall, Advent, and Christmas seasons. *Part V: Blessings Related to Feasts and Seasons* is dedicated to a series of blessings that are specifically related to the liturgical year. Some of these blessings serve to emphasize the great mysteries of redemption in Christ, while others take their inspiration from the lives of the saints.

The first rite that may appropriately be used is the *Order for Visiting a Cemetery on All Souls Day* (Chapter 57). This rite may be celebrated on November 2 or on another day during the month of November. It may be used at a public celebration or by family members when they visit the cemetery. In some cases, it may be a suitable alternative to cemetery Masses during the month of November, when the weather often makes the celebration of the eucharist difficult or impossible. Many of the texts of the rite are taken from the *Order of Christian Funerals.*

Chapter 47 of the *Book of Blessings* contains the *Order for the Blessing of an Advent Wreath.* This blessing may be celebrated on the First Sunday of Advent either in a church or in a home. Three orders for the blessing are given: Order of Blessing within Mass; Order of Blessing within a Celebration of the Word of God; Shorter Rite. The shorter rite is appropriate for use in homes, and a version of this rite is found in *Catholic Household Blessings and Prayers.* When the Advent Wreath is used in a church, on the Second and succeeding Sundays of Advent the candles are lighted either before Mass begins or immediately before the opening prayer; no additional rites or prayers are used. All contrary practices should be discontinued. The prayers that were previously used for the lighting of the candles were actually the opening prayers of the

Mass for each Sunday of Advent. These prayers are appropriate for use at home, but are duplications of the opening prayers when used at Mass.

An *Order for the Blessing of Food for Thanksgiving Day* is provided in Chapter 58. As with the previous rite, there are three forms given, and the third is appropriate for use at home. The blessing may be celebrated at Mass to bless food for the family Thanksgiving dinner or for distribution to the poor either the evening before Thanksgiving Day or on the day itself. The Order of Blessing within a Celebration of the Word of God may be used, with suitable adaptations, for ecumenical services.

Three blessings are appropriately used during the Christmas season: *Order for the Blessing of a Christmas Manger or Nativity Scene* (Chapter 48); *Order for the Blessing of a Christmas Tree* (Chapter 49); *Order for the Blessing of Homes during the Christmas and Easter Seasons* (Chapter 50). These three blessings recognize common customs associated with Christmas.

The blessing of a Christmas Manger or Nativity Scene may take place at home or in church. If the manger is set up in church, it must not be placed in the presbyterium. A place should be chosen that is suitable for prayer and devotion and is easily accessible by the faithful. The practice of placing the manger under or on the altar is not proper since it devalues the nature of the altar and makes it only a setting for the crib. A form of the shorter rite is found in *Catholic Household Blessings and Prayers*.

The Christmas tree may be blessed on or before Christmas during a celebration of the Word of God, or during Morning or Evening Prayer. This later provision is appropriate for religious communities. In the home the Christmas tree may be blessed by a parent or another family member, in connection with the evening meal on the Vigil of Christmas or at another suitable time on Christmas Day; the shorter rite in *Book of Blessings* or the rite contained in *Catholic Household Blessings and Prayers* may be used for this purpose. When Christmas trees are used in church, the decoration of the trees should be appropriate to their use in church, and care should be taken that they do not interfere with the requirements of the liturgical space.

In many places it is customary for the priest to visit homes during the Christmas season, especially on the solemnity of the Epiphany, and to bless them. The *Order for the Blessing of Homes during the Christmas and Easter Seasons* contains specific texts which may be appropriately used for the seasonal blessing of homes and families. If there are many homes to visit, the shorter rite may be used.

1989 National Meeting of Diocesan Liturgical Commissions

Marking the 20th anniversary of the first meeting of the Federation of Diocesan Liturgical Commissions, more than two hundred delegates and guests from dioceses throughout the United States met on October 9-12, 1989, in Pittsburgh, PA, to discuss the topic "Active Participation." The meeting was sponsored jointly by the Bishops' Committee on the Liturgy and the Federation of Diocesan Liturgical Commissions and was hosted by the Diocese of Pittsburgh and the dioceses of Region 3.

Along with the customary business sessions, several major presentations and a variety of workshops and showcases developed different aspects of the conference topic. Fred Moleck, Ph.D., and Marchita Mauch, Ph.D., gave a humorous presentation reviewing the musical and artistic developments that have taken place in the American liturgical renewal since the initial postconciliar reforms. A broader understanding of how the liturgy has been unconsciously inculturated in the United States was discussed by Dr. Mark Searle. And Irene Nowell, OSB, traced the roots of active participation in the Hebrew understandings of covenant, community and worship and brought out their implications for Christian worship. The conference concluded with the presentation of the Most Reverend Rembert G. Weakland, Archbishop of Milwaukee, entitled "A Bridge in Time."

Reports by the Chair of the FDLC, Reverend Richard Ward, and various committee heads briefed those present on the progress of several FDLC projects. The current activities of the Bishops' Committee on the Liturgy were presented by the Most Reverend Joseph P. Delaney, Chairman, who took the opportunity to congratulate the FDLC for its twenty years of contributions to renewal and promotion of the liturgy in the United States.

NCCB Administrative Committee Meeting

The Administrative Committee of the National Conference of Catholic Bishops met at the new NCCB/USCC headquarters building in northeast Washington, DC, on September 26-28, 1989. The members approved the following items submitted by the Committee on the Liturgy: (1) Lakota as a liturgical language for use in the dioceses of the United States of America; the interim Spanish translation of texts found in the American *Sacramentary* but not contained in the Mexican edition of the *Roman Missal;* (3) the interim English translation of the remaining 34 masses in honor of the Blessed Virgin Mary originally published by the Congregation for Divine Worship and the Sacraments during the 1987-1988 Marian year. These three decisions have been forwarded to the Congregation for Divine Worship and the Discipline of the Sacraments for the requisite confirmation.

The Administrative Committee also agreed to place on the agenda of the plenary assembly of the National Conference of Catholic Bishops in November 1989 three action items (see above).

New Publications

Texto unico, Catholic Book Publishing Company—the common Spanish translation of the Order of Mass in a hardcover liturgical book with ribbons and tabs, suitable for use at the chair and altar. Available through local religious bookstores. Approximate cost: $25.00.

Music in Christian Funerals, Office of Worship of the Diocese of Buffalo—musical guidelines based on the principles of the *Order of Christian Funerals* with specific musical selections for appropriate parts of the funeral liturgy; recommended hymns, solos, and organ music; bibliography and resources. Contact Rev. Msgr. Edward Grosz, Office of Worship, 795 Main St., Buffalo, NY 14203. Telephone: 716/847-5545. $3.00.

1990 editions of several liturgical publications of Liturgy Training Publications of the Archdiocese of Chicago are now available.

At Home with the Word—1990 edition contains the Sunday scripture readings for cycle A in addition to formats for morning, evening and night prayer, seasonal psalms, and the Order of Mass for those who participate in televised Masses or for those who participate in Mass outside the church. $3.25.

Workbook for Lectors and Gospel Readers 1990, Celebrating Liturgy: Cycle A contains readings for Sundays, holy days, vigil Masses, Ash Wednesday and Easter Triduum of cycle A. Also contains suggested pause indicators and emphasis markings as well as a pronunciation guide. $6.50.**

Sourcebook for Sundays and Seasons 1990, An Almanac of Parish Liturgy draws on the Lectionary, Sacramentary, and other liturgical resources to assist liturgy planners in shaping liturgical celebrations. $5.95.

Liturgical Calendar for 1990 is a poster for home, classroom, sacristy and planning areas providing a circular calendar of the liturgical year. $4.00.

These publications are available, with quantity discounts, from: Liturgy Training Publications, 1800 North Hermitage Avenue, Chicago, IL 60622-1101. Telephone: 800/933-1800.

BISHOPS' COMMITTEE ON THE LITURGY
NEWSLETTER
NATIONAL CONFERENCE OF CATHOLIC BISHOPS

**1989
VOLUME XXV
DECEMBER**

November Liturgy Committee Meeting

The NCCB Liturgy Committee (bishop members and consultants) met on Saturday, November 4, 1989 in Baltimore, MD, to consider several matters. After reviewing both the action items approved by the NCCB Administrative Committee in September (Lakota as a liturgical language; Spanish translation of prayers from the *Sacramentary; Collection of Masses of the Blessed Virgin Mary*) and those which were to be presented during the November plenary assembly of the National Conference of Catholic Bishops, the Committee discussed several issues: the ICEL revision of the *Sacramentary* and the process for its approval; the proposed creation of a Task Group to study possible adaptations in the USA edition of the *Sacramentary;* the request to include Blessed Miguel Pro in the Proper Calendar for the Dioceses of the United States of America (to be included on the agenda of the June 1990 meeting); the request of Archbishop Roger Mahony and Bishop Joseph Sullivan concerning appropriate commemoration of the centennial anniversary of *Rerum Novarum* in 1991; and a varium concerning back-to-back Sundays and holy days of obligation. The Committee approved for submission to the NCCB Administrative Committee the English translation of the liturgical texts for the obligatory memorial of Saints Andrew Dung-Lac and Companions. It also reviewed the position statements approved by the delegates to the 1989 National Meeting of Diocesan Liturgical Commissions (see below), and agreed to place on the agenda of its June meeting a proposal for the development of additional liturgical texts for the optional memorial of Blessed Katharine Drexel.

Oral information reports were made concerning the National Workshop on the *Ceremonial of Bishops*; the October 1989 visit of the NCCB officers to the Congregation for Divine Worship and Discipline of the Sacraments; the work of the Liturgy Secretariat; and the activities of the various subcommittees and task groups of the Liturgy Committee.

Future meetings of the Committee will be held at the Dallas-Fort Worth airport on February 10, 1990 (bishop members and consultants), in Menlo Park, CA, from June 17-19, 1990 (members, consultants and advisors), and in Washington, DC, on November 11, 1990 (bishop members and advisors).

Seasonal Blessings

The *Book of Blessings* and the *Sacramentary* contain several blessings for use during the period of Ordinary Time which precedes Lent and during the Lenten season itself.

The blessing of candles is celebrated on the Feast of the Presentation of the Lord, February 2. This blessing, contained in the *Sacramentary,* is celebrated in the context of either a procession to the church from some gathering place or a solemn entrance rite which begins at the church door or at the rear of the church. Unlit candles are held by those present and then are lighted while the antiphon in the *Sacramentary* or a hymn is sung. After the greeting and brief introduction, the priest says one of the two prayers of blessing, and he sprinkles the candles with holy water. The priest, accompanied by at least some of the people, processes through the church. The people go directly to their seats, and the priest goes to the altar. After venerating the altar in the usual way, he may incense it, and he then goes to his chair. The Gloria and Opening Prayer follow as usual.

Chapter 31 of the *Book of Blessings* contains the Order for the Blessing of Throats on the Feast of Saint Blase (February 3). This blessing, a longstanding custom in the United States, was not included in the revised

Roman edition of *De Benedictionibus*. Consequently, the Bishops' Committee on the Liturgy issued a *Rite of Blessing of Throats* in 1985. This rite was later revised and included in the American edition of the *Book of Blessings*.

The blessing of throats may be given by a priest, a deacon, or a lay minister who has been so designated by the bishop. The rite may be celebrated within Mass (after the homily) or within a celebration of the Word of God. A special form of the blessing is provided for use by lay ministers.

According to tradition the blessing is given by touching the throat with two blessed candles which have been joined together in the form of a cross. The use of the candles probably arose from the fact that candles were blessed the previous day on the Feast of the Presentation of the Lord, also known as Candlemas Day. It is Christ, the Light of the world, who conquers sin, sickness, and death.

The blessing of throats is an opportune time for prayer for the sick and those who care for them. It should be noted that this blessing is related to the memorial of Saint Blase (February 3). It should not normally be transferred to another day.

The Order for the Blessing and Distribution of Ashes on Ash Wednesday, Chapter 52 of the *Book of Blessings*, is for use when the blessing takes place outside Mass. The *Sacramentary* contains the rite for use within Mass. It also indicates the order this rite should take when celebrated outside Mass, but does not include all the necessary texts. The *Book of Blessings* indicates that the blessing of Ashes is restricted to priests and deacons, but they may be assisted by lay ministers in the actual distribution of the ashes. The full order, with the exception of the blessing of the ashes, may be used by a lay minister for the distribution of ashes in hospitals, nursing homes, or other places.

Chapter 53 of the *Book of Blessings* contains the Order for the Blessing of Saint Joseph's Table on the solemnity of Saint Joseph (March 19). This blessing is common in families of Italian descent, yet it is appropriate for use by all. As the rite recalls the bounty enjoyed by the participants and their responsibility to share what they have with the poor, it also looks forward to the eschatological banquet. The blessing may be used by a priest, a deacon, or a lay minister who has been designated by the bishop. The blessing takes place within a celebration of the Word of God, and the intercessions may be replaced by the litany of Saint Joseph.

Finally, the *Sacramentary* contains the rite for the commemoration of the Lord's entrance into Jerusalem on Passion (Palm) Sunday. This rite includes the blessing of palms or other branches and a procession to or through the church. The *Sacramentary* provides three forms for the rite: the Procession and Solemn Entrance are basically the same, whereas the Simple Entrance differs from the usual entrance rite only by the inclusion of a special entrance antiphon and verses of Psalm 23.

The faithful assemble in another church, chapel, or other suitable place and hold palms or other branches. If this is not possible, at least some of the people assemble in front of the church door or inside the church. After the proper antiphon or a suitable hymn is sung, the priest greets the people and briefly explains the meaning of the commemoration of the Lord's entrance into Jerusalem. Then, with hands extended, he says the prayer of blessing, using one of the two formularies provided. After the blessing the branches are sprinkled with holy water in silence. The deacon, another priest, or, if there is no deacon or other priest, the celebrant himself reads the gospel. A brief homily may be given. The deacon or another minister gives the invitation to begin the procession (to the church or down the aisle). The procession is accompanied by appropriate song. When the priest comes to the altar, he venerates it and, if desired, he incenses it. He then goes to the chair, where he puts on the chasuble (if he wore the cope for the procession) and says the opening prayer of the Mass.

Resolutions of the National Meeting of Diocesan Liturgical Commissions

The following Position Statements and Resolutions of Immediate Concern were adopted by the delegates to the 1989 National Meeting of Diocesan Liturgical Commissions, held in Pittsburgh, PA, October 9-12, 1989. The degree of commitment to each statement is indicated in parentheses. The voting scale is graded from +3 (highest degree of commitment) to -3 (completely opposed to the statement). A commitment of +1.5 was required for acceptance. Timelines and procedures for implementation of the approved resolutions will be set by the FDLC Board of Directors at its January, 1990 board meeting.

Resource tool for the assembly on active participation (P.S. 1989 A)

It is the position of the delegates to the 1989 National Meeting of Diocesan Liturgical Commissions that the Eucharist and Liturgical Year Committee and the Liturgical Arts Committee of the FDLC develop a resource tool for parish liturgy committees and a companion bulletin insert series for parish assemblies which address the principles of full, conscious, and active participation, including the areas of the arts and the environment, and apply those principles to the Order of Mass in a way that is understandable to the assembly. (Passed +1.99)

Seminary Formation in Liturgical Music (P.S. 1989 B)

It is the position of the delegates to the 1989 National Meeting of Diocesan Liturgical Commissions that the Bishops' Committee on the Liturgy, through its subcommittee on music, formulate guidelines for the full implementation of the *Instruction on Liturgical Formation in Seminaries* with regard to music in all seminaries of the United States, both diocesan and those under the charge of religious orders.(Passed + 2.47)

Hispanic Cultural Adaptation Resource (P.S. 1989 C)

It is the position of the delegates to the 1989 National Meeting of Diocesan Liturgical Commissions that the Prayer Committee of the National Board of Directors of the FDLC develop a printed resource which will interpret primary liturgical customs of Hispanic cultures and provide pastoral recommendations. (Passed +2.41)

Liturgy of the Hours (P.S. 1989 D)

It is the position of the delegates to the 1989 National Meeting of Diocesan Liturgical Commissions that Diocesan Liturgical Commissions/Offices develop strategies and programs on the significance of the *Liturgy of the Hours* as the prayer of the Church and to catechize all in the assembly as to the "full, conscious, and active participation" in this "Prayer of the Church," especially the principal hours of morning and evening prayer; and that the FDLC Prayer Committee prepare a bulletin insert, which will assist in this process. (Passed +1.66)

Tridentine Mass (R.I.C. 1989 E)

Whereas the Mass according to the 1962 *Roman Missal,* commonly referred to as the Tridentine Mass, has aired weekly on national television since the summer of 1989;

Whereas several diocesan bishops have received notice that the "Tridentine Mass" would be held with or without their permission in their diocese or archdiocese;

Whereas some dioceses or archdioceses have been forced to increase the number of locations and the frequency of the celebration of said "Tridentine Mass;"

Whereas active and full participation of the assembly is normative for Roman Catholic worship (CSL 14);

The delegates to the 1989 National Meeting of Diocesan Liturgical Commissions are resolved that: the abuse of the 1984 indult *Quattuor abhinc annos,* especially by those who seek to reverse the Vatican II liturgical reforms, is undermining and jeopardizing the liturgical renewal mandated by the Second Vatican Council. (Passed +2.86)

Episcopal Appointments

Pope John Paul II has recently named Auxiliary Bishop Patrick R. Cooney of Detroit as Bishop of Gaylord, Michigan; Monsignor Edward M. Grosz, Executive Secretary of the Buffalo Diocesan Office of Worship, as an Auxiliary Bishop of Buffalo; and Father Roger L. Schwietz, OMI, Director of the Duluth Diocesan Office for Liturgy and Spirituality, as Bishop of Duluth. The appointments were announced by Archbishop Pio Laghi, Apostolic Pro-Nuncio in the United States, on November 20, December 4, and December 11, 1989, respectively.

Bishop Cooney, a member of the Bishops' Committee on the Liturgy, received primary, secondary, and college education in Detroit followed by theological training at the Gregorian University in Rome, where he was ordained a priest on December 20, 1959. He served in various parochial assignments in the Archdiocese of Detroit, as Vice-Chancellor, Director of the Liturgy Commission, and Rector of Blessed Sacrament Cathedral prior to his appointment as Auxiliary Bishop of Detroit on December 7, 1982.

Bishop-elect Grosz was born February 16, 1945, in Buffalo, New York. After attending the Diocesan Preparatory Seminary, he studied philosophy and theology at Saint John Vianney Seminary in East Aurora. He was ordained a priest on May 29, 1971.

Bishop-elect Grosz received a Master of Arts degree in liturgical studies from the University of Notre Dame in 1972. He has served as Executive Secretary of the Buffalo Office of Worship since 1975 and has represented Region 2 on the board of directors of the Federation of Diocesan Liturgical Commissions since 1988.

Bishop-elect Schwietz was born July 3, 1940, in Saint Paul, Minnesota. He studied at Oblate College in Pine Hills and at the Gregorian University in Rome, where he was ordained a priest on December 20, 1967. In addition to his current assignment as Pastor of Holy Family Church in Duluth, Bishop-elect Schwietz has served as Director of the Duluth Office of Worship and Spirituality, Dean of the Duluth Deanery, and President of the Diocesan Presbyteral Council.

The members, consultants, advisors, and Secretariat staff of the Bishops' Committee on the Liturgy offer Bishop Cooney and Bishops-elect Schwietz and Grosz heartfelt prayers and best wishes for many fruitful and fulfilling years in Christ's service as bishop.

In Memoriam: Stephen J. Hartdegen, OFM

On December 19, 1989, Father Stephen J. Hartdegen, OFM, the internationally renowned scripture scholar, died after a year-long battle with cancer. He was 82 years old. Well known for his contribution as editor of the *New American Bible,* Father Hartdegen also played a major role in the development of the 1970 U.S. edition of the *Lectionary for Mass.* Until his illness made it impossible for him to continue working, he had devoted countless hours to the Liturgy Committee's Lectionary Subcommittee in the preparation of the upcoming revised edition of the *Lectionary for Mass.*

Father Hartdegen, a native of Philadelphia, entered the Franciscan Order in 1925 and studied for the priesthood in Washington, DC, where he was ordained in 1932. He earned an S.T.B. degree from The Catholic University of America and a Licentiate in Sacred Scripture from the Pontifical Biblical Institute in Rome. In 1939 he graduated *summa cum laude* from the Franciscan Biblical Institute in Jerusalem.

Through his many years of ministry, Father Hartdegen was a leader in the promotion of the biblical apostolate in the United States. From 1957-58 he served as president of the Catholic Biblical Association of America. Until his retirement this year, he was Director of the United States Center for the Catholic Biblical Apostolate in the Department of Education of the United States Catholic Conference. He also served as vice chairman of the World Catholic Federation for the Biblical Apostolate, based in Stuttgart, West Germany, from 1972-1978. And in recent years he was Executive Secretary to the Board of Editors responsible for the revised translation of the *American Bible.*

He was the recipient of numerous honors and awards, which give testimony to the valuable contribution he made toward the growing appreciation of the Scriptures in the English-speaking world.

Father Hartdegen will be greatly missed by all who had the good fortune to experience his expansive knowledge, his lively wit, his priestly zeal and, most of all, his abundant charity. His contribution to the liturgical and scriptural apostolates will long be remembered with gratitude to God.

> Faithful God,
> we humbly ask your mercy for your servant and priest, Stephen,
> who worked so generously to spread the Good News:
> grant him the reward of his labors
> and bring him safely to your promised land.
>
> We ask this through Christ our Lord.
> Amen.

BISHOPS' COMMITTEE ON THE LITURGY

NEWSLETTER

NATIONAL CONFERENCE OF CATHOLIC BISHOPS

1990
VOLUME XXVI
JANUARY

Chairman-elect and New Advisors to the Committee

At the November 1989 plenary assembly of the National Conference of Catholic Bishops in Baltimore, MD, the members elected the Most Reverend Wilton D. Gregory, Auxiliary Bishop of Chicago, as the next chairman of the Bishops' Committee on the Liturgy. Bishop Gregory's three-year term of office will begin in November 1990.

Bishop Gregory was ordained a priest of the Archdiocese of Chicago on December 7, 1973, and a bishop ten years later on December 13, 1983. After completing his seminary training at the North American College, Rome, he earned an S.L.D. degree in liturgical studies from the Pontifical Institute of Saint Anselm, also in Rome. He has served as a member of the Bishops' Committee on the Liturgy since 1984 and is currently chairman of its Black Liturgy Subcommittee. Bishop Gregory also serves on several other NCCB/USCC committees, including the Economic Concerns of the Holy See Committee, Priestly Life and Ministry Committee, the Standing Committee of Bishops for the North American College, and the National Advisory Council.

Two new advisors to the Liturgy Committee have recently been appointed by Bishop Joseph P. Delaney, the present Chairman of the Committee, to replace outgoing advisors Father William M. Cieslak, OFM Cap, Franciscan School of Theology, Berkeley, CA, and Sister Kathleen Loewen, OP, formerly director of the Office of Worship of the Archdiocese of Milwaukee.

Appointed to three year terms as at-large advisors are Sister Linda Gaupin, CDP, director of the Office of Worship for the Diocese of Wilmington, DE, and the Reverend John Baldovin, SJ, Associate Professor of Historical and Liturgical Theology at the Jesuit School of Theology, Berkeley, CA.

Sister Linda Gaupin is a member of the Sisters of Divine Providence of Pittsburgh. She earned a Ph.D. in Religious Education from The Catholic University of America in 1985 and has served as director of the Wilmington Office of Worship since 1984. She is also an Adjunct Professor of Religious Studies at La Salle University. Father Baldovin, a member of the Society of Jesus, received a Ph.D. in Theology from Yale University in 1982. In addition to teaching at the Jesuit School of Theology, Berkeley, he has served as an associate editor of Worship and presently serves as president of the North American Academy of Liturgy and as a member of the Oakland Diocesan Liturgical Commission.

The Bishops' Committee on the Liturgy and its Secretariat wish to express their appreciation for the assistance and advice given by Sister Kathleen Loewen and Father William Cieslak during their terms as advisors and look forward to the future collaboration of the Committee's chairman-elect and its newly-appointed advisors.

Hispanic Liturgy Subcommittee Meeting

The Hispanic Liturgy Subcommittee of the Bishops' Committee on the Liturgy met on November 29-30, 1989, at the Cathedral Hill Hotel in San Francisco, CA. Agenda items included the review and approval of several sections of the Spanish-language *Sacramentario,* discussion of the proposals for bilingual editions of the *Rite of Marriage, Rite of Baptism for Children,* and *Order of Christian Funerals,* and progress reports on the Spanish editions of the *Rite of Christian Initiation of Adults* and the *Order for Sunday Celebrations in the Absence of a Priest.*

3211 4TH STREET, N.E. • WASHINGTON, D.C. 20017

Most of the meeting was devoted to the *Sacramentario,* the Spanish edition of the *Roman Missal* being prepared for use in the dioceses of the United States, a project which has received the greatest amount of attention from the subcommittee since the Congregation for Divine Worship, in a decree dated 19 January 1985 (Prot. N. CD 382/84), confirmed the decision of the Administrative Committee of the National Conference of Catholic Bishops (11 September 1984) that Spanish be authorized as a liturgical language in the United States of America.

Even prior to this approval of Spanish as a liturgical language in the United States, the Subcommittee for Hispanic Liturgy of the Bishops' Committee on the Liturgy had recommended to the Liturgy Committee that a Spanish edition of the Roman Missal be prepared for use in the dioceses of the United States. The Liturgy Committee concurred with this request at its June 1983 meeting, as did the Administrative Committee on September 13, 1983. The Hispanic Liturgy Subcommittee then began the work of preparing the translations and gathering the required texts. The Liturgy Committee decided that the Missal should be called the "*Sacramentario*" to show a clear relationship with the English edition of the *Roman Missal* which bears the title, *Sacramentary.*

The *Sacramentario* will contain the "*texto unico*" or common Spanish translation of the Order of Mass and the additional eucharistic prayers which were approved by the National Conference of Catholic Bishops at its November 1986 meeting. (This common translation must be used in all Spanish-speaking countries by March 30, 1992. In September of 1988, the Administrative Committee set the First Sunday of Advent, December 3, 1989, as the mandatory effective date for the use of the "*texto unico*" in the United States.) The other liturgical texts of the *Sacramentario* will be taken from the Mexican edition of the *Misal Romano.* The decision to use the Mexican translation was based on the results of a survey of the Hispanic offices of the country conducted by the Hispanic Liturgy Subcommittee in January 1987. The survey included sample prayers taken from the various Spanish editions of the *Roman Missal* without any indication of the source of each prayer. The respondents were asked to indicate the texts they preferred, and the majority chose the Mexican translation of the Missal.

With the exception of the "*texto unico*" the *Sacramentario* will mirror the English edition of the *Sacramentary* presently in use in the United States. Therefore, it has been necessary to translate into Spanish all the prayer texts proper to the dioceses of the United States, as well as particular rubrics and introductory material. The Administrative Committee approved the translations of these liturgical texts during its September 1989 meeting, and the requisite confirmation of this action has been requested of the Congregation for Divine Worship and the Discipline of the Sacraments. The new texts were translated into Spanish by Father Wilfredo Guinea, SJ, director of the Obra Nacional de la Buena Prensa, Mexico City, the office which was responsible for the Mexican edition of the *Misal Romano.*

It is the hope of the Liturgy Committee and its Subcommittee for Hispanic Liturgy that the first U.S. edition of the Sacramentario will be published toward the end of 1990 or shortly thereafter.

Rereading the Constitution (art. 33-36)

The liturgy is above all things the worship of God. But it also has an important pedagogical value for the development of faith. God speaks through the liturgy; Christ proclaims his Gospel though it. And the people respond to God through song and prayer.

The Fathers of the Council of Trent, to underscore the element of catechesis inherent in the liturgy, directed that the parts of the Mass could be explained during its celebration. The Fathers of the Second Vatican Council, reflecting the same concern, took a different approach. They directed that the rites should be revised in such a way that through their celebration their meaning and instructional value be clearly evident. The two differing orientations are most clearly revealed in the discussion of the use of vernacular languages.

At the twenty-second session of the Council of Trent (September 1562), at which the doctrine of the sacrifice of the Mass was declared, the Council Fathers thought it inopportune to permit the use of the vernacular. At the same time they encouraged explanations, even during the Mass itself. "Though the Mass contains much instruction for the faithful, it has, nevertheless, not been deemed advisable by the Fathers that it should be celebrated everywhere in the vernacular tongue. Wherefore, the ancient rite of each Church, approved by the holy Roman Church . . . , being everywhere retained, . . . the holy council commands pastors and all who have the care of souls, that they, either themselves or through others, explain frequently during the celebration of the Mass some of the things read during the Mass, and that among other things they explain some mystery of this most holy sacrifice, especially on Sundays and festival days."[1]

A different approach in addressing this concern for liturgical catechesis is found in the *Constitution on the Liturgy* of the Second Vatican Council. Although short directives are allowed during liturgical celebrations (CSL 35.3), the primary didactic element is not to be these directives interpreting the liturgy. Rather it is to be the composition of the rites themselves that make perceptible the meaning of what is being celebrated. Accordingly, the Council Fathers declared that the rites to be revised are to be "distinguished by noble simplicity; . . . short, clear, and unencumbered by useless repetition; . . . within the people's powers of comprehension, and as a rule not requir(ing) much explanation" (CSL 34).

This revision, even radical simplification, of the rites for the sake of the people's understanding has been one of the great successes of the modern liturgical reform. One needs only to participate in one of the revised rites to experience its depth and to understand its personal and communal significance. Religious depth and significance were certainly present in the rites revised by mandate of the Council of Trent. But because these rites were celebrated in Latin, a language that most of the people could not readily understand, their fullness could not be easily grasped without added explanation.

The Fathers of the Second Vatican Council found it opportune to permit the introduction of vernacular languages into the liturgy. It is with this decision that some would claim that the Council of Vatican II compromises the teaching of Trent. But, in fact, both Councils display the same desire to make the liturgy intelligible to the people. They take different approaches, however. Trent provided for frequent explanations; Vatican II sought to have the rites speak for themselves. For both the use of the Latin language was to be preserved (CSL 36).

The decision in 1963 to allow the use of vernacular languages was greeted so enthusiastically that, subsequent to the Council, the Apostolic See and competent territorial bodies of bishops gave permission for all liturgical rites to be celebrated in the vernacular. In October 1963 a meeting was held in Rome of the "English Liturgical Committee," chaired by Archbishop Paul J. Hallinan of Atlanta who represented the bishops of the United States. Because the responsibility of translating liturgical texts into the vernacular languages was to be given to episcopal conferences and consultation between neighboring regions was to take place as part of the process of introducing the vernacular (CSL 36.3), it became clear that some form of collaboration among English speaking countries was necessary. Recognizing the varying literary styles of such diverse conferences as the United States, Great Britain, and English-speaking African countries, representative bishops sought to provide a framework that would respect the integrity of the various idioms. What ultimately evolved from their foresight is the International Commission on English in the Liturgy (ICEL).

Celebrating its twenty-fifth anniversary recently, ICEL continues its work as set forth in the mandate given by its 11 member and 15 associate member conferences of bishops. The translation of new liturgical texts and the revision of earlier translations continues as a means to assist episcopal conferences in the work of insuring the fuller understanding of the liturgy by the faithful.

It is not only in the use of the vernacular that the liturgy is to be more comprehensible. The Liturgy Constitution notes the importance of preaching based on Scripture and liturgical sources (CSL 35.2). Although continuous attention needs to be paid to homiletic development and style, according to a recent study, much progress has already been made in this regard. The *Notre Dame Study of Catholic Parish Life* describes the differing styles of homilies at several kinds of parishes. According to the study, "homilies generally were marked by a strong application to daily life and by their openness to change, rather than by their stress on traditional doctrine."[2] Most homilies were scripturally oriented, even though the extent of that orientation varied according to the type of parish studied. It seems as if great strides have been made among those charged with proclaiming and preaching to Gospel to make Scripture applicable to daily life. Possibly, as homiletic skills develop, there will be a better integration of doctrinal teaching as it flows from Scripture and the Tradition of the Church.

This emphasis on renewing the place of Scripture in the life of the faithful can be seen again in CSL 35.4 as it encourages scripture services. To complement the celebration of the eucharist, separate celebrations of the word are seen as an important means of catechizing people and renewing the Church. During Advent and Lent such services are particularly appropriate to emphasize the special character of the seasons. Although it would appear this article was written for missionary lands, because bible services are particularly commended where priests are not available, it actually should be seen as complementing, rather than substituting for, the ministry of priests. The article also directs that the bishop, who is the overseer of the liturgy in the diocese, be the one to authorize those who are to preside at these services.

The desire of the Council Fathers that the liturgy be comprehensible to the people and authentic to the Church's tradition led to a careful examination of what were thought to be even the most long standing practices. Certainly the charge to simplify the rites, to allow the use of the vernacular, to stress the importance of scripturally and doctrinally sound sermons, and to encourage bible services took much of the Church by surprise. But the wisdom of this direction now can be seen two and one half decades later. The faith of Christian people continues to be renewed principally when the Church gathers at prayer. The words and actions, now ever more connected with each other, reveal the basic understanding that the law of praying is the law of believing.

Notes

1. Council of Trent, Session XXII, September 17, 1562. Doctrine concerning the Sacrifice of the Mass, chap. 8.

2. See Mark Searle and David C. Leege, *The Notre Dame Study of Catholic Parish Life,* Report 5: "The Celebration of Liturgy in the Parishes," August, 1985.

New Responsibilities for Archbishops Kada and Noé

On March 1, 1989, the provisions of the apostolic constitution *Pastor Bonus* on the restructuring of the various congregations, secretariats, councils, and offices of the Roman Curia took effect. One of those provisions was the combining of the Congregation for Divine Worship with the Congregation for the Discipline of the Sacraments. Connected with this reorganization, the secretaries of the two former dicasteries have recently been given new responsibilities in the Curia.

In May 1989 Pope John Paul II confirmed as Secretary of the reorganized Congregation for Divine Worship and the Discipline of the Sacraments the Most Reverend Lajos Kada, titular Archbishop of Tibica.

Archbishop Kada was born in Budapest on November 16, 1924. After completing secondary education in Budapest, he studied philosophy and theology at Esztergom, Budapest, and Rome, finishing with degrees in theology and canon law. On October 10, 1948, he was ordained a priest and, completing his studies at the Pontifical Ecclesiastical Academy, he entered the diplomatic service of the Holy See. He served in Pakistan, Denmark, Germany, and Argentina before being named archbishop on June 20, 1975. At that time Archbishop Kada was named Apostolic Nuncio in Costa Rica. In 1980 he was given additional responsibility as Apostolic Nuncio in El Salvador. In April 1984 Pope John Paul II named him Secretary of the Congregation for the Discipline of the Sacraments.

On May 15, 1989, Pope John Paul II named the Most Reverend Virgilio Noe, titular Archbishop of Voncaria, as Coadjutor to His Eminence Aurelio Cardinal Sabattani, Archpriest of the Basilica of Saint Peter. Archbishop Noé, formerly the Secretary of the Congregation for Divine Worship, was also named Delegate of the *Fabbrica di San Pietro* (the office in charge of construction matters relating to the Basilica of Saint Peter) and a member of the Congregation for Divine Worship and the Discipline of the Sacraments.

Archbishop Noé, who held the position of Master of Liturgical Ceremonies for Popes Paul VI, John Paul I, and John Paul II between 1969 and 1982, served for twenty years in the dicastery responsible for promoting the liturgical reform: from 1969-1977 as Under-Secretary, from 1977-1982 as Associate Secretary, and ultimately, from 1982-1989, as Secretary of the Congregation. His contribution to the Universal Church in overseeing many aspects of the liturgical reform will long be appreciated with gratitude.

LDS 8: *Order of Christian Funerals:* Correction

The *Liturgy Documentary Series 8: Order of Christian Funerals,* published by the United States Catholic Conference (Publication No. 990-4), incorrectly states in paragraph 133 on page 30 that the Easter candle may be carried before the coffin in the procession at the Funeral Liturgy. The last line of paragraph 133 should be corrected to read as follows: ". . . If the Easter candle is used on this occasion, it may be placed beforehand near the position the coffin will occupy at the conclusion of the procession."

BISHOPS' COMMITTEE ON THE LITURGY

NEWSLETTER

NATIONAL CONFERENCE OF CATHOLIC BISHOPS

1990
VOLUME XXVI
FEBRUARY

Confirmation of Lakota as a Liturgical Language

On January 9, 1990, the National Conference of Catholic Bishops received the decree of the Congregation for Divine Worship and the Discipline of the Sacraments, dated December 12, 1989, confirming the decision of the Administrative Committee of the NCCB to approve the Lakota language for use in the liturgy in the dioceses of the United States of America. The following is an unofficial English translation of the decree.

Prot. N. 779/89

At the request of His Excellency, the Most Reverend Daniel E. Pilarczyk, Archbishop of Cincinnati and President of the National Conference of Catholic Bishops, in a letter dated November 28, 1989, and by virtue of the faculties granted to this Congregation by the Supreme Pontiff, Pope John Paul II, after having given attention to what was set forth, we willingly concede that the Lakota language may be used in liturgical celebrations. Liturgical texts confirmed by the Apostolic See will be used in these celebrations.

Anything to the contrary notwithstanding.

From the Congregation for Divine Worship and the Discipline of the Sacraments, 12 December 1989.

+ Eduardo Cardinal Martinez
Prefect

+ Lajos Kada
Titular Archbishop of Tibica
Secretary

Homily of Pope John Paul II on the Liturgical Reform

On Sunday, January 14, 1990, Pope John Paul II made a pastoral visit to the Church of Saints Fabian and Venantius in Rome. During his homily at Mass he addressed the liturgical dimensions of the upcoming diocesan pastoral Synod of the Church of Rome. The complete text of the homily may be found in L'Osservatore Romano, *No. 5, January 29, 1990. Selected paragraphs follow.*

The work of salvation, accomplished by Christ the Lord through his paschal mystery, is not an event belonging exclusively to the past; it is also present in the Church's "today," impelling her towards its future fulfillment. This is possible through the power of the Spirit, who acts through the sacred signs of the liturgy, a living and effective memorial of the mystery of redemption. Celebrating the sacred rites, the Church, faithful to the command of her Spouse, "opens up to the faithful the riches of her Lord's powers and merits, so that these are in some way made present for all time; the faithful lay hold of them and are filled with saving grace" (*Constitution on the Sacred Liturgy* [hereafter CSL] 102).

This is especially true of the celebration of the eucharist, center and hinge of the liturgy. In fact, "for as often as the death of the Lord is proclaimed, his word of redemption is continued" (Prayer over the Gifts, Second Sunday in Ordinary Time). For the Church, this is the mystery celebrated in the divine liturgy: memory and prophecy, proclamation and listening, a gift offered and received.

Precisely by reason of this dimension of "memorial" upon which the Council particularly insisted, the celebration of the mysteries of redemption is revealed as the "summit towards which the activity of the

3211 4TH STREET, N.E. • WASHINGTON, D.C. 20017

Church is directed; it is also the font from which all her power flows" (CSL 10): the privileged experience of communion of people with God and among themselves, and, at the same time, an inexhaustible source of missionary involvement.

All of this, naturally, not in an automatic or quasimiraculous way, but in relation to the faith and the inner disposition of those who participate in it. The liturgy, in fact, presupposes faith and conversion in order to be a lived experience of salvation.

The diocesan pastoral Synod, which plans, among other things, to review and deepen the study of the Council's teachings in order to fulfill its spirit and directives with greater consistency, should therefore verify and relaunch the liturgical renewal in the Church of Rome; this renewal is considered by the Second Vatican Council's *Constitution on the Sacred Liturgy* as a "sign of the providential dispositions of God in our time, and as a movement of the Holy Spirit in his Church" (CSL 43).

The liturgical celebration is a meeting, dialogue, and communion between the Risen Christ and the Church, his Spouse; he is present and acts in it to give the Spirit. It is the sacred action par excellence (see CSL 7). The Church cannot live this communion and be engaged in the mystery of salvation without drawing from this inexhaustible font.

It is in the assiduous, ordered, and active participation in the liturgical assembly, especially on Sunday, that the community of believers lives the experience of ecclesial communion, overcoming temptations to being isolated or closed; from Christ it learns how to be a servant, through the many forms of service envisaged in the liturgical action; Christ's charity asks, as he does, to give its life for the world's salvation. To put it briefly, in the celebration of the divine mysteries, the school of faith and Christian life, the Church is manifested and built up as "a people brought into unity from the unity of the Father, the Son and the Holy Spirit" (*Lumen Gentium* 4) and is impelled by the same Spirit to go into the world to proclaim to all people that only in Christ, who died and is risen, is it possible to be saved.

In this perspective we can clearly see some of the objectives of the synod journey of the Church of Rome, in such a way that all of this may become a reality.

Although the work of liturgical reform which the Council desired is now concluded, much remains to be done so that the spiritual and pastoral renewal may proceed in an orderly manner, with renewed awareness and great vigor, and produce the fruits which are to be hoped for.

Not everyone understood its spirit and accepted its implications and pastoral and spiritual demands, as they appear especially in the valuable "Introductions" of the new liturgical books. Thus can be explained, on the one hand, the headlong haste and, on the other, the resistance of some people to accept the reform. Therefore it is necessary to continue in the effort, which has already begun and is bearing fruit, for a more adequate liturgical formation, not only of the faithful, but also of all those, especially the priests, who so laudably place themselves at the service of their brothers and sisters, for their more active, joyful, and conscious involvement in the mystery.

In this perspective there is still much to be done to bring about a more harmonious relationship between catechesis and liturgy, so as to interpret, in the light of the word of God, the signs which reveal and fulfill the mystery of salvation, and thus to make clear all of its consequences for the life of faith and missionary involvement.

However, that is still not all. If we truly desire the liturgical experience to be a fruitful time of communion with God, we must reevaluate the sense of the sacred in the celebration, using to advantage silence, the ability to listen, the intimate joy of contemplating and meeting the Lord, and thereby banishing everything that distracts and that calls attention to the merely human and exterior aspects of the liturgical action.

Finally, we must strive to ensure that the celebration of the divine mysteries be given its central place in the organization of pastoral activity in such a way that all apostolic activity, in a certain sense, will have its beginning and fulfillment therein, precisely because the liturgy is the "summit and font" of the Church's life and mission.

This does not mean that the Church's entire task is limited to the liturgy; rather it is necessary that all that the ecclesial community proclaims and does to bring the gift of salvation to people should be harmonized with the liturgical-sacramental celebration, and flow from it and lead to it. This is true especially of the other forms of worship and piety, rich in human value and educational potential, by which the Christian people expresses its faith and devotion.

February Meeting of the Liturgy Committee

The members of the Bishops' Committee on the Liturgy met in Fort Worth, TX, on February 10, 1990. The Committee reviewed and approved the plans and programs for 1991 which will be submitted to the National Conference of Catholic Bishops for final approval at the November, 1990, Plenary Meeting. Many of the plans approved for 1990 will be carried over into 1991.

In addition to the ongoing work of the Secretariat—which includes the publication of the *Newsletter,* preparation of liturgical books for approval and publication, response to liturgical inquiries, and the review of participation aids and other liturgical materials—work will continue on the following activities: the development of guidelines to address several areas of pastoral concern: cremation and other funeral practices, posture and gesture at Mass and in other liturgical celebrations, and the role and training of presiding liturgical ministers; possible sponsorship of regional workshops to present the *Order of Sunday Celebrations in the Absence of a Priest*; a study of possible adaptations to the *Order of Mass* for use in the United States; collaboration with the Federation of Diocesan Liturgical Commissions on statements concerning liturgy and social justice, televised masses, and liturgical preparation of candidates for ordination; participation in ecumenical liturgical consultations, such as the North American Consultation on Common Texts (CCT), the English Language Liturgical Consultation (ELLC), North American Academy of Liturgy (NAAL), and the Worship Commission of the National Council of Churches of Christ.

The Secretariat will continue to be involved in the publication, implementation, and/or promotion of the following in 1991: *Order of Sunday Celebrations in the Absence of a Priest;* the complete *Collection of Masses of the Blessed Virgin Mary*; the *Lectionary for Masses and Other Celebrations with Children*; the *Sacramentario* (the Spanish language Sacramentary); the *Lectionary for Mass* (2nd typical edition); *Rito de la Iniciación Cristiana para Adultos* (the Spanish language *Rite of Christian Initiation of Adults*); the *Order for the Solemn Exposition of the Holy Eucharist; Study Texts:* No. 13: *Blessings in the Life of the Church,* No. 14: *Holy Week and the Eastern Triduum,* No. 15: *Order for Sunday Celebrations in the Absence of a Priest,* and No. 16: *Order for the Solemn Exposition of the Holy Eucharist*; and *Liturgy Documentary Series:* No. 9: *Book of Blessings, Introduction and Pastoral Notes,* No. 10: *Sunday Celebrations in the Absence of a Priest,* and No. 11: *Order for Solemn Exposition of the Holy Eucharist; Gathered in Steadfast Faith: a Statement of the Bishops' Committee on the Liturgy concerning Sunday Celebrations in the Absence of a Priest; Plenty Good Room: African Americans and Catholic Worship,* a joint statement of the Secretariats for the Liturgy and Black Catholics.

The Committee will continue to study trends affecting the sacramental life of the parish community in collaboration with the Committee on Pastoral Research and Practices. Areas of possible study include: lay preaching, holy days of obligation, Sunday Mass schedules, and the age of Confirmation.

The members of the Committee then discussed the proposed draft of *Gathered in Steadfast Faith: a Statement of the Bishops' Committee on the Liturgy concerning Sunday Celebrations in the Absence of a Priest.* After making several modifications that reflected the recommendations and concerns that were raised at the November, 1989, Plenary Meeting of the National Conference of Catholic Bishops, the Committee decided to present the revised statement to the NCCB Administrative Committee at its March, 1990, meeting.

The Statement on the Pastoral Challenge of Implementing the Rite of Christian Initiation of Adults for Children of Catechetical Age, which is a joint statement of the Bishops' Committee on the Liturgy, the Committee on Education, and Committee on Pastoral Research and Practices, was discussed. This statement had been approved by the Liturgy Committee at its June, 1989, meeting. The statement contains no new policy; rather it takes note of the diverse family situations which often present a challenge to the implementation of the *Rite of Christian Initiation of Adults* for children of catechetical age.

Father Ronald F. Krisman, Executive Director of the Secretariat for the Liturgy, reported that confirmation of the decisions of the NCCB to approve the use of Lakota as a liturgical language and the change of the date of the Optional Memorial of Blessed Junipero Serra to July 1, had been received from the Congregation for Divine Worship and Discipline of Sacraments. He also indicated that the following texts and decisions of the NCCB have been sent to the Congregation and await confirmation: *Order of Sunday Celebrations in the Absence of a Priest;* the complete *Collection of Masses for the Blessed Virgin Mary*; and the use of *ustedes* in Spanish liturgical texts.

A shorter edition of the *Book of Blessings* containing only the blessings that are celebrated outside Mass is being edited for publication. The *Lectionary for Mass and Other Celebrations with Children* is being reviewed by selected catechists to identify strengths and weaknesses of the pericopes for use with children.

Bishop Wilton Gregory, chairman of the Black Liturgy Subcommittee, reported that the statement *Plenty Good Room: African Americans and Catholic Worship* should be completed for presentation to the Bishops' Committee on the Liturgy at its June, 1990, meeting. The structure of the Black Liturgy Subcommittee will be reviewed after completion of the statement to determine the most appropriate way to investigate possible African-American liturgical adaptations.

The Hispanic Liturgy Subcommittee will meet in May, 1990. The *Ordinario de la Misa,* containing the "*texto unico,*" has been published by the Catholic Book Publishing Co., New York. The Spanish translation of the *Rite of Christian Initiation of Adults* has been completed and will be sent to the NCCB Administrative Committee for approval at its September, 1990, meeting. Work is just starting on the Spanish translation of the *Order of Christian Funerals.*

For the remainder of the meeting, the Committee discussed the liturgical sections of the draft of the *Catechism for the Universal Church.* Analyses of these sections are being prepared for the Ad Hoc Committee on the Catechism for presentation to the NCCB Administrative Committee at its March, 1990, meeting.

The next meeting of the members, consultants, and advisors of the Bishops' Committee on the Liturgy will take place at Saint Patrick Seminary, Menlo Park, CA, on June 17-19, 1990.

Confirmation of Change of Date for Blessed Junipero Serra, Priest

The Congregation for Divine Worship and the Discipline of the Sacraments, in a decree dated December 9, 1989, confirmed the decision of the National Conference of Catholic Bishops to transfer the date of the optional memorial of Blessed Junipero Serra from August 28, which is the obligatory memorial of Saint Augustine, bishop and doctor, to July 1. The following is an unofficial English translation of the decree.

Prot. N. 1609/88

At the request of His Excellency, the Most Reverend Daniel E. Pilarczyk, Archbishop of Cincinnati and President of the National Conference of Catholic Bishops, in a letter dated November 28, 1989, and by virtue of the faculties granted to this Congregation by the Supreme Pontiff, Pope John Paul II, after having given attention to what was set forth, we most happily concede that in the Proper Calendar for the dioceses of the United States of America the celebration of Blessed Junipero Serra, priest, may be transferred from August 28 to July 1.

Anything to the contrary notwithstanding.

From the Congregation for Divine Worship and the Discipline of the Sacraments, 9 December 1989.

> \+ Eduardo Cardinal Martinez
> Prefect
>
> \+ Lajos Kada
> Titular Archbishop of Tibica
> Secretary

Ordinario de la Misa

Ordinario de la Misa, an interim liturgical book containing the common ("*texto unico*") Spanish translation of the Order of Mass, fourteen eucharistic prayers (including the five-fold "Swiss Synod" prayer), and several additions to the *Roman Missal,* is now available. The effective date for the mandatory use of *Ordinario de la Misa* in the dioceses of the United States was the First Sunday of Advent, December 3, 1989, as set by the Administrative Committee of the National Conference of Catholic Bishops at its November 11, 1986, meeting.

The *Ordinario de la Misa* is a hardcover liturgical book with ribbons and tabs, designed for use at the chair and altar. It is published by the Catholic Book Publishing Co. and may be purchased at religious bookstores and religious good supply companies. The recommended retail price of the book is $25.00.

BISHOPS' COMMITTEE ON THE LITURGY

NEWSLETTER

NATIONAL CONFERENCE OF CATHOLIC BISHOPS

1990
VOLUME XXVI
MARCH

NCCB Administrative Committee Meeting

On March 20-22, 1990, the Administrative Committee of the National Conference of Catholic Bishops met at the NCCB/USCC headquarters building in Washington, D.C. The members of the Committee approved the following action items submitted by the Committee on the Liturgy:(1) the provisional English translation of the liturgical texts for the obligatory memorial of Andrew Dung-Lac, priest and companions, martyrs (November 24); (2) the publication of *Gathered in Steadfast Faith: Statement of the Bishops' Committee on the Liturgy on Sunday Worship in the Absence of a Priest,* to be released once the *Order of Sunday Celebrations in the Absence of a Priest* has received the requisite confirmation of the Congregation for Divine Worship and the Discipline of the Sacraments; and (3) the publication of the joint statement of the NCCB Committees on the Liturgy and on Pastoral Research and Practices and the USCC Committee on Education concerning the pastoral challenge of implementing the *Rite of Christian Initiation of Adults* for children who have reached catechetical age.

The Administrative Committee also approved an action item proposed by the NCCB Committee on Pro-Life Activities that either a special Mass for Life or other liturgical texts in thanksgiving for God's gift of life be composed and submitted for approval. The liturgical texts, if approved by the National Conference of Catholic Bishops and confirmed by the Congregation for Divine Worship and the Discipline of the Sacraments, would be made available for use in dioceses of the United States.

RCIA for Children of Catechetical Age

On March 20, 1990, the members of the Administrative Committee of the National Conference of Catholic Bishops approved the publication of the joint statement of the NCCB Committees on the Liturgy and on Pastoral Research and Practices and the USCC Committee on Education, entitled Statement on the Pastoral Challenge of Implementing the Rite of Christian Initiation of Adults for Children Who Have Reached Catechetical Age. *That statement follows.*

With the implementation of the final translation of the *Rite of Christian Initiation of Adults* (RCIA) on September 1, 1988, and the increased understanding that has been gained of this rite during the past few years, there has arisen the pastoral challenge of implementing that portion of the RCIA (Part 2, Chapter 1) which applies to the "particular circumstances" of children who have reached catechetical age and who have not yet been initiated.

There are now many families whose adult members are being initiated, or are returning to the practice of the faith, and who have children of varying ages who have not received one or more of the sacraments of initiation. There are often, in the same family, older baptized but uncatechized children, and younger children who have been neither baptized nor catechized. According to the requirements of the RCIA, these family members are to be initiated in diverse ways. Unbaptized adults will be enrolled in the catechumenate and ultimately will receive all the sacraments of initiation at the same time. Baptized but uncatechized adults will be given the necessary catechetical formation and, if circumstances warrant, may be enrolled in an adapted form of the catechumenate for the already baptized; at the appropriate time they will receive the eucharist and/or confirmation. Baptized but uncatechized children will receive the necessary catechesis for confirmation and the eucharist and will receive these sacraments, insofar as possible, at the same time as their classmates. Unbaptized children of catechetical age will participate in a suitably adapted form of the

3211 4TH STREET N.E. ● WASHINGTON, D.C. 20017

catechumenate and, after the necessary period of formation, will receive all three sacraments of initiation at the same time. Unbaptized infants and small children will be baptized and then will participate in the usual catechetical and sacramental formation programs for those baptized in infancy.

Thus, within the same family individuals may be initiated at different times and in different ways, depending upon their age, whether or not they have been baptized, and the extent to which they have previously been formed in the Christian life. Those responsible for catechesis must clearly explain to families the various approaches to the Christian formation and sacramental initiation of their family members which correspond to these different factors.

The NCCB/USCC Committees on Pastoral Research and Practice, Liturgy, and Education recognize the challenge which these varying situations present for pastors and religious educators. Nevertheless, the initiation of unbaptized children who have reached the age of discretion must always conform to the requirements of the *Rite of Christian Initiation of Adults*. These persons are to be admitted into a form of the catechumenate which has been adapted to the particular needs of children (see RCIA, nos. 252-259). They will receive the three sacraments of initiation once they have been suitably formed in the Christian way of life and have established that they are ready for the sacraments (see RCIA, no. 256). The confirmation of such children should not be separated from the other sacraments of initiation to which it is integrally related.

Because the members of the National Conference of Catholic Bishops have not set a uniform age for confirmation of those who were baptized as infants, it will be necessary for pastors and religious educators to explain that varying practices regarding the age of those to be confirmed and the sequence of the reception of confirmation and eucharist exist in our country. They should provide the appropriate catechesis and rites of initiation necessary for the initiation of individuals into the sacramental life of the Church in conformity to diocesan regulations.

The Committees on Pastoral Research and Practices, Liturgy, and Education also recognize the need for new instructional materials, methods, and models to compensate for the lack of published sacramental preparation materials for older children preparing for confirmation and for lectionary-based catechesis. The Department of Education's Task Force preparing guidelines for catechetical materials will keep this in mind and share these needs with the publishers of catechetical materials.

The Committees on Pastoral Research and Practices, Liturgy, and Education express their appreciation for all that religious educators are striving to do in the face of these pastoral challenges, and encourage them to continue informing the NCCB/USCC Committees of their pastoral experiences so that the Church may provide for the faith formation of our people.

Reception of the Holy Oils

On March 21, 1988, the members of the NCCB Administrative Committee approved the rites contained in the United States edition of the *Book of Blessings* (see *Newsletter*, Vol. XXIV, pp. 22-23). They also gave approval to three additional rites relating to the liturgical year which may be celebrated during the eucharistic liturgy: Order for the Proclamation of the Birth of Christ (on Christmas); Order for the Proclamation of the Date of Easter on Epiphany; Order for the Reception of the Holy Oils. These brief rites were confirmed by the Congregation for Divine Worship when it also confirmed the *Book of Blessings* (Prot. N. 699/88, dated January 27, 1989). The rites will be incorporated into the next edition of the *Sacramentary*. However, since that edition is not expected to be available for several years, the rites will soon be published in the form of a fascicle which can be inserted into the present edition of the *Sacramentary*. The date of publication and the publishers will be indicated in a future issue of the *Newsletter*.

Order for the Reception of the Holy Oils*

Introduction

1. It is appropriate that the oil of the sick, the oil of catechumens, and the holy chrism, which are blessed by the bishop during the Chrism Mass, be presented to and received by the local parish community.

2. The presentation of the holy oils may take place at the Mass of the Lord's Supper on Holy Thursday or, if the oils are not blessed on Holy Thursday, on another day.

3. The oils should be reserved in a suitable repository in the presbyterium or near the baptismal font.

Reception of the Holy Oils

4. The oils, in suitable vessels, are carried in the entrance procession by ministers or other persons. The vessels of oil are placed on a table which has been prepared for them in the sanctuary. The priest may incense the oils after he has incensed the altar.

5. After the greeting of the Mass the priest may briefly explain the significance of the blessing of the oils and their use. The oils are then placed in the repository where they are to be reserved and the Mass continues in the usual manner.

6. The following, or other words, may be used to explain the significance of the oils:

Oil of the Sick

This oil of the sick has been blessed by our bishop for the healing of body, mind, and soul. May the sick, who are anointed with it, experience the compassion of Christ and his saving love.

Oil of Catechumens

This oil of catechumens has been blessed by our bishop for the anointing of those preparing for baptism. Through this anointing they are strengthened by Christ to resist the power of Satan and reject evil in all its forms, as they prepare for the saving waters of baptism.

Holy Chrism

This holy chrism, a mixture of olive oil and perfume, has been consecrated by our bishop and the priests of our diocese. It will be used to anoint infants after baptism, those who are to be confirmed, bishops and priests at their ordination, and altars and churches at the time of their dedication.

Blessings During the Easter Season

Previous issues of the *Newsletter* have presented commentary on some of the blessings related to feasts and seasons which are contained in the new *Book of Blessings* (see *Newsletter,* Vol. XXV, pp. 42-43, 45-46). Several other blessings may fruitfully be celebrated in the Easter season and in early summer.

Chapter 54 of the *Book of Blessings* provides an Order for the Blessing of Food for the First Meal of Easter. The practice of blessing food for Easter arose in connection with the discipline of the Lenten fast and the special Paschal fast during the Easter Triduum. Easter was the first day when meat, eggs, cheese, and others foods could again be eaten, and so the return of these foods to the daily diet was celebrated with special blessings. Although the Paschal fast during the Triduum is no longer of obligation (except on Good Friday), its observance is highly encouraged especially to support the elect who will be initiated at the Easter Vigil.

The blessing of the food which was used to break the Paschal fast had customarily taken place during the morning or early afternoon of Holy Saturday. The *Circular Letter Concerning the Preparation and Celebration of the Easter Feasts* (January 16, 1988) notes that "festive customs and traditions associated with this day [Holy Saturday] because of the former practice of anticipating the celebration of Easter on Holy Saturday should be reserved for Easter night and the day that follows" (no. 76). Accordingly, food may be blessed before or after the Easter Vigil on Holy Saturday or on Easter morning for consumption at the first meal of Easter, when fasting is ended and the Church is filled with joy. The *Book of Blessings* provides an order of blessing within a celebration of the Word of God and a shorter rite that may appropriately be used after the Easter Vigil. The blessing may be used by a priest, a deacon, or a properly designated layperson. A form of this blessing for use in the home is given in *Catholic Household Blessings and Prayers* (p. 152).

The blessing of homes may be celebrated during the Christmas season (see *Newsletter,* Vol. XXV, p. 43). The same order of blessing, Chapter 50 of the *Book of Blessings,* also provides proper texts for the blessing of homes during the Easter season. An adapted form of this blessing is given in *Catholic Household Blessings and Prayers* (pp. 153-156).

The *Book of Blessings* contains two additional blessings that may be celebrated during the Easter season or shortly thereafter: Order for the Blessing of Mothers on Mother's Day; Order for the Blessing of Fathers on Father's Day. Since Mother's Day occurs during the Easter season, the Mass of the Sunday of Easter is always to be celebrated. However, in order to provide some recognition of this annual observance during the liturgy, three model intercessions are given and a prayer over the people is provided for use at the blessing which concludes the Mass. This prayer may replace the simple blessing or the solemn blessing of the Easter season. Similar provisions are made for Father's Day. Prayers for blessing mothers and fathers are also contained in *Catholic Household Blessings and Prayers* (pp. 197-198).

Berakah Award to Theophane Hytrek, OSF

Sister Theophane Hytrek, a School Sister of Saint Francis, has been named the recipient of the 1990 Berakah Award given by the North American Academy of Liturgy. The award is presented annually in recognition of outstanding contribution in the field of liturgy. Previous recipients have included Catholic, Protestant, and Jewish liturgists from the United States and Canada.

For fifty years Sister Theophane has been a leader in the development of liturgical music. Throughout this time, as a member of the faculty of Alverno College in Milwaukee, she has taught and composed music principally for liturgical use. Among her many compositions, the "Pilgrim Mass," which was composed for use during the 1976 International Eucharistic Congress in Philadelphia, demonstrates the quality of her contribution to the liturgical life of the English-speaking Church.

The Bishops' Committee on the Liturgy congratulates Sister Theophane on receiving this well deserved honor and acknowledges with gratitude the significant contribution she continues to make to liturgical renewal in the Church.

New Musical Resources

Flor y Canto, a hymnal for monolingual Spanish and bilingual Spanish/English communities, contains traditional and contemporary music from several Spanish speaking countries, including Mexico, Cuba, Puerto Rico, Spain, and the United States. The collection is arranged according to the liturgical seasons and, in addition to nearly 500 hymns, contains 75 psalm settings, 6 Mass settings, and 40 bilingual compositions. A total of 711 musical selections is included in the collection.

Oregon Catholic Press publishes *Flor y Canto* in two perfect-bound formats: the People's Edition (text and music, 692 pages) at $6.95, and the People's Edition (text only, 548 pages) at $2.95. The cost of the Accompaniment Edition (Guitar/Vocal) is $29.95. Quantity discounts are also available. For further information contact: Oregon Catholic Press, P. O. Box 18030, Portland, OR 97218-0030. Telephone: 800/547-8992 (in Oregon, 800/422-3011).

Hymnal for the Hours is a collection of 316 hymns with organ accompaniment for Morning and Evening Prayer and general use arranged for use throughout the liturgical year. It was prepared by a committee of poets, liturgists, and musicians from various religious communities. Its cost is $12.95 per copy. Available from: GIA Publication, Inc., 7404 South Mason Avenue, Chicago, IL 60638.

BISHOPS' COMMITTEE ON THE LITURGY

NEWSLETTER

NATIONAL CONFERENCE OF CATHOLIC BISHOPS

1990
VOLUME XXVI
APRIL/MAY

Confirmation of Spanish Language Liturgical Texts

On April 20, 1990, the National Conference of Catholic Bishops received the decree of the Congregation for Divine Worship and the Discipline of the Sacraments, dated March 12, 1990, confirming the decision of the NCCB to approve the Spanish translation of several liturgical texts proper to the dioceses of the United States which will be included in the *Sacramentario,* the Spanish language edition of the *Misal Romano* for use in the United States. (For more information concerning the publication of the *Sacramentario,* see *Newsletter,* vol. 26, January 1990, pp. 1-2). The following is an unofficial English translation of the decree.

Prot. N. CD 794/89

At the request of His Excellency, the Most Reverend Daniel E. Pilarczyk, Archbishop of Cincinnati and President of the National Conference of Catholic Bishops, in a letter dated 28 November 1989, and by virtue of the faculties granted to this Congregation by the Supreme Pontiff, Pope John Paul II, we gladly approve, that is, confirm the Spanish translation of certain texts of the Proper of Masses as they appear in the attached copy.

This decree, by which the requested confirmation is granted by the Apostolic See, is to be included in its entirety in the published text. Two copies of the printed text should be sent to this Congregation.

Anything to the contrary notwithstanding.

From the Congregation for Divine Worship and the Discipline of the Sacraments, 12 March 1990.

> \+ Eduardo Cardinal Martinez
> Prefect
>
> \+ Lajos Kada
> Titular Archbishop of Tibica
> Secretary

Fifth Centenary Liturgical Texts

The year 1992 will mark the five hundredth anniversary of the arrival of Christopher Columbus to the Americas under the patronage of the Catholic monarchs of Spain. On Columbus' return voyage the following year efforts to evangelize those who inhabited the "New World" were initiated. To observe this event and to commence a decade of evangelization leading to the beginning of the third millennium in the year 2000, the bishops of the United States, at their June 1989 plenary meeting at Seton Hall University, approved the proposal of the ad hoc Committee for the Observance of the Fifth Centenary of Evangelization in the Americas to develop liturgical and pastoral materials to assist in the continuing priority of evangelization of all people in the Americas. These materials will be contained in a booklet offering a three-part program of action (history, observance, and evangelization) for dioceses and parishes. The booklet is scheduled for publication by the USCC Office of Publishing Services in late 1990.

3211 4TH STREET, N.E. ● WASHINGTON, DC 20017

Liturgical texts for a Mass in Celebration of the Fifth Centenary of the Evangelization of the Americas were composed as part of the liturgical component of the observance. On November 15, 1988, the National Conference of Catholic Bishops approved these new liturgical texts—in both English and Spanish—for use at celebrations of the Fifth Centenary. After NCCB consultation with CELAM (Consejo Episcopal Latinoamericano), the Congregation for Divine Worship and the Discipline of the Sacraments on 10 April 1990 issued the requisite confirmation of the NCCB decision.

An unofficial translation of the decree of confirmation and the approved liturgical texts follow.

Prot. N. CD 1608/88

At the request of His Excellency, the Most Reverend John L. May, Archbishop of Saint Louis and President of the National Conference of Catholic Bishops, in a letter dated 20 December 1988, and by virtue of the faculties granted to this Congregation by the Supreme Pontiff, Pope John Paul II, we gladly approve, that is, confirm the English and Spanish versions of the text of the Mass "In Celebration of the Fifth Centenary of the Evangelization of the Americas" as they appear in the attached copy.

This decree, by which the requested confirmation is granted by the Apostolic See, is to be included in its entirety in the published text. Two copies of the printed text should be sent to this Congregation.

Anything to the contrary notwithstanding.

From the Congregation for Divine Worship and the Discipline of the Sacraments, 10 April 1990.

+ Eduardo Cardinal Martinez
Prefect

+ Lajos Kada
Titular Archbishop of Tibica
Secretary

MASS IN CELEBRATION OF THE FIFTH CENTENARY OF THE EVANGELIZATION OF THE AMERICAS

Introductory Rites　　May God bless us in his mercy; may he make his face shine upon us (alleluia). (Ps. 66:2)

OPENING PRAYER

O God, whose saving love embraces all peoples,
you sent your Son to gather into one family
the scattered children of earth.
As we give thanks for the evangelization of the Americas;
renew within us the grace of conversion,
that we may live more fully the gospel we have received
and manifest your Church more clearly to the world
as the universal sacrament of salvation.

We ask this through our Lord Jesus Christ, your Son,
who lives and reigns with you and the Holy Spirit,
one God, for ever and ever.

LITURGY OF THE WORD

First Reading

Isaiah 2:1-5　　　　All the nations will stream to the mountain of the Lord God.

or:
Zechariah 8:20-23　　Many great nations will come to seek the Lord God in Jerusalem.

or, in Eastertime
Acts 11:19-26　　　The disciples started preaching to the Greeks, proclaiming the Good News of the Lord Jesus.

Responsorial Psalm

Ps. 67: 2-3, 5,7-8
R. (4) O God, let all the nations praise you!

or:
Ps. 96: 1-2, 2-3, 7-8, 9-10
R. (3) Proclaim his marvelous deeds to all the nations.

or:
Ps. 98: 1, 2-3, 3-4, 5-6
R. (2) The Lord has revealed to the nations his saving power.

or:
R. (3) All the ends of the earth have seen the saving power of God.

Second Reading

Romans 10:8-18

How will they hear without someone preaching? How will they preach unless they are sent?

or:
Ephesians 2:13-22

You are strangers and aliens no longer.

Gospel Acclamation

Go and teach all people my gospel.
I am with you always, until the end of the world. (Mt. 28:19-20)

Gospel

Matthew 28:16-20

Go and teach all nations.

or:
Mark 16:15-20

Go into the whole world and preach the gospel.

or:
Luke 24:44-53

In the name of Jesus, repentance for the forgiveness of sins should be preached to all the nations.

or:
John 17:11, 17-23

As you sent me into the world, I have sent my followers into the world.

LITURGY OF THE EUCHARIST

PRAYER OVER THE GIFTS

Lord,
the suffering and death of Christ your Son
won your salvation for all the world.
May the prayers and gifts of your Church
come before you and be pleasing in your sight.
We ask this through Christ our Lord.

Communion Rite

All you nations, praise the Lord, proclaim him all you peoples! For steadfast is his kindly mercy to us, and everlasting his fidelity (alleluia). (Ps. 116: 1-2)

PRAYER AFTER COMMUNION

Lord God,
nourished by this gift of redemption, we pray:
may we faithfully live the gospel
that has taken root in our midst,
zealously sharing with others its promise of reconciling love
and the Good News that Jesus Christ is Lord for ever and ever.

SOLEMN BLESSING

May God, who has called you out of darkness
    into his marvelous light,
strengthen you to make known his saving deeds
in the sight of all peoples.

May Jesus Christ, who has called you as members of his one body,
direct you in the ways of peace
and reign always in your hearts.

May the Holy Spirit, who fills the Church
    with a diversity of gifts
make you joyful in faith and bold in bearing witness.

May almighty God bless you,
the Father, and the Son, + and the Holy Spirit.

MISA PARA CELEBRAR EL QUINTO CENTENARIO DE LA EVANGELIZACION DE LAS AMERICAS

Rito Iniciales

El Señor tenga piedad y nos bendiga, ilumine su rostro sobre nosotros (aleluya). (Sal 66:2)

ORACION

O Dios, que amas a todos los pueblos,
Tú enviaste a tu Hijo Jesús a unir en una familia
a tus hijos dispersos por el mundo.

Te damos gracias por la evangelización de las Américas
y te pedimos que renueves en nosotros la gracia de la conversión.
Concédenos vivir a plenitud el Evangelio que hemos recibido
y manifestar tu Iglesia al mundo
como sacramento universal de salvación.

Por nuestro Señor Jesucristo, tu Hijo,
que vive y reina contigo
en la unidad del Espíritu Santo y es Dios
por los siglos de los siglos.

LITURGIA DE LA PALABRA

Primera Lectura

Isaías 2:1-5

Todas las naciones acudirán a la montaña del Señor Dios.

o:
Zacarías 8:20-23

Muchas grandes naciones vendrán buscando al Señor Dios en Jerusalén.

o, en tiempo de Pascua
Hechos 11:19-26

Los discípulos empezaron a predicar a los griegos, proclamando la Buena Nueva del Señor Jesús.

Salmo Responsorial

Sal 67: 2-3, 5,7-8
R. (4) ¡Oh Dios, que te alaben todas las naciones!

o:

Sal 96: 1-2, 2-3, 3-4, 5-6
R. (3) Proclamen sus maravillas a todas las naciones.

o:

Sal 98: 1, 2-3, 3-4, 5-6
R. (2) El Señor ha revelado a las naciones su salvación.

o:

R. (3) Los confines de la tierra han visto la salvación de Dios.

Segunda Lectura

Romanos 10:8-18   ¿Cómo oirán sin que alguien les predique? ¿Cómo predicarán sin ser enviados?

o:

Efesios 2:13-22   Ustedes ya no son extranjeros ni huéspedes.

Aclamación antes del Evangelio

Vayan y enseñen mi evangelio a todos los pueblos.
Yo estaré con ustedes hasta el fin del mundo. (Mt. 28:19-20)

Evangelio

Mateo 28:16-20   Vayan y enseñen a todas las naciones.

o:

Marcos 16:15-20   Vayan por todo el mundo y prediquen el evangelio.

o:

Lucas 24:44-53   En nombre de Jesús, el arrepentimiento para el perdón de los pecados debe predicarse a todas las naciones.

o:

Juan 17:11,17-23   Como me enviaste al mundo, yo envío a mis discípulos al mundo.

LITURGIA EUCARISTICA

ORACION SOBRE LAS OFRENDAS

Acepta, Señor,
los dones que te ofrece tu Iglesia,
como te dignaste aceptar la gloriosa muerta de tu Hijo
por la salvación del mundo.

Por Jesucristo nuestro Señor.

Rito de la Comunión   Alaben al Señor todas las naciones, aclámenlo todos los pueblos. Firme es su misericordia con nosotros, su fidelidad permanece por siempre (aleluya). (Sal 116:1-2)

ORACION DESPUES DE LA COMUNION

Alimentados con el sacramento de la salvación,
te pedimos, Señor, vivir fielmente el Evangelio
        que en nosotros se ha encarnado
y compartir con entusiasmo
la promesa del amor que nos reconcilia
y la Buena Nueva que Jesucristo es Señor
por los siglos de los siglos.

BENDICION SOLEMNE

Dios, que les ha llamado de las tinieblas
    a su incomparable luz,
los fortalezca para manifestar a todos los pueblos
su obra de salvación.

Jesucristo, que los ha llamado a ser
    miembros de un mismo cuerpo,
dirija sus pasos en el camino de la paz
y reine siempre en sus corazones.

El Espíritu Santo, que llena la Iglesia
    con la variedad de sus dones
les conceda gozo en la fe y fortaleza en el testimonio.

La bendición de Dios todopoderoso,
Padre, Hijo y + Espíritu Santo,
descienda sobre ustedes.

Rereading the Constitution on the Liturgy (art. 37-40)

Recently a group of Afro-Brazilian bishops received approval from the Congregation for Divine Worship to begin investigating the possibility of adapting the *typica editio* of the Roman Missal to incorporate Afro-Brazilian cultural elements. A year earlier, in April 1988, the bishops of Zaire had received confirmation of their adaptation of the Missal after twenty years of development. Meanwhile increasingly it is heard in the United States that the liturgy needs to be adapted not only for African Americans, but for the many distinct cultural groups that make up the American population. These three situations, on three continents, point to the fact that the liturgical renewal has now entered upon a new phase, namely, the cultural adaptation of the reformed Roman liturgy.

This is not a new issue for the Church. In fact, except for the period after the Council of Trent, the liturgy has always been adapted to the culture of the people. The early Church at Jerusalem gave Christian interpretations to its Jewish rituals and, in the process, transformed them. The eucharist developed out of the rites which surrounded the Jewish meal. The baptism of John took on new meaning in light of Jesus' instructing the apostles to go forth and baptize all nations. An entire sacramental economy took shape as religious and cultural practices were transformed to become the foundation for the liturgy of the Church.

In Rome, with the Edict of Milan and the legalization of Christianity during the 4th century, the liturgy took on many aspects of Roman culture. The Christian meeting place moved from the house church to the basilica. Bishops, priests and deacons donned the dress of Roman officials. And the liturgy incorporated ceremonial elements of the Roman court which were not contrary to Christian values. Ancient festivals acquired new Christian meaning and were added to the developing Roman calendar. Roman bathing practices were used to supplement and explain the rites of initiation. And while Christians were quick to reject pagan ritual celebrations, they treated the culture of the people with respect and incorporated into Christian practice whatever was not alien to their faith.

It was during this period up to the eighth century that the classical form of the Roman liturgy took shape. The interplay between Christian religious practices and Roman culture led to a liturgy with structural qualities that influenced future liturgical developments, including the reforms mandated by the *Constitution on the Liturgy*. The attention to brevity, sobriety, simplicity, and nobility became the hallmark of the Roman liturgy. Naturally, as the Roman liturgy spread to other locales, it was embellished as it encountered the new cultures. But underlying these cultural adaptations, as one would perceive them today, were attempts to do exactly what the Church had done in Rome, that is, incorporate ritual and prayer practices which were consonant with Christian theological understandings.

Even the liturgical direction of the Council of Trent was an attempt to adapt the liturgy to the ecclesial situation of that time. It was thought that the unity of the Church, which was being threatened by the innovations of Protestant reformers, could best be preserved through a uniform liturgical practice. It is no wonder that Pope Pius V, in his apostolic constitution *Quo primum* (July 19, 1570) promulgating the Roman Missal of 1570, wrote that nothing in the missal, ceremonies or prayers could be changed. Even the slightest accommodation might be viewed as a threat to the unity of the Church. Liturgical rigidity was the result of such a perception, and more than a few commentators have remarked that such inflexibility ultimately contributed to the failure of missionary efforts in China during the 17th century.

The more traditional view concerning accommodation to culture began to reemerge with the publication of *Summi Pontifice,* the 1939 encyclical letter of Pope Pius XII which repeated insights from a 1659 instruction of the Congregation for the Propaganda of the Faith concerning faith and its cultural expressions. *Summi Pontifice,* stating the Church strives for unity rather than uniformity, became the conduit for this renewed sensitivity to the culture and traditions of peoples which became enshrined in articles 37-40 of the *Constitution on the Liturgy.*

Articles 37-40 should be seen as a necessary component of the liturgical reform rather than simply an option, if the objective of encouraging full and active participation is to be realized. The *typica editio* of the Roman Missal, as reformed according to the directives of the Constitution, contains a structure as well as prayers (euchology) that present well the Roman liturgical tradition. The texts are historically, theologically, and pastorally grounded; they are noble, simple, brief, and usually unencumbered with any sort of embellishment. The ritual is flexible and lends itself to the simplest or the most elaborate celebration. These attributes manifest the genius of the Roman rite, allowing its acceptance by a broad range of peoples and cultures. But because it is celebrated in diverse cultures, the rite requires adaptation if it is to "respect and foster the genius and talents of the various races and peoples" (CSL 37).

Adaptation can take place in a variety of ways. The first avenue has been provided for in the rites themselves. To paraphrase articles 38 and 39, provisions have been made in the revised liturgical books for variations and adaptations for different groups, regions and peoples, especially, but not exclusively, in mission areas "provided the substantial unity of the Roman rite is preserved." The *praenotanda* of each rite delineates possible ways in which national episcopal conference might adapt the ritual (as well as ways in which the minister presiding over an actual celebration might adapt certain texts to the circumstances of the participants). In the United States such minor adaptations of the Roman Missal have included originally composed opening prayers for Sundays, a variation in the posture of the assembly during the eucharistic prayer, the authorization to use other song in place of the entrance and communion antiphons, the extension of the practice of communion under both forms, the option of receiving communion in the hand, etc. The *Order of Christian Funerals* incorporates a number of adaptations, such as the additional rituals for Gathering in the Presence of the Body, Transfer of the Body to the Church or to the Place of Committal, and numerous original prayer texts composed to meet pastoral needs. As the other rites are revised, additional adaptations will no doubt be proposed which correspond to cultural practices in the United States.

Another avenue of adaptation is the admission of local cultural practices into the liturgy itself. In some cultures Western European postures at prayer may not be consonant with the cultural practices of the people. Conferences of bishops may propose that these postures and gestures be replaced by those more amenable to the customs of the people. And while the Roman euchology is brief and to the point, some cultures may have different styles of prayer that are more elaborate. Spontaneous acclamations may also be a natural part of communal prayer in some cultures. Such elements may be harmonized with the liturgy so that the people might participate intelligently and fully in the Church's worship.

More radical adaptations of the liturgy are envisioned by article 40, as are the corresponding difficulties. Such adaptations might include the transformation of non-Christian rituals that are "not indissolubly bound up with superstition and error," modifications in the structure of the Roman rite, or significant adaptations that go beyond those allowed in articles 38 and 39 or the *praenotanda* of a particular ritual book. Article 40 outlines the procedure for approval of these variations in the liturgy. Episcopal conferences are first to determine those elements from the traditions of the people that might be admitted into the liturgy of the Church. This review would include the liturgical worthiness, theological soundness, and pastoral sensitivity of those elements proposed. After review by the Apostolic See, a period of experimentation (which, according to no. 12 of the 5 September 1970 instruction *Liturgicae instaurationes,* is not to go beyond a year) may be recommended for a particular limited group of people. Liturgical experts are to be involved in the formulation of these adaptations since possible conflicts with existing liturgical rites and legislation might arise. Ultimately, upon approval of the episcopal conference and confirmation by the Holy

See, the rites could become part of the official liturgy of the Church for that local area. This is the process which led to the approval of the adaptation of the Roman rite for the dioceses of Zaire, and it is the process recently initiated by the bishops of Brazil.

Although the methods of accomplishing more radical adaptations are sketchy, the Congregation for Divine Worship and the Discipline of the Sacraments has indicated that it is in the process of preparing a directory on cultural adaptation of the liturgy (see *Newsletter,* vol 25, January 1989, p. 4). This document should assist the discussion of the directions that need to be taken to make the liturgy an expression of the Latin Church as well as the particular local worshiping community. Certainly, the next several decades will be devoted to the issues of cultural adaptation here in the United States and throughout the world. It will be important not to lose sight of the ultimate objective, which is to encourage that full, conscious, and active participation of the Christian faithful which ultimately leads to the spiritual renewal of the Church.

Liturgical Programs/Conferences

Notre Dame Center for Pastoral Liturgy

"Disciples at the Crossroads, Who Shall Lead Them? Liturgical Leadership in the Church of the 90's," has been chosen as the theme of the nineteenth annual liturgical conference sponsored by the Notre Dame Center for Pastoral Liturgy. The conference, which will explore the various perspectives of lay presiding, will be held at the University of Notre Dame on June 18-21, 1990. Major speakers include Richard P. McBrien, Kathleen Hughes, RSCJ, John Brooks-Leonard, James and Evelyn Whitehead, and John Baldovin, SJ. A variety of special focus sessions will also be offered. For further information contact the Notre Dame Center for Pastoral Liturgy, Center for Continuing Education, Box 1008, Notre Dame, IN 46556. Telephone: 219/239-6691.

National Association of Pastoral Musicians

Regional conventions of the National Association of Pastoral Musicians will be held in Phoenix, AZ, June 6-9 (The Ministry of Music in the Church in America), Chicago, IL, June 27-30 (Liturgy in Dialogue with the World), and Washington, DC, August 1-4 (Blessed are Those Who Gather the Children). NPM also offers a variety of summer programs and institutes throughout the country; these include week-long intensive programs for parish guitarists, organists, choir directors, and cantors and lectors. For further information consult the April/May, 1990 issue of Pastoral Music or contact NPM, 225 Sheridan Street, NW, Washington, DC 20011. Telephone: 202/723-5800.

Rensselaer Program of Church Music and Liturgy

The annual summer session of the Rensselaer Program of Church Music and Liturgy at Saint Joseph College will be held June 19-August 2, 1990. Undergraduate and graduate sequences are available, as well as a three-summer program leading to a Diploma in Pastoral Liturgy. Tuition is $98 per undergraduate credit and $107 per graduate credit.

The summer curriculum will includes Historical and Theological Perspectives of Christian Worship, Hymnody and Metrical Psalmody, Music as Pastoral Prayer, Musical Theory, Conducting, and Composition. A mini-session on the Order of Christian Funerals will be offered June 18-29, 1990 (2 credit hours).

For further information and/or applications contact: Rev. Lawrence Heiman, CPPS, Director of the Rensselaer Program of Church Music and Liturgy, Saint Joseph College, P. O. Box 815, Rensselaer, IN 47978. Telephone: 219/866-6272.

Detroit Conference On Liturgy

"The New Evangelization and the Future of Worship" will be the theme of the tenth annual Detroit Conference on Liturgy to be held August 6-9, 1990, in Detroit. Major speakers will be Aidan Kavanagh, OSB, J-Glenn Murray, SJ, Fred Moleck, Alan Detscher, Mary Frances Reza, and Michael Joncas.

For further information contact: Department of Christian Worship, 305 Michigan Avenue, Detroit, MI 48226. Telephone: 313/237-5932.

BISHOPS' COMMITTEE ON THE LITURGY

NEWSLETTER

NATIONAL CONFERENCE OF CATHOLIC BISHOPS

1990
VOLUME XXVI
JUNE

The Ordination of Bishops, Presbyters, and Deacons

In a decree, dated 29 June 1989, His Eminence Eduardo Cardinal Martinez, Prefect of the Congregation for Divine Worship and the Discipline of the Sacraments, promulgated the editio *typica altera* (second typical edition) of the rites for the ordination of bishops, presbyters, and deacons. The revised rites are expected to be available in Latin in the next few months. Before the rites will be published in English, they will have to be translated by the International Commission on English in the Liturgy, approved by the National Conference of Catholic Bishops and confirmed by the Congregation for Divine Worship and the Discipline of the Sacraments.

Reasons for Revision

The decree of promulgation provides the rationale for producing a new edition of the ordination rites, which may be summarized as follows:

1) The new edition contains an introduction (*praenotanda*), lacking in the first edition, which explains the doctrine of the sacrament and clarifies the structure of the celebration.

2) The order of the rites is changed so that the ordination of a bishop comes first, since the bishop has the fullness of holy orders. This also allows for a better understanding of presbyters as the bishop's cooperators and deacons as his ministers.

3) The prayers of ordination for presbyters and deacons have been modified to better express the nature of these orders and their functions. Words have been changed, sentences have been added, and references to the New Testament have been included.

4) References to the exercise of the ministry of reconciliation and the celebration of the eucharist have been inserted in the examination of the candidates for the presbyterate.

5) The rite for the commitment to celibacy, which was prepared by the Congregation for Divine Worship according to the norms of the Apostolic Letter *Ad pascendum,* of Pope Paul VI, in 1972, has been inserted into the rite for the ordination of deacons (as was done in the 1978 English edition of the Roman Pontifical). By virtue of a special mandate of Pope John Paul II, the current discipline has been changed so that religious in perpetual vows are now to take part in this rite during their ordination to the diaconate. This derogates from the prescriptions of canon 1037 of the 1983 *Code of Canon Law* which states that "an unmarried candidate for the permanent diaconate and a candidate for the presbyterate is not to be admitted to the order of diaconate unless in a prescribed rite he has assumed publicly before God and the Church the obligation of celibacy or professed perpetual vows in a religious institute."

6) Members of institutes of consecrated life are to promise obedience and respect to the diocesan bishop as well as their own superiors in the rites of ordination to the diaconate and presbyterate: "Do you promise respect and obedience to the diocesan bishop as well as your own legitimate superiors?"

7) The Rite for Admission to Candidacy for Ordination as Deacons and Presbyters has been included as an appendix in a slightly modified form.

Effective Date for Use

As soon as the Latin second typical edition of *De Ordinatione Episcopi, presbyterorum et diaconorum* has been published, it may be used for ordinations. The episcopal conference is to set the effective date for the use of the vernacular edition, once the translation has been approved by the conference of bishops and confirmed by the Apostolic See.

Structure and Content of the Book

The General Introduction (*Praenotanda Generalia*) consists of three sections: I. Sacred Ordination (nos. 1-6); II. Structure of the Celebration (nos. 7-10); III Adaptations for Various Regions and Conditions (no. 11).

The rites for each of the three orders of the ministry are contained in separate chapters. Each chapter has an introduction which follows the same pattern: I. Meaning and Significance of the Ordination (a brief theological treatment of the order and its functions) [nos. 12-14, 101-102, 173-178]; II. Offices and Ministries (the roles of the various ministers required for the ordination) [nos. 15-18, 103-106, 179-180]; III. Celebration of the Ordination (particular notes concerning the actual celebration of the rite of ordination) [nos. 19-27, 107-114, 181-189]; IV. Preparations (the objects, vestments, seats, etc., that must be prepared for the celebration) [nos. 28-30, 115-117, 190-192].

Chapter I: Ordination of Bishops—the rites for the ordination of a single bishop [nos. 31-64] and for several bishops [nos. 65-100].

Chapter II: Ordination of Presbyters—the rites for the ordination of several presbyters [nos. 118-144] and for only one presbyter [nos. 145-172].

Chapter III: Ordination of Deacons—the rites for the ordination of several deacons [nos. 193-219] and for only one deacon [220-247].

Chapter IV: Ordination of Deacons and Presbyters Conferred in the Same Liturgical Action—an introduction [nos. 248-259] and the rites for the ordination of several deacons and presbyters [nos. 260-300] and for one deacon and one presbyter [nos. 301-341].

Chapter V: Texts for Use in the Celebration of Ordinations—the texts for special ordination Masses for each of the orders and for the ordination of deacons and priests at the same time (nos. 342-345); and a lectionary of Scripture readings for use during the ordination Masses (nos. 346-351).

Appendix: I. Chants; II. Rite for Admission to Candidacy for Ordination as Deacons and Presbyters.

Although the actual liturgical texts for ordinations have not yet been published, there do not appear to be many changes in the rites. The more significant changes are contained in the texts of the ordination prayers of consecration and the provision of complete Mass formularies for each of the orders. Proper intercessions are now included for each of the eucharistic prayers (rather than just the Roman Canon), and new prefaces and solemn blessings are given for each order.

Rites of Ordination and the Synod of Bishops

The February 1990 issue of *Notitiae*, the review of the Congregation for Divine Worship and the Discipline of the Sacraments, contains the introduction (*praenotanda*) of the revised edition of the *Rites of Ordination of Bishops, Presbyters, and Deacons* (see the article in this issue which describes the new book for ordinations). The first edition of this portion of the *Roman Pontifical* was promulgated in 1968 by Pope Paul VI and was one of the first fruits of the conciliar reform of the liturgy.

The editor of *Notitiae* notes that it is appropriate that the actual publication of this new edition of the ordination rites will coincide with the Synod of Bishops which will take place in the fall of this year. He indicates five ways in which the new book relates to the themes of the Synod.

1) The second edition highlights in various ways the notion of the presbyterate as cooperator in the ministry of the bishop. This is evidenced with greater intensity in how the vocation to the sacred ministry differs from the vocation to the religious life. The first is, in fact, so essentially bound to the call of the bishop that none of the faithful is able to have a true and proper right to it. For religious vocations, the cooperation with the episcopal order always exists, in each case, in strict pastoral obedience to the one who is the apostolic sign of unity in a particular Church.

2) The description of the functions and responsibilities of the presbyteral ministry is explained more

explicitly in the new edition. Thus the liturgy, following from the conciliar documents and from the daily experience of the presbyteral ministry, presents a clear response to the question that is often repeated: What does the priest do?

3) In order to explicate the desire of the Holy Father, the bond between celibacy and presbyteral ordination appears more clearly in the ordination of deacons who are candidates for the presbyterate. The requirement of making the promise of celibacy also by those who have already taken religious vows or who have a similar juridical responsibility is made more evident to the gathered assembly. The revised rite shows that ecclesiastical celibacy is not only a personal question of a spiritual relationship between the Christian and God, but that, in the case of sacred ministers, besides being an eschatological sign it is also an ecclesiological sign. The presbyter is impelled to a love of and total dedication of his whole person to the Church, of which he is minster and pastor, in communion with and in imitation of the spousal love of Christ.

4) The second typical edition more clearly underlines the "plural" character of presbyters by putting the ordination of several presbyters in the first place and indicating, as noted also in the *Code of Canon Law* and the *Ceremonial of Bishops,* that the ordination of presbyters is preferably celebrated in the cathedral. There certainly can be reasons for celebrating it in another church and also for celebrating the ordination of only one presbyter. But one cannot deny the fact that the ordination of a group of presbyters, done in the cathedral church, more clearly shows, on the one hand, that the presbyters are a collegial reality (a presbyterate) in the local (diocesan) Church before being a reality in a particular parish, and on the other hand, it helps to avoid making the ordination of a single priest appear to be a sort of honorific elevation of the person of the candidate.

5) In accord with the Church's tradition, this new edition confirms once again the principle of giving preference to the celebration of ordinations on Sunday. There is, first of all, a Christological motive for this. It was the risen Lord who invited the apostles to announce and actualize the work of salvation, and it is logical that in the context of this weekly "appearance" of the Lord, which is Sunday, there be celebrated the sacrament which continues the apostolic succession.

There is also an ecclesiological and eucharistic motive for preferring the celebration of ordinations on Sunday. The sacred ministers are for the Church of the present time. It is important that the Church be visibly present. On Sunday the Church receives and is able to express the proper acceptance and approval of the ordination. Sunday is the day of the eucharistic assembly, and on that day the priest does what he is specifically commissioned to do for the Church, that is, celebrate the eucharist. In the Sunday eucharistic assembly the common priesthood of the faithful and the ministerial priesthood are mutually encountered in one sacrificial memorial, in one offering, in one praise to the Father, and in the same invocation of the Holy Spirit.

Readings the Gospel in Parts

Q. Is it permissible to read the Gospel in parts at the celebration of the Eucharist? If so, must a deacon or a priest always be involved?

R. This matter is not specifically treated in the *General Instruction of the Roman Missal.* In principle the gospel is proclaimed by a deacon, a priest other than the principal celebrant or, in their absence, the celebrant himself (GIRM 34). However, the gospel is not "reserved" to a deacon or priest as the homily is. Lay readers are specifically mentioned in the Sacramentary for *Passion Sunday, Liturgy of the Word* (p. 126, Catholic Book edition). While the part of Christ is ordinarily to be proclaimed by an ordained minister, allowance is made for an exception at times to this practice. This might particularly be called for when the Passion is to be sung by three lay chanters.

The *Directory for Masses with Children* provides for proclamation in parts (no. 47) when a reading lends itself to this. It follows that, at a Sunday Eucharist at which a large number of children participate, this norm might be applied at times. One must be careful, however, that this manner of proclamation not be overdone or abused. Often times those who prepare Masses with children actually hinder effective proclamation by using inadequately prepared children as readers or by reducing proclamation in parts to mere play-acting.

The proclamation of the gospel by several readers might be used effectively on the 3rd, 4th, and 5th Sundays of Lent (Year A) and on other occasions when the gospel lends itself to this manner of proclamation because of the dialogue between Jesus and other persons. However, such manner of proclamation should be used judiciously, and its use at "adult" Masses must be regarded as beyond the present norms, although not specifically contrary to them.

Liturgical Programs/Conferences

North American Conference on Cultural Awareness in Liturgy

A conference designed to provide a forum in which grassroots liturgical inculturation experiences and needs can be shared is scheduled for November 13-20, 1990, in Rome. Speakers for the North American Conference on Cultural Awareness in Liturgy will include His Eminence Francis Cardinal Arinze of the Apostolic See, Bishop Wilton Gregory (Chairman-elect of the Bishops' Committee on the Liturgy), Fathers Ronald F. Krisman, Murray Kroetsch, Tran Van Kha, and Cuthbert Johnson, OSB, Sister Francesca Thompson, OSF, Mary Frances Reza, and conference organizer, Grayson Brown. The cost of the conference, which includes round-trip air transportation, hotel accommodations, ground transportation, meals, and conference fees, ranges from $1,589 from New York to $1,789 from Los Angeles.

For further information contact Rev. Louis Vallone, St. Benedict the Moor Church, 91 Crawford Street, Pittsburgh, PA 15219. Telephone: 412/281-3141.

Form/Reform

The National Conference on Environment and Art for Catholic Worship will be held on October 28-31, 1990, in Albuquerque, NM, with the theme "A House for the Church in the Global Village." Sponsored by the Form/Reform National Committee in collaboration with the Georgetown Center for Liturgy, Spirituality and the Arts, the conference is designed for those involved in a church building or renovation project, diocesan building and liturgical commissions, liturgical and technical consultation, as well as architects, artists, craftspeople, and students who seek further knowledge and enrichment in the forum of environment and art.

For further information contact: Conference Services by Loretta Reif, P. O. Box 5084, Rockford, IL 61125. Telephone: 815/399-2150.

National Association of Pastoral Musicians

"Blessed are those . . . who Gather the Children" is the theme of the second national Pastoral Musicians convention addressing the concerns of the formation of children in liturgy, religious education, and music education. Major speakers will be Raymond Studzinski, OSB, Helen Kemp, Elizabeth McMahon Jeep, and Christiane Brusselmans. Christopher Walker and Ronald Krisman will also present an in-depth look at the Part II of the *Rite of Christian Initiation of Adults* for children who have reached catechetical age. A variety of other speakers will address issues pertaining to celebration and education of children.

The convention will be held at the Ramada Renaissance/Techworld Hotel, Washington, DC, on August 1-4, 1990. For further information, contact: National Association of Pastoral Musicians, 225 Sheridan Street, NW, Washington, DC 20011. Telephone: 202/723-5800.

Federation of Diocesan Liturgical Commissions

The 1990 National Meeting of Diocesan Liturgical Commissions will be held from October 15-18, 1990, in Chicago, IL. Cosponsored by the NCCB Committee on the Liturgy and the Federation of Diocesan Liturgical Commissions, the national meeting will have as its theme "Liturgical Ministries: Changes and Challenges" and will feature as speakers: Dr. Fred Moleck, Chicago; Sr. Mary Collins, OSB, The Catholic University of America; Sr. Kathleen Hughes, RSCJ, The Catholic Theological Union, Chicago; Sr. Barbara O'Dea, DW, Provincial, Daughters of Wisdom. Several workshops will focus on the special concerns and needs of diocesan liturgical commissions and offices of worship.

For additional information, please contact: Office for Divine Worship, Archdiocese of Chicago, 1800 North Hermitage Avenue, Chicago, IL 60622-1101. Telephone: 312/486-5153.

BISHOPS' COMMITTEE ON THE LITURGY

NEWSLETTER

NATIONAL CONFERENCE OF CATHOLIC BISHOPS

1990
VOLUME XXVI
JULY

Norms for Minor Basilicas

The Congregation for Divine Worship and the Discipline of the Sacraments has issued a decree, dated November 9, 1989, concerning the concession of the title of minor basilicas to churches outside the city of Rome. This title is granted to certain churches which manifest an active liturgical and pastoral life in accord with the norms, directives, and laws of the Church and thereby have a special bond to the Roman Church and the Supreme Pontiff.

After the Second Vatican Ecumenical Council norms for minor basilicas were issued by the Sacred Congregation of Rites in the decree *Domus Dei* (6 June 1968). These norms are now superseded by those of November 9, 1989. A summary of the new norms follows:

Conditions for Obtaining the Title of Minor Basilica

1. A Church which is proposed for the title of minor basilica must be dedicated according to the proper liturgical rite. It should be a center of liturgical and pastoral life in the diocese, especially in regard to the celebration of the eucharist, penance, and the other sacraments. These celebrations should be exemplary both in their preparation and execution, faithfully observing liturgical norms, and with the active participation of the people of God.

2. In order that worthy and exemplary celebrations might be carried out, the church must be large enough and have a presbyterium (sanctuary) of sufficient size. The various elements which are required for the liturgical celebration (altar, ambo, presidential chair) should be situated according to the requirements of the restored liturgy (see *General Instruction on the Roman Missal,* nos. 253-280).

3. The church should be renowned throughout the diocese. For example, it has been built and dedicated to God on the occasion of some historical-religious event, or it contains the body or relics of a saint, or it houses a sacred image which is particularly venerated.

The church also should be considered valuable because it is an historical monument or because of its artwork.

4. In order that the various celebrations in the course of the liturgical year might be laudably carried out in the church, it is necessary that it have a number of priests who are responsible for liturgical-pastoral care, especially in the celebration of the eucharist and penance (for which a suitable number of confessors should be present at set times to meet the needs of penitents).

In addition, it is required that the church have a sufficient number of liturgical ministers as well as an adequate choir to encourage the faithful's participation in the music and sacred song.

Documents Needed for Granting the Title of Minor Basilica

The following documents must be sent the Congregation for Divine Worship and the Discipline of the Sacraments:

1) *Petition* of the local Ordinary, even if the church is under the care of a religious community;

2) *Nihil obstat* or favorable judgment of the National Conference of Catholic Bishops;

3) *Report* on the origin, history, and religious activity (worship and pastoral activities, organizations, and works of charity) of the church;

3211 FOURTH STREET, N.E. ● WASHINGTON, D.C. 20017

4) *Slides or photographs* which show the exterior and interior of the church, particularly the arrangement of the presbyterium (altar, ambo, presidential chair) and other places and seats destined for the carrying out of the celebrations (chairs for the ministers; baptistry or baptismal font; place for the reservation of the eucharist, and place for the celebration of the sacrament of penance);

5) *Information* concerning the church as indicated in the "Questionnaire" which is to be completed and returned to the Congregation for Divine Worship and the Discipline of the Sacraments.

Liturgical and Pastoral Offices and Works

1. In the minor basilica liturgical instruction of the Christian faithful should be promoted by means of conferences and particular courses of instruction, serious discussions, and other similar attempts.

Within the basilica great effort should be given to studying and making available the documents of the Supreme Pontiff and the Holy See, especially those concerning the liturgy.

2. Great care should be shown in preparing and carrying out the celebrations of the liturgical year, especially those during Advent, Christmas, Lent, and Easter.

During Lent, where the practice of gathering the local Church in the form of the "Roman stations" is observed (see *Sacramentary,* note at the beginning of the Lenten season, and the *Ceremonial of Bishops,* nos. 260-262), it is recommended that the basilica be one of these "stations."

The Word of God should be zealously proclaimed both in liturgical homilies and in preaching on other occasions.

The active participation of the faithful should be promoted both in the celebration of the eucharist and in the celebration of the Liturgy of the Hours, especially Morning and Evening Prayer.

In addition, approved and worthy forms of popular devotion should be cultivated.

3. Since the liturgy has a more noble form when it is sung, care should be taken to see that the assembly of the Christian faithful be able to sing the parts of the Mass, especially those found in the Ordinary of the Mass (see Constitution on the Liturgy *Sacrosanctum Concilium,* no. 54; Sacred Congregation of Rites, Instruction *Musicam Sacram,* 5 March 1967).

In a basilica where the faithful from various nations or language groups frequently gather it is desirable that they know how to sing the profession of faith and the Lord's Prayer in Latin (see *General Instruction of the Roman Missal,* no. 19) set to simple melodies, such as those of Gregorian chant proper to the Roman liturgy (Constitution on the Liturgy *Sacrosanctum Concilium,* no. 116).

4. In order to make clear the particular bond of communion which unites the minor basilica to the chair of Peter, the following should be celebrated with particular care:

a) the feast of the Chair of Peter (February 22);
b) the solemnity of Peter and Paul (June 29);
c) the anniversary of the election of the beginning of the pastoral ministry of the Supreme Pontiff.

Concessions Granted to Minor Basilicas

1. The day on which the granting of the title of basilica by the Apostolic See is publicly announced should be prepared for and festively carried out with suitable preaching, prayer vigils, and other celebrations, either on the days before or after the proclamation of the title.

On these days the Mass and Liturgy of the Hours may be of the title of the church, of the saint or sacred image which receives special veneration in the church, or "for the local Church" or "for the Pope," if these days do not occur on the days indicated in I, 1-4; and II, 5-6 of the table of liturgical days according to their order of precedence (see *General Norms for the Liturgical Year and the Calendar,* no. 59).

On the day itself on which the title is proclaimed the Mass of the day or one of the Masses indicated above, according to the rubrical norms, is celebrated. At the beginning of the celebration the apostolic letter or the decree raising the church to the status of a basilica is read in the vernacular before the Gloria.

2. The faithful who piously visit the basilica and there participate in a sacred rite or at least recite the Lord's Prayer and the Creed may, under the usual conditions (sacramental confession, eucharistic communion and prayer for the intentions of the Supreme Pontiff), obtain a plenary indulgence on the following days:

1) anniversary of the dedication of the basilica;
2) day of the liturgical celebration of the titular;
3) the solemnity of Peter and Paul;
4) the anniversary of granting the title basilica;
5) once a year on the day determined by the local ordinary;
6) once a year on the day that each of the faithful is free to choose.

3. The pontifical insignia, that is, "the crossed keys," may be used on banners, on furnishings, and in the seal of the basilica.

4. The rector of the basilica, or the person who presides over the basilica, may licitly in the exercise of his office wear over the cassock or religious habit and surplice a black mozzetta with trim, button holes, and buttons of red.

The decree is dated November 9, 1989, the feast of the Dedication of the Lateran Basilica, and is signed by Eduardo Cardinal Martinez, Prefect, and Lajos Kada, Secretary.

Papal Liturgical Fascicles

Responding to numerous requests for copies of the liturgical participation booklets prepared for the celebrations of Pope John Paul II, the Office of the Liturgical Celebrations for the Supreme Pontiff has recently announced the availability of collections containing the booklets from 1989 and 1990, respectively. The 1989 collection may be purchased either in a complete set (35 fascicles) for 100,000 lire or in a smaller set (30 fascicles) for 70,000 lire. (Copies of the year's first five fascicles are limited.) Subscriptions for the 1990 set may also be requested.

To purchase either of the 1989 collection or to subscribe to the one for 1990, write: Ufficio della Celebrazioni Liturgiche del Sommo Pontefice, 00120 Vatican City State, Europe.

Confirmation of Liturgical Texts for Andrew Dung-Lac and Companions

On June 14, 1990, the National Conference of Catholic Bishops received the decree of the Congregation for Divine Worship and the Discipline of the Sacraments, dated July 8, 1990, confirming the decision of the NCCB Administrative Committee to approve the English translation of liturgical texts for the memorial of Saints Andrew Dung-Lac, priest, and Companions, martyrs, for use in the dioceses of the United States. The following is an unofficial English translation of the decree along with the approved Mass formulary. The texts for use in the Liturgy of the Hours will be printed in the August 1990 issue of the *Newsletter*. (See the August 1989 issue of the *Newsletter*, volume 25, pp. 29-30, for the decree promulgating the inclusion of the new memorial in the General Roman Calendar.)

Prot. N. CD 475/90

At the request of His Excellency, the Most Reverend Daniel E. Pilarczyk, Archbishop of Cincinnati and President of the National Conference of Catholic Bishops, in a letter dated May 8, 1990, and by virtue of the faculties granted to this Congregation by the Supreme Pontiff, Pope John Paul II, we gladly approve, that is, confirm, *ad interim* the English texts for Mass and the Liturgy of the Hours in honor of Saints Andrew Dung-Lac, priest, and Companions, martyrs, as they appear in the attached copy.

In the publication of these texts mention should be made of the confirmation granted by the Apostolic See. In addition two copies of these printed texts are to be sent to this Congregation.

Anything to the contrary notwithstanding.

From the Congregation for Divine Worship and the Discipline of the Sacraments, 8 June 1990.

+ Eduardo Cardinal Martinez
Prefect

+ Lajos Kada
Titular Archbishop of Tibica
Secretary

THE ROMAN MISSAL

24 November
ANDREW DUNG-LAC, priest, and COMPANIONS, martyrs
Memorial

ENTRANCE ANTIPHON   We should boast of nothing but the cross of our Lord Jesus Christ. For to us who are saved the word of the cross is the power of God.

Galatians 6:14a; 1 Corinthians 1:18

OPENING PRAYER

O God,
the source and origin of all fatherhood,
you kept the blessed martyrs Andrew and his companions
faithful to the cross of your Son
even to the shedding of their blood.
Through their intercession
enable us to spread your love among our brothers and sisters,
that we may be called and may truly be your children.

We ask this through our Lord Jesus Christ, your Son,
who lives and reigns with you and the Holy Spirit,
one God, for ever and ever.

PRAYER OVER THE GIFTS

Father most holy,
accept the gifts we bring
as we honor the sufferings of the Vietnamese martyrs.
Amid the trials of life
help us to remain faithful to you
and to present our lives
as an offering that is pleasing in your sight.

We ask this through Christ our Lord.

COMMUNION ANTIPHON   Blessed are those who suffer persecution for the sake of justice; the kingdom of heaven is theirs.

Matthew 5:10

PRAYER AFTER COMMUNION

Nourished by the one bread that we have received
on this feast of the holy martyrs,
we beg you, Lord,
that we may remain in your love,
and through patience inherit your promised reward.

We make this prayer through Christ our Lord.

BISHOPS' COMMITTEE ON THE LITURGY
NEWSLETTER

NATIONAL CONFERENCE OF CATHOLIC BISHOPS

1990
VOLUME XXVI
AUGUST

June Meeting of the Bishops' Committee on the Liturgy

The annual plenary meeting of the NCCB Committee on the Liturgy (members, consultors, advisors, and Secretariat staff) took place at Saint Patrick's Seminary, Menlo Park, CA, on June 17-18, 1990. The Committee approved the following action items to be presented at the September meeting of the NCCB Administrative Committee: 1) the Order of Mass in the Lakota language; 2) the Spanish translation of the *Rite of Christian Initiation of Adults (Rito de la Iniciación Cristiana de Adultos)*; 3) Mass texts for Blessed Junipero Serra (July 1), and Mass and Office texts for Blessed Katharine Drexel (March 3). One change of date and two additions to the Proper Calendar for the Dioceses of the United States were also approved for presentation at the November plenary meeting of the National Conference of Catholic Bishops: the transfer of the optional memorial of Saint Paul of the Cross from October 19 to October 20, and the addition of optional memorials commemorating Blessed Miguel Augustin Pro (November 23) and Blessed Juan Diego (December 9).

The Committee also: 1) reviewed a revised draft of the Introduction to the *Lectionary for Masses and Other Celebrations with Children*; it is to be further revised, reviewed by the Lectionary Task Group, and presented to the Committee for approval in June, 1991; 2) approved the publication of *Plenty Good Room: The Spirit and Truth of African-American Catholic Worship* as a joint statement of the NCCB Secretariats for the Liturgy and Black Catholics; 3) approved using the ICEL translation of responsorial psalms and alleluia verses in the second edition of the *Lectionary for Mass*; 4) reviewed the draft of the *Norms for Preaching by Lay Persons in Churches and Oratories* prepared by the Committee for Pastoral Research and Practices; 5) discussed a letter from the Committee for Pastoral Research and Practices concerning the scheduling of the Rite of Reconciliation of Individual Penitents prior to the celebration of Sunday Mass; 6) approved the *Criteria for the Evaluation of Inclusive Language in Biblical Translations Proposed for Liturgical Use* prepared by the Joint Committee (Liturgy and Doctrine) on Inclusive Language; the criteria will be submitted to the Administrative Committee for approval in September; 7) approved a survey of the approximately 50 dioceses in the United States that have Sunday celebrations in the absence of a priest to determine the need to authorize lay persons to preside at the funeral liturgy in the absence of a priest or deacon; 8) discussed a request from the Committee on Pro-Life Activities that a Mass in thanksgiving for God's gift of life be prepared and directed the Secretariat to work on this matter.

Father Ronald Krisman, Executive Director of the Secretariat for the Liturgy, reported that the Reverend Andrew Anderson, a priest of the Archdiocese of Miami, has been appointed to the staff of the Congregation for Divine Worship and the Discipline of the Sacraments. Prior to his appointment Father Anderson served as Judicial Vicar of the Archdiocese of Miami.

Bishop Wilton Gregory reviewed the work of the Black Liturgy Subcommittee and discussed ways in which the liturgical needs of African-American Catholics might continue to be addressed in light of the NCCB's present budgetary constraints. Bishop Ricardo Ramirez reported that the Hispanic Liturgy Subcommittee continues its major work of translation of liturgical texts into Spanish. The *Ordinario de la Misa* was published at the end of 1989, and the Spanish translation of texts from the English version of the *Sacramentary* have recently been confirmed by the Apostolic See. It is hoped that the *Sacramentario* might still be published in 1990, but the project may be held up if the question of the use of *ustedes* is not resolved soon. With the completion of *Rito de la Iniciación Cristiana de Adultos* (the Spanish language version of the *Rite of Christian Initiation of Adults*), the next major project of the Subcommittee will be the translation into Spanish of the *Order of Christian Funerals*. Monsignor Detscher, in the absence of Archbishop Whealon, presented the report of the Lectionary Subcommittee, which has completed work on all the Sunday readings and most of the weekday readings of the second edition of the lectionary; the book is to be presented for the approval of the NCCB in late 1991. Bishop Patrick Cooney and Father Kenneth Jenkins reported that the Task Group on Cremation and Other Funeral Practices had been formed and that its first meeting is scheduled for September, 1990. Task Groups yet to be formed include those for the Revision and Adaptation of the *Sacramentary* and for Televised Masses.

Reports from organizations associated with the Liturgy Committee were also given. Father Krisman stated that the International Commission on English in the Liturgy continues its major project of revising the *Sacramentary*. The Presentation of Texts Subcommittee has completed the pastoral notes, the rubrics for the Order of Mass and Holy Week, and other rubrical material. The Original Texts and Translations Subcommittees continue their work. The vast number of texts and financial constraints prevents a more rapid progress on this project. Father Michael Spillane, Executive Secretary of the Federation of Diocesan Liturgical Commissions, reviewed the Resolutions of the 1989 National Meeting of Diocesan Liturgical Commissions (see the *Newsletter*, December 1989, pp. 46–47) and the ongoing work and special projects of its committees. He invited the comments of the Committee on a revised version of the FDLC pamphlet, *Take and Drink*. Sister Rosa Maria Icaza, CCVI, President of the Instituto de Liturgia Hispana, presented a report on the work of the Institute. Projects include the October 25-28, 1990 national conference to be held in Phoenix, AZ, a booklet on images of Christ and Mary honored by Hispanics, listings of resources of Hispanic music, a booklet and videotape on the Quinceañera, a pamphlet on Hispanic customs at weddings, and the regular publication of its newsletter *Amen*.

An additional report was given by Father Krisman on the North American Conference on Cultural Awareness in the Liturgy scheduled for November 13-19, 1990, in Rome (Italy) that is being organized by Mr. Grayson Brown (see the *Newsletter*, June 1990, p. 24).

Future meetings of the Liturgy Committee will be held in Washington, DC, on November 11, 1990, and in February, 1991, on a date to be determined. The Committee will meet with its consultants and advisors in June, 1991. The date and place have yet to be determined.

Blessings that Pertain to Catechesis and to Communal Prayer

Chapter 4 of the *Book of Blessings* contains blessings for catechists, for a catechetical or prayer meeting, and for catechumens. Chapter 5 contains the blessing for students and teachers. The first two blessings come from the Latin edition of the *Book of Blessings*, the third is taken from the *Rite of Christian Initiation of Adults*, and the last blessing was composed for use in the dioceses of the United States.

The Order for the Blessing of Those Appointed as Catechists is intended for those who are to undertake the role and ministry of catechesis on either the diocesan or the parochial level. It may be celebrated during Mass or at a celebration of the Word of God and may be used by either a priest or a deacon. The blessing is appropriately celebrated on Catechetical Sunday. (The materials prepared by the USCC for the 1990 Catechetical Sunday contain this blessing.) Some dioceses may wish to use this blessing exclusively for those persons who have been certified as catechists by the diocese. Two forms are provided for the prayer of blessing; the second formulary is proper to the United States.

The Order of Blessing for a Catechetical or Prayer Meeting is especially appropriate for meetings that are planned for the purpose of catechesis or communal prayer, e.g., with catechumens. The blessing is not used when the celebration of the eucharist precedes the meeting. The order of blessing usually comes at the end of the meeting, and it may be given by a priest, a deacon, or a layperson who uses the rites and prayers designated for a lay minister.

The Blessings of Catechumens are taken from Part 1 of the *Rite of Christian Initiation of Adults*. These nine prayers of blessing may be given by a priest, a deacon, or a qualified catechist appointed by the bishop. These blessings are usually used at the end of a celebration of the Word of God, although they may also be given at the end of a meeting for catechesis. In particular circumstances they may be given to catechumens outside those usual times.

The Order for the Blessing of Students and Teachers (Chapter 5) has been prepared for use when it is desirable to invoke God's blessing on students and teachers alike. It may be used for the beginning of the school year, either at Masses on the Sunday before schools open or at school celebrations as the academic year begins. The celebration may take place during Mass or within a celebration of the Word of God. A shorter rite is also provided for less formal circumstances. The rite may be adapted for blessing either students or teachers alone. The blessing may be given by a priest, deacon, or a lay minister.

Liturgical Texts for Andrew Dung-Lac and Companions

In the July 1990 issue of the *Newsletter* (pp. 27-28) the approved English translation of the Mass formulary for the memorial of Saints Andrew Dung-Lac, priest, and Companions, martyrs, was published. The following texts are for use in the celebration of the Liturgy of the Hours for the memorial.

THE LITURGY OF THE HOURS

24 November
ANDREW DUNG-LAC, priest, and COMPANIONS, martyrs
Memorial

The beginning of the sixteenth century saw the first sowing of the Gospel of Christ among the Vietnamese people, and this seed grew through the blood of martyrs and the spiritual joy of the newly baptized faithful. During the seventeenth, eighteenth, and nineteenth centuries, particularly during the reign of the Emperor Minh-Mang (1820-1840), many Christians received the martyr's crown; these included bishops, priests, men religious and women religious, and members of the laity. All of these suffered torments of various kinds for their Christian faith and fidelity to the cross of Christ and bore witness to Christ's Church and true religion. Some were decapitated, others hanged, others burned or whipped to death, others died during their imprisonment.

Of these the Supreme Pontiff John Paul II on 19 June 1988 declared one-hundred seventeen martyrs to be among the ranks of the saints.

From the common of several martyrs, except for the following:

OFFICE OF READINGS

SECOND READING

From a letter of Saint Paul Le-Bao-Tinh sent to students of the Seminary of Ke-Vinh in 1843 (A. Launay, *Le clergé tonkinois et ses prêtres martyrs* [Paris Foreign Mission Society, Paris, 1925], pp. 80-83)

The martyrs' share in Christ's victory

I, Paul, in chains for the name of Christ, wish to relate to you the trials besetting me daily, in order that you may be inflamed with love for God and join with me in his praises, "for his mercy is for ever." The prison here is a true image of everlasting hell: to cruel tortures of every kind—shackles, iron chains, manacles—are added hatred, vengeance, calumnies, obscene speech, quarrels, evil acts, swearing, curses, as well as anguish and grief. But the God who once freed the three children from the fiery furnace is with me always; he has delivered me from these tribulations and made them sweet, "for his mercy is for ever."

In the midst of these torments, which usually terrify others, I am, by the grace of God, full of joy and gladness, because I am not alone—Christ is with me.

Our Master bears the whole weight of the cross, leaving me only the tiniest, last bit. He is not a mere onlooker in my struggle, but a contestant and the victor and champion in the whole battle. Therefore upon his head is placed the crown of victory, and his members also share in his glory.

How am I to bear with the spectacle, as each day I see emperors, mandarins, and their retinue blaspheming your holy name, O Lord, "who are enthroned above the Cherubim and Seraphim"? Behold, the pagans have trodden your cross underfoot! Where is your glory? As I see all this, I would, in the ardent love I have for you, prefer to be torn limb from limb and to die as a witness to your love.

O Lord, show your power, save me, sustain me, that in my infirmity your power may be shown and may be glorified before the nations: grant that I may not grow weak along the way, and so allow your enemies to hold their heads up in pride.

Beloved brothers, as you hear all these things may you give endless thanks in joy to God, from whom every good proceeds; bless the Lord with me, "for his mercy is for ever." "My soul proclaims the greatness of the Lord, my spirit rejoices in God my Savior, for he has looked with favor" on his lowly servant and from this day all generations will call me blessed, "for his mercy is for ever."

"O praise the Lord, all you nations, acclaim him, all you peoples," for "God chose what is weak in the world to confound the strong, God chose what is low and despised" to confound the noble. Through my mouth he has confused the philosophers who are disciples of the wise of this world, "for his mercy is for ever."

I write these things to you in order that your faith and mine may be united. In the midst of this storm I cast my anchor toward the throne of God, the anchor that is the lively hope in my heart.

Beloved brothers, for your part "so run that you may attain the crown," put on the "breastplate of faith" and take up "the weapons" of Christ "for the right hand and for the left," as my patron Saint Paul has taught us. "It is better for you to enter life with one eye or crippled" than, with all your members intact, to be cast away.

Come to my aid with your prayers, that I may have the strength to fight according to the law, and indeed "to fight the good fight" and to fight until the end and so finish the race. We may not again see each other in this life, but we will have the happiness of seeing each other again in the world to come, when, standing at the throne of the spotless Lamb, we will together join in singing his praises and exult for ever in the joy of our triumph. Amen.

RESPONSORY

See Hebrews 12:1-3

Through patience let us run the race that is set before us.
—Looking to Jesus the pioneer and perfecter of our faith.

Consider him who from sinners endured such hostility against himself,
so that you may not grow weary or fainthearted.
—Looking to Jesus . . .

PRAYER

O God,
the source and origin of all fatherhood,
you kept the blessed martyrs Andrew and his companions
faithful to the cross of your Son
even to the shedding of their blood.
Through their intercession
enable us to spread your love among our brothers and sisters,
that we may be called and may truly be your children.

We ask this through our Lord Jesus Christ, your Son,
who lives and reigns with you and the Holy Spirit,
one God, for ever and ever.

Shorter Book of Blessings

The *Shorter Book of Blessings,* an abridged edition of the *Book of Blessings,* has recently been published by The Catholic Book Publishing Company, New York. Containing 576 pages, this 4½ by 6⅞ inches book with flexible cover contains all the blessings from the complete *Book of Blessings* except for those celebrated during Mass or within a church, or ones celebrated with greater solemnity apart for a church (such as the blessings of new seminaries, universities, libraries, etc.). For ease of use, the reference numbers to the complete *Book of Blessings* are given for those blessings which may also be celebrated within Mass. The *Shorter Book of Blessings* is available at local religious supply houses and bookstores. For information write: The Catholic Book Publishing Company, 257 West 17th Street, New York, NY 10011.

BISHOPS' COMMITTEE ON THE LITURGY
NEWSLETTER

NATIONAL CONFERENCE OF CATHOLIC BISHOPS

**1990
VOLUME XXVI
SEPTEMBER**

NCCB Administrative Committee Meeting

The Administrative Committee of the National Conference of Catholic Bishops met on September 11-13, 1990 at the NCCB/USCC headquarters building in Washington, DC. The members of the Committee approved the following action items submitted by the Committee on the Liturgy that require the confirmation of the Congregation for Divine Worship and the Discipline of the Sacraments: (1) the provisional English and Spanish liturgical texts for the optional memorials of Blessed Katharine Drexel, virgin (March 3), and Blessed Junipero Serra, priest (July 1); (2) the provisional Spanish translation of the *Rito de Iniciacion Cristiana de Adultos;* and (3) the provisional Lakota translation of the *Order of Mass* and Eucharistic Prayer II.

The Committee also approved placing on the agenda of the November plenary meeting of the National Conference of Catholic Bishops the following items: (1) the inclusion of the optional memorials of Saint Paul of the Cross, priest (October 20), Blessed Miguel Austin Pro, priest and martyr (November 23), and Blessed Juan Diego (December 9) in the Proper Calendar for the Dioceses of the United States; (2) the request that diocesan bishops be authorized to permit laypersons to preside at funerals outside of Mass when there is no priest or deacon available; (3) the principles of the Lectionary Subcommittee of the Bishops' Committee on the Liturgy which guide the preparation of pericopes from the *New American Bible* in the second edition of the *Lectionary for Mass;* and (4) *Criteria for the Evaluation of Inclusive Language Translations of Scriptural Texts Proposed for Liturgical Use,* a document of the Joint Committee (Liturgy and Doctrine) on Inclusive Language.

Emendation of No. 5 of the GNLYC

The March-April 1990 issue of *Notitiae,* the journal published by the Congregation for Divine Worship and the Discipline of the Sacraments, contains a decree of the congregation emending no. 5 of the *General Norms for the Liturgical Year and the Calendar,* promulgated by the Sacred Congregation of Rites (Consilium) on March 21, 1969. The practical effects of this emended norm for the General Roman Calendar are that in the future when December 8 occurs on a Sunday, the solemnity of the Immaculate Conception will be celebrated on *Monday,* December 9 [instead of Saturday, December 7], and when either the solemnity of Saint Joseph (March 19) or the Annunciation of the Lord (March 25) occur on a Sunday of Lent, they will be celebrated on the following Monday, except when either occurs on Passion (Palm) Sunday or Easter Sunday, in which case they will be transferred to the Monday after the Second Sunday of Easter. [As conceded by the Congregation for Divine Worship and the Discipline of the Sacraments, this emended norm will *not* be observed in the dioceses of the United States in 1991, since calendars have already been prepared. Thus, the Solemnity of the Immaculate Conception will be observed on Saturday, December 7, 1991.] The decree, in a translation prepared by the International Commission on English in the Liturgy, follows.

Prot. N. CD 500/89

DECREE

Sunday, the foundation and nucleus of the entire liturgical year, should be proposed to the devotion of the faithful and taught to them as the first holyday of all (see *Sacrosanctum Concilium,* no. 106).

3211 FOURTH STREET, N.E. • WASHINGTON, D.C. 20017

The norm thus laid down by the Constitution on the Liturgy restored to the Lord's Day its primacy over all other celebrations "unless they be truly of greatest importance" (ibid.).

This applies above all to the Sundays of Advent, Lent, and the Easter season, which have precedence over all other celebrations, even those observed with the rank of solemnity.

According to the "General Norms of the Liturgical Year and the Calendar," no. 5, solemnities occurring on these Sundays are to be observed on the Saturday preceding.

But pastoral experience has shown that this solution raises certain problems, particularly in regard to the evening Mass and evening prayer II of some solemnity coinciding with the evening Mass and evening prayer I of a Sunday.

To keep as complete as possible the celebration both of the Sundays in question and of those solemnities to which the faithful are particularly devoted, the Congregation for Divine Worship and the Discipline of the Sacraments, by virtue of the present Decree, emends no. 5 of "General Norms for the Liturgical Year and the Calendar" as follows:

"Because of its special importance the Sunday celebration gives way only to solemnities or feasts of the Lord. The Sundays of the seasons of Advent, Lent, and Easter, however, take precedence over all feasts of the Lord and all solemnities. Solemnities occurring on these Sundays are *transferred to the following Monday*, except in the case of their occurrence on Palm Sunday or on Easter Sunday."

Hereafter all are to observe the norm as thus emended.

As to the particular calendars of nations, dioceses, or religious institutes already drawn up for 1991, the concession is hereby granted to follow the solution (in cases of occurrence) that these calendars have already provided on the basis of the norm in force up to the present.

The Supreme Pontiff John Paul II has approved and confirmed the contents of this Decree prepared by this Congregation, and has ordered publication of the same Decree.

All things to the contrary not withstanding.

From the Congregation for Divine Worship and the Discipline of the Sacraments, April 22, 1990, Second Sunday of Easter, *in albis*.

+ Eduardo Cardinal Martinez
Prefect

+ Lajos Kada
Titular Archbishop of Tibica
Secretary

Congregation for Divine Worship Consultation

A special meeting of consultors and invited guests took place at the Congregation for Divine Worship and the Discipline of the Sacraments from April 24-30, 1990. The guests included the editors of liturgical reviews, directors of liturgical institutes, and other experts. Monsignor Frederick R. McManus, Consultant to the Secretariat for the Liturgy, and Father Ronald F. Krisman, Executive Director of the Secretariat, attended the meeting from the United States.

The purpose of the consultation was to help prepare for a plenary meeting of the Congregation which is to take place later this year. Several important topics were discussed in the course of the meeting: a General Instruction to the Book of Sacraments; the revision of the Rite for the Baptism of Children, the Rite of Christian Initiation of Adults, Confirmation, Penance, Anointing of the Sick, and Funerals; preparation of a third edition of the Roman Missal; reflection on liturgical formation and the present status of the liturgical renewal.

The participants at the meeting were provided with a draft of a proposed General Instruction to the Book of the Sacraments. The purpose of this General Introduction is to help unify the various liturgical books which comprise the Roman Ritual and the Pontifical and have appeared as individual volumes during the course of the liturgical reform and renewal. Related to the General Instruction is the question of a "one volume" edition of the Roman Ritual. It was proposed to collect together the rites for the sacraments, blessings, exorcisms, and supplications. (These later two have yet to be published). Various suggestions were made in this regard: some of those present were opposed to a single volume because of the vast amount of material that would have to be collected in one volume; others were concerned that such a collection would not distinguish between the sacraments and the sacramentals. On the positive side, it was suggested that the term "one volume" does not necessarily mean only one book, but rather a collection of several books under the same title, e.g., the *Roman Missal* (*Sacramentary, Lectionary for Mass, Roman Graduale*) and the four volume *Liturgy of the Hours*. Those present acknowledged the importance of a General Instruction, even if it is not part of a "one volume" edition, that would underline the conciliar vision of the sacraments. There did not seem to be any common agreement on the publication of a "one volume" edition of the liturgical books.

Individual study groups were formed to discuss the possibility of new editions of the rites for initiation, penance, anointing and pastoral care of the sick, and funerals. The groups later reported to the whole assembly and noted the various aspects of each of the rites that need to be considered in any revision that might be undertaken. One possibility that was discussed was a single liturgical book that would contain all the rites of initiation: children, adults, and confirmation.

The third major topic of the meeting was the preparation of a third edition of the *Roman Missal.* Various presentations were made on each section of the missal. Corrections need to be made in the General Instruction of the Roman Missal. The missal needs to be updated in light of the revision of the *Code of Canon Law,* the new edition of the *Ceremonial of Bishops,* changes in the General Roman Calendar, the new ritual Masses for ordinations, etc. In response, several additional suggestions were made. It was proposed that music be put in place throughout the Latin book. It was also suggested that a new edition of the missal take into consideration the various adaptations approved for different countries. Suggestions were made about the revision of the introductory rites, the presentation of the gifts, the communion rite, and the dismissal. Separate presentations were also made on the prayers of the missal and the eucharistic prayers. Lastly, there was a discussion of the *Lectionary for Mass* and some possible revisions of the order of readings. Some problems were also mentioned in relation to the lectionary which are connected to the *Ordo Cantus Missae* and the *Roman Gradual.*

The meeting concluded with a common reflection on liturgical formation and renewal and presentations on the work of international commissions for the translation of liturgical texts, the work of the liturgical institutes, and liturgical periodicals.

Ordination of Presbyters and Deacons: Imposition of Hands

Recently, questions have been raised regarding the participation of bishops, who are present at the ordination of deacons or presbyters, in the imposition of hands and the prayer of ordination. May these bishops join the ordaining bishop in imposing hands on each of the candidates and then participate in the prayer of consecration?

The various rubrics found the liturgical books for the imposition of hands on bishops, presbyters, and deacons can be traced back to the *Apostolic Tradition* of Hippolytus (c. 215). He notes that all the bishops present impose or lay hands on a candidate for the episcopacy; that the presbyters present join the bishop in laying hands on candidates for the presbyterate, not to ordain, but to signify their common order and task; and that only the bishop lays hands on deacons, since they are ordained for service to the bishop. This ancient practice is expressed in our present ordination rites where the bishops present are invited to participate in the ordination of a bishop by laying hands on the candidate and reciting the essential form of the sacrament. In the rite of ordination to the presbyterate, the presbyters in attendance are invited to impose hands on the candidates after the bishop has done so and before the prayer of ordination is proclaimed. In the rite for ordination to the diaconate, the bishop alone imposes hands.

The Congregation for the Doctrine of the Faith, in a letter dated May 16, 1972, and published in the May 1980 edition of *Notitiae,* posed the following question: "In the ordination of presbyters, may not bishops who are present for the rite of ordination participate in the imposition of hands after the principal celebrant and join him in saying the essential part of the consecratory prayer?"

The Congregation gave as its response: "It is not expedient."

Thus, in keeping with ancient practice, bishops should concelebrate the sacrament of order only in the case of the ordination of a bishop. The participation of presbyters in the imposition of hands at the ordination of presbyters is a corporate sign of welcome into the order of presbyters. It is, therefore, inappropriate for bishops who are present to participate in the laying of hands, since they no longer belong to the order of presbyters, but rather to the order of bishops. Similarly, bishops other than the ordaining bishop should not join in the imposition of hands at the ordination of deacons.

In Memoriam: Luigi Cardinal Dadaglio

His Eminence Luigi Cardinal Dadaglio, Secretary of the Congregation for Divine Worship and the Sacraments from 1980-1984, died at the age of 75 on August 22, 1990, several weeks after he had suffered a heart attack. His service to the Church as a diplomat and curial official spanned forty-five years. Four years before his retirement his contribution was recognized with his selection as a Cardinal Deacon.

Entering the diplomat service of the Holy See in 1937, three years after his ordination, he served as a member of the official Vatican delegation in Haiti, the United States, Canada, Australia, New Zealand and Colombia. Ordained a bishop in 1961 with the personal title of archbishop, he was assigned as nuncio to Venezuela and served there until 1967, when he was transferred to Spain. It was in Spain that his diplomatic skills may best be remembered. He is credited with supporting the Spanish bishops' conference during turbulent years when tensions between the bishops and the Franco government strained the relationship that had developed over the centuries. To his credit he spoke clearly of the right of political dissent and the need for improved labor conditions. Ultimately he oversaw the acceptance of a redesigned concordat that preserved and strengthened the Church's role in that developing country.

In 1980 Cardinal Dadaglio was assigned to the Congregation for Sacraments and Divine Worship, where he served for four years as Secretary of the Section for Sacraments. It was during this period that the final text of *Pastoral Care of the Sick* was approved and confirmed for use in the United States. After his brief tenure at the Congregation, he was named to head the Apostolic Penitentiary, a post he held until his retirement in April 1990.

First a diplomat in the international community and later a leader in internal Church affairs, Cardinal Luigi Dadaglio contributed abundantly to the stability and development of the Church in the years surrounding the Second Vatican Ecumenical Council. The respect and esteem earned from his colleagues will remain an inestimable witness to the faith and prowess of this twentieth century churchman.

> God of mercy and love,
> grant to Luigi, your servant and priest,
> a glorious place at your heavenly table,
> for you made him here on earth
> a faithful minister of your word and sacrament.
> We ask this through Christ our Lord.

Southwest Liturgical Conference 1991 Study Week

The Southwest Liturgical Conference, which comprises the dioceses of Arizona, Colorado, New Mexico, Oklahoma, Texas, Utah, and Wyoming, will hold its 29th annual study week at the Hilton Hotel, Grand Junction, CO, on January 21-24, 1991. The theme of the conference is "Marriage: Celebrating the Promise."

Major topics and speakers include: "Liturgical Implications of Marriage" by Vicki Klima; "Readiness for Marriage/Family Systems Perspective" by Eileen Raffaniello; "Spirituality of the Engaged" by Austin Fleming; "Sacramentality of Marriage" by John Baldovin, SJ; "Cultural Implications of Marriage" by Bishop Ricardo Ramirez; and "The Parish as a Support Community" by David Thomas.

A variety of workshops are planned for clergy, pastoral musicians, marriage preparation teams, youth and young adult ministers, and those interested in marriage enrichment.

For further information contact: 1991 SWLC Study Week, Diocese of Pueblo, Office of Worship, 1001 North Grand Avenue, Pueblo, CO 81003. Telephone: 719/544-9861.

BISHOPS' COMMITTEE ON THE LITURGY

NEWSLETTER

NATIONAL CONFERENCE OF CATHOLIC BISHOPS

1990
VOLUME XXVI
OCTOBER/NOVEMBER

November Plenary Assembly of the NCCB

The National Conference of Catholic Bishops met in plenary assembly, November 11-15, 1990, at the Omni Shoreham Hotel, Washington, DC. During the course of their meeting, the bishops approved several liturgical action items presented by the Committee on the Liturgy.

Those items approved by the required two thirds majority vote of the *de jure* members and which now require confirmation by the Apostolic See were: the inclusion of the optional memorials of Blessed Miguel Agustin Pro, priest and martyr (November 23) and Blessed Juan Diego (December 9) in the proper calendar for the dioceses of the United States and the change of date for the optional memorial of Saint Paul of the Cross (from October 20 to October 19) in the proper calendar. The English translation of the opening prayer for use at Mass on the optional memorial of Blessed Juan Diego was also approved.

Finally the bishops approved a set of principles for preparing pericopes from the *New American Bible* for use in the second edition of the *Lectionary for Mass,* as well as *Criteria for the Evaluation of Inclusive Language Translations of Scriptural Texts proposed for Liturgical Use* (proposed by the Joint Committee [Liturgy and Doctrine] on Inclusive Language).

The request that diocesan bishops be authorized to permit lay persons to preside at the Funeral Liturgy outside of Mass, in accordance with the 1969 *Ordo Exsequiarum,* nos. 19 and 22:4, failed to receive approval by the requisite two thirds majority vote.

November 1990 Liturgy Committee Meeting

The NCCB Liturgy Committee met in Washington, DC, on November 11, 1990. The committee reviewed the six liturgical action items on the agenda of the NCCB Plenary meeting and also discussed: 1) a draft statement regarding policy, procedures and status of national shrines; 2) the translation of the psalter of the *New American Bible;* 3) the position statements adopted by the delegates to the 1990 National Meeting of Diocesan Liturgical Commissions; and 4) the first draft of a proposed Mass in Thanksgiving for the Gift of Human Life. In response to three varia concerning holy days of obligation, the Committee approved surveying the bishops together with the Committee on Pastoral Research and Practices to determine if examining this issue once more would be worthwhile at this time.

Reports were made on several activities, including: 1) the completion of the revised *Lectionary for Mass;* 2) the progress of the Children's Lectionary Task Group on the *Lectionary for Mass and other Occasions with Children;* 3) the work of the Hispanic Subcommittee; 4) the final reports of the Black Liturgy Subcommittee and the Joint Committee on Inclusive Language; 5) the initial work of the Task Group on Cremation and Other Funeral Practices; and 6) the status of the NCCB-approved *Order of Sunday Celebrations in the Absence of a Priest.*

Criteria for the Evaluation of Inclusive Language

On November 15, 1990, during the plenary assembly of the National Conference of Catholic Bishops, the members approved the Criteria for the Evaluation of Inclusive Language Translations of Scriptural Texts proposed for Liturgical Use. *These criteria, developed by the Joint Committee (Liturgy and Doctrine) on Inclusive Language over the past three years, are intended to assist bishops in evaluating the suitability of inclusive language translations of scriptural texts proposed for liturgical use. The text follows:*

Introduction: The Origins and Nature of the Problem

1. Five historical developments have converged to present the Church in the United States today with an important and challenging pastoral concern. First, the introduction of the vernacular into the Church's worship has necessitated English translations of the liturgical books and of sacred scripture for use in the liturgy. Second, some segments of American culture have become increasingly sensitive to "exclusive language," i.e., language which seems to exclude the equality and dignity of each person regardless of race, gender, creed, age or ability.[1] Third, there has been a noticeable loss of the sense of grammatical gender in American usage of the English language. Fourth, English vocabulary itself has changed so that words which once referred to all human beings are increasingly taken as gender-specific and, consequently, exclusive. Fifth, impromptu efforts at inclusive language, while pleasing to some, have often offended others who expect a degree of theological precision and linguistic or aesthetic refinement in the public discourse of the liturgy. Some impromptu efforts may also have unwittingly undermined essentials of Catholic doctrine.

These current issues confront a fundamental conviction of the Church, namely, that the Word of God stands at the core of our faith as a basic theological reality to which all human efforts respond and by which they are judged.

2. The bishops of the United States wish to respond to this complex and sensitive issue of language in the English translation of the liturgical books of the Church in general and of sacred scripture in particular. New translations of scriptural passages used in the liturgy are being proposed periodically for their approval. Since the promulgation of the 1983 Code of Canon Law these translations must be approved by a conference of bishops or by the Apostolic See.[2] The question confronts the bishops: With regard to a concern for inclusive language, how do we distinguish a legitimate translation from one that is imprecise?

3. The recognition of this problem prompted the submission of a varium to the National Conference of Catholic Bishops requesting that the Bishops' Committee on the Liturgy and the Committee on Doctrine be directed jointly to formulate guidelines which would assist the bishops in making appropriate judgments on the inclusive language translations of biblical texts for liturgical use. These two committees established a Joint Committee on Inclusive Language, which prepared this text.

4. This document, while providing an answer to the question concerning translations of biblical texts for liturgical use, does not attempt to elaborate a complete set of criteria for inclusive language in the liturgy in general, that is, for prayers, hymns, and preaching. These cognate areas will be treated only insofar as they overlap the particular issues being addressed here.

5. This document presents practical principles for the members of the National Conference of Catholic Bishops to exercise their canonical responsibility for approving translations of scripture proposed for liturgical use. However, just as this document does not deal with all cases of inclusive language in the liturgy, neither is it intended as a theology of translation. The teaching of *Dei Verbum* and the instructions of the Pontifical Biblical Commission prevail in matters of inspiration, inerrancy, and hermeneutics and their relationship with meaning, language, and the mind of the author. While there would be a value in producing a study summarizing these issues, it would distract from the immediate purpose of this document.

6. This document treats the problem indicated above in four parts: General Principles; Principles for Inclusive Language Lectionary Translations; Preparation of Texts for Use in the Lectionary; Special Questions, viz., naming God, the Trinity, Christ, and the Church.

Part One: General Principles

7. There are two general principles for judging translations for liturgical use: the principle of fidelity to the Word of God and the principle of respect for the nature of the liturgical assembly. Individual questions, then, must be judged in light of the textual, grammatical, literary, artistic, and dogmatic requirements of the particular scriptural passage, and in light of the needs of the liturgical assembly. In cases of conflict or ambiguity, the principle of fidelity to the word of God retains its primacy.

I. Fidelity to the Word of God

The following considerations derive from the principle of fidelity to the Word of God.

8. The People of God have the right to hear the Word of God integrally proclaimed[3] in fidelity to the meaning of the inspired authors of the sacred text.

9. Biblical translations must always be faithful to the original language and internal truth of the inspired text. It is expected, therefore, that every concept in the original text will be translated within its context.

10. All biblical translations must respect doctrinal principles of revelation, inspiration, and biblical interpretation (hermeneutics), as well as the formal rhetoric intended by the author (e.g., Heb 2: 5-18). They must be faithful to Catholic teaching regarding God and divine activity in the world and in human history as it unfolds. "Due attention must be paid both to the customary and characteristic patterns of perception, speech, and narrative which prevailed at the age of the sacred writer and to the conventions which the people of his time followed."[4]

II. The Nature of the Liturgical Assembly

The following considerations derive from the nature of the liturgical assembly.

11. Each and every Christian is called to, and indeed has a right to, full and active participation in worship. This was stated succinctly by the Second Vatican Council: "The Church earnestly desires that all the faithful be led to that full, conscious, and active participation in liturgical celebrations called for by the very nature of the liturgy. Such participation by the Christian people as 'a chosen race, a royal priesthood, a holy nation, God's own people' (1 Pt 2:9, see 2:4-5) is their right and duty by reason of their baptism."[5] An integral part of liturgical participation is hearing the word of Christ "who speaks when the scriptures are proclaimed in the Church."[6] Full and active participation in the liturgy demands that the liturgical assembly recognize and accept the transcendent power of God's word.

12. According to the Church's tradition, biblical texts have many liturgical uses. Because their immediate purposes are somewhat different, texts translated for public proclamation in the liturgy may differ in some respects (cf. Part Two) from those translations which are meant solely for academic study, private reading, or *lectio divina*.

13. The language of biblical texts for liturgical use should be suitably and faithfully adapted for proclamation and should facilitate the full, conscious, and active participation of all members of the Church, women and men, in worship.

Part Two: Principles for Inclusive Language Lectionary Translations

14. The Word of God proclaimed to all nations is by nature inclusive, that is, addressed to all peoples, men and women. Consequently, every effort should be made to render the language of biblical translations as inclusively as a faithful translation of the text permits, especially when this concerns the People of God, Israel, and the Christian community.

15. When a biblical translation is meant for liturgical proclamation, it must also take into account those principles which apply to the public communication of the biblical meaning. Inclusive language is one of those principles, since the text is proclaimed in the Christian assembly to women and men who possess equal baptismal dignity and reflects the universal scope of the Church's call to evangelize.

16. The books of the Bible are the product of particular cultures, with their limitations as well as their strengths. Consequently not everything in scripture will be in harmony with contemporary cultural concerns. The fundamental mystery of incarnational revelation requires the retention of those characteristics which reflect the cultural context within which the Word was first received.

17. Language which addresses and refers to the worshiping community ought not use words or phrases which deny the common dignity of all the baptized.

18. Words such as "men," "sons," "brothers," "brethren," "forefathers," "fraternity," and "brotherhood" which were once understood as inclusive generic terms, today are often understood as referring only to males. In addition, although certain uses of "he," "his," and "him" once were generic and included both men and women, in contemporary American usage these terms are often perceived to refer only to males. Their use has become ambiguous and is increasingly seen to exclude women. Therefore, these terms should not be used when the reference is meant to be generic, observing the requirements of n. 7 and n. 10.

19. Words such as 'adam, anthropos, and homo have often been translated in many English biblical and liturgical texts by the collective terms "man," and "family of man." Since in the original languages these words actually denote human beings rather than only males, English terms which are not gender-specific, such as "person," "people," "human family," and "humans," should be used in translating these words.

20. In narratives and parables the sex of individual persons should be retained. Sometimes, in the Synoptic tradition, the gospel writers select examples or metaphors from a specific gender. Persons of the other sex should not be added merely in a desire for balance. The original references of the narrative or images of the parable should be retained.

Part Three: The Preparation of Texts for Use in the Lectionary

21. The liturgical adaptation of readings for use in the lectionary should be made in light of the norms of the Introduction to the *Ordo Lectionum Missae* (1981). Incipits should present the context of the various pericopes. At times, transitions may need to be added when verses have been omitted from pericopes. Nouns may replace pronouns or be added to participial constructions for clarity in proclamation and aural comprehension. Translation should not expand upon the text, but the Church recognizes that in certain circumstances a particular text may be expanded to reflect adequately the intended meaning of the pericope.[7] In all cases, these adaptations must remain faithful to the intent of the original text.[8]

22. Inclusive language adaptations of lectionary texts must be made in light of exegetical and linguistic attention to the individual text within its proper context. Blanket substitutions are inappropriate.

23. Many biblical passages are inconsistent in grammatical person, that is, alternating between second person singular or plural ("you") and third person singular ("he"). In order to give such passages a more intelligible consistency, some biblical readings may be translated so as to use either the second person plural ("you") throughout or the third person plural ("they") throughout. Changes from the third person singular to the third person plural are allowed in individual cases where the sense of the original text is universal. It should be noted that, at times, either the sense or the poetic structure of a passage may require that the alternation be preserved in the translation.

24. Psalms and canticles have habitually been appropriated by the Church for use in the liturgy, not as readings for proclamation, but as the responsive prayer of the liturgical assembly. Accordingly, adaptations have justifiably been made, principally by the omission of verses which were judged to be inappropriate in a given culture or liturgical context. Thus, the liturgical books allow the adaptation of psalm texts to encourage the full participation of the liturgical assembly.

Part Four: Special Questions

25. Several specific issues must be addressed in regard to the naming of God, the persons of the Trinity, and the Church, since changes in language can have important doctrinal and theological implications.

I. Naming God in Biblical Translations

26. Great care should be taken in translations of the names of God and in the use of pronouns referring to God. While it would be inappropriate to attribute gender to God as such, the revealed word of God consistently uses a masculine reference for God. It may sometimes be useful, however, to repeat the name of God, as used earlier in the text, rather than to use the masculine pronoun in every case. But care must be taken that the repetition not become tiresome.

27. The classic translation of the Tetragrammaton (YHWH) as "LORD" and the translation of Kyrios as "Lord" should be used in lectionaries.

28. Feminine imagery in the original language of the biblical texts should not be obscured or replaced by the use of masculine imagery in English translations, e.g., Wisdom literature.

II. Naming Christ in Biblical Translations

29. Christ is the center and focus of all scripture.[9] The New Testament has interpreted certain texts of the Old Testament in an explicitly christological fashion. Special care should be observed in the translation of these texts so that the christological meaning is not lost. Some examples include the Servant Songs of Isaiah 42 and 53, Psalms 2 and 110, and the Son of Man passage in Daniel 7.

III. Naming the Trinity in Biblical Translations

30. In fidelity to the inspired Word of God, the traditional biblical usage for naming the Persons of the Trinity as "Father," "Son," and "Holy Spirit" is to be retained. Similarly, in keeping with New Testament usage and the Church's tradition, the feminine pronoun is not to be used to refer to the Person of the Holy Spirit.

IV. Naming the Church in Biblical Translations

31. Normally the neuter third person singular or the third person plural pronoun is used when referring to the People of God, Israel, the Church, the Body of Christ, etc., unless their antecedents clearly are a masculine or feminine metaphor, for instance, the reference to the Church as the "Bride of Christ" or "Mother" (cf. Rev 12).

Conclusion

32. These criteria for judging the appropriateness of inclusive language translations of sacred scripture are presented while acknowledging that the English language is continually changing. Contemporary translations must reflect developments in American English grammar, syntax, usage, vocabulary, and style. The perceived need for a more inclusive language is part of this development. Such language must not distract hearers from prayer and God's revelation. It must manifest a sense of linguistic refinement. It should not draw attention to itself.

33. While English translations of the Bible have influenced the liturgical and devotional language of Christians, such translations have also shaped and formed the English language itself. This should be true today as it was in the age of the King James and Douay-Rheims translations. Thus, the Church expects for its translations not only accuracy but facility and beauty of expression.

34. Principles of translation when applied to lectionary readings and psalm texts differ in certain respects from those applied to translations of the Bible destined for study or reading (see nos. 22-25 above). Thus, when submitting a new or revised translation of the Bible, an edition of the lectionary or a liturgical psalter for approval by the National Conference of Catholic Bishops, editors must supply a complete statement of the principles used in the preparation of the submitted text.

35. The authority to adapt the biblical text for use in the lectionary remains with the conference of bishops. These criteria for the evaluation of scripture translations proposed for use in the liturgy have been developed to assist the members of the National Conference of Catholic Bishops to exercise their responsibility so that all the People of God may be assisted in hearing God's Word and keeping it.

Notes

1. Cf. Bishop Members of the Pastoral Team, Canadian Conference of Catholic Bishops, *To Speak as a Christian Community,* (August 16, 1989), p. 2.

2. Code of Canon Law [hereafter CIC], 825.1.

3. CIC 213.

4. Second Vatican Ecumenical Council, Constitution on Divine Revelation *Dei Verbum,* no. 12.

5. Second Vatican Ecumenical Council, Constitution on the Sacred Liturgy *Sacrosanctum Concilium,* n. 14. English translation is from *Documents on the Liturgy 1965-1979: Conciliar, Papal and Curial Texts* [hereafter DOL], (Collegeville, MN: The Liturgical Press, 1982), 1, no. 14.

6. *Ibid.,* no. 7.

7. Secretariat for Christian Unity (Commission for Religious Relations with Judaism), *Guidelines and Suggestions* for the application of no. 4 of the conciliar declaration *Nostra aetate,* December 1, 1974 [AAS 67 (1975) 73-79].

8. Sacred Congregation of Rites (Consilium), Instruction *Comme le Prevoit* on the translation of liturgical texts for celebrations with a congregation (January 25, 1969) [DOL 123], nos. 30-32.

9. Cf. *Dei Verbum,* no. 16.

Principles for Preparing NAB Pericopes

The National Conference of Catholic Bishops, meeting in plenary assembly on November 11-15, 1990, approved the Principles for Preparing Pericopes from the New American Bible for Use in the Second Edition of the Lectionary for Mass. *These nine principles are designed solely to assist the Lectionary Subcommittee in preparing the biblical texts for inclusion in the* Lectionary for Mass *in conformity to the liturgical requirements of the* editio typica altera *of the* Ordo Lectionum Missae *(1981). The approved introduction and principles follow:*

Nine Principles for Preparing Pericopes from the *New American Bible* for Use in the *Lectionary for Mass*

The following principles have been formulated to assist the Lectionary Subcommittee of the Committee on the Liturgy in the preparation of the pericopes from the *New American Bible with the Revised New Testament* which will be used in the second edition of the *Lectionary for Mass*. It is understood that these principles are to be applied with great care and that the adapted texts never alter the meaning of the biblical text.

Principle A: An incipit is supplied, expressing the context of the reading in accord with lectionary tradition.

Principle B: A pronoun is replaced by a noun for purposes of clarity or facility in public reading.

Principle C: A clause is put into the plural so as to be inclusive in language, without affecting the meaning of the clause.

Principle D: A clause is changed from the third person singular to the second person so as to be inclusive in language, only when it does not affect the meaning of the clause.

Principle E: The expression "the Jews" in the Fourth Gospel is translated as "the Jewish authorities" or "the Jewish religious leaders" or "the Jewish leaders" or the "Jewish people," etc., in accord with the *Guidelines on Religious Relations with the Jews* (December 1, 1974), Part II: Liturgy, of the Apostolic See's Council on Religious Relations with the Jews.

Principle F: The Greek word *adelphoi* is translated as "brothers and sisters" in a context which, in the judgment of Scripture scholars, includes women as well as men.

Principle G: In those instances where the meaning of the text would not be altered, a word which is exclusive in meaning is replaced by an inclusive word or words when the context includes women as well as men.

Principle H: Individuals are not described by their disability ("a paralytic," "a leper," etc.), but as a man (woman) who is paralyzed, a man (woman) with leprosy, etc.

Principle I: In occasional instances a word which is difficult to read publicly or to understand is replaced by a simpler or easier word, without affecting the meaning of the sentence.

1990 National Meeting of Diocesan Liturgical Commissions

The annual National Meeting of Diocesan Liturgical Commissions, sponsored by the Federation of Diocesan Liturgical Commissions and the Bishops' Committee on the Liturgy, was held from October 15-18, 1990, in Chicago, IL. The site was chosen to commemorate the fiftieth anniversary of the first National Liturgical Week which took place at Holy Name Cathedral. The three hundred and twenty-five delegates, representing diocesan liturgical commissions and offices of worship throughout the United States, recalled the achievements of past liturgical leaders and heard a variety of speakers address the theme of the meeting, "Liturgical Ministries: Changes and Challenges."

Speaker Mary Collins, OSB, in addressing the theological foundations of liturgical ministry, stressed the essential connection between service at the altar and service in the community. Kathleen Hughes, RSCJ, offered an analysis of the present cultural climate by making reference to the dynamic work of the early leaders of the liturgical reform in the United States. And Barbara O'Dea, DW, discussed current national and diocesan ministerial needs in the Church.

During the business sessions of the meeting, the delegates passed five position statements. They are published in this issue of the *Newsletter*.

Resolutions of the National Meeting of Diocesan Liturgical Commissions

The following Position Statements were adopted by the delegates to the 1990 National Meeting of Diocesan Liturgical Commissions, held in Chicago, Illinois, October 15-18, 1990. The degree of commitment to each statement is indicated in parentheses. The voting scale is graded from +3 (highest degree of commitment) to -3 (completely opposed to the statement). A commitment of +1.5 is required for acceptance. Resolutions P.S. 1990 A, 1990 C, and 1990 E, directed to the Committee on the Liturgy, were briefly considered at its November 11, 1990, meeting. A timeline and procedure for implementation of each resolution will be set by the FDLC Board of Directors at its January 1991 Board Meeting.

Sequence of the Sacraments of Initiation for Children Baptized in Infancy

P.S. 1990 A

It is the position of the delegates to the 1990 National Meeting of Diocesan Liturgical Commissions that the Bishops' Committee on the Liturgy and the Federation of Diocesan Liturgical Commissions invite the National Conference of Diocesan Directors and the North American Forum on the Catechumenate to join with them in forming a task force: a) to seek the support of the bishops of the United States for the uniform practice of the celebration of the initiation sacraments for children baptized in infancy in the sequence of baptism, confirmation and eucharist; b) and simultaneously develop a parish process of catechesis designed to implement this refined practice; c) and foster a comprehensive view of formation for youth of catechetical age. (Passed +2.714)

Ongoing Liturgical Education for Priests and Deacons

P.S. 1990 B

It is the position of the delegates to the 1990 National Meeting of Diocesan Liturgical Commissions that the Ministry Committee of the FDLC Board of Directors compile a printed resource which lists liturgical institutes, seminars, workshops, mini-courses, and resource persons who are available for presentations in support of the ongoing liturgical education of the clergy, and distribute it to bishops, major superiors of communities of priests, those responsible for continuing education of priests and deacons and to Diocesan Offices of Worship/Commissions. (Passed +1.722)

Posture During the Eucharistic Prayer

P.S. 1990 C

It is the position of the delegates to the 1990 National Meeting of Diocesan Liturgical Commissions that the BCL Task Force on American Adaptation of the Roman Missal provide for the assembly to stand throughout the Eucharistic Prayer in the revised Sacramentary for use in the United States. (Passed +2.853)

Lay Presence in Episcopal, Presbyteral, and Diaconal Ordinations

P.S. 1990 D

It is the position of the delegates to the 1990 National Meeting of Diocesan Liturgical Commissions that the Sacraments Committee of the FDLC study the rites for the ordination of bishops, presbyters, and deacons with a view to highlighting elements that can visibly and symbolically enhance the ordination liturgies as celebrations in which all the baptized have a legitimate, active part. (Passed +2.156)

Images of God

P.S. 1990 E

It is the position of the delegates to the 1990 National Meeting of Diocesan Liturgical Commissions that diocesan liturgical commissions, the Board of Directors of the FDLC, and the BCL acknowledge and address by means of publications and dialogue the limitation of our understanding of God caused, in part, by the systemic poverty of expression in the use of feminine imagery and language regarding God, and that these groups acknowledge and address the necessity of both feminine and masculine metaphors for understanding God and humanity. (Passed +2.000)

Newsletter Subscription Renewals

All subscribers to the Bishops' Committee on the Liturgy Newsletter will be sent computerized renewal notices in late November for the 1991 calendar year. To avoid interruption in service, the completed forms should be returned with payment before December 21, 1990. (Subscriptions which have not been renewed by the time of the January 1991 *Newsletter* goes to press will be placed on an inactive list and reinstated once payment is received.) Subscription rates for 1991 will remain the same as in the past few years. The individual subscription price is $9.00 domestic mail and $11.00 foreign mail. Bulk rates also will remain the same.

In order that subscribers' accounts may be properly credited, the instructions accompanying the renewal forms should be followed. The "renewal coupon" portion of the invoice must be included with payment. Coupon and payment should be returned in the self-mailer envelop which has been provided. This envelop is preaddressed for direct deposit to the bank. Payment should not be sent to the NCCB Secretariat for the Liturgy because it needlessly slows the renewal process.

Subscribers who have not received a renewal notice by December 7, 1990, should contact the Liturgy Secretariat so that a duplicate invoice can be sent. (*Newsletter* recipients whose subscription number is 205990, 205995, or 205999 are receiving gratis copies and therefore, will receive no renewal notice.)

The gratitude of the Liturgy Secretariat is extended to all subscribers for their cooperation in the *Newsletter* renewal process.

In Memoriam: D.S. Amalorpavadass

On the day after Ascension Thursday, May 25, 1990, Father D. S. Amalorpavadass, priest, scholar and internationally respected promoter of cultural adaptation of the liturgy, was tragically killed in an automobile accident in his native India. Both nationally and internationally recognized for his contributions to the liturgical reform and spiritual renewal of the Church he will no doubt be counted among those deserving major attention when the history of the post-Vatican II liturgical movement is written.

Ordained a priest in 1959, Father Amalorpavadass enjoyed a career that spanned the era of dynamic reform initiated by the Second Vatican Council. Earning an STD at the Catholic Institute, Paris, as well as a Master's Degree in Pastoral Catechetics in 1965, he returned to India to establish the National Biblical, Catechetical and Liturgical Center under the auspices of the Catholic Bishops' Conference of India. Under his fifteen year leadership, the center gained worldwide recognition and continues to serve as a dynamic force for renewal and cultural adaptation in the life of the Church of India. In 1983 Father Amalorpavadass resigned as director of the Center to found the Anjali Ashram where he lived as a priest, spiritual guide, and holy man. It was at this time, to his tribute, that he was named chair of Christian Studies at the University of Mysone, the first such chair at a state-run university in India.

Father Amalorpavadass authored numerous books and articles and lectured extensively on the subjects of catechetics, liturgy and Indian spirituality. He served as a consultor to several Roman discasteries, including the Congregation for Worship, the Congregation for the Evangelization of Peoples, and the Secretariat for Dialogue with non-Christians. As a Special Secretary to the 1974 Synod of Bishops on Evangelization in the Modern World, he played an important role in shaping the documents of that Synod. Also, as a member of the Advisory Committee of the International Commission on English in the Liturgy, he was noted for his focused attention to presentations as well as his rare but intense interventions that demonstrated yet again his manifest conviction to the promotion of the liturgical reform and the spiritual renewal of the Church.

Ascetic, calm, unhurried in his demeanor, D. S. Amalorpavadass spent his years intent on pluming the depth of the spiritual life through his unselfish contribution to the Church. By his colleagues, family, friends, and admirers who gained strength from his intense dedication to the spiritual life, this holy man will long be remembered with gratitude to God. Dead at age 57 years.

BISHOPS' COMMITTEE ON THE LITURGY

NEWSLETTER

NATIONAL CONFERENCE OF CATHOLIC BISHOPS

1990
VOLUME XXVI
DECEMBER

Confirmation of *Rito de la Iniciación Cristiana de Adultos*

On November 21, 1990, the National Conference of Catholic Bishops received the decree of the Congregation for Divine Worship and the Discipline of the Sacraments, dated November 6, 1990, confirming the decision of the Administrative Committee of the NCCB to approve the Spanish language translation of the Rite of Christian Initiation of Adults (Rito de la Iniciación Cristiana de Adultos) *for use in the dioceses of the United States. The following is an unofficial English translation of the decree.*

Prot. N. 770/90

At the request of His Excellency, the Most Reverend Daniel E. Pilarczyk, Archbishop of Cincinnati, in a letter dated September 27, 1990, and by virtue of the faculties granted to this Congregation by the Supreme Pontiff, Pope John Paul II, we gladly approve, that is, confirm for a period of five years the Spanish language translation of the *Ordo initiationis christianae adultorum,* entitled in the vernacular, the *Rite of Christian Initiation of Adults,* as it appears in the attached copy.

In the publication of this text, this decree granting the confirmation requested of the Apostolic See is to be included in its entirety. Two copies of the printed text are to be sent to this Congregation.

Anything to the contrary notwithstanding.

From the Congregation for Divine Worship and the Discipline of the Sacraments, November 6, 1990.

+ Eduardo Cardinal Martinez
Prefect

+ Lajos Kada
Titular Archbishop of Tibica
Secretary

New Chairman, Members, Consultants, and Advisors to the Committee

On November 15, 1990, the Most Reverend Wilton D. Gregory, Auxiliary Bishop of Chicago, assumed the chairmanship of the Liturgy Committee of the National Conference of Catholic Bishops. Having been elected to a three-year term by the member bishops of the NCCB at their November 1989 Plenary Assembly, Bishop Gregory replaces outgoing chairman, the Most Reverend Joseph P. Delaney, Bishop of Fort Worth, who served as chairman of the Committee since November 1986.

As chairman, Bishop Gregory has appointed several new members and consultants to the Committee. New members include: the Most Reverend Norbert M. Dorsey, CP, Bishop of Orlando; the Most Reverend Roberto O. Gonzalez, OFM, Auxiliary Bishop of Boston; the Most Reverend Jerome Hanus, OSB, Bishop of Saint Cloud; the Most Reverend Frank J. Rodimer, Bishop of Paterson; the Most Reverend Francis B. Schulte, Archbishop of New Orleans; and the Most Reverend Emil A. Wcela, Auxiliary Bishop of Rockville Centre. Those who have agreed to serve as consultants to the Committee are: His Eminence Joseph Cardinal Bernardin, Archbishop of Chicago and member of the Congregation for Divine Worship and the Discipline of the Sacraments; the Most Reverend Daniel E. Pilarczyk, Archbishop of Cincinnati and NCCB representative to the Episcopal Board of the International

Commission on English in the Liturgy; the Most Reverend Patrick R. Cooney, Bishop of Gaylord and Chairman of the BCL Task Group on Cremation and Other Funeral Practices; the Most Reverend Enrique San Pedro, SJ, Auxiliary Bishop of Galveston-Houston and member of the BCL Subcommittee on Hispanic Liturgy; the Most Reverend Roger L. Schwietz, OMI, Bishop of Duluth; and the Most Reverend John F. Whealon, Archbishop of Hartford and Chairman of the BCL Lectionary Subcommittee.

Bishop Gregory has also appointed three new advisors to the Committee: Dr. Marchita Mauck, professor of art history at Louisiana State University, Baton Rouge, LA; Sister Barbara O'Dea, DW, provincial superior of the Daughters of Wisdom of the American Province, Islip, NY; and the Reverend Michael G. Witczak, SLD, Saint Francis School of Pastoral Ministry, Milwaukee. Each has been appointed to a three-year term except for Dr. Mauck, who will have a four-year term. They replace outgoing advisors Monsignor Douglas Ferraro, Los Angeles; Sister Nancy Swift, RCE, Boston; and Sister Jennifer Glen, Boulder, CO.

Grateful appreciation is expressed to Bishop Delaney and the former members, consultants, and advisors of the Liturgy Committee who have served these past several years.

FDLC Address of Bishop Joseph P. Delaney

On Wednesday, October 17, 1990, the Most Reverend Joseph P. Delaney, Bishop of Fort Worth and Chairman of the Liturgy Committee of the National Conference of Catholic Bishops, reported on the agenda of the Committee to the delegates and guests attending the annual National Meeting of Diocesan Liturgical Commissions in Chicago, IL. The full text of Bishop Delaney's report follows:

In September 1964 the Sacred Congregation of Rites issued *Inter Oecumenici,* its first of three instructions on the orderly carrying out of the Constitution on the Liturgy. Reading that document today brings back more than a little nostalgia for the euphoria—and in some cases the sense of dread—felt in the Church when the first liturgical changes resulting from the Second Vatican Council were finally mandated.

We've traveled a good distance since 1964. *Inter Oecumenici* is hardly required reading any more. It was concerned principally with the interim changes between the Council and the revision of the various liturgical books. And those revisions are generally completed.

But *Inter Oecumenici* should be consulted from time to time by those of us in this room since it elaborates on article 45 of *Sacrosanctum Concilium,* which deals with diocesan liturgical commissions. *Inter Oecumenici* provides a listing of the various duties of a diocesan liturgical commission as it supports the diocesan bishop as moderator, promoter, and custodian of the liturgical life of the diocese. These responsibilities are: 1) to be fully informed about the state of pastoral-liturgical activity in the diocese, 2) to carry out faithfully those proposals in liturgical matters made by competent authority and to keep abreast of the studies and programs taking place elsewhere in this field, 3) to suggest and promote practical programs which will contribute to the advancement of liturgical life in the diocese, especially programs which will aid priests, 4) to suggest a graduated program for liturgical renewal of individual parishes, and even the entire diocese, and to provide the suitable means and resources for this program, and 5) to see that the program of liturgical renewal in the diocese receives the broadest cooperation and collaboration from other groups in the diocese and that it be in consonance with the promotion of the liturgy by the conference of bishops.

These responsibilities boil down to three interrelated activities: ongoing formation in the liturgy, liturgical research and adaptation, and multilevel collaboration. I have chosen to highlight these responsibilities because I believe that they still have as much importance and immediacy today as they did when they were first stated more than 25 years ago. In the next few years several important liturgical developments will affect the local Churches in the United States. Liturgical commissions and offices of worship will have to lend their support if these developments are to achieve their full potential for ongoing liturgical renewal.

The most important of these developments is the complete revision of the Roman Missal by the International Commission on English in the Liturgy. This revision should appear in 1993 and 1994. Before that time, ICEL will issue two more progress reports on the revision. These reports, the first of which you will receive in another month or so, should be carefully studied, and suggestions should be forwarded back to ICEL.

But revising the Missal isn't only ICEL's responsibility. The Bishops' Committee on the Liturgy counts on your assistance during the next few years as it studies the question of further adaptation of the Missal for the dioceses of the United States. The results of the *Ordo Missae* study which was conducted by the FDLC almost ten years ago will provide a direction for the BCL's work. But additional suggestions for adaptation will be gratefully received from each of you.

Commentators across the ideological spectrum have remarked that the first efforts at liturgical formation after the Second Vatican Council met with spotty success. Thus, the revised Missal will present a fresh opportunity for further liturgical catechesis. Diocesan liturgical commissions and offices of worship will have a large part to play in the effectiveness of this second catechesis.

Other liturgical books to be issued during the next few years will present additional opportunities for continuing liturgical formation. During the next year or so we will see the English translations of the second editions of the Rites of Ordination and the Rite of Marriage. Who would deny that we need much more understanding of these revised liturgical books, particularly the Rite of Marriage?

The *Lectionary for Mass,* based on the 1981 revised edition of the *Ordo Lectionum Missae,* and the *Lectionary for Masses and Other Occasions with Children*—both scheduled for completion by November 1991—will provide opportunities for renewed practical programs for formation of liturgical readers, and for the general formation of the Church regarding the importance of the word of God in our liturgical celebrations. These two books, which will be sensitive to inclusive language, hopefully will usher in a time when the liturgical assembly can open itself completely to the transforming power of the redemptive word of God.

The Church in the United States is multicultural, multilingual, and ethnically diverse. We have known this for a long time, but the effective avenues have yet to be explored to give full expression to the multicultural nature of many of our liturgical assemblies. We can take pride in the fact that for several years now we have been developing a full set of liturgical books in Spanish as well as in English. Several Native American languages have been approved for liturgical use, and the Order of Mass has now been prepared in Navajo, Choctaw, and Lakota. It seems safe to assume that several other Native American languages will also be developing their own liturgical resources in the years ahead.

And we are becoming more and more aware of additional cultural, ethnic, and language groups in the United States. Repeatedly we are hearing of the growing need for liturgical materials in the Hmong and Vietnamese languages.

But this activity, as important as it is, barely scratches the surface of what we believe must be done for cultural adaptation of the liturgy. Is there, in fact, an American cultural perspective which can be brought to liturgy? While we grapple with that question, we have taken our first "baby steps" at liturgical adaptation with the *Rite of Christian Initiation of Adults* and the American *Book of Blessings.* At the same time our African-American Catholics brothers and sisters are being invited through two documents of the BCL Secretariat—*In Spirit and in Truth,* and the soon-to-be-published *Plenty Good Room*—to explore more culturally-rooted expressions of the liturgy. Our American centers for pastoral liturgy must contribute to the ongoing research, the dialogue and ultimately, the development of indigenous forms for Catholic worship in America in the twenty-first century. The need for cultural adaptation of the liturgy is well known. But how we go about it is not so easily understood.

Diocesan liturgical commissions can also be of assistance in assuring that the liturgical reform continues on track and that the emphases of that reform are kept ever in mind. Part of our continuing liturgical agenda for the United States is the formation of the entire liturgical assembly, particularly the liturgical ministers of the assembly. This formation is intended to assist the assembly in rightfully carrying out its full, conscious and active participation in the liturgy. The hallmarks of that liturgical reform are a renewed understanding of the paschal dimension of all Christian worship, the liturgical assembly as the locus of God's activity in the world, the fuller appreciation of the proclamation of the word of God in the liturgy, the recovery of Sunday as the original and preeminent feast day of the Church, and the sanctity of times and places since the definitive reign of God has broken in upon them.

It is easy to overlook one or more aspects of this reform as new problems and questions present themselves to us. In too many of our parishes the critical questions about Christian conversion, ecclesial identity and mission, and ongoing mystagogy are sadly overlooked as the catechumenate is reduced to only one more mandated program for renewal. In too many of our dioceses the immediate practical task of having to train lay ministers for Sunday celebrations in the absence of a priest interferes with carefully addressing the fundamental questions, such as, the nature of the Christian Sunday assembly, the Eucharist as constitutive of the Church, the nature of the ordained ministry in the Church. Let us not be afraid to take up those questions.

As I conclude my four-year term as chairman of the Bishops' Committee on the Liturgy, I look back with gratitude for the support which the Federation of Diocesan Liturgical Commissions has given to me personally, to the Committee, and to its Secretariat. Each November, as a sign of that gratitude, I have urged my fellow American bishops to continue supporting their diocesan liturgical commissions and offices of worship. Yet, sad to say, worship offices and commissions continue to close around the country.

The liturgical renewal mandated by the Second Vatican Council is far from over. And the work of diocesan commissions and offices in liturgical formation, research and adaptation, and multilevel collaboration remains an ever-present challenge. The Church in the United States needs your experience and your wisdom. And the Church needs the voice of your Federation more than ever.

What is the most important benefit of being a diocesan member of the Federation of Diocesan Liturgical Commissions? It is this: being able to collaborate with other dioceses to voice the grassroots hopes, dreams and liturgical concerns of the persons you serve in your dioceses. Don't undersell the importance of your contribution to the liturgical agenda of our country. I assure you, the Bishops' Committee on the Liturgy welcomes and values that contribution from all of you.

Fr. Ronald Krisman Named NCCB Delegate to 1993 Eucharistic Congress

The Most Reverend Daniel E. Pilarczyk, Archbishop of Cincinnati and President of the National Conference of Catholic Bishops, has appointed Father Ronald F. Krisman as the National Delegate to the 45th International Eucharistic Congress, to be held from June 7-13, 1993, in Seville, Spain. The theme of the Congress is "Christ, the Light of the Nations" ("*Christus Lumen Gentium*"). Father Krisman is the Executive Director of the NCCB Liturgy Secretariat and is a priest of the Diocese of Lubbock.

International Eucharistic Congresses combine liturgical services with catechetical programs on devotion to Christ in the Eucharist and on the relationship between the liturgy of worship and witness to life. Participants are clergy, religious and laity and representatives of national and international Catholic organizations from throughout the world.

The idea of a eucharistic congress was first put forth by Marie Marthe Emilia Tamisier (1834-1910) who because of her eucharistic devotion had encouraged pilgrimages to the various sites in France known for eucharistic miracles. After several initial attempts at organizing a congress, Msgr. Louis Gaston de Ségur (1820-81), with the approval of Pope Leo XIII and patronage of Philibert Vrau, succeeded in convening the first international congress. That gathering was held at the University of Lille, France, in June 1881, the same year that Msgr. de Ségur died. It was attended by approximately 800 people from Belgium, England, Spain, France, Holland and Switzerland. A permanent committee charged with arranging future congresses was formed at the conclusion of the event.

Eucharistic congresses were held sporadically through the years until the 1922 congress held in Rome, when Pius XI decreed that meetings would be held every two years. Since then, except during the years of World War II and resuming in 1952, international eucharistic congresses have been held regularly.

Congresses have taken place on every continent and at times have been the occasion for significant historic events. The 1908 Congress in London marked the first time a Papal Legate had entered England since Cardinal Reginald Pole (1500-58). The 1964 Congress in Bombay, attended by Pope Paul VI, was the first to be held in a country where the Catholic population was less than 2 per cent. The international character of that congress took on a new dimension with 20 foreign cardinals, several hundred foreign bishops, and over 30,000 foreign visitors attending. The most recent Congress took place in October 1989 in Seoul, Korea. Pope John Paul II was principal concelebrant of the closing Mass.

INDEX